Unwin Critical Library

GENERAL EDITOR: CLAUDE RAWSON

POUND'S CANTOS

Pound's Cantos

PETER MAKIN

Kansai University, Osaka, Japan

London
GEORGE ALLEN & UNWIN

Boston   Sydney

George Allen & Unwin (Publishers) Ltd,
40 Museum Street, London WC1A 1LU, UK

George Allen & Unwin (Publishers) Ltd,
Park Lane, Hemel Hempstead, Herts HP2 4TE, UK

Allen & Unwin, Inc.,
Fifty Cross Street, Winchester, Mass. 01890, USA

George Allen & Unwin Australia Pty Ltd,
8 Napier Street, North Sydney, NSW 2060, Australia

First published in 1985

British Library Cataloguing in Publication Data

Makin, Peter
  Pound's Cantos. – (Unwin critical library)
  1. Pound, Ezra. Cantos, The
I. Title
811'.52   PS3531.O82C2
ISBN 0-04-811001-9
ISBN 0-04-811002-7 Pbk

Library of Congress Cataloging in Publication Data

Makin, Peter.
  Pound's Cantos.
(Unwin critical library)
Bibliography: p.
Includes index.
1. Pound, Ezra, 1885–1972. Cantos. I. Title.
II. Series.
PS3531.O82C2863 1984 811'.52 84-6477
ISBN 0-04-811001-9 (alk. paper)
ISBN 0-04-811002-7 (pbk.: alk. paper)

Set in 10 on 12 point Plantin by Graphicraft Typesetters Limited
and printed in Great Britain by Billing and Sons Ltd, London and Worcester

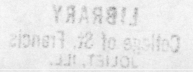

ACKNOWLEDGEMENTS

I wish to thank Professor C. J. Rawson, General Editor of this series, for his encouragement and for his tact in editing, which have resulted in a better book than would have come from my impulse unbridled.

Obiter dicta of Mr Basil Bunting and Professor Hugh Kenner have provided the backbone of a good deal of the argument here; to their thought and that of Pound I have added little but my own naïve zeal. But every writer who writes about Pound must try to educate himself in various un-English fields. Dr Peter Goldsbury of Hiroshima has wrestled with my ignorance in philosophy, Dr John Rignall of Warwick has patched up my German, and Professor Charles Vernon of Ehime has done his best for my sinology. David L. Mansell, a Senior Librarian at Westminster City Libraries, and John L. Makin, Senior Assistant Librarian at Trent Polytechnic, have done all that professional skill in tracing information could do. To each of these I owe books, learning and the stimulation of fellow over-curious minds.

I owe a considerable debt for support and advice to colleagues at Kansai University; and also to members of the English Department at Hiroshima University, for this book was largely written there. At Hiroshima, the late and much regretted Professor Masami Tanabe and Professors Hiroshige Yoshida and Hiroshi Matsumoto gave me every assistance, Professor Michio Kawai was especially generous with resources, and Professor Nobuyuki Yuasa was also a critical audience for several of the expositions attempted here. I have profited a great deal from contact with the Ezra Pound Society of Japan: especially from the humane culture of Professor Akira Yasukawa, and from Professor Akiko Miyake's scholarship (to her I owe several rare items of Poundiana).

My good friend Professor Tan-ichi Takezawa of Hiroshima kindly consented to give the Chinese characters in this book the clarity that Western eyes require.

Dr Donald Gallup, formerly Curator of the Pound Collection at Yale, provided me, and rapidly, with otherwise-unobtainable material. Among librarians at Hiroshima I should particularly like to thank for unfailing kindness Ms Hiroko Hashimoto (now of the National Institute for Women's Education), Mr Hironobu Masumoto, Ms Hideko Tadehara, Ms Hatsue Otsuki and Mr Masanobu Osawa. In the English Department office, Mr Osamu Hamaguchi (now of the Faculty of Education) and Mr Kazuhira Maeda (now of Shimane University) devoted much time to acquiring materials for me, and assistants in many departments of the Faculty of Arts went out of their way to help.

U.S.A. and Canada permission to quote from *Confucius: The Great Digest, The Unwobbling Pivot, The Analects,* from *The Spirit of Romance,* from *Guide to Kulchur,* and from *Pavannes and Divagations,* by Ezra Pound, has been granted by New Directions Publishing Corporation, New York; British and Commonwealth (excluding Canada) permission to quote from *Confucius: The Unwobbling Pivot and the Great Digest,* from *Confucius: The Analects,* from *The Spirit of Romance,* from *Guide to Kulchur,* and from *Pavannes and Divagations,* by Ezra Pound, has been granted by Peter Owen Ltd., London; U.S.A. and Canada permission to quote from *The Confucian Odes/The Classic Anthology Defined by Confucius,* by Ezra Pound, has been granted by Harvard University Press; British and Commonwealth permission (excluding Canada) permission to quote from *The Classic Anthology Defined by Confucius,* by Ezra Pound, has been granted by Faber and Faber Ltd., London.

'Oread' and 'Hermes of the Ways', by H. D., copyright © 1916 by H. D., published in *The Collected Poems of H. D. 1912–1944,* copyright © 1982, 1983 by The Estate of Hilda Doolittle, are reprinted by permission of Carcanet Press Ltd., Manchester, for the British Commonwealth (excluding Canada) and New Directions Publishing Corporation, New York, for the U.S.A. and Canada.

Extracts from 'No Second Troy', copyright 1912 by Macmillan Publishing Co., Inc., renewed 1940 by Bertha Georgie Yeats, from 'The Valley of the Black Pig', from 'The Madness of King Goll', from 'Who Goes With Fergus?', from 'Cuchulain's Fight with the Sea', from 'He Thinks of Those Who Have Spoken Evil of his Beloved', all by W. B. Yeats, published in *The Poems of W. B. Yeats* edited by Richard J. Finneran, and from *A Vision* by W. B. Yeats, copyright 1937 by W. B. Yeats, renewed 1965 by Bertha Georgie Yeats, are reprinted by permission of Michael Yeats and Macmillan London Limited, for the world excluding the U.S.A., and Macmillan Publishing Company, New York, for the U.S.A.

Extracts from *Briggflatts,* copyright © 1968,1970, 1978 by Basil Bunting, from 'All the cants they peddle', copyright © 1969, 1978 by Basil Bunting, are reprinted by permission of Oxford University Press as publishers of the revised edition (1978) of Basil Bunting's *Collected Poems.* Permission to reproduce extracts from a letter to the author, © 1971 by Basil Bunting.

GENERAL EDITOR'S PREFACE

Each volume in this series is devoted to a single major text. It is intended for serious students and teachers of literature, and for knowledgeable non-academic readers. It aims to provide a scholarly introduction and a stimulus to critical thought and discussion.

Individual volumes will naturally differ from one another in arrangement and emphasis, but each will normally begin with information on a work's literary and intellectual background, and other guidance designed to help the reader to an informed understanding. This is followed by an extended critical discussion of the work itself, and each contributor in the series has been encouraged to present in these sections his own reading of the work, whether or not this is controversial, rather than to attempt a mere consensus. Some volumes, including those on *Paradise Lost* and *Ulysses*, vary somewhat from the more usual pattern by entering into substantive critical discussion at the outset, and allowing the necessary background material to emerge at the points where it is felt to arise from the argument in the most useful and relevant way. Each volume also contains a historical survey of the work's critical reputation, including an account of the principal lines of approach and areas of controversy, and a selective (but detailed) bibliography.

The hope is that the volumes in this series will be among those which a university teacher would normally recommend for any serious study of a particular text, and that they will also be among the essential secondary texts to be consulted in some scholarly investigations. But the experienced and informed non-academic reader has also been in our minds, and one of our aims has been to provide him with reliable and stimulating works of reference and guidance, embodying the present state of knowledge and opinion in a conveniently accessible form.

C.J.R.
University of Warwick,
December 1979

CONTENTS

to Corrêa

TEXTS AND ABBREVIATIONS

Translations throughout are mine, unless otherwise stated; but those from Dante are based on the translations in the Temple Classics, and those from Ovid on *The Metamorphoses of Ovid*, trans. Henry T. Riley (London: Bell, 1915).

Passages in the Cantos are referred to by Canto number (in roman numerals) and the number of the page in *The Cantos of Ezra Pound* (New York: New Directions, 1972; and London: Faber, 1975 [i.e. 1976]). However, Cantos up to and including those of *Thrones* are generally given in the text of *The Cantos of Ezra Pound* (London: Faber, 1964). (See below, Chapter 16.) Reference to Pound's short poems is by title only, where these are included in *Collected Early Poems*, ed. Michael John King (New York: New Directions, 1976; and London: Faber, 1977), or *Personae* (New York: New Directions, 1971). For poems included in *Collected Early Poems* and *Personae*, the text of the former is preferred.

Other abbreviations are as follows:

ABC   Ezra Pound, *ABC of Reading* (London: Faber, 1961)

BFT   Massimo Bacigalupo, *The Forméd Trace: The Later Poetry of Ezra Pound* (New York: Columbia University Press, 1980)

BG   Ronald Bush, *The Genesis of Ezra Pound's Cantos* (Princeton, NJ: Princeton University Press, 1976)

C   Ezra Pound, *Confucius: The Great Digest; The Unwobbling Pivot; The Analects* (New York: New Directions, 1969)

DE   H. D., *End to Torment: A Memoir of Ezra Pound* (New York: New Directions, 1979)

E   Ezra Pound, *Literary Essays of Ezra Pound*, ed. T. S. Eliot (London: Faber, 1960)

EPS   Ezra Pound, *'Ezra Pound Speaking': Radio Speeches of World War II*, ed. Leonard W. Doob (Westport, Conn./London: Greenwood Press, 1978)

GB   Ezra Pound, *Gaudier-Brzeska: A Memoir* (Hessle: The Marvell Press, 1960)

GK   Ezra Pound, *Guide to Kulchur* (London: Peter Owen, 1966)

Ibb   Ezra Pound, *Letters to Ibbotson, 1935–1952*, ed. Vittoria I. Mondolfo and Margaret Hurley (Orono, Me: National Poetry Foundation, 1979)

Int   D. G. Bridson, 'An interview with Ezra Pound', in *New Directions in Prose and Poetry*, no. 17 (1961), pp. 159–84

J/M   Ezra Pound, *Jefferson and/or Mussolini: L'Idea statale: Fascism as I Have Seen It* (New York: Liveright, 1970)

KP   Hugh Kenner, *The Poetry of Ezra Pound* (Millwood, NY: Kraus Reprint, 1974)

KPE   Hugh Kenner, *The Pound Era* (Berkeley, Calif.: University of California Press, 1971)

CHAPTER 1

The Beginning

Ezra Pound was born in Hailey, Idaho, in 1885, and therefore his 'Epitaph' by Rex Lampman (*PD*, vii) makes him a frontiersman:

> Here he lies, the Idaho kid,
> The only time he ever did.

But from the age of 3 he grew up in suburban Pennsylvania, where his father at that time became an assayer in the United States Mint. By 1892 they had moved into the house where Pound spent most of his youth. The local paper proclaimed: 'Some of the best known and wealthiest Philadelphia business people live in these elegant mansions, and a person residing here should consider himself blessed as few others are so far as residence location is concerned.' It was noted that 'Mr and Mrs Pound entertained the Wyncote Musicale on Friday night. An unusually fine programme was given by the members, nearly all of whom were present.'[1]

Pound thus had something to escape from, like Hemingway in Oak Park, Illinois, or like Hanno the Carthaginian in Canto XL:

> flaps, farthingales, fichus, cuties, shorties, pinkies
> et cetera
> > Out of which things seeking an exit
> PLEASING TO CARTHEGENIANS: HANNO
> that he ply beyond pillars of Herakles
> > > (XL, p. 199)

The modern Western suburb may be near the nadir of all civilisation, and artists – 'the antennae of the race' – have reacted to it with some violence in this century. At a certain point the *raison d'être* for the whole economic structure was the Sunday-afternoon tea and chat, this being the ideal end of the consumer chain: for this heavy industry fed light

industry, that ultimately some might sit among the latter's products
and chat, and others might aspire to. Pound's suburb had virtues, but
by the time he was thirty 'the word "Presbyterian" had become for him
a term of abuse'.[2]

The frontier birth has a signifiance, since it represents a rebellion
against the proper life on the part of Pound's father. He was 'accepted
for West Point but descended from the train before it arrived, returned
home, and went to work in a Chippewa Falls butcher's shop'; and
thence to Hailey (*SL*, 3). Descriptions of Homer L. Pound suggest
Daniel Touchett in *The Portrait of a Lady*: a quiet independence from
surrounding values. In the success culture of Pennsylvania he seems
never to have wasted emotional energy on the fact that he was poorer
than his neighbours. His wife compensated for poverty by cultural
means; she was 'a beautiful woman, well-bred, somewhat affected in
manner' (*DE*, 22); 'when Ezra was about five the maid would call him
so that his mother could read him "the classics" before his afternoon
nap' (*SL*, 6).

Pound began his travels in 1898, at the age of 12, in the wake of his
massive and undeflectable Aunt Frank, who took him to the Tower of
London, to Warwick Castle, 'which he was impressed to discover was
"still" the home of the Earl of Warwick' (*SL*, 13), to Heidelberg,
Florence, Naples, Rome and Venice. The routes of such cultural
Odysseys can be traced in the journals and letters of Melville,
Hawthorne, James, and a thousand of their aftercomers. The sites take
on their meaning because of the Baedekers, and because of the books
behind the Baedekers (Ruskin, Shelley); conversely the sites give
meaning to the books. So at the same time Pound was beginning his
Odyssey through books and the voices and scenes implied in them: at
the age of 13, as the Cantos remember,

> it was old Spencer (, H.) who first declaimed me the Odyssey
> with a head built like Bill Shepard's
> on the quais of what Siracusa?
>   or what tennis court
> near what pine trees?   (LXXX, p. 512)

He was enrolled at the University of Pennsylvania in 1901, at the age
of 15. He was admitted to the university because of his ability in Latin,
and he had a gusto for the reading that was hidden among the
uncharted archipelagos of hard tongues. At Pennsylvania and at

Hamilton College in New York State he was taught by scholars like Felix Schelling (Shakespeare) and W. P. Shepard (Provençal), men of great distinction; and if he had followed the path made ready for him in Romance philology, as William Paden has observed, 'he would have been a member of the first generation of philologists trained through the doctoral level' in America.[3] But Pound lacked the urge to 'master the field' that professional scholarship requires; he was gifted with a lack of any sense of 'fields', though not of any sense of relations, which is another thing.[4] And he cultivated a great inexactitude. He took what he wanted, and moved on. Another kind of reading was giving him its sense of values: William Morris, Blake, Ibsen and Pater. His friend Hilda Doolittle (later the poet 'H.D.') remembered:

> He read me 'The Haystack in the Floods' with passionate emotion.
> He brought me the Portland, Maine, Thomas Mosher reprint of the Iseult and Tristram story. He called me Is-hilda and wrote a sonnet a day; he bound them in a parchment folder. (*DE*, 12)

Pound withdrew from the postgraduate course at Pennsylvania in 1907; and after four months in a teaching post in Crawfordsville, Indiana, he was thrown out for scandalous behaviour. Well before that he was a master poet. Among the poems hard-bound in vellum for Hilda Doolittle was this (*circa* 1905?):

> Soul
> Caught in the rose hued mesh
> Of o'er fair earthly flesh
> Stooped you again to bear
> This thing for me
> And be rare light
> For me, gold white
> In the shadowy path I tread?
> (*DE*, 70: 'La Donzella Beata')

The Platonic conceit, and even its 'mesh'/'flesh' rhyme, were common enough, and could have come from Arthur Symons ('Rosa Mundi', 1894), Browning's 'By the Fire-Side', or even the Episcopalian hymnal. But the verse grows, aurally: each line develops a more emotional utterance out of a sound-seed planted in the line before. And indeed in subtlety of sound by 1906 Pound almost equalled his master Yeats, as 'The Tree' shows:

> I stood still and was a tree amid the wood,
> Knowing the truth of things unseen before;
> Of Daphne and the laurel bow
> And that god-feasting couple olde
> That grew elm-oak amid the wold.
> 'Twas not until the gods had been
> Kindly entreated, and been brought within
> Unto the hearth of their heart's home
> That they might do this wonder thing;
> Nathless I have been a tree amid the wood
> And many new things understood
> That were rank folly to my head before.

I have taken the liberty of punctuating the poem according to Pound's final version, because the breaklessness of the original punctuation obscures the movement. The poem has Yeats's extraordinary variation in speed: great length of vowel, shifting to great brevity:

> I stood   still   (   )   and was a tree   (   )   amidthewood

Few others would have dared that as a first line. The metre throughout the poem (the ideal pattern, the rhythmic expectation maintained in the mind) is iambic, and the second line establishes this safely; but the only way of taming the first line would be to cut it to 'I stood still, was a tree amid the wood', which is not what it says. Compare this by Yeats, the opening to a poem in iambic hexameters:

> The dews drop slowly and dreams gather: unknown spears
> Suddenly hurtle before my dream-awakened eyes[5]

The art of the rest is that of not repeating the cadence. It may be seen in the whole of a fifty-two-line poem called 'La Fraisne' (1906/7), which begins:

> For I was a gaunt, grave councilor
> Being in all things wise, and very old,
> But I have put aside this folly and the cold
> That old age weareth for a cloak.
>
> I was quite strong – at least they said so –
> The young men at the sword-play

Yet it is not as skilled as Yeats had been ten years before, which is not surprising. Yeats in 1895 was the product of three-quarters of a century of work by his predecessors in the same materials: a special area of images (tender, woven, mouse-grey, solitary, gold, silver, wandering, veils) and of diction ('chaunt', 'high'; 'boughs' and not 'branches'; 'seek' and not 'look for', 'cry' and not 'shout', 'breast' not 'chest', 'wend' not 'go'). Also of sound: the consonants and vowels in those words, for example, help to select them as being suitable for collocation in patterns of the soft and keening alternating with sharp sudden cries. It took most of the nineteenth century to get from Keats via Tennyson and Morris to this particular development (in Yeats) of Keats's sophistication:

> I sat on cushioned otter skin:
> My word was law from Ith to Emen,
> And shook at Invar Amargin
> The hearts of the world-troubling seamen

The head of the average worker in English iambics conceives, without thinking, a series of feet incorporating stressed syllables pretty much equal in length. The following syllables do not differ much, either in their lengths or in their stress-levels:

> one
> draw
> thru
> node
> things

That is the fodder for a very average pentameter. The poet (here Pound) strings them together, displaces one stress, and thinks he has made an interesting line:

> As one/ that would/ draw thru/ the node/ of things
> ('Plotinus')

The metre, being iambic, expects regularly alternating stresses; it largely gets them, here. And stresses in English speech tend towards recurring at regular time-intervals, regardless of intervening syllables; there is nothing in the natural durations of these syllables that works against that tendency. The line jogs. But consider the Yeats. By itself this line seems unremarkable in its durations:

My word was law from Ith to Emen

But it is in violent contrast with what opens the poem: a line with not
one single *long* stressed syllable, which therefore (to maintain distance
between stresses) bunches itself up like this:

I saton   cushioned   otterskin

To keep the regularity of beat in the mind, when the natural lengths of
the important syllables are violently at variance with each other, shakes
the mind alert; the voice then dances between flurries of rapidity and
immense drawled syllables:

I ˙saton   cushioned   otterskin:
My word   was law   from Ith   toEmen,
And shook   at InvarAmargin
The hearts   oftheworld   troubling   seamen

Along with his fertility in image and dramatic articulation, Yeats
developed such tricks as keeping his dance alive by a run of unstressed
syllables in the latter half of a line, followed immediately by a stressed
short syllable –

And dance ŭpŏn thĕ lével shore
His heart hung all ŭpŏn ă sílken dress

– or a pair of short unstresseds in the midst of massive longs:

Or do you lōng fŏr thĕ dīm sleēpў groūnd?

It is not surprising that Joyce's sound-besotten Stephen treasured in his
mouth this masterpiece:

And no more turn aside and brood
Upon Love's bitter mystery

Pound could, with comfort, have remained a skilled 'Nineties'
lyricist all his life, like Symons, whom in 1910 he called 'the subtlest
living translator' (*SR*, 144), and who survived until 1945. And perhaps
Pound made no progress at all between 1907 and 1915 (that is, during all
his struggles to become 'modern') in the sense of raising his 'absolute'

level of craftsmanship. If the use of verse is that it articulates specific resources of language along the grain of entirely specific matter, then Pound had this at the start. Of course a large part of both the language and the experience was borrowed ready-assembled from predecessors; and soon Pound decided to drop them. Having to build an entirely new language for himself, the matter that he could get into it, during the early years of 'modernity', was often crude by comparison – mere epigram, as Eliot said (*SP*, 16). Meanwhile the apprenticeship to the Yeatsian tradition had shown Pound a standard in the exploitation of verse's aural dimension (which was for him, simply, the defining characteristic of verse: *PF*, 35). It also probably developed his ear for the duration of syllables, or in other words 'quantity', which was to be a key to the versification of the Cantos.

For the young Pound, Yeats was music. Now, music in verse, ideologically speaking, represented a certain specific Good: it was equivalent to evocation of the underlying, the subtle, the unstatable. One part of nineteenth-century culture had analysed all existence in terms of discrete computable physical entities; by implication, as any poet could see, it excluded that which the human regards as his self, namely the autonomous part of him. The Western boom in material wealth was obviously allied with this tendency, as being technology- and computation-based. Public and prosperous culture followed out no implications, but accepted the whole by glossing it with a breezy magazine faith of inherited religious motions and evolutionary optimism.

Music and all 'subtlety' were ways of striking back at this ethos, because they escaped measuring. Thus Pound set them against the whole physical, normal, measurable, atomic and democratic world when he attacked the universities, which 'train scientific specialists for utility, and the fugitive fragrance of old song-wine is left to the chance misfit or the much-scorned *dilettante*' (*SL*, 57). Allied with subtlety were solitude, and that old Platonic doctrine of an immaterial soul caught in the net of an 'accidental' body:

> But for all that, I am homesick after mine own kind
> And would meet kindred e'en as I am,
> Flesh-shrouded bearing the secret [...]
>   ye, that hide
> As I hide most the while
> And burst forth to the windows only whiles or whiles
> For love, or hope, or beauty or for power,

> Then smoulder, with the lids half closed
> And are untouched by echoes of the world.

This poem, 'In Durance', posits a scattered secret society, whose secret is:

> 'Beyond, beyond, beyond there lies ...

It was written in Crawfordsville, Indiana.

The high priests of subtlety had been Pater and Swinburne; Yeats and Lionel Johnson now carried their flame. Pater had had a positive aesthetic programme, which largely corresponds to Pound's in his earliest critical prose – for example, in *The Spirit of Romance: An Attempt to Define Somewhat the Charm of the Pre-Renaissance Literature of Latin Europe* (1910). The book is thoroughly imbued with Paterism, in its language (key words are 'fine', 'subtle'), its choice of materials (small, private, craftsman-like objects, such as Arnaut Daniel's lyrics and the church of San Zeno), and its hidden assumptions.

> The objects with which aesthetic criticism deals – music, poetry, artistic and accomplished forms of human life – are indeed receptacles of so many powers or forces: they possess, like the products of nature, so many virtues or qualities.[6]
>
> Pater assumed, first that each entity had its 'virtue' (in the Neoplatonic sense), its efficient specific nature.

This 'virtue' was pre-eminently an unstatable, a subtlety, and corresponded more to a way of acting and feeling than to anything static. It 'organised' – activated and gave shape to – the essential part of the entity; the rest was dross. And, in exactly the same way, the artist had his 'virtue', which informed the essential part of him. His job was to perceive the virtues of things, so that he could get them into his work. But he could only do so at moments when he was himself at maximum efficiency – when he was most fully organised by his own inner nature, his virtue.

> Take, for instance, the writings of Wordsworth. The heat of his genius, entering into the substance of his work, has crystallised a part, but only a part, of it [. . .] scattered up and down it, sometimes fusing and transforming entire compositions [. . .] sometimes, as if at

random, depositing a fine crystal here and here, in a matter it does not wholly search through and transmute, we trace the action of his unique, incommunicable faculty, that strange, mystical sense of a life in natural things, and of man's life as a part of nature [. . .]

Thus that virtue, as we see it in Wordsworth's poetry, is both him and his perception of something outside him. So the trace of the artist's own virtue will necessarily be left in the art-work whenever he succeeds in getting into his work the virtue of its subject. The works of the school of della Robbia

bear the impress of a personal quality, a profound expressiveness, what the French call *intimité*, by which is meant some subtler sense of originality – the seal on a man's work of what is most inward and peculiar in his moods, and manner of apprehension [. . .]

And so Pound wrote in 1912 (*P*, 29) that the artist's virtue might be anything – 'It may be something which draws Catullus to write of scarlet poppies, of orange-yellow slippers, of the shaking, glorious hair of the torches; or Propertius to [. . .] "The honey-coloured light"' – but 'So far as mortal immortality is concerned, the poet need only discover his *virtù* and survive the discovery long enough to write some few scant dozen verses' – provided that he gain the technique to do so. And a chapter added in 1912 to *The Spirit of Romance* offers the theory that the troubadour and his lady are electromagnetic poles, whose effect on the troubadour is to excite him into a heightened existence in which he will 'register' (almost accidentally) what is in the interstices of the nature-world around him, so that we may in turn perceive it in the interstices of his verse, 'registered' there along with the sign of his own efficient thisness. For the artist, functioning, fits this description by Pater in 1869 of certain figures in Leonardo da Vinci:

They are the clairvoyants, through whom, as through delicate instruments, one becomes aware of the subtler forces of nature, and the modes of their action, all that is magnetic in it, all those finer conditions wherein material things rise to that subtlety of operation which constitutes them spiritual, where only the finer nerve and the keener touch can follow. It is as if in certain significant examples we actually saw those forces at their work on human flesh. Nervous, electric, faint always with some inexplicable faintness, these people

seem to be subject to exceptional conditions, to feel powers at work
in the common air unfelt by others, to become, as it were, the receptacle of them, and pass them on to us in a chain of secret influences.

Thus it is that the artist becomes prophet (or, in one of Pound's later
modernising statements, 'the antennae of the race': *E*, 58). When
Pound found this idea more or less restated by Allen Upward as
anthropological observation of the witchdoctor's function, he seized on
it (1913: *P*, 403) and drew it thus into the bases of the Cantos.

As for Pound's critical programme, he agreed essentially with Pater's
belief that the critic's job was to decide in which particular work by an
artist his 'virtue' was most strongly manifest, and to decide in which
artist the 'virtue' of a given age was most strongly manifest.[7] Having
found them, the critic would compare their 'virtues' on a sort of
Specific Intensity scale – which is how Pound will 'weigh Theocritus
and Yeats with one balance' (*The Spirit of Romance*, 'Praefatio'). Since
the whole point about this activable specific nature is that it is not the
sum of various quantifiables, the critic can only communicate it by a
non-literal language: by a kind of secondary art, or prose-poetry. Pater
instructs us to note, in a *Madonna and Child* by Leonardo, the 'curves
of the head of the child, following the little skull within, thin and fine as
some sea-shell worn by the wind'. One imagines his ecstasy when he
had created this mimetic cadence to express Leonardo's subject-matter:
'the smiling of women and the motion of great waters'. Yeats in his
critical prose cultivated these gems, which, once found, were worth
re-using,[8] and Pound also at first: Dante's *Vita Nuova* was 'this ivory
book' (*SR*, 120, cf. 126). Though he abandoned these preciosities, in
all his later critical activity Pound never abandoned the assumption that
critical prose could only hint at an unstatable: it was to the student to
read, or listen, or look, and experience for himself what was in the
art-work.[9]

Pound managed to steal the riches of 'the age of Pater' without falling
into any of its traps. In Pater's case these arise from a profound
relativist scepticism, which flatly denies his own assumption of a
specific nature, a 'virtue', in things: there is in fact, he believes, only
the individual impression, in the eyes of a particular observer at a
particular moment. And the observer himself, introspectively, discovers that he has no specific nature. As defences against the terrors of
this sceptical void, arise all the aspects of Pater's aesthetic activity: his
Neoplatonism, his cult of control, smallness, perfection, religion and

craft as ritual – in the end a stifling Gilbert Osmond-ism, treasuring and caressing qualities as *objets trouvés*.[10] Even in *The Spirit of Romance*, Pound escapes this, with an epic breadth and gusto in his analysis of Dante and Villon, with (as Marianne Moore described it) 'his definiteness, his indigenously unmistakable accent'.

To cultivate subtlety was a mode of rebellion; but that form of post-Romanticism assumes the futility of effort. To it, what is in fact constructable cannot be valuable, for it enters the solid, measurable, explicable. Only the kingship in decline, the kingship that can be no more, or the kingship that no one understands can evoke infinite dreams; only 'the fugitive fragrance of old song-wine' stays adequately suggestive. (Hence Yeats's dishevelled, old-hearted young men wandering lonely among fallen leaves, soft breasts and dim stars.) Pound had a habit of energy that was hard to fit with this. Problems were to be solved. 'I am by natr thank god IMPATIENT, if I hadn't been, I shd. still be teaching half wits in a desert beanery, at Crawfurd'sville, Indiana, which is lowern hell' (letter of 1935).[11] 'Tell him to go away, tell him to go home, he always makes too much noise, that young Mr Browning' (D*E*, 49) – thus a relic of the Pre-Raphaelite clans in London, complaining of Pound in about 1912.

Pound deeply believed that dead ends, sorrow, darkness could not be other than 'accidental' in the significant scheme of things.[12] The primal sin was to 'shut out the light'; it followed that the light was essentially there. From cowardice, and greed which was a form of fear, men refused to let it pour in, breeding pain, damage, evil. To the question 'Why is it, disgraced, they seem to relish life the more?' Pound made Browning's Fifine answer:

> we wastrels that the grey road's call
> Doth master and make slaves and yet make free,
> Drink all of life and quaffing lustily
> Take bitter with the sweet without complain
> And sharers in his drink defy the pain
> That makes you fearful to unfurl your souls.
> ('Fifine Answers')

This was the use of Browning, for Pound: the anti-obscurantist intelligence, confident of its power to clarify all corners of a fundamentally un-evil world. Browning strode in everywhere and proclaimed 'Let the light pour', like the Cantos (XCIV, p. 635) in 1955. He had a tic of exposing the manifold ways that people find to obtund their own faculties: the heroic grammarian's, the over-sensual bishop's. His Fra Lippo Lippi taught the immanence of God in a sunlit world. Much of what Emerson might have meant to Pound probably came to him through Browning, and

> Said Mr Charles Francis Adams [. . .]
> They take Browning for an American,
> he is unenglish in his opinions and carriage.
>   (XLVIII, p. 240)

The point at which snobbery, and dread of anything that moves, became 'Fear, father of cruelty' (CXIV, p. 793) had been shown to Pound by Browning in 'My Last Duchess'. The Duke writhes because his wife smiles too readily; his ' "Just this/ Or that in you disgusts me" ' is exactly the voice of Gilbert Osmond, again, in *The Portrait of a Lady* of that American investigator of psychocrimes, Henry James – a tone also related to connoisseurship, which is Osmond's line, and also Pater's ('For the way to perfection is through a series of disgusts . . .'[13]). And Pound eventually came to feel that these were a peculiarly English disease.

Against these stiflings, ambition. Energy becomes a moral duty. And the inbuilt urge in a poet to open, to bring light, to rectify, to be responsible to a real and pre-existent world, when backed with enough energy, turns into an epic ambition: to clarify and set in relation the whole world. Browning had this in his youth. In middle age he fought out the moral battle of energy, setting the young Raphael who

> was flaming out his thoughts
> Upon a palace-wall for Rome to see

against the sense of limitation in Andrea del Sarto's 'low-pulsed forthright craftsman's hand' that colours life and painting:

> A common greyness silvers everything, –
> All in a twilight, you and I alike

But at the same time 'Andrea del Sarto' shows the common ground between the Yeats tradition and Browning, and the reason why Pound could write in 1928 that above all he stemmed from Browning (*L*, 218). For these descendants of the Romantics, the 'beyond' exists; that which cannot be rationally accounted for exists; and it is in the struggle to reach to it (which is impossible) that man becomes meaningful/ spiritual/godlike, and may also leave a trace (in art) through which this quality shows, though the art 'breaks down' in the process:

> Reaching, that heaven might so replenish him,
> Above and through his art – for it gives way;
> That arm is wrongly put

Pound's Cantos are about a series of heroes who fail to reach their goals, in voyaging *past* the limits set for them. One of them is Sigismondo Malatesta, and when Pound tries in 1938 to explain what Malatesta is about he quotes (*GK*, 160) 'Andrea del Sarto':

> Ah, but a man's reach should exceed his grasp,
> Or what's a heaven for?

Since this element of vigour was in Pound from the start, it is not surprising that back in these earliest times we find in him illimitable, epic aims. The speaker of 'Scriptor Ignotus', written in July 1906, sees his

> greater soul-self bending
> Sibylwise with that great forty-year epic
> That you know of, yet unwrit

In 1904 the young Pound apparently wanted to write an epic about a *femme fatale* called Marozia.[14] In 1905 he challenged his mother to 'Find me a phenomenon of any importance in the lives of men and nations that you cannot measure with the rod of Dante's allegory [. . .]' (*SL*, 26). And by 1909 he had worked out a plausible theory of an epic's requirements (*SL*, 96–7).

If Browning was one major model (at least until about 1919) for the epic that Pound was meditating, it was quite settled from the beginning that Dante was another. Pound was later to write that his Cantos were merely footnotes to the *Divine Comedy*. This was because Dante has, in contradiction to some of his own theology, a religious sense that in its various aspects can variously be called pantheist, Neoplatonic, Thoreauvian–Transcendentalist, or (as I have said in Browning's case) the sense of God's immanence in a sunlit world: the sense that the world is charged with God. God is its cohering, structuring principle. (This is not an argument from design; God is not the designer, but the Design.) Pound felt that the *Divine Comedy* of Dante showed differentiated values inherent in the universe. This leads to larger relations, and grand Structure; and also to microcosmic structure. Romantic writing also, in some ways a resurgence of these same Neoplatonist tendencies found in Dante, liked the idea of a vast macrocosm structured and substructured down to the minutest detail – which detail is thus a microcosm. Romantic attempts at stating macrocosmic relations are common. But the Romantic failing was in microcosmic relations. Emerson's verse might say that 'A subtle chain of countless rings/The next unto the farthest brings', but it could not show this, for it had subtlety neither of cadence nor of suggested sensual apprehension. The same must be said at least of Coleridge's and Blake's (compare *E*, 72). The presenting of microcosmic relations (a matter of texture, of particular) would have threatened these writers' sense of the Ideal. Dante, on the other hand, clearly showed a vast structure of value-relations, from the 'vigor of sunlight·in the *Paradiso*' to 'the still malignity of the traitor's wallow' (*SR*, 150, 134). And he could enact microcosm in the intimate detail of his language. Hugh Kenner has shown that Pound, from his earliest studies at Hamilton, approached Dante as a linguist, caring for the single phrase, individual simile, suggestive etymology, and sharply seen detail:[15]

> e sì ver noi aguzzavan le ciglia,
> come il vecchio sartor fa nella cruna

> and towards us they sharpened their vision,
> as an aged tailor does at the eye of his needle.
> (*Inferno*, 15.20–1)

In 1934, Pound wrote of

> the progressive tightening of poet's attention from Homer to Ovid, to Dante [and] the almost uninterrupted decadence of writers' attention for centuries after Dante, until the gradual struggle back toward it in Crabbe, Stendhal, Browning and Flaubert. (*E*, 210)

Browning here coincides with Dante. In this sense both are 'modern', as Yeats never was. But before Pound could make a successful start to his twentieth-century epic he had to peel off elements in the manners both of Yeats and of Browning that have nothing to do with this kind of perception.

NOTES: CHAPTER 1

1 Noel Stock, *Ezra Pound's Pennsylvania* (Toledo, Ohio: Friends of the University of Toledo Libraries, 1976), p. 11.
2 ibid., p. 14.
3 William J. Paden, jun., 'Pound's use of troubadour manuscripts', *Comparative Literature*, vol. 32, no. 4 (Fall 1980), p. 403.
4 Paden (ibid., pp. 405–6) shows how Pound was well in advance of the philologists of his time in his sense of the relations between Provençal verse and Provençal music, ignoring the limits of the Provençal 'field' as then accepted.
5 'The Valley of the Black Pig' (text here as in 1899). 'The Madness of King Goll', below, is quoted in the text of 1895.
6 Walter Pater, *The Renaissance: Studies in Art and Poetry*, ed. Donald L. Hill (Berkeley/Los Angeles, Calif.: University of California Press, 1980), p. xix. For the following quotations, see pp. xxi–xxii, 56, 91.
7 cf. ibid., pp. xxii, xxi.
8 cf. W. B. Yeats, *Uncollected Prose*, ed. John B. Frayne and Colton Johnson, Vol. 2 (London: Macmillan, 1975), pp. 117, 90, 89.
9 cf. *L*, p. 261; his criticism largely amounted to 'There digge!'
10 See especially Pound's remarks of 1932 in *VA*, p. 222.
11 Quoted in C. David Heymann, *Ezra Pound: The Last Rower* (London: Faber, 1976), p. 11.
12 cf. 'Letters to Viola Baxter Jordan', ed. Donald Gallup, *Paideuma*, vol. 1, no. 1 (Spring–Summer 1972), p. 110.
13 Pater, *Renaissance*, p. 81.
14 The date appears to be disputed: see *SL*, p. 25; *NEP*, p. 356; *KPE*, p. 354; *Ibb*, p. 114 (where the note seems to conflict with the text).
15 Hugh Kenner, 'Dante à travers Pound et Eliot', *Les Cahiers de l'Herne*, no. 7 (May 1966), pp. 473–6.

CHAPTER 2

London: Preparation

(i) HARDNESS

Pound received his MA in June 1906, and was then appointed to a Harrison Fellowship in Romanics, which gave him a summer in Europe and a further year of postgraduate work. A quarrel arose with the University , and he left without proceeding to a doctorate. In August 1907 he was appointed to be in charge of all Romance-language teaching at Wabash College, Crawfordsville, Indiana. There he tried to build a poet's career: he sent a collection of poems to T. B. Mosher, the leading publisher in America of 'Nineties' verse. The poems were rejected, and Pound did not find congenial company in Crawfordsville. Instead he drew emotional sustenance from scandalising the citizens, and was, perhaps deliberately, so careless of their opinion in the matter of harbouring a certain actress that he was dismissed.

He then asked his father for backing in starting a poetic career in Europe. The pragmatic Homer L. Pound sent him with some of his verse to a competent authority, to see whether the boy's talent would justify this step. The answer was yes, and Pound left America for Venice in February 1908, taking his poems with him.

In Venice there were doubts, and poverty. But Pound had a book of poems privately printed – *A Lume Spento* – and with it travelled to London, arriving in September 1908. He wrote, then and later, that his purpose in going to London was to meet Yeats; which took him about six months. The introductions began with Elkin Mathews, publisher to Lionel Johnson, to Yeats, and to the 'Nineties' poets in general, who saw from *A Lume Spento* that Pound was a poet. Pound was well received; his poems were well reviewed. In spring 1909 he was already checking the proofs of his poem 'Sestina: Altaforte', to appear in Ford Madox Hueffer's *English Review*, which also published Conrad, Hudson, Galsworthy, George Moore and Henry James.

Soon Pound was active both as a poet and as an organiser of the literary world. His purposes were to learn every poetic skill, and to

bring about a second Renaissance. These were one aim, which was to
prepare for the Cantos, since Pound perceived that involvement in a
new Renaissance would not drain but feed his talent.

A critic of genius, he seemed to have an immediate understanding of
what the writer was trying to do, in every piece of new manuscript he
read. This is very rare; critics normally either do not see the new and
unforeseen element, or try to eliminate it: '[. . .] I know that one of the
temptations against which I have to be on guard', T. S. Eliot wrote, 'is
trying to re-write somebody's poem in the way in which I should have
written it myself if I had wanted to write that poem. Pound never did
that [. . .]' (*SEP*, 23).

Pound's effort also demonstrated the power of American or Emersonian sincerity, as against cosmopolitan insincerity in the service of
divided emotions – as Pound partly knew (compare *C*, 95). But perhaps
it just never occurred to him to add, in his criticism, the inevitable
admixtures: cleverness, flattery, competition. When writers met with
the 'irreverent, intuitive exactness' of his comments (Charles Tomlinson's phrase), they felt the draw of an audience that would understand
the best they could possibly produce in their own mode. The effect of
Pound's presence was very great. He lifted into activity some who
might not otherwise have become poets (H.D., William Carlos
Williams). He brought forward unknowns (Marianne Moore, Basil
Bunting). He changed the writing of the firmly established (Yeats).
Also, in matters of art, he was practical and constructive in a selfless
and in fact impersonal way: we owe the existence of both *Ulysses* and
The Waste Land in considerable degree to his timely help.

In 1908, Pound had not yet found that his Renaissance must also be a
revolution in the arts. At that time he seems to have thought chiefly of
'excellence' in modes he already knew. His *A Lume Spento* (1908), with
its fine ear and definite personal vigour, was followed by the somewhat
thinner *A Quinzaine for This Yule* in the same year, and *Personae* in
1909. Pound continued to write more self-conscious and less vigorous
Swinburnian–Yeatsian verse: *Exultations* (1909), *Provença* (1910),
Canzoni (1911). His business was, in one part, to evoke certain ways of
anti-being, felt to be in contradiction to the ways of being that are
bound by mass and time. There might be a precision in this; for,
though the goal might be Plato's One, impalpabilities turn out in
practice to be particular, and poems are valued in this mode in so far as
they attain delicate individuation of them. In 1911, Pound was
extremely skilled at this Swinburnian art:

THE HOUSE OF SPLENDOUR

'Tis Evanoe's,
A house not made with hands,
But out somewhere beyond the worldly ways
Her gold is spread, above, around, inwoven,
Strange ways and walls are fashioned out of it [. . .]

There are there many rooms and all of gold,
Of woven walls deep patterned, of email,
Of beaten work; and through the claret stone,
Set to some weaving, comes the aureate light.

Here am I come perforce my adoration of her,
Behoid mine adoration
Maketh me clear, and there are powers in this
Which, played on by the virtues of her soul,
Break down the four-square walls of standing time.

The stone is woven of light; the lady is woven of light; the light is of gold, solid, woven: 'And all her robe was woven of pale gold.' And all the sound is a weaving. It is a gem for treasurers of the exquisite – like the young Stephen Dedalus again, with his 'day of dappled seaborne clouds'.

This came out in *Canzoni* in July 1911, and in August Pound proudly took the book along with him to show his friend Ford Madox Hueffer (who later changed his name to Ford Madox Ford), who was then in Germany. Now Ford knew all about this kind of verse. His father, Francis Hueffer, had married into the interconnected clans of the Rossettis and Madox Browns, centres of the Pre-Raphaelite movement. Francis was a close friend of Dante Gabriel Rossetti, whose works gave Pound much of his early insight into the Italian poets; and in whose 'The Blessèd Damozel' (1850) Mary's handmaidens sit in heaven

Into the fine cloth white like flame
Weaving the golden thread

Ford Madox Ford, at least in his criticism, rejected the whole Pre-Raphaelite tendency, and went to its opposite. He reacted to Pound's new subtleties with a mockery that was clearly a great shock to Pound, and for some time threatened to spoil their relationship (*P*, 461–2; *PF*, 8–9). In later years Pound repeatedly expressed his gratitude.

Ford was a bearer of the gospel of continental Realism to England at a time when continental Realism was still, to England, a gospel. He sat at the feet of James, who had made contact with Turgenev, Flaubert, Zola and even the Goncourts. He used phrases from Flaubert to browbeat his opponents, much as Petrarch had once used the name of Plato to browbeat his. Ford's Realism comported a set of worlds as well as a language; and Pound, though he tended to speak only of the language, had to learn both.

The Pre-Raphaelites and the Nineties had been interested in non-causal worlds; the Realists were interested in causal worlds, which of course they said were the only ones. Thus in Ford's novel-criticism one of his terms was *'justification'*, to be pronounced as a French word, which meant:

> Before everything a story must convey a sense of inevitability: that which happens in it must seem to be the only thing that could have happened. Of course a character may cry, 'If I had then acted differently how different everything would now be.' The problem of the author is to make his then action the only action that character could have taken.[1]

Certain chains of *justification* in Ford's *The Good Soldier* (1914–15) explain the characters Florence and Leonora by events of 400 years before – as the reader is prompted to think when they are confronted over the manuscript of Luther's Protest. From that document come Florence's New England moral ruthlessness and lack of finer integration of sensibility and ideation; and from it (via the particular reaction to it of English Catholicism) comes Leonora's frozen terror of her husband's erring desires. It is a well-worked example of the craft, and one that both Flaubert and James might have been pleased with. This might be a craft that ought to be mastered by one like Pound whose aims had epic scope; but it had made very little impression on him so far, though he had read Ibsen before he left Pennsylvania. Pound's first reading of Flaubert was in 1912 – at Ford's instigation. Pound could not handle any suggestion of far-reaching human causalities until he had an antidote to what they seemed to imply, and that was to be provided by Remy de Gourmont and by Frazer.

Like all those of the 'Nineties', Pound had taken it that far-reaching causalities amounted to determinism. Like them, he had devoted much verbiage in excess of its occasions to denying all such things. This was no doubt because, in all-too-visible fact, the Explainable, and chains of explainables, had been gaining ground all through the nineteenth century. That they would end (perhaps had already ended) by conquering everything was as much the underlying and unspeakable belief of *symbolistes*, of Yeats and of Pater, as it was the open propaganda of the most thoroughgoing Realist.

For almost any *poet* of the nineteenth century, things ceased to be valid subject-matter as soon as they entered the explainable. This Yeatsian assumption suggests that the advances of the Great Explainable had been stopped by sacrificing the whole visible world to it.

This inexorable advance made Realists exult. 'Thus there is absolute determinism in the conditions of existence of natural phenomena both for living beings and for inert matter'; 'All that we can say is that there is an absolute determinism for all human phenomena' (Zola). 'We are workers – we leave to the speculators the unknown of the *why* in which they have been struggling in vain for centuries – to confine ourselves to the unknown of the *how*, which each day diminishes before our investigation.'[2] The great goal: final eradication of all pretension to autonomous, self-existent motives; and by the same token, to their opponents, final denial of the value of the human.

Yet worse (for poets), each chain of causes threatened to lead not only from the explainable to the explainable, but from the banal to the horrific. One set of chains led to the merely alien, the cold sea that had thrown up life by accident. Others led from civilised greed in slum, drawing-room and factory to 'Homeric struggles' (Stephen Crane) on darkling plains; and yet further, to Mesozoic greed fossilised in cliffs. And always confused with these was the great horror of the unspoken: sexuality.

Dull lust and ambition are inextricable in Zola's *Thérèse Raquin* (1867). Sister Carrie is moved at all crucial points by desire for glitter, glamour; which (internal evidences suggest) Dreiser conceived to be the main or only manifestation of female sexuality. In 1899, Ford's collaborator Conrad published *Heart of Darkness*, in which Kurtz's propensity to lust is essentially the same thing as his propensity to grasp, murder and cannibalise. (They are all suggested at once and indiscriminately by that airport-art image of a bronze-limbed queen surrounded by heads on stakes.) These exist in all of us, or (metaphorically) under all of us, in that great unknown sea of our dark bellies or (dare one say?) loins. 'The hysteria! The hysteria!' one might say; for in this lineage the author is unable to sort out the subject; his faculties are paralysed.[3]

The discovering of causalities, outside the area of any supposed free will, is an important part of Ford; it is also a big part of Pound's writing from about 1913. In both of them, sexual causalities are among the most important. In direct comment, Pound plays down this question of a content, stressing instead language concerns; and Ford plays down the particular matter of the sexual element. But the chief *justification* of the horrors that transpire in *The Good Soldier* leads back to the quiet, naïve, sentimental and utterly unstoppable urge of Edward Ashburnham to bed weak-looking women as a gesture of protection. The discovery of all this under the solid English officer and gentleman is the unfolding of the novel. And the discovery of this kind of thing is offered as example by Ford when he describes the proper matter of the Novel.[4] In Pound's collection *Lustra* (1916), the following was suppressed:

THE TEMPERAMENTS

Nine adulteries, 12 liaisons, 64 fornications and something approaching
  a rape
Rest nightly upon the soul of our delicate friend Florialis,
And yet the man is so quiet and reserved in demeanour
That he passes for both bloodless and sexless.
Bastidides, on the contrary, who both talks and writes of nothing save
  copulation,
Has become the father of twins,
But he accomplished this feat at some cost;
He had to be four times cuckold.

The plot of a Ford novel, or two. But this is different: where Ford is self-consciously glum, this has an urbane gaiety.

To see why Pound's poem has this gaiety is to see why at last he is able to handle these Realist preserves. He had, as it were, found order in Africa. (We can take Africa, as seen in Conrad or suggested in Melville's 'Benito Cereno', as a main variant on that seething meaningless dark sea.) With the help of Frazer and Gourmont he had been able to absorb, as significant, the fact that the civilised walker of London streets and dreamer of lake isles exists in a web of relationships that contains Congolese tribesmen as well as ants, and that this fact was not necessarily to his disadvantage; the shared patterns might be life-givers. Voltaire had probed into Western religion and found it a cardboard; but Frazer and many aftercomers, especially (for Pound) Upward (see *P*, 403–12), found that its dead and half-living forms were the survival of ritual shapes that had a thousand echoes in a thousand cultures, all

enacting, stimulating the patterns of life and growth. A dozen post-
Darwinians had read their own culture's crudeness into Darwin, and
found sexuality a gross and blind battering-ram throughout humanity
and nature; but Gourmont, a relic of that finer cult of the female that
'Calvin never blacked out/en l'Isle [de France]' (XCV, p. 647), read his
Fabre carefully and found in 'nature' and in man an endless range of
subtle and beautiful variants on the flowers of culture that sexuality's
urges lead to (*E*, 344–5; *NPL*). If (as Pound later said) the cultural
level was 'the determinant', it was not at all easy to say whether the
1914 Congolese level was higher than the British or lower. He had, as it
were, discovered that what to Conrad's Victorian provincialism was a
sea of horror was patterns. Hence his amusement, but also exhilaration,
at observing how here, in 1914,

> The gilded phaloi of the crocuses
> > are thrusting at the spring air.
> Here is there naught of dead gods
> But a procession of festival [. . .]
> Dione, your nights are upon us.
>
> The dew is upon the leaf.
> The night about us is restless.   ('Coitus')

Pound learned 'realism' at the same time as he learned a Catullan irony,
and he combined the two to express an amused superiority: taunting
the stuffed shirts as he played the fawn on the crags.[5]

Chains of hard facts were thus made acceptable as poetic matter. But
they could hardly be dealt with in a language evolved to project
penumbras of misty anti-fact. Pound now began, under Ford's guidance, to discover the virtues of prose – especially that prose developed
by the non-melodramatic branch of Realism, Stendhal, the Goncourts,
Flaubert and Maupassant. 'Poetry must be *as well written as prose*.' How
was prose written? A certain word-order is natural to it; and a certain
type of diction is natural to it – roughly, those of a natural speech that
has been somewhat trimmed and standardised to maximise the number
of distinctions it can cover, and its universal sharedness. As, in speech,
deviations from this word-order and vocabulary do not generally occur
when a man has something important to say, so we associate deviations
from them (of which Swinburne's archaic-poetick is full) with frivolity
and evasion. 'Now in this genre one only moves the reader by clarity',
as Pound never tired of repeating from Stendhal; only the articulation

of thought-sequence and the precision of image will have any effect on the reader.

And Ford trained Pound to pay attention to the prose vocabulary's resources: the kind of emotional nuance on which whole worlds turn, and how it could be concentrated (to have effect, must be concentrated) in the articulation of a single phrase.

> And as Ford said: get a dictionary
> and learn the meaning of words.
> (XCVIII, p. 689)

– Ford's advice to young writers at Rapallo in 1932 (*PD*, 155). Thus

> [...] all that de Maupassant finds it necessary to say is : 'C'était un monsieur à favoris rouges qui entrait toujours le premier.'
> [...] Maupassant's gentleman with red whiskers, who always pushed in front of people when it was a matter of going through a doorway, will remain, for the mind of the reader, that man and no other. The impression is as hard and as definite as a tin-tack.[6]

And thus Ford's 'discovery' of Lawrence by reading the first paragraph of 'Odour of Chrysanthemums'; there was no need to read more. (The explanation of how the words showed genius may be *post facto*; but the immediate recognition by such means need not have been any the less genuine.) Pound transmitted his lesson:

> [...] Poetry must be *as well written as prose* [...] There must be no book words, no periphrases, no inversions. It must be as simple as De Maupassant's best prose, and as hard as Stendhal's.
> There must be no interjections. No words flying off to nothing [...]
> Rhythm MUST have meaning [...]
> There must be no cliches, set phrases, stereotyped journalese. The only escape from such is by precision, a result of concentrated attention to what one is writing [...]
> Objectivity and again objectivity, and expression: no hindside-beforeness, no straddled adjectives (as 'addled mosses dank'), no Tennysonianness of speech; nothing – nothing that you couldn't, in some circumstance, in the stress of some emotion, actually say. Every literaryism, every book word, fritters away a scrap of the

reader's patience, a scrap of his sense of your sincerity. When one really feels and thinks, one stammers with simple speech; it is only in the flurry, the shallow frothy excitement of writing, or the inebriety of a metre, that one falls into the easy – oh, how easy! – speech of books and poems that one has read.*

And all this 'hardness' goes back to Ford:

*1937. It should be realized that Ford Madox Ford had been hammering this point of view into me from the first time I met him (1908 or 1909) and that I owe him anything that I don't owe myself for having saved me from the academic influences then raging in London. (*L*, 49 n.)

(ii)   IMAGE

Pound retained his scorn for the self-immolators before the Remorseless, for the 'red-blood school' as he called them. He saw how selective was their 'real world': '"[...] do you call that corner of a pig-sty in which you happen to live, *the world*?"' was James's imagined answer to Zola-ism.[7] And for those like Melville, Crane and Twain, who drew excitement from ever-newly annulling the Christian deity, Pound quoted a sage old relic of pre-Victorian civilisation:

> 'Why flay dead horses?
> 'There was once a man called Voltaire.'
> ('I Vecchii'; cf. *GK*, 227)

But he was now able to learn from the true prose analysts of humanity, the ones who set out with no lusts for denial to satisfy, merely wishing to find out. He also took from these predecessors of Ford an idea of the writer's function. To them, the measurable world being the important one, the only function of the artist was to render it so that it could be measured. This had a social function, in Zola: writers must be content to find out what determines social phenomena, 'leaving to legislators, to those with power of application, the task sooner or later of directing these phenomena in such a way as to develop the good and reduce the bad from the standpoint of human utility'.[8] Thus we find it in Pound in 1913, when he is very much under Ford's influence:

It is obvious that ethics are based on the nature of man [...]

It is obvious that the good of the greatest number cannot be attained until we know in some sort of what that good must consist. In other words we must know what sort of an animal man is, before we can contrive his maximum happiness [...]

The arts give us a great percentage of the lasting and unassailable data regarding the nature of man, of immaterial man, of man considered as a thinking and sentient creature. They begin where the science of medicine leaves off or rather they overlap that science. The borders of the two arts overcross. (*E*, 41–2)

Thus Ford, some years later:

[...] your business with the world is rendering, not alteration. You have to render life with such exactitude that more specialised beings than you, learning from you what are the secret needs of humanity, may judge how many white-tiled bathrooms are, or to what extent parliamentary representation is, necessary for the happiness of men and women.[9]

Like Zola, Pound in 1913 appeals to medicine as a model, to the magic of the 'experiment' and of the 'analysis' of emotions, and to Stendhal as the founding example.

In this tradition, the artist must render a pre-existing world so that it may be grasped; he must render it 'precisely'. The word 'precise' is much in Pound's vocabulary around 1912:

Mr Yeats has been subjective; believes in the glamour and associations which hang near words [...] Mr Hueffer [i.e. Ford] believes in an exact rendering of things. He would strip words of all 'associations' for the sake of getting a precise meaning [...] You will find his origins in Gautier or in Flaubert. (*SL*, 159)

How is the artist to be 'precise'? The Impressionist wing of Realism tended to assume that experience was divisible, and words were units, and the one could be matched in series to the other.

The world was out there; it sent its pictures into the brain; the writer's job was to match his words to these pictures, as they came, without 'idealist' distortion. '[We] saw,' Ford recalls of himself and Conrad, 'that Life did not narrate, but made impressions on our

brains'; '[. . .] the general effect of a novel must be the general effect
that life makes on mankind. A novel must therefore not be a narration,
a report. Life does not say to you: In 1914 my next-door-neighbour, Mr
Slack, erected a greenhouse and painted it with Cox's aluminium paint
. . .'[10]. This is perhaps as far as literati in general had got by the late
nineteenth century in understanding 'science': the notion that the
world was 'things', existent but more or less unknowable, in motion,
sending images into a brain which then computed them. It was Crane's
position in *The Red Badge of Courage* (1895), Ford still stood by it in
1924, and Virginia Woolf in *The Waves* was still valiantly labouring
with it. (*Tristram Shandy* had reduced it to an absurdity in 1760, and
Ulysses repeated the demonstration from 1917 onwards; but the
London descendants of Utilitarians and Pre-Raphaelites seemed to
prefer two-dimensional worlds.)

Literary Impressionism was suitable for baffled and paralysed minds.
In *The Red Badge of Courage* the soldier is the passive victim of all
experience: all is a threat, rapid and confusing, coming from nowhere
known and changing without reason. The movements and the utterances of what he manages to perceive as a colonel on a white-horse
giving orders are as half-grasped as the movements of the blue blur on
the hillside which is the enemy. Temperaments are attracted to
techniques. Virginia Woolf's cauterised soul seeks, among blurs, for
wisps from a pre-cauterised childhood; Ford Madox Ford finds his
truest self-projection in the impotent and bewildered Dowell, peeling
layer after layer of baseness from those around him, and never
expecting to reach the end of it. Hence the excessive (and not in the
least 'scientific') emphases: in Crane on lumps of vaguely perceived
colour, in Woolf on glitterings of sharply perceived colour. Pound was
not subject to this Impressionist limitation to visuality, as we shall see.
In 1923 he observed:

> I think Hueffer goes wrong because he bases his criticism on the eye,
> and almost solely on the eye. Nearly everything he says applies to
> things *seen*. It is the exact rendering of the visible image, the cabbage
> field *seen*, France *seen* from the cliffs.
>
> Man is an animal, and as Winzer says, 'no better than woman or
> any other animal'; he is affected by interstitial pressures, from seven
> sets of glands, and from the sensations of taste, sight, hearing, touch,
> etc., etc.
>
> All of which leave a residuum, dangerous to Mr Hueffer's theories
> [. . .]

[...] there is the quality that Yeats calls 'intensity'; there is a more dissociable agglomerate of things that can be called the musical properties of verse, quantity, stress, syncopation, etc., etc., etc., etc., et cetera.[11]

From this temperamental attraction to the idea of passively receiving blurs also comes all the fuss, in Ford, of trying to produce consistently, on the page, the illusion of a verbal record *as* enunciated by a consciousness that itself 'received' the experience. To put it another way, hence all his effort, as conscious technician, to keep a consistent narrative frame: that of oral recall by the man who saw. When asked why he tries to produce this illusion, Ford can only reply: 'Why then write?'[12] The consistent illusion of a record by the man who received the impressions matters more than a sense of a thing 'known' through those impressions, for, indeed, through them nothing *is* known: '[...] on the whole, the indirect, interrupted method of handling interviews is invaluable for giving a sense of the complexity, the tantalisation, the shimmering, the haze, that life is.'[13]

Pound from the first impact of Ford's ideas had registered some doubt: 'A ball of gold and a gilded ball give the same "impression" to the painter. [But] Poetry is in some odd way concerned with the specific gravity of things, with their nature [...] The *conception* of poetry is a process more intense than the *reception* of an impression [...]' Trying to clarify his objection, he wrote in 1920 to Ford:

And certainly one backs impressionism, all I think I wanted to do was to make the cloud into an animal organism. To put a vortex or concentration point inside each bunch of impression and thereby give it a sort of intensity, and goatish ability to butt. (*PF*, 10, 43)

He complained to Ford in 1921 (*PF*, 59) that, while Ford had been right to push for clear ordering of the verbal (syntactical, dictional) qualities of writing, in Ford's own writing these amounted to a charming surface that hid all sorts of slithers and archaisms of ideation. Ford, in return, refused to interest himself in 'subject' rather than 'treatment'. The difference between them ultimately was that Pound believed in understructure: in the world, knowable through and beyond impressions; in writing, knowable through and beyond words. The 'goatish ability to butt' in each written 'bunch of impression' would be that overcharge arising from inner structure,[14] the force or directional energy of a thing, its tense 'significance' in its relations with a world containing other charged structures.

But in 1911 and 1912 Ford was the most valuable shock Pound could receive. He held up, as a model, prose, where word-worlds analogous to important experience were analysed causally; as against verse, where worlds analogous to nothing important were created by the play of 'opalescent words'. The effect can be seen in Pound's next book of verse, *Ripostes*, in October 1912:

AN OBJECT

This thing, that hath a code and not a core,
Hath set acquaintance where might be affections,
And nothing now
Disturbeth his reflections.

A small causality shown. The matter is very simple and unspecific compared to that of Pound's Swinburnian achievements, but the poem is a step in the new direction.

This aspect of Pound's progress received much less publicity than Imagism, which seemed easier; for, to many, Imagism was simply two-line Impressionism. In 1909 a group consisting of Pound, T. E. Hulme, F. S. Flint, Edward Storer, Joseph Campbell and others was discussing all sorts of innovations in English verse, under the influences particularly of recent French *vers libre* and traditional Japanese *haiku*. T. E. Hulme is said to have insisted on 'absolutely accurate presentation and no verbiage'. His theories suggested that words should correspond to impressions combined:

Thought is prior to language and consists in the simultaneous presentation to the mind of two different images.
[. . .] Language is only a more or less feeble way of doing this.

But the two might become divorced:

All emotion depends on real solid vision or sound. It is physical.
But in *rhetoric* and expositional prose we get words divorced from any real vision [. . .]

Compare in algebra, the real things are replaced by symbols. These symbols are manipulated according to certain laws which are independent of their meaning. N. B. At a certain point in the proof we cease to think of x as having a meaning and look upon it as a mere counter to be manipulated [...]

Poetry is always the advance guard in language. The progress of language is the absorption of new analogies. (Scout, so nearest to flux and real basic condition of life.)[15]

This theory of Impressionism was a very useful anti-rhetorical 'acid'. Yet all we have so far is two images overlaid. That is what Hulme's verse presented in 1908:

> ### AUTUMN
> A touch of cold in the Autumn night –
> I walked abroad,
> And saw the ruddy moon lean over a hedge
> Like a red-faced farmer.
> I did not stop to speak, but nodded,
> And round about were the wistful stars
> With white faces like town children.

(See Hulme's 'Complete Poetical Works', in Pound's *Personae*.) The town children acquire a certain pathos of lostness; it is compensated by the jolly moon-as-farmer, avuncular, and made more whimsical by the speaker's nodding to it. There is something of the cosiness of Arnold Bennett's *Grim Smile of the Five Towns*.

Pound coined the term 'Imagiste' in 1912, for his old friend H.D., who had brought him this:

> ### HERMES OF THE WAYS
> The hard sand breaks,
> And the grains of it
> Are clear as wine.
>
> Far off over the leagues of it,
> The wind,
> Playing on the wide shore,
> Piles little ridges,
> And the great waves
> Break over it

Here was a new language-quality. This, and his own thinking about *haiku* and metaphor, inspired Pound to a new 'Imagist' doctrine, which he announced in March 1913, and which quickly attracted to it a large number of writers. An anthology called *Des Imagistes*, edited by Pound in 1914, included Richard Aldington, Skipwith Cannell, John Cournos, H.D., F. S. Flint, James Joyce, Amy Lowell, Pound, and William Carlos Williams. When Amy Lowell edited another anthology, *Some Imagist Poets* (1915), D. H. Lawrence was added. The 1913 doctrine demanded chiefly verbal economy, metrical invention – and the Image:

> An 'Image' is that which presents an intellectual and emotional complex in an instant of time [. . .]
> It is the presentation of such a 'complex' instantaneously which gives that sense of sudden liberation; that sense of freedom from time limits and space limits; that sense of sudden growth, which we experience in the presence of the greatest works of art. (*E*, 4)

Thus Pound's own 'Liu Ch'e' (*Des Imagistes*) is not a mere overlay of two images, or collation of two planes. The entities juxtaposed must be significant ones, which I take to mean at one and the same time having a sensed inner structure and a sensed directional potential. They will not, in other words, be Ford Madox Ford's mere 'cloud of impressions'. When Pound said he wanted 'to put a vortex or concentration point inside each bunch of impression and thereby give it a sort of intensity, and goatish ability to butt', he added:

> Structure, inner form, (thence departmentilization, which ultimately demands a metric, a rhythmic organization, each part necessarily of the whole, just as in prose (H. J[ames].) each word must have its functioning necessary part). (*PF*, 43)

Finding (selecting) and presenting one of these entities is likely to be as difficult, precisely, as writing the first five lines of 'Liu Ch'e'.

LIU CH'E
>The rustling of the silk is discontinued,
>Dust drifts over the court-yard,
>There is no sound of foot-fall, and the leaves
>Scurry into heaps and lie still,
>And she the rejoicer of the heart is beneath them:
>
>A wet leaf that clings to the threshold.

A woman and a leaf: two nouns (one implied). That is all that the hasty student, his head pre-stuffed with the Imagist theories, sees. But the woman's life was an expensive one, since it was involved in rustlings of silk and with the quiet to-and-fro ('footfall') of girls (presumably) like this particular rejoicer of the heart, whose sight and touch pleased. It is gone now, evidently with the prosperity of a great household, now touched only the wind; the caressing of dust-wisps and the sudden movement of leaves mock absent excitement. A life is implied in the five lines, too specific to be exhausted by mere critical prose, which does not enact a shape of movement in its cadence as this verse does. Consonant-blocks create silences, which we may notate crudely:

> Dust // drifts // over the court-yard
> There is no sound of foot-fall [pause], and the
> leaves [build-up]
> Scurry into heaps   and   lie   still

Thus are contrasted the silence and the absent movement. A voice, which presents this girl in terms tending to attract one to her past, itself offers no gush, but instead keeps its reserve in phrases like 'is discontinued', 'the rejoicer of the heart'.

And this 'she', thus sharply defined, meets the leaf, which is the end-point of its own processes. Fall of leaf: autumn; time, beauty gone, hence sense of transience; the gaiety, but the lightness (fragility) of the spring leaf implied in the past, ancient metaphor for being beautiful and young. This leaf is cold because wet, and – by now the mind is full of incipient bridgings between the two processes – 'clings' to the locus of past warmth, solitary, under threat of final exclusion by the wind.

Thus this Imagist poem does not collocate two discrete images. 'Leaf-plus-woman' would be quite void on its own. Each has to be qualified by word-structure, subsidiary image-structure, breath-structure, to build in the process of which it, at this point, is merely a complex glimpse seen in a single flash. As Ernest Fenollosa said, in what Pound was to take as his own *Ars Poetica*, 'Things are only the terminal points, or rather the meeting points, of actions, cross-sections cut through actions, snap-shots'; '[. . .] all truth is the *transference of power*. The type of [the?] sentence in nature is a flash of lightning. It passes between two terms, a cloud and the earth. No unit of natural process can be less than this.'[16]

To the magazine critics, Imagist poetry seems to have been a noting of visual images, with a *frisson* of perceived resemblance such as the

iconographer experiences when he finds a group of buildings in
Carpaccio prefigured in some Dutch woodcut. It was the interesting
collocation of fixed units, passively received, and illustrating the truth
of Impressionism (out of Locke). To Pound, the whole poem-Image
was the *result* of the interaction (by 'super-position') of two epitomised
processes, and it led 'beyond': a whole group ('intellectual and
emotional') of understandings burst upon the reader, giving that 'sense
of sudden liberation; that sense of freedom from time limits and space
limits', and 'sudden growth'.

In this writing the Image is sufficient: Pound wrote that 'The point of
Imagisme is that it does not use images *as ornaments*. The image is itself
the speech. The image is the word beyond formulated language' (*GB*,
88). And May Sinclair in 1915 defended the Imagists thus:

> The Victorian poets are Protestants. For them the bread and the wine
> are symbols of Reality, the body and the blood. They are given 'in
> remembrance'. The sacrament is incomplete. The Imagists are
> Catholic; they believe in Transubstantiation [. . .] For them the
> bread and the wine are the body and blood. They are given. The
> thing is done. *Ite Missa est.*

She quoted an Image in Dante, to which Pound had earlier drawn
attention in another context: the crowded souls of the damned who
pour into Charon's boat to cross into Hell:

> Come d' autunno si levan le foglie
> L' una appresso dell' altra infin che il ramo
> Vede alla terra tutte le sue spoglie.
>
> As leaves of autumn fall one after one
> Till the branch seeth all its spoils upon
> The ground....
>   (*SR*, 156; *Inferno*, 3.112–14)

The tendency is to abstract the self from writing, making it in one
sense 'impersonal'. To place one process-implying visual image next to
another, without comment; and to have the result found significant,
even moving, by readers; is to suggest that important structures can
exist out there, in a world that is in some ways the same for all of us,
and that they do not gain their importance from what the poet or the
poem's speaker thinks of them. This avoids one deep Romantic

assumption: that, since the universe is no more than a bundle of contingencies, the only possible significant relation between any of them is the relation that happens to interest oneself at a given moment. The poet's excuse for then foisting this to-him-interesting relation on the public is that *he* is an Interesting Person: a hero, an overreacher, a Sordello. Hence Romantic plasterings of autobiography all over the other subject-matter of the poem; or Expressionist gratuitous manipulation of the subject-matter by the proudly displayed neurosis of the artist, whether Munch or Vlaminck or the later D. H. Lawrence.

Along with the withdrawal of the (exalted) ego, at the Imagist moment, goes a shift towards the concrete. It had always been felt that Art was the profound; it now began to be felt that this profound (as, for example, 'an intellectual and emotional complex in an instant of time') could come from the concrete, and not only from the noble, the ideal, the purified-of-all-particularity. One may compare Yeats's 'No Second Troy' (apparently written in 1908)

> What could have made her peaceful with a mind
> That nobleness made simple as a fire,
> With beauty like a tightened bow, a kind
> That is not natural in an age like this,
> Being high and solitary and most stern?

with H.D.'s 'Oread' (*Some Imagist Poets*, 1915)

> Whirl up, sea –
> Whirl your pointed pines,
> Splash your great pines
> On our rocks,
> Hurl your green over us,
> Cover us with your pools of fir.[17]

The difference immediately expresses itself in words like 'crisp', 'gristly'. The texture of the experience in 'Oread' is sensed in minute particular. Some of this comes by synaesthetic suggestion: the angular difficulty of oral conjunctions like 'pines,/Splash' provokes a sense of differentiated existences. Yeats's legato 'high and solitary and most stern' by contrast evokes Ideal finish. But such specificity is also a particular power of metaphor, whose mechanism is close to that of the Image. Without enumerating flecks and strigillations, caressing textures and heaped volumes, the mere interaction of pines and sea can give immediate and exact sense of multiple aspects of these kinds. Simile also has that potential, but Yeats does not put into his the material to exploit it: 'a tightened bow' interacting with 'beauty' is gloss interacting with gloss.

For a few Imagists, for some reason, the touchable world was now acceptable. It had been evaded with the Greek-inherited concept of the Ideal: the plane above, and away from, what one stumbles over or rubs one's finger on in living; the plane to which necessarily belonged any woman (including Yeats's Maud Gonne) who could be found in verse, or any deed or setting. With that, in nineteenth-century verse, went often the sense of a special emotional strain in which such things were known: a sort of drunken abstraction or subjective loftiness that closed the vision to all spiky detail that would 'lower' it. One might enter this state by chaunting the hypnotic rhythms of poetry (see Yeats, 'The Symbolism of Poetry'[18]) or by obeying in imagination the instruction 'Half close your eyelids, loosen your hair' (Yeats, 'He thinks of Those who have spoken Evil of his Beloved') or a thousand sensory equivalents; or by merely dwelling on the noble, the high, that is, the detail-elided. The result was the sense of the whirling shimmering glassy bubble that Pound in early days called the 'phantastikon', namely the sphere of subjective vision that the ego projects from itself.[19] Thus the Ideality or loftiness of the poetic world, and the heightened or entranced state of the subject, tend to be found together.[20]

Imagist meditations on metaphor and *haiku* led Pound to the central formal discovery of the Cantos, which he later called the theory of the 'ideogram'. It is: that a statement may consist of the placing-together of two verbal 'things'. The interaction between them need not be described, and indeed cannot adequately be described. It seems that the interaction arises because things, in so far as they are felt to be significant, are also felt to be 'in process', to contain potency for particular action. Or to put it another way: integral structure, direction, and (for the human observer) significance, are inseparable.

The 'ideogram' is the Chinese written character. Pound drew his interest in the Chinese ideogram from a manuscript of the late orientalist, Ernest Fenollosa, which in 1919 he was to edit as *The Chinese Written Character as a Medium for Poetry*.

According to Pound, the Chinese ideogram does not merely represent a word, but pictures a thing (usually indissociable from its action).[21] This is put together with another picture of a thing, creating a third entity, which is a knowledge equivalent to the relations(s) between these two things and/or their actions. Instead of writing 'the cup is bright', the Chinese – Fenollosa said – wrote 'cup sun-moon', which can be read as 'the cup does what the sun and moon do'.[22]

The advantage of the 'ideogramic method', Pound tells us, is that it avoids this:

> In Europe, if you ask a man to define anything, his definition always moves away from the simple things that he knows perfectly well, it recedes into an unknown region, that is a region of remoter and progressively remoter abstraction.
>
> Thus if you ask him what red is, he says it is a 'colour'.
>
> If you ask him what a colour is, he tells you it is a vibration or a refraction of light, or a division of the spectrum.
>
> And if you ask him what vibration is, he tells you it is a mode of energy, or something of that sort, until you arrive at a modality of being, or non-being, or at any rate you get in beyond your depth, and beyond his depth. (*ABC*, 19)

This is defining by class- (or concept-) naming. Red belongs to that delimitable class of entities called colours, which belongs to that delimitable class of entities that incorporate the characteristic 'light', which belongs to that delimited class of entities called modes of energy. And thus if we say 'the sea is green' we are saying that the sea belongs to a class of entities identical in one aspect, which aspect we may abstract (from this and other phenomena) and call 'greenness'. But if we write

> Whirl up, sea –
> Whirl your pointed pines [. . .]
> Cover us with your pools of fir

we are telling the sea to 'fir', do what the fir does; and telling the fir to 'sea', do what the sea does. What does the fir do? It buries us in masses of bristly fronds, or drowns us in green; but the things that the fir is felt to do cannot be limited in number, and the irrelevant actions among them are relevant.

The problem with class-naming is that it leaves untouched three-quarters of our knowledge – the unspoken knowledge, for example, by which we can know whether assertions are right before we can work out 'why'. It cuts out those multiple 'irrelevancies' that the intelligence needs to work on, if it is to make any advances beyond what it already understands. (Precisely because these irrelevancies are concrete, they evoke the specificity of the things in question, and thus call in all our other knowledge of them.) And further: class-naming posits the existence *in the world* of finally delimitable classes of things, corresponding to concepts we can arrive at by a sort of mental computation of phenomena observed.

Such finality corresponds neither to the understanding of science nor to the processes by which men 'think'. (Scientists cannot decide the border between life and non-life: whether the virus, for example, is a living thing.) But that such finality is possible, and should be our aim, is a fixed prejudice of Greek-derived Western culture; which further suggests to us that that which cannot be so categorised does not really exist. The impoverishing effects of this, from Descartes through to John Stuart Mill, have been pithily described by Hugh Kenner (K*P*, 81–3, 95–101), to whom the present discussion is indebted.

For reasons like these, partly worked out after the event, Pound was to structure his Cantos 'ideogramicly' by juxtaposing concretenesses of all kinds: civilisations, vicissitudes, psychic states, philosophic images, lyrics, arms, men. Instead of working at one remove with terms denoting fallaciously posited classes, the reader would get 'a type of perception, a kind of transmission of knowledge obtainable only from [...] concrete manifestation' (*GK*, 28).

(iii) FORCE

Pound himself had produced, some time previously, verse that was strongly emotional (as the bulk of Imagist poetry, for example, was not), while yet moving towards the impersonal by an extreme reticence on the part of the speaking voice. In 1911 he had translated 'The Seafarer' from the Anglo-Saxon:

> May I for my own self song's truth reckon,
> Journey's jargon, how I in harsh days
> Hardship endured oft.
> Bitter breast-cares have I abided,
> Known on my keel many a care's hold,
> And dire sea-surge, and there I oft spent
> Narrow nightwatch nigh the ship's head
> While she tossed close to cliffs. Coldly afflicted,
> My feet were by frost benumbed.

Chill its chains are; chafing sighs
Hew my heart round and hunger begot
Mere-weary mood. Lest man know not [. . .]

As Pound said in 1936: 'As to POERTY// it just ain't till it is lived/ Best of it has to be knocked out a man; *at* the end of his tether/ no matter what tether// The real thing is the LAST resource' (*Ibb*, 56). The situation denoted in 'The Seafarer' is solitude, sea-battering, extremes of temperature, uncertainty. The man speaks, but only when forced to; and the sign of this is in diction, cadence and image. '*J*ourney's *j*argon [. . .] *h*arsh days/*H*ar*d*ship endured': grating alliterated consonants, hard vowels repeated. A whole world of 'shaggy' sounds (Dante's term), evoking hard rope, wood, ice against flesh: '*Ch*ill its *ch*ains are; *ch*afing *s*ighs/*H*ew my *h*eart round [. . .]' These consonants build up in blocks so that no flow is possible, instead heavy marching: 'tossed close to cliffs. Coldly afflicted [. . .]' But this heightens a tendency already present in diction, which strictly avoids 'the' and 'a' and polysyllabic flannelling, so that the strong-stress count is at a maximum. Added to systematic alliteration, hammering the harsh consonants, this makes (as Bunting has said) 'a MARCH'.[23]

Sound-structure is highly affective in the Old English 'Seafarer', and so Pound had decided not to translate in the usual sense. Instead he copied cadence and vowel–consonant pattern closely, perforce letting the 'things meant' more or less go hang. The resulting changes in literal meaning change the emotional direction of the poem, but not much. The real losses occur elsewhere. 'Chill its chains are' is emotively weaker than 'caldum clommun' not because the meaning is quite different (as indeed it is), but because of the inversion, which is 'literary'. 'Mere-weary mood' bends the meaning of 'merewerges mod', yet it is not that factor which causes the emotional leakage, but the archaism. And these losses are trivial, compared to the majesty of force and self-control that still remains in movement and image. In 1916 Pound wrote:

'The beginnings of English poetry . . . made by a rude war-faring people for the entertainment of men-at-arms, or for men at monks' tables.' [. . .] has the writer of this sentence read *The Seafarer* in Anglo-Saxon? Will the author tell us for whose benefit these lines, which alone in the works of our forebears are fit to compare with Homer – for whose entertainment were they made? They were made

for no man's entertainment, but because a man believing in silence
found himself unable to withhold himself from speaking. And that
more uneven poem, *The Wanderer*, is like to this, a broken man
speaking [. . .] an apology for speaking at all [. . .] (*E*, 64)

An influence from an entirely different direction met with this Anglo-
Saxon. The widow of Ernest Fenollosa in 1913, and again in 1915, gave
Pound batches of Fenollosa's papers, seeing in him the non-scholar
who might have imagination to perceive the force in Fenollosa's notes
from Chinese poetry and Japanese drama. Within eighteen months
from receiving the first batch, Pound had published 'Exile's Letter':

> And the girls singing back at each other,
> Dancing in transparent brocade,
> And the wind lifting the song, and interrupting it,
> Tossing it up under the clouds.
> > And all this comes to an end.
> > And is not again to be met with.
> I went up to the court for examination,
> Tried Yō Yū's luck, offered the Chōyō song,
> And got no promotion,
> > and went back to the East Mountains
> > White-headed.
> And once again, later, we met at the South bridge-head.
> And then the crowd broke up, you went north to San palace,
> And if you ask how I regret that parting:
> It is like the flowers falling at Spring's end
> > Confused, whirled in a tangle.
> What is the use of talking, and there is no end of talking,
> There is no end of things in the heart.
> I call in the boy,
> Have him sit on his knees here
> > To seal this,
> And send it a thousand miles, thinking.

In 1923 Pound classed this with his 'Seafarer' and *Homage to Sextus
Propertius* as translations that 'would have a literary existence of their
own even if no originals existed'.[24]

Nothing is said about the girls; but the song referred to is fused with
their transparent brocade, lifted and tossed. There is no need to say
anything. 'And all this' (unqualified) 'comes to an end'. Diction is
eclectic enough to allow for uncolloquial precisions of image, but its
ground-tone is simplicity, neither courtly nor showily popular, and

when the delighting images are done there is only the flat statement, in an improvised-looking sentence-structure, setting down the fact and implying the emotion. Years later Charles Reznikoff, associated with Pound via Zukofsky's 'Objectivists' group, found occasion to quote A. C. Graham's introduction to his translations of T'ang poetry: an eleventh-century Chinese wrote that 'Poetry presents the things in order to convey the feeling. It should be precise about the thing and reticent about the feeling.'[25]

(iv) IRONY

Pound also had to develop his urbane voice; that gay irony that he used to mock the ossified, in 1913 and 1914, as he 'mated with his free kind upon the crags',[26] now had to be sharpened for more savage purposes. There was the war. Trainloads of earnest and healthy young men had left for the Front, and among them, against Pound's judgement, his friend, the sculptor Gaudier-Brzeska. For years there was the newspaper war, and the real war; and, in the climate of public opinion at home, returning survivors hardly dared mutter of what they had really seen. But Pound was receiving letters from Gaudier-Brzeska, in which the emotional wearing-down from his first zest is even more painful than the things described. December 18, 1914:

When we took the trenches after the march it was a sight worthy of Dante, there was at the bottom a foot deep of liquid mud in which we had to stand two days and two nights, rest we had in small holes nearly as muddy [. . .]

May 25, 1915:

We killed 1,250, but the horrid side is the stench now.

The last letter that Pound received, ?3 June, 1915:

Right and left they lead Rosalie [the bayonet] to the dance, but we have the ungrateful task to keep to the last under a hellish fire [. . .] It is a gruesome place all strewn with dead, and there's not a day without half a dozen fellows in the company crossing the Styx. We are betting on our mutual chances [. . .] I have read nothing, a

desert in the head a very inviting place for a boche bullet or a shell
[...] (*GB*, 59–64)

Then Gaudier was killed, and there are signs that Pound continued to
be affected by this loss throughout his life.

Poung began to associate with the radical *New Age* group, and to read
things like this pamphlet that was later used in his poem *Hugh Selwyn
Mauberley*:

Some saw adventure like an old Pied Piper [...] Some came from
fear of cowardice, a few at the bidding of the Church; one, here and
there, at the command of starvation. And for liberty they have
suffered the torments of the damned. They have been shot and
stabbed to death. They have been blown to pieces. They have been
driven mad. They have been burned with liquid fire. They have been
poisoned with phosgene. They have been mutilated beyond description. They have slowly drowned in mud. They have endured modern
war.

To what end? For what liberty?[27]

Two enormous congeries of human culture, economics and history, had
come into collision, without any real idea of purpose or of likely result;
having come into collision, so that now they were losing some of their
best elements, they were unable to admit what was happening, or (in so
far as it was admitted) to do anything about it. To Pound this suggested
great motive forces and an absence of controlling power. Controlling
power had to do with communication, hence with words, Pound's
medium. Hence his attack on the public language.

Men in comfortable places, desirous of prolonging their ease, had
sifted their words, collecting velleities and large ambiguities, words that
seemed to bring all history in on the side of the way things were, words
whose august suggestions defied all challenge, words that awed the
pedestrian reader as the lofty façades around the Parc Monceau in the
1890s dared any humble passer-by to think that life behind them might
not be the peak of human existence.

The British Empire was supported by words: like 'annalists',
'reputations', 'monumental effigies', 'expound', 'historical data'.Collo-
cated in sonorous subordinations in *The Times*, they might serve to
apportion merit in some North-West Frontier war; or they might

discuss some crux of Roman history; or they might conveniently imply both, for indeed an implicit comparison with the Roman Empire was one of the great self-assurers of that on which the sun never set. Such language is impervious to actuality, to the local particularity and gristle of what takes place (on the North-West Frontier or anywhere). What can one do with it?

To kill it with irony is one of the purposes of Pound's collage-translation taken from Propertius' *Elegies, Homage to Sextus Propertius* (1919). Any such language, being evasion, hides some concrete aim. One can juxtapose its befogging generalities with words that specify particular aims, of the kind being hidden:

> Annalists will continue to record Roman reputations,
> Celebrities from the Trans-Caucasus will belaud Roman celebrities
> And expound the distentions of Empire,
> But for something to read in normal circumstances?

'Celebrities' is unfortunate: then the significance of these foreign satraps is merely their fame? And 'distentions': is the virtue of Empire merely its size? 'Belaud' – rather close to 'bedaub': is that what our historians do? These words fit uncomfortably well into the thought-sequence; and this close fitting is the ironist's great weapon, his shirt of Nessus.

The vocabulary 'of Empire', grandiosity and vagueness, shrivels upon juxtaposition with the real. One can place it with a vocabulary that is mentally one degree too elevated for it; for it is after all a glorified journalese. A word that is somewhat scientific, a little learned, neutrally precise – like 'elucidation' – will leave it staggering:

> Neither expensive pyramids scraping the stars in their route,
> Nor houses modelled upon that of Jove in East Elis,
> Nor the monumental effigies of Mausolus,
>   are a complete elucidation of death.

Or one can juxtapose with it matters, experiences, that are specific, have the smell of things personally and genuinely known. Propertius' own chief personally important matter is love:

> Now with bared breasts she wrestled against me,
>   Tunic spread in delay;
> And she then opening my eyelids fallen in sleep,

Her lips upon them; and it was her mouth saying:
Sluggard!

His second is the tooth of time:

When, when, and whenever death closes our eyelids,

Moving naked over Acheron
Upon the one raft, victor and conquered together,
Marius and Jugurtha together,
one tangle of shadows.

But Pound's Sextus is not content to let even his own realities stand,
lest they inflate themselves – or be thought to. Irony cuts them down.
He advertises the fact that he is a fool in his pursuing of a mistress who
makes a fool of him. She herself is a bundle of postures answering his
self-mocking insincerities:

Damp woolly handkerchiefs were stuffed into her undryable eyes,
And a querulous noise responded to our solicitous reprobations.

The two 'personal' subject-matters are fused, frequently, in irony; his
love is as bathetic as his imagined death:

You, sometimes, will lament a lost friend,
For it is a custom:
This care for past men

Cynthia falls ill:

Great Zeus, save the woman,
or she will sit before your feet in a veil,
and tell out the long list of her troubles.

Yet even when the ironist thus punctures himself his irony stands as
a bulwark against public fatuousness. When the reader is shown on the
one hand a man who knows his own experience and his own follies, and
on the other a public that has no idea of its own follies, there is only one
decision. As Eliot had shown in 1914, between the man who tells us he
does not know how to spit out all the butt-ends of his days and ways,
and the women who 'come and go/Talking of Michelangelo', there is no
confusion. Private self-doubt is a weapon against stupid public certainty.

Pound was extremely conscious that poets supply novelists, who supply popular novelists and hence newspapermen, with phrases and images to think in; as it were Joyce – Burgess – novel-reviewer – leader-writer – and so on. If somehow in 1915 a population of newspaper-readers, sending their sons from mine and factory to die in ditches, were able to tolerate even for a moment the suggestion that they were thereby defending a shared British lifestyle that consisted of bugles calling from sad shires and honey still for tea, it was because there had instantly arisen in 1914 a generation of subpoets and hymn-writers who offered these images to them, building on the efforts of Newbolts before them. These bestselling poetasters habitually started from generalities and moved to generalities: from the stern and proud mother and her bosom, to the war implicitly waged in her name. They were willing to set off on great public themes before they had mastered the textures, faced the intimate realities, of their own lives. A public accustomed to a diet of large rhetoric has its demands, which, acting on the politicians they elect, become political forces. Thus, in his excellent poem 'They All Made Peace – What Is Peace?' (1922), Hemingway connected the minds of newspapermen, cliché, the minds of statesmen, and treaties that cause wars.

From these realisations it was not far to the position that no expression public or political, or indeed concerning anything larger than the pain- or pleasure-stimulant in front of one's nose, could ever be genuine. Hemingway reached that position. So did Pound's Propertius: it is implied by *Homage to Sextus Propertius* as a whole that *any* public utterance is bombast. This was, by and large, the position of the ironists that Pound had learned such writing from: Eliot, Laforgue, James and Gourmont. Of his own generation as a whole, Pound later wrote that they were

> a generation of experimenters [. . .] which was unable to work out a code for action. We believed and disbelieved 'everything', or to put it another way we believed in the individual case.
>
> The best of us accepted every conceivable 'dogma' as a truth for *a* situation, as the truth for a particular crux, crisis or temperament. (*GK*, 291)

In his *Homage to Sextus Propertius*, Pound took a Latin text in which he saw verbal ironies which few others saw; compressed the whole violently, leaving out sections of (to him) unnecessary mythological protestation; imitated the verbal ironies, not where they occurred but

wherever he could, allowing new ones to be suggested by all sorts of
minor associations in the Latin; likewise created punning banalities for
a ground-tone to the irony, and even joked frequently about the game
of translating; and allowed sound to overrule denotation in support of
the tone that he wanted.[28] He probably heightened the disparity
between language-registers (for example, American vocabulary perhaps
for the first time enters his verse on a large scale here, acting as the plain
blunt debunker: 'door-yard', 'boom', 'erasers', 'scraping the stars',
'stumbles' (noun), 'quiet hour', 'interment', 'plumb in the middle'), so
as to lay on the irony with a trowel. Thus he violently wrenched his
'translation' into something like a heightened equivalent for the
original's meaning: a man setting intimate awareness of his own life and
follies against a threatening public vacuity. This way of proceeding with
the Classics was not understood. Readers fled to the arms of professors,
who confirmed their worst suspicions: the text contained Howlers.

So, Pound said (*L*, 239), he wrote *Hugh Selwyn Mauberley (Contacts
and Life)* (1920) as a popularisation of *Propertius* (though he may
have said so in mere irritation). The layout of emotional centres in the
two poems is somewhat similar. There is the same fatuity of the press
and public life, worshipped then as the Gross National Product is
worshipped in our day:

> Faun's flesh is not to us,
> Nor the saint's vision.
> We have the press for wafer;
> Franchise for circumcision.

(The irony has become sharper by becoming less heavy in contrasts.
There is no transition of language-register here, but instead a brutally
unremarked shift of subject-matter). In this poem, again, there is war
as the result of public crassness, but it is no longer merely matter for
joking, a matter of a Tibet 'full of Roman policemen':

> Died some, pro patria,
>   non 'dulce' non 'et decor'. . . .
> walked eye-deep in hell
> believing in old men's lies, then unbelieving
> came home, home to a lie,
> home to many deceits,
> home to old lies and new infamy;
> usury age-old and age-thick
> and liars in public places.

The pamphlet *The Right to Live* had said soldiers had come 'From suburbs and from hovels [. . .] Some attested the promptings of duty [. . .] And for liberty they have suffered the torments of the damned [. . .] To what end? For what liberty?' The poem now answers as bluntly as possible:

> For an old bitch gone in the teeth,
> For a botched civilization,
>
> Charm, smiling at the good mouth,
> Quick eyes gone under earth's lid,
>
> For two gross of broken statues,
> For a few thousand battered books.

Set against this menacing public horror there is again the private; as in *Propertius*, it is love, again threatened with the 'tooth of time':

> *Tell her that sheds*
> *Such treasure in the air,*
> *Recking naught else but that her graces give*
> *Life to the moment,*
> *I would bid them live*
> *As roses might, in magic amber laid,*
> *Red overwrought with orange and all made*
> *One substance and one colour*
> *Braving time.*

But between these poles of the lying and botched public life, and the specific and valued private, comes a complicated ballet of cultures and sensibilities.

There is Mauberley himself, who has a sensibility such as civilisation needs, but is battered into inaction by the grossness around him – like the 'helpless few in my country,/O remnant enslaved![. . .] You who can only speak,/Who can not steel yourselves into reiteration', whom Pound had tried to encourage in 1913 ('The Rest'). But Mauberley's extreme inability to fight back against pervading crudity is associated with a personal impotence in him that includes sexual and literary indecision; and (by image) it is also associated with the Nineties – another era of fine sensibilities, producing portraits with eyes 'Thin like brook-water,/With a vacant gaze', to match Mauberley's medallion of his mistress's 'face-oval beneath the glaze,/Bright in its suave bounding-line, as,/Beneath half-watt rays,/The eyes turn topaz'.

There is also Mr Nixon, apparently suggested by Arnold Bennett, representative of the culture-level of bestselling subpoets and hymn-writers, that is to say elevated hacks with a nose for what the public wants. It wants bluffness, blandness, solidity; and Mr Nixon is thus associated with the Buchanans and the Gladstonian official culture that battered Rossetti and his successors into insensibility.

And Mauberley and Nixon kick about between them a football which is 'Ezra Pound'.

'Mauberley buries E.P. in the first poem; gets rid of all his trouble-some energies,' Pound wrote in about 1954.[29] Mauberley sees E.P. as someone born in a 'half-savage' America, and, for that reason, attempting something that his wiser and more cosmopolitan London world has given up long ago, namely

> to resuscitate the dead art
> Of poetry; to maintain 'the sublime'
> In the old sense.

Mr Nixon and his like are of the opinion that E.P. is in fact trying to do exactly what 'the Nineties' did:

> 'And give up verse, my boy,
> 'There's nothing in it.'
> . . . .
> Likewise a friend of Blougram's once advised me:
> Don't kick against the pricks,
> Accept opinion. The 'Nineties' tried your game
> And died, there's nothing in it.

Mauberley does not make that mistake, exactly; he says E.P. is using harder men for models, like Flaubert and Homer; but he detects in E.P. no wider aims than the Nineties had, credits him with a desire to wring Nineties-ish lilies from the acorn, and with a proper Nineties scorn for philology as opposed to 'the elegance of Circe's hair'. Mauberley's only objection to E.P. in fact appears to be that, instead of giving up (like the more sophisticated Mauberley himself), E.P. is going into action, doing what he aims to do, thus proving finally his American grossness.

Both Mauberley and Mr Nixon are wrong: for the E.P. of *Hugh Selwyn Mauberley* does in fact show an advance over the Propertius of *Homage to Sextus Propertius*. Whereas that Propertius disbelieves totally in the value of any public concerns or energies, such energies are implicit everywhere in the sensibility behind *Mauberley*. The slaughter is connected by the poem with public lies; the lies are connected with the grossness of the public culture, whether in 'tea-rose tea-gown etc.', in the 'mould in plaster,/Made with no loss of time', in Mr Nixon's buttering of reviewers, or the ignoring of the prose stylist (Ford). The speaker's portrait of Mauberley connects his inability to combat these things with an impotence that is personal, and need not be universal. And it continues by giving (in negative form) a concrete and coherent programme of actions that should be undertaken to defeat the grossness, when it says that Mauberley is

> Incapable of the least utterance or composition,
> Emendation, conservation of the 'better tradition',
> Refinement of medium, elimination of superfluities,
> August attraction or concentration.
>
> Nothing, in brief, but maudlin confession

Pound, in the 1910s, by interesting himself in oddities like tone colours and Sapphics, allowed himself to be taken for a collector of cameos. *Hugh Selwyn Mauberley* was written to show, no doubt partly to Pound himself, that he was not that. By 1920, when *Mauberley* was published, the concrete proof of Pound's ability to use larger energies was already being attempted, in the Cantos.

NOTES: CHAPTER 2

1 Ford Madox Ford, *Joseph Conrad: A Personal Reminiscence* (Boston, Mass.: Little, Brown, 1925), p. 128.

2 Emile Zola, 'The experimental novel' (1880), in George Becker (ed.), *Documents of Modern Literary Realism* (Princeton, NJ: Princeton University Press, 1963), pp. 163, 172, 186.

3 Crane ('Maggie', *Black Riders*), Jack London (*The Iron Heel*) and Twain ('The Mysterious Stranger') gloom didactically, exult, or exult under the cover of gloomy preaching. By contrast, Melville (in *Benito Cereno*) and Hardy are often clear-sighted if insistent.

4 See Ford, *Joseph Conrad*, pp. 136–7.

5 cf., e.g., 'Phasellus Ille', published in 1912 next to 'An Object' (for which, see above, p. 28).

6 Ford Madox Hueffer, 'On impressionism' (1913), reprinted in *Critical Writings of Ford Madox Ford*, ed. Frank McShane (Lincoln, Nebr.: University of Nebraska Press, 1964), pp. 38–9.

7 Becker (ed.), *Documents*, p. 239.

8 ibid., p. 180.

9 Ford, *Joseph Conrad*, p. 223.

10 ibid., pp. 194, 192; cf. esp. p. vi.

11 'On criticism in general', *Criterion*, vol. 1, no. 2 (January 1923), p. 146.

12 *Critical Writings of Ford Madox Ford*, p. 44.

13 Ford, *Joseph Conrad*, p. 204.

14 See *PF*, p. 43, and above, p. 30.

15 'Notes on language and style', in Michael Roberts, *T. E. Hulme* (London: Faber, 1938), pp. 281, 273, 272, 277. This essay was first published (partially) in 1925.

16 Ernest Fenollosa, *The Chinese Written Character as a Medium for Poetry*, ed. Ezra Pound (San Francisco, Calif.: City Lights, n.d.), pp. 10, 12.

17 Reprinted in Peter Jones (ed.), *Imagist Poetry* (Harmondsworth: Penguin, 1972), p. 62; for May Sinclair, see ibid., pp. 31–2.

18 W. B. Yeats, *Essays and Introductions* (New York: Macmillan, 1961), p. 159.

19 'Three Cantos: I', *Poetry*, vol. 10, no. 3 (June 1917), p. 120; cf. *SR*, p. 92.

20 But withdrawal of a specified subject (as we see in many Imagist poems) need not, on its own, destroy this aesthetic.

21 But see e.g. *KPE*, pp. 223–9, and Scott Johnson, 'The "tools" of the ideogramic method', *Paideuma*, vol. 10, no. 3 (Winter 1981), pp. 525–32.

22 Fenollosa, *Chinese Written Character*, p. 18.

23 Letter to the author, 31 October 1971.

24 'On criticism in general', p. 152.

25 Quoted in L. S. Dembo (ed.), 'The "objectivist" poet: four interviews', *Contemporary Literature*, vol. 10, no. 2 (Spring 1969), p. 193, from A. C. Graham, *Poems of the Late T'ang* (Harmondsworth: Penguin, 1965), p. 7.

26 'Tenzone' (1913).

27 Quoted by Ernest Griffin in *Paideuma*, vol. 5, no. 2 (Fall 1976), pp. 269–70.

28 J. P. Sullivan, *Ezra Pound and Sextus Propertius* (London: Faber, 1965), p. 97.

29 In *Accent* (Winter 1956), quoted by A. L. French in J. P. Sullivan (ed.), *Ezra Pound: A Critical Anthology* (Harmondsworth: Penguin, 1970), p. 334. Pound seems to have intended the first poem of the first sequence to be Mauberley's epitaph for E.P.; the rest of the first sequence to be E.P.'s portrait of his times, spoken in the first person; and the second sequence (beginning with the subtitle 'Mauberley/1920') to be E.P.'s portrait of Mauberley. But this is controversial in the extreme: see esp. Ezra Pound, *Hugh Selwyn Mauberley*, ed. Massimo Bacigalupo (Milan: Il Saggiatore, 1982), pp. 9–12 (and refs) for other views.

The evidence for Pound's plan is chiefly as follows. Pound stated twice in the 1950s that the opening 'Ode' was an epitaph for E.P. (see above, and Terri Brint Joseph, 'The Decentered Center of Ezra Pound's *Hugh Selwyn Mauberley*', *The Yearbook of Research in English and American Literature*, vol. 1 (1982), p. 125). Pound further stated c.1954 (see above) that it was Mauberley who 'buried' E.P. (For the usage, cf. *L*, 323.) Most critics agree that some non-Poundian sensibility is, with scorn, 'burying' E.P. in this 'Ode' (it might be a British commentator: *KP* 170; or it might be E.P. himself, speaking ironically). Mauberley seems the perfect candidate for the role of expressing this sensibility (even though he was not created till after these lines were written). His 'burial' of E.P. at the outset is then balanced by E.P.'s burial of him at the end of the work. The subtitle 'E.P. Ode pour l'Election de son Sépulchre' properly applies only to the first poem, though it was wrongly placed in many editions: see J. J. Espey, *Ezra Pound's 'Mauberley'* (Berkeley, Calif.: University of California Press, 1974), p. 20. It is ambiguous, but must have been intended to mean 'E.P.: Ode for the Selection of His Tomb', i.e. 'Ode for the Selection of E.P.'s Tomb'; that is in fact the only possible interpretation of the remarks cited by Joseph (see above), where Pound is saying that this subtitle says, precisely, that it is E.P.'s sepulchre that the 'Ode is for.

CHAPTER 3

'Ur-Cantos'

At first the proof of Pound's powers, in epic, was being attempted on the model of Browning, whom Pound associated with constructive, world-penetrating energy – or 'a revivalist spirit' (*GK*, 290). Pound had been very quiet on the subject of writing epics since about 1907. Then suddenly, on 21 September 1915, he wrote to an American friend that he was at work on 'a cryselephantine poem of immeasurable length which will occupy me for the next four decades unless it becomes a bore'. 'By mid-December', Noel Stock tells us, 'Pound had drafted the first three cantos of his long poem and was working on canto 5. In a letter of 18 December 1915 he warned Homer that he had better begin reading Browning's *Sordello* to prepare himself for the "big long endless poem" with which he was then struggling. Such preparation was necessary, he said, because it alluded much to Browning's poem' (*SL*, 231, 237).

It appears that these writings are much the same as the 'Three Cantos' that appeared in *Poetry* in June, July and August 1917, which have every fault that Pound could possibly have inherited from Browning.[1]

The first of these 'Ur-Cantos' discusses (with Browning) the form to be used for the long poem, the relation between the speaker-author and the things presented, and the right place to start from. Should one use the device of the showman's booth, parading visions of history? Are these visions of gods too subjective? Should one begin with ancient Egypt, or China? Most poetry loses a great deal by paraphrase. But what this poetry would lose would be merely: (*a*) further qualifications to the argument; (*b*) historical 'atmospheres'; and (*c*) local colour, merging with autobiography:

> Beaucaire's slim gray
> Leaps from the stubby base of Altaforte –
> Mohammed's windows, for the Alcazar
> Has such a garden, split by a tame small stream.

Pound's stage-manager casts before our eyes *his* history-visions, qual-
ifying description of one historical site by noting its visual cross-
reference to another. He divagates to attack the evasion in Browning's
method of presenting himself through his hero Sordello. He qualifies
his attack on Browning's method by reference to his own lively parallel
experiences. For the main opponents are philosophical sophistication
and cultural sophistication; they are the reason for all the defensive
qualifications. We must pause to have it shown clearly that the speaker
realises how 'naif' Ficino was, and how *awful* the quoted piece of
Wordsworth is, with a thousand extraneous observations of detail to
show the fineness of the speaker's eye. He finally arrives at this
conclusion concerning gods and subjectivities:

> Oh, we have worlds enough, and brave *décors*,
> And from these like we guess a soul for man
> And build him full of aery populations.

Having said that, he finds his pentameters so grandiose that, in a later
edition, he must show his awareness of that, too; and adds a paren-
thesis: '(Panting and Faustus)' (*QPA*, 23).

Under all these things there are certain 'matters' which are not
concerned with the speaker's relationship with reality, historicity,
Robert Browning, or his own soul. The first Canto eventually gets
around to presenting gods, around us in the air. The second presents
passion. The third offers various late, thin visions-with-Neoplatonic-
philosophy, and judges their thinness by comparison with a vigorous
Lorenzo Valla and a robust Homer. This *robustezza* (simply knowing
that its gods exist) is the point that the whole of the three 'Ur-Cantos'
were intended to arrive at.

Pound wanted to show himself by showing his worlds (which, in his
case, included the rather embarrassing, defensive-making matter of the
gods). And he wanted to show his discovery of himself by showing his
discovery of his worlds. According to the logic of Romantic verse
(which extends to *Sordello*), writing such poems was justified only in so
far as the self was a Special self, not caught in the ruck of the ordinary,
the explicable, of politicians manufacturing votes, or Naddos manufacturing verse. So passion and vigour must peep from every cranny.
Everywhere in these Cantos is demonstrated the vigorous intervention
of the poet, vigorously seizing scraps of history and giving them
imaginative life. Likewise, dramatic actions must be squeezed by
Pound through Browning's vigour-apparatus:

And the young prince loved her – Pedro,
Later called the cruel. And other courtiers were jealous.
Two of them stabbed her with the king's connivance,
And he, the prince, kept quiet a space of years –
Uncommon the quiet.
And he came to reign, and had his will upon the dagger-players,
And held his court, a wedding ceremonial –
He and her dug-up corpse in cerements
Crowned with the crown and splendor of Portugal.

Pound uses Browning's Elizabethan stage-language and metre, glamour of chiaroscuro ('chinks', 'flashes') that lights dark deeds, dramatic pace-change ('Uncommon the quiet.'), grim humour ('dagger-players'). But Browning, who believed in this kind of thing, was able to fuse his action into a whole:

> Glide we by clapping doors, with sudden glare
> Of cressets vented on the dark [...]
>   Why strange
> Such a recess should lurk behind a range
> Of banquet-rooms? Your finger – thus – you push
> A spring, and the wall opens, would you rush
> Upon the banqueters, select your prey,
> Waiting (the slaughter-weapons in the way
> Strewing this very bench) with sharpened ear
> A preconcerted signal to appear
>   (*Sordello*, I. 313–24)

But the vigour imparted even here is that of the ego, which struts and frets and generally considers its position; it is not that of the self. Nineteenth-century poets called their beloved ego 'the self' or 'the imagination' from sheer ignorance of the rest of the human faculties. (Pound later quoted Remy de Gourmont: 'My true life is in the unspoken words of my body' – *E*, 342.) Since the self is more intricate and deeper than the ego, its knowing of worlds is deeper; it is not the mere concepts of them (in an Aristotelian sense), or even merely the uncogitated sights of them (as in Ford and Impressionists). It is grain, odour, and other unknowns that can amount to sense-of-isness. If he read Rimbaud's remark that he intended to study himself by cultivating visions,[2] Pound might well have taken him to mean 'visions' in this sense – including the fullest kind of daylight knowing, as well as that kind reflected in the *Illuminations*. For Pound wrote in 1928 that the method Rimbaud had arrived at by intuition he (Pound) had erected into a systematic aesthetic; and he had in mind the more Catullan of Rimbaud's poems (*L*, 217).

Language that can impart such knowing must pull together a mass of uncogitated resources that the poet does *not* understand rationally in the moment of composition (however much he may have laboured with their analogues in his self-training). And since good versification is an activity that demands the resources of the whole self, it follows that to discover what one can properly versify is to discover what one genuinely knows, apprehends. The rest should follow: knowledge of the things, the worlds, the world, the self. And thus it is that those passages from the 'Ur-Cantos' that are fully integrated as verse (which are the ones that Pound was to keep for the Cantos proper) can be felt (from the perspective of the later work) to be 'genuine Pound', part of a whole self-portrait. They scarcely mention the poet:

> Gods float in the azure air,
> Bright gods, and Tuscan, back before dew was shed [. . .]

> 'And then went down to the ship, set keel to breakers,
> Forth on the godly sea [. . .]'

(Compare the present III, p. 11, and I, p. 3.) Voice-rhythms achieved, worlds presented, and, necessarily, portions of the self discovered.

Pound's job was to cut out of the poem everything but what he felt most intensely. To discover what that was a technical problem: discovering what he could get into integrated verse. The poet, as visible self, is irrelevant. Pound had reached this point, *as theory*, in the first 'Ur-Canto' of 1917:

> Say that I dump my catch, shiny and silvery
> As fresh sardines flapping and slipping on the marginal cobbles?
> (I stand before the booth, the speech; but the truth
> Is inside this discourse – this booth is full of the marrow of wisdom.)

And that passage was to be reprinted in the foreword, written fifty years 'ater, to *Selected Cantos*.

And now, having in June–August 1917 published these three Cantos, ntended to be the basis of his life's main work, Pound received in December the manuscript of this:

He watched her pour into the measure and thence into the jug rich white milk, not hers. Old shrunken paps. She poured again a measureful and a tilly. Old and secret she had entered from a morning world, maybe a messenger. She praised the goodness of the milk, pouring it out. Crouching by a patient cow at daybreak in the lush field, a witch on her toadstool, her wrinkled fingers quick at the squirting dugs. They lowed about her whom they knew, dewsilky cattle. Silk of the kine and poor old woman, names given her in old times. A wandering crone, lowly form of an immortal serving her conqueror and her gay betrayer, their common cuckquean, a messenger from the secret morning. To serve or to upbraid, whether he could not tell: but scorned to beg her favour.

This language in Joyce's *Ulysses*, not limited by a stagey iambic in its suggestion of the textures of the world, can enact them orally ('They lowed about her whom they knew') and in image ('her wrinkled fingers quick at the squirting dugs'). It is also highly wrought, collecting echoes of magniloquence in word ('*whether* he could not tell') and phrasing ('he could not tell: but scorned'). But that posturing is only part of the portrayal of one of the 'objects' of the book, Stephen Dedalus; though the one refracts the other. With a series of such complex and objective precisions, Joyce was about to build *the* epic of the twentieth century; while all Pound's Renaissance-building had led to nothing but flummery in a hundred-year-old mode.

Pound probably did his relations with his public a lot of harm by publishing these three draft Cantos; and this may have contributed to his eventual isolation. The reading public for modern verse in 1917 was small, but existed, thanks partly to Pound's own efforts. For these draft Cantos, he used *Poetry*, an organ effectively created by himself, that would reach a good number of these readers. He placed before them material that (it was immediately obvious to them, but not to him) was not only prehistoric but preposterous; and then he continued to throw it at them. Retinkered versions of these three Cantos appeared in *Lustra*, his collection of October 1917; in the *Future* (February–April 1918);[3] and in his book *Quia Pauper Amavi* (October 1919 – this time with elucidations in the margin, just as Browning had added them to *Sordello* because the public had expressed its incomprehension). New Cantos material was then published that was not in nineteenth-century modes: *The Fourth Canto*, published separately, October 1919; Cantos V and VII, in the *Dial*, August 1921. But this material was obscured by the republication of the first three, and even by the publication of new material in a nineteenth-century-medieval manner (the original version of Canto VI, published together with Cantos V and VII). If hereafter a Joyce or an Eliot should think of Pound's Cantos, the thought would be coloured willy-nilly by this painful Browning resurrection that Pound had offered as the launching of the work.

It was no doubt a nadir in Pound's life. When he perceived that the retinkerings offered no exit from the crisis, there followed two years of increativity (early 1920 to early 1922). The crisis was then resolved rather suddenly, and a new order sprang into being in Pound's mind.

There is no clear evidence of structural plans for the whole of the Cantos between the formation of 1917 and the final order that began to issue fully formed in 1924, culminating in the text which is the subject of this book. It is now time to consider that text as a whole, beginning with its structural aspect.

NOTES: CHAPTER 3

1   'Three Cantos. I', 'Three Cantos. II' and 'Three Cantos. III', *Poetry*, vol. 10, no. 3 (June 1917), pp. 113–21; no. 4 (July 1917), pp. 180–8; no. 5 (August 1917), 248–54.
2   Rimbaud to Paul Demeny, 15 May 1871.
3   The *Future* versions are improved by much deletion; but those in *Quia Pauper Amavi* bring the deleted material back.

CHAPTER 4

Structures

(i) AGAINST BLUEPRINTS

In the vast mass of the 'final' version of the Cantos, as published in the successive collections from *A Draft of XXX Cantos* (1930)[1] to *Drafts & Fragments of Cantos CX–CXVII* (1969), it is possible to find certain principles governing structure, though they may contain a contradiction. One is: the journey, as analogy for the writer's life. The poem begins 'And then went down to the ship'. The hero is to be as Odysseus; but the shape of the journey as that of Hanno the Carthaginian.

One has Browning energy; one wants to encompass and affect the world in one's verse. Like Browning's Paracelsus, one wants to grasp the Secret, which somehow will take in the whole world. The meaning of existence is the goal; but it is assumed from the start, in Whitmanian manner, that the meaning is in/among/through the world, not elsewhere; the relations of the whole world, when understood, will themselves be the secret. One must experience the world until the meaning is perceived. One cannot sit around and wait. And since the meaning will arise from these experiences they must be recorded. But how to show these experiences, which will not be fully understood until the goal of godlike understanding is reached? And which way to set off, how to order one's experiences, when one will not know the true Order till the whole is known? Answers came, positively, from Browning and from Hanno; in negative form, from Dante.

The hero of Browning's *Pauline* searches for some aim commensurate with his immense, his unlimited talents. Under Shelley's sign, he sets off, big with energy:

> 'Twas in my plan to look on real life,
> The life all new to me; my theories
> Were firm, so them I left, to look and learn
> Mankind, its cares, hopes, fears, its woes and joys;

> And, as I pondered on their ways, I sought
> How best life's end might be attained – an end
> Comprising every joy. I deeply mused.

Before long an obscure crisis occurs, and all his afflatus evaporates. He speaks one last despairing, wondering time of his grandiose aims. At this point in the text Pauline, as it were his literary executrix, adds a footnote, explaining something important about these aims – presumably because Browning had not managed to get it into the young man's poetic testament. I translate from Pauline's French:

> I think that in what follows he alludes to an examination of the soul he once undertook – or rather of his soul. He wanted to discover the series of objects it would be possible to attain, each of which, once attained, would form a kind of plateau from which one could perceive other aims, other projects, other delights, which, in their turn, were to be surmounted [. . .][2]

Each success leads to battles previously unimagined, thence to successes of a nature not dreamed of at the start. This idea comes up again in *Sordello* in a different guise. Sordello, frame and soul, is one of the favoured few, who throw all their weight of love into every new object. They might discover that it is all useless – has no meaning – to the frail vehicle which is the thing they love; and so they pour their own souls into the beloved object, in an attempt to give it life.

> Nor rest they here; fresh births of beauty wake
> Fresh homage, every grade of love is past,
> With every mode of loveliness: then cast
> Inferior idols off their borrowed crown
> Before a coming glory. Up and down
> Runs arrowy fire, while earthly forms combine
> To throb the secret forth; a touch divine –
> And the scaled eyeball owns the mystic rod;
> Visibly through his garden walketh God.

Sordello-like heroes lend life to their beloveds; their beloveds form a chain of ascending love-arousings, each arousing fresh awareness; finally leading to the awareness of God in His creation. Each step is necessary before the hero is even aware of the existence of the next and higher. To go back to the metaphor of the journey, Pound said in 1934:

'I am leaving Rome in the direction of China: along the way I shall become increasingly different from what I was when I left. At Peking I shall be presented with a vast and unforeseen horizon. I would not have been able to reach that point [achieve that scope] if I had not departed in the first place' (R'76, 11).

By the 1930s, Pound was expressing this idea by writing of *periplous*. This is the kind of journey undertaken by the Hanno who, in Canto XL, cuts loose from a Victorian suburbia Pound has there imagined for him, and voyages coastwise via many wonders till he returns to post up the record of his journey in Kronos' temple.

Hanno was a Carthaginian of the fifth century BC, whose account of his journey, surviving in a Greek translation, is the source of that part of Canto XL. The work is called a *periplous*, 'circumnavigation', 'account of a coasting voyage'. Victor Bérard (who led both Joyce and Pound to these matters) tells us that *periploi* are like the 'Nautical Instructions' that modern Oceanographic Bureaux publish to accompany their maps, tide-tables and lighthouse manuals, to 'describe the coasts, indicate notable points whose recognition may help navigation, and give notes on winds, tides, currents, beacons, pilots, routes, commerce [...]' But *periploi* like Hanno's, since they were records of first-time exploration of more or less unknown shores, had to be more flexible, improvised. They resembled 'modern sailors' shipboard journals, or the travel accounts that they draw from them'.[3]

These *periploi* were records of explorations; that was their value to the sailors who used them. Therefore they got down whatever might help the next comer. Therefore they are not systematic (like the modern Instructions); their contents might be as those of Canto XL: headlands, seaboard marshlands, elephant herds, misshapen men swifter than horses, flames flowing into the sea – whatever was encountered, of whatever kind. And the *periploi*, Bérard insists,[4] got these things down from the point of view of the sailors who saw them; as it says in a later Canto:

> periplum, not as land looks on a map
> but as sea bord seen by men sailing.
> (LIX, p. 324)

And that is Pound's description of his poetic method. As a model for a cosmos-poem, a map falsely suggests that a final overall view is possible, indeed normal. (A map supposes theoretical multiple viewpoints suspended over the landmass, arrived at by measuring it from all angles.) By contrast, a *periplous*-like poem will give the trace of a concrete series of actions, from which one will be able to intuit all the information that such actions can validly afford.

A poem like a *periplous* will not give encyclopaedic information about life; but will suggest how one might act, for example, in the absence of such complete information. (That, it is suggested, is now our case.) Early *periploi* are all 'Notes by a Very Ignorant Man' (Pound's title for one of his own writings). Hanno reported that 'our Lixtae' said the 'folk hairy and savage' were called Gorillas; he noted it down; he could not stop for ten years' ethological or ethnological study to pass an opinion as an expert. He was after a sense of larger relations, such as later discoveries might lead to. And the accepted basis for the journey was that one did not know where one was going. Early *periploi* are liable to tail off, like Hanno's in Canto XL:

> Went no further that voyage,
> as were at end of provisions.
> (XL, p. 201)

The explorer-writer's (Pound's) energy must finally fail him, and his last *Drafts & Fragments* be as inconclusive as the journey.

The comparison supposes that a modern poet can explore on behalf of a 'tribe' in similar ignorance; a tribe with no map. And the particular map that Pound said was '*not* valid now'[5] was the one provided by old Aquinas: the one that Dante had used sketch out the geography of the universe for *his* epic journey, and in accordance with which (Pound said) Dante had Mount Purgatory sticking forty miles up in Australian sheepland (*L*, 190).

Pound, as I have said, acknowledged that his Cantos were 'footnotes' to the *Divine Comedy*; he felt that Dante's epic poem could show not only value-relations and structures on the microcosmic scale, but also a sense of the larger value-relations that amounted to universal structure. But these larger relations were *not* validly presented by the cosmic geography of the *Divine Comedy*, and the poem's more visible form, which bore quite unacceptable implications.

Dante's geography, and his action in general, are partly fantasy intended to illustrate moral truths, and partly more-or-less literal depiction of the universe as then understood. Both morally and physically they present a universe that is, in general layout, known.

The fixed point from which Dante's map is drawn is God, as purpose of journey, as absolute moral limit to the knowable world, and as source of known moral law. Physically, the Empyrean, the abode of God, is the end of the universe. Morally, God lays down rules that delimit the area of human understanding: questions about the fate of pagans in Limbo, and the apportioning of grace, we are warned, are off limits to our speculation. The committing of the Original Sin, as presented in *Paradiso*, 26.117, was simply the crossing of a barrier God had laid down. Moral and physical senses are combined when Dante's Ulysses urges his crew to explore regions that are forbidden. He and his crew seem preternaturally to waste away; and when they are tantalisingly in sight of the Mount of Purgatory,

> '[. . .] We rejoiced, and the rejoicing soon turned to weeping
>   for from the new land a storm rose,
>   and struck the bows of our ship.
> It turned her round three times with all the waters,
>   [and] at the fourth [made] the poop rise up
>   and the prow go down, as it pleased Another,
> until the sea was closed over us.'   (*Inferno*, 26.136–42)

No reasons are given, or need be, for so it pleased Another, who is himself the primal Limit. (Eliot accepted that, with all its implications, for he thought that only such a Limit could give moral meaning to actions.)

The physical world of Dante reflects this moral and spiritual known-ness and demarcation. In Job, 38:4, God, a craftsman house-builder, uses stretched string to lay out his creation; but Dante's God is a geometer:

> 'He who turned the arc
>   round the limits of the universe, and within it
>   marked out so much that is hidden and revealed [. . .]'

He naturally used these compasses to place the city where His Son was to be born 90° from one edge of the inhabited globe (the Pillars of Hercules) and 90° from the other (the mouths of the Ganges).[6] Purgatory is a sort of protruding plug corresponding exactly to the hole of Hell, for it was pushed out when Satan fell down there. We begin to understand what fearful symmetry Ulysses was disturbing when he set out to explore beyond the Pillars of Hercules – those Pillars that in

Pound are the natural *jumping-off point* for Hanno, for Columbus and himself:

> 'the great periplum brings in the stars to our shore.'
> You who have passed the pillars and outward from Herakles
> when Lucifer fell in N. Carolina.   (LXXIV, p. 425)

And history also in Dante is foreknown, leads to a fixed point, and works out within symmetries. In the Celestial Rose, which is formed by the places for the souls of the saved in the tenth heaven, there are precisely as many petals (seats) reserved for those who shall have worshipped Christ since His coming as are already filled by those who foresaw Him before He came.

Only God can know all about the universe; and yet it is clear that Dante can know pretty much everything significant that man will ever be permitted to know. Whether or not we should take Dante literally when, in the letter to Can Grande, he refers to his memories of Paradise, he has certainly 'been there' in the sense that he has had experiences which (he feels) have shown him the Secret. They have made him, like Chaucer's Troilus, look down and understand by and large everything that matters; and the scheme of it fits in with that great world-view offered by Aristotle and modified by Averroes, Albertus and Aquinas, a world-view in which the moral and physical layout of the world is delimited and, within these limits, largely known. Thus he has a kind of God's-eye view. Having been there, and knowing the fixed point from which 'it all' can be measured, he can organise his poem, his life-map, as a unity, a totality, reflecting that singleness of view. He divides the past and present population of the world into moral classes, and arranges them in layers, against the backdrop of a heaven, hell and purgatory imposed on the Aristotelian cosmology. Then all he has to do is to walk up through it; his plot, as Pound says, is 'a walk upstairs' (SL, 458). The journey could in principle be a straight line, which would take him to each layer, for any encounter with any individual on a given level would necessarily be an encounter with a moral representative of the whole of that level.

As to symmetries on the page: 100 is a round number, so 100 cantos in all. Hell, Purgatory and Paradise ought to have exactly one-third each, but Hell can have an extra Canto as prologue to the whole poem, giving it thirty-four Cantos in all, and the other cosmic regions thirty-three each. Morally/geographically, each region must (naturally) be divided into ten layers; but Hell's moral states (as a matter of human observation) are rather easier to distinguish; so rather than have an un-Godly (un-Platonic) number like seventeen or eighteen, Dante sub-divides some of them. All this then leaves him with the immense task of getting his *actual* human, anarchic wealth of moral distinction and spiritual awareness into these straitjackets; bending the geography and action so as to allow for interest of dramatic encounter, etc.; working his later, inopportunely hellish diatribes into the Paradise cantos; in other words, like the author of *Ulysses* (as described by Hugh Kenner[7]), expending vast ingenuity in fitting humanity to a potentially Procrus-tean bed that he himself has created. Which involves, among other things, smoothing over, or ignoring, *differences of evaluation* of the same events and persons expressed at different moments in the writing of the work – caused both by changes in the author himself and by changes in the world around him since the first lines were written.

In Dante's day, every great thinker was constructing, and every little thinker was tinkering with modifications to, a map of the universe in all its aspects, using the same materials: a small pinch of empirical observation and a waggonload of reasoning. It was possible to theorise so far beyond known fact because *new* known fact came so rarely to disturb theory. In the twentieth century the lifetime of a fundamental theory in physics is short, for new observation comes too fast.[8] As for man's place 'in it all' – and a morality arising therefrom (if any) – most writers shrink from all that.

Therefore Pound, wanting to find and tell a tale that shall be useful to his tribe, must voyage, not in a straight line to a foreknown goal, but like Odysseus (who at one point sets out on a raft he has built mid-journey, *chez* Calypso, with his own hands), accepting the deflec-tions of new circumstance:

> By no means an orderly Dantescan rising
> but as the winds veer
> 　　　　　　　　　　tira libeccio
> now Genji at Suma　　, tira libeccio
> 　　as the winds veer and the raft is driven
> 　　and the voices　　, Tiro, Alcmene
> 　　with you is Europa nec casta Pasiphaë
> 　　　　　　Eurus, Apeliota as the winds veer in periplum
> 　　　　　　　　　　　(LXXIV, p. 443)

Every new juncture arrived at is *new*; modifies the aspect of what went before; requires rethinking of the whole direction to be taken. The veering of the wind, the sudden inturn of the headland are part of the actuality of the world he is discovering, as opposed to the hypothetical world he might have brought with him on the blueprint provided by the head office. Treated as new information, they will lead to places not even dreamed of by the voyager when he set off.

'As the winds veer and the raft is driven': this line was written in the prison camp at Pisa, where Pound was rethinking. The Pisan Cantos are the record of his rethinking, considering, like Henry James, where he and we have,

> in a manner of speaking,
> arrived.
> Got to, I think he says 'got to, all got to.'
> The ubicity, ascertaining.   (LXXXVII, p. 576)

For his setting out from Philadelphia, and his scribal setting out from Homer's Aiaia in Canto I ('And then went down to the ship'), had brought him to understanding an Italian Odysseus (Malatesta) with a constructive element superadded. That in turn had led him to 'seeing' another Italian Odysseus (Niccolò d'Este) with *socially* constructive aims; which had brought him, via many new discoveries, to a revaluing downwards of mere wandering in itself, to perceiving in eighteenth-century Tuscany a socially constructive exploring, yielding a sense of non-parasitical state activity. This helped him to 'see' John Adams – whom he might have mugged up on in the college library in Crawfordsville, or, after a successful academic career, in New Haven or Cambridge, without ever leaving his native shores. And the mugging-up would have been as meaningless to him as to the dozen other research students set to dig the stuff out 'blind, ham-strung, as blacks in a diamond mine' (*GK*, 221) every year by the history departments of their universities.

To perceive the significance of John Adams in a really existent modern world meant discovering, first, a great many other significant 'points de repère' – as opposed to going round regions once significant, now excellently charted, and without any real bearing on modern necessities. Pound had to come to Italy to 'see' Adams. But one does not properly know any stage on the journey without involvement; Hanno did not observe the hairy 'Gorillae' through a telescope. The involvement is itself an *étape* that teaches. One of the stages on Pound's journey of understanding was Mussolini, and that, with other vicissitudes, was why he was now in a United States Army Disciplinary Training Centre with the dregs of the army's criminals, having been (in some degree) in the war on the wrong side, and having seen collapse the Italy that all his previous steps of learning had persuaded him was the only sure hope for the West's future.

A rethink was necessary. It must take in the disaster, and all the extrapolations-from-the-so-far-known that he the explorer had drawn up at every previous stage of the journey, back to the first mental chart of goals laid hold of at the start. To help the next man, these Cantos must get down the quality of the circumstances in which this rethink is forced:

> The form of the poem and main progress is conditioned by its own inner shape, but the life of the D.T.C. passing OUTSIDE the scheme cannot but impinge, or break into the main flow. The proper names given are mostly those of men on sick call seen passing my tent [. . .][9]

Which leads to a thought, arising out of earlier considerations, but made possible by openness to the experience of this new situation: concerning the particular categories of Americans oppressed by the current un-Adamsian system . . .

The journey, therefore, is one of the main structural principles of the Cantos. But is it 'structural' or anti-structural?

(ii) FOR BLUEPRINTS

'"You mean it didn't come off?" [. . .] "Of course it didn't. That's what I mean when I say I botched it." He then went on to describe a shop window full of various objects: "I picked out this and that thing that interested me, and then jumbled them into a bag. But that's not the way," he said, "to make" – and here he paused – "*a work of art*."'[10]

These are the remarks of an aged Pound in the grip of chronic remorse. Yet the *periplous* might only be the last of a series of excuses for merely amassing everything the poet knows – necessarily in the order that he comes across it. After its philosophical ground-clearings, the first of the 1917 draft Cantos sets off on a Cook's Tour of the poet's worlds:

How shall we start hence, how begin the progress?
Pace naif Ficinus, say when Hotep-Hotep
Was a king in Egypt [...]
                              Say it was Moses' birth-year?
Exult with Shang in squatness? The sea-monster
Bulges the squarish bronzes.

He strung up other washing-lines on which to hang them all out: the Chaucerian dream, of which there is still a trace in Canto XX; the phantastical History-Amphitheatre, through which all ages will parade as we spectate, a creaking transition-device of which variants still dot the first thirty Cantos.[11] The 'matters' that are thus strung together will be selected by the criterion I have already described: whether they can be got into good verse. That will give them the cohesion of being, all of them, pictures of elements of the poet's soul, for he can fully poetise only what he understands. But nothing in all this makes for a sequence, or any one way of putting these things together. Or for an end: for the poet is curious, and '[it is never late, for an attempt on the unknown]' (XCIII, p. 629), which his curiosity will heap up endlessly, interesting rubble, variegated sand, a mind's Sargasso Sea.

Very well, the open-ended, ongoing situation – 'leaky as an unstanched wench' – is our era; at least, our era's view of itself. But it was not Pound's view. He assumed that while no one here will get a God's-eye view of a neat and mappable Creation, yet there is a shape in what-there-is, and that not merely the shape that the human Creative Eye happens to lend it. There is an order (not a symmetry). Now major structure in any medium is affective; therefore it should enact the meaning. The meaning in this case is 'order'. Pound in 1938:

The function of music is to present an example of order, or a less muddied congeries and proportion than we have yet about us in daily life. Hence the emphasis in Pythagoras and Confucius. (*GK*, 255)

Further,

The phrase 'paroles en liberté' was not perfect. It leaves room for words that are loose; not made organic. In a fine piece of prose, in a fine poem, the complex forms as it were one word. Made organic.

Brancusi's ideal, that in perfect architecture one should be able to turn the building upside down, push it to and fro as the ship is pushed by the wind, turn it roof down, or side down, without giving the effect of disequilibrium. (Translated from *OS*, 1265)

This ideal is attainable only by inner cohesion. Therefore, partly in contradiction to the principle of the journey, we find in Pound's writings a bundle of principles of organisation; of local ordering of the relations of elements with one another.

There is a general blueprint for the content: hellish, purgatorial and paradisal states of man; and an idea that they must be tackled in that order. In 1944 Pound wrote: 'For forty years I have schooled myself [. . .] to write an epic poem which begins "In the Dark Forest" crosses the Purgatory of human error, and ends in the light, "[among the masters of those who know]". For this reason I have had to understand the NATURE of error.'[12] First came a study of man's historical hells, though with flashes of paradisal matter at intervals. About the middle of the 1930s Pound began to consider that he had more or less done with the economic inferno. Canto XLVI opens with an admission that the poem was didactic, and a warning that the reader might need such a Guide to Hell. It speaks of the economic argument –

> 19 years on this case first case. I have set down part of
> The Evidence.   (XLVI, p. 234)

– and links the shaping of the whole poem to the resting of that case:

> This case, and with it
> the first part, draws to a conclusion,
> of the first phase of this opus
> (XLVI, pp. 233–4)

In 1939 Pound tells Santayana, 'I have [. . .] got to the end of a job or part of a job (money in history) and for personal ends have got to tackle philosophy or my "paradise", and do badly want to talk with some one who has thought a little about it' (*L*, 331). End of Hell, opening of Paradise; Purgatory already illustrated variously. And so, tentative explorings of paradisal coasts. He has a go at Scotus Erigena, of whom he has heard travellers' tales: 'I haven't yet found anything that fits what I had read about what he thought [. . .]' (*L*, 334). There is an idea of a distant goal ('I have heard that to sail coastally or plow you fix yr. eye on a distant point or two points in a line': *L*, 343) which is the land of Paradise.

And these mutterings of entry into Paradiseland, leaving Inferno, come *after* the writing of LII–LXXI. The set of Cantos before those, as above quoted, had rested the case in paradigmatic form, with the Blake-like chants against Evil ('*With Usura*'), contrasted with an achieved opposite, the Sienese reforms. LII–LXXI then gave two extended examples (from Chinese history and the life of John Adams) of the battle against this evil. Now (though pieces of Paradise have come before, and pieces of Hell will come after) we have reached a conscious turning-point[13] – in intention. (The war will upset this.)

There is a general idea of form on the printed page: 100 Cantos perhaps (1917); 100 or 120 (1922) (P*B*, 299; *L*, 180). And of fitting the content to this form, perhaps: Pound's talk of leaving Inferno comes after the writing of LII–LXXI, thus leaving slightly less than a third of the 100 Cantos for Paradise. Also of the writing schedule: 'There are not likely to be more than two cantos each year [. . .]' (P*B*, 301). From, say, 1917, this would have brought him to 1967 for the completion of his 100.

Within these immense outlines one should not look for 'form' in the sense of 'forms', that is, symmetries. Dante has plenty of these; but, just as they do not dictate real subject-matter (why does a diatribe against Florence belong in the entrance to Purgatory?), so they do not dictate major form, which is a movement of emotivities. '[. . .] Dante's sense of main construction is perhaps rudimentary in comparison with Flaubert's' (*E*, 211).

Therefore, a general sense of a Paradiso standing in a certain relation to a Hell; taken from Dante. Within that, the Cantos are to be published in groups of about ten, each with a 'simultaneously-planned' internal order, yet somehow adding accretively to a pre-existing order already inherent in the sets of Cantos previously published.

Pound's analogies for this order were chiefly musical; but the rhythms of this musical order were to be made up of aesthetic (and therefore 'moral') distinctions.

All aesthetic structures are built out of differentiations: in architecture, between angle and angle, or angle and plane, or mass and void; in music, between tonality and tonality, sound and silence. Pound's 'material' is aesthetic discriminations, which connote the moral, for 'A revelation is always didactic' (*L*, 180). As Zukofsky noted in respect of *Mauberley*, aesthetic and moral structurings are not incompatible.[14]

Two things placed together set up an interaction; make us 're-see' both; create an aesthetic/moral category that was not present in either seen alone. This is the aesthetic of the Ideogram, which sets out concrete instances, not smoothing them to an authorial abstraction, and allows their interaction to be the meaning.

So Pound will yoke together Thomas Jefferson (1743–1826), of Monticello, Virginia, and Lawrence Medici (1449–1492), of Florence, Italy. Lorenzo 'the Magnificent' speaks plain American:

> And from '34 when I count it, to last year,
> We paid out 600,000 and over,
> That was for building, taxes and charity.
> Nic Uzano saw us coming. Against it, honest,
> And warned 'em.   (XXI, p. 97)

Linguistic sleight of hand? Well, Lorenzo wrote a blunt and pithy Italian – which is now quoted in the Canto. Three lines after it ends, we come to Jefferson's words:

> 'Could you', wrote Mr Jefferson,
> 'Find me a gardener
> Who can play the French horn? [. . .]'

The 'point' here is obvious: here are two men in the act of intelligent and creative patronage. There is also a cultural tension, which we are likely to bring to the text. We are accustomed to thinking of Jefferson as the quizzical and down-to-earth inquirer, certainly interested in the Arts, but hardly so in a way, or an environment, that might have any such significance as Lorenzo's. Conversely, culture-training has given us a sense that Art is somehow inevitable in that Florentine air and time; it goes with that patrician *disdegno* and splendour that Medici portraits invest Cosimos and Pieros with. But seeing Jefferson, ever in tangles of political construction, seizing the chance to build an art-Vortex; seeing Lorenzo listing his political battles with artistic expenses; we begin to isolate from them both that element of *choice*, of volition, the seeing of the moment and the chance amid a mess where no one else would have seen it. Perhaps we begin to hoist Jefferson up from the apple-cheeked inventor of new designs for goblets and fences, to a creative level where he belonged – but for circumstance.

But identity in itself gives nothing to structure, and this is also a differentiation. Lorenzo speaks of a 'we', a clan; he is a magnate, spending vastly; that he is much more of a businessman than Jefferson is even implied in the diction, for Jefferson's, though modified from the original by Pound, is still Austenian, gentlemanly. There is here a contour, a demarcation, a difference, even where Pound is pointing out a shared element.

For a more violent angle:

> And Kung said, 'Without character you will
> be unable to play on that instrument
> 'Or to execute the music fit for the Odes.
> 'The blossoms of the apricot
> blow from the east to the west,
> 'And I have tried to keep them from falling.'
>
> (XIII, p. 60)

On the opposite page:

> Io venni in luogo d'ogni luce muto;
> The stench of wet coal, politicians
> Lloyd George and Wilson, their wrists bound to
> their ankles,
> Standing bare bum,
> Faces smeared on their rumps,
> wide eye on flat buttock,
> Bush hanging for beard,
> Addressing crowds through their arse-holes
>
> (XIV, p. 61)

If we think of negatives in relation to Confucius' preachments, we are likely to think of Oriental, antique villains: peculating counsellors in long gowns, or baroquely sadistical courtesans, such as Chinese mytho-history seems to breed. We do not think of our times. But Confucius here is talking about straight (or other) inner motivation, and how it shows through; in his case (as in the blossom parable) it clearly includes a sense of the real proportion between oneself and the world's larger processes. His quiet language reflects this. It clearly judges what is found on the opposite page: men who have no sense of their own insignificance; who wish to impose their personalities on the world at all repellent costs; and whose motivation shows through, as Confucius said it would. The satirist (Pound) needs only to extend the obvious metaphor ('What a fart that man is').

Thus (*a*) Confucius is brought alive, (*b*) Lloyd George is condemned by emanation from pre-Han China. There is a certain cultural shock here, its degree depending on how much we personally inherit the dignified and prating China of Pope and of James Legge, the great Victorian translator of the Chinese classics. It is not the main point, for if we and all succeeding Pound readers had to step back into Legge's blinkers so as to be able to note the shock of having the Cantos make them fall away, the Cantos would be already half-dead, like *This Side of Paradise*, where we must strive to imagine both 'petting' and its prohibition. That main contrast, here, between a proper self-knowledge and fretful assertion, will last when the cultural surprise has gone.

Difference is what Pound wants; it creates 'discharge' between 'charged surfaces', one of his governing images in physics, sexual relations, and the aesthetics of art. Already, in the *haiku*-ish poems of Imagism, each 'half' was itself a complex of events within a suggested changing complex which was its situation. But in the Cantos each complex may be an immense set of ramifications. Lorenzo is a whole page of complication, suggested by such concentrated means as Ford had shown were available in prose ('abrupt' waves, he said, would suggest, precisely, a boat, not a ship: *PD*, 155), and intensified by verbal music. But Lorenzo existed ('exists in history'). Our sense of what Italy and Florence were, what the Medici were – a sense that is of course gradually evolving – is inevitably there as we read, and adds to this intricate entity. Pound began to speak of 'blocks', which term suggests at least the *mass* of any one of these mutually charging complexes.

Some might be simple, some might be otherwise, some might rely on 'what we all know', some might require the previous establishing of a whole era in our minds. (The Marecchia does not spring to mind as might the Arno.) Pound's area of subject is the entire world that *can be* brought within the culture-field of an active twentieth-century man, armed with the British Museum catalogue and an alert set of faculties. He has his theory: that divinity inheres, *in una parte più, e meno altrove*, more here, and less there, in an immense gradation of values. To make clear what this divinity consists of, and how it inheres in all things, thus cohering them, it is necessary to bring out the bones of all knowable universes. We need a thousand juxtapositions. We need to be able to see Confucius not only against a lying hen-house of politicians resembling the 'Aeolus' chapter in *Ulysses*, but also against other states, more and less creative and fulfilled, in other unexpected worlds. So Confucius is placed next after Baldy Bacon, a small-time wheeler-dealer whom Pound once knew, whose first wheeze was about cornering small coinage: '"No interest in any other kind uv bisnis,"/Said Baldy.'

But that is already the limit for the block 'Confucius': Baldy on one side and Lloyd George on the other. It cannot, physically, be juxtaposed with any more.

Suppose now that Pound wants to rejuxtapose Confucius, with a different block. He can bring him before us again by repeating the whole Canto – unendurable. He can print 'REPEAT CANTO XIII', which will have much the same effect as a pause in a recording of Stravinsky's *Orpheus*, where an admirably BBC voice shall say: 'Please now recall, if you will, the theme stated in the first movement.'

Or, following the suggestions of simultaneity in some recent music scores, he can print the Cantos as a huge fold-out map, so as to juxtapose Confucius with as many complexes as he can legibly fit in a circle round him. But those surrounding complexes in turn have to be juxtaposed with their own circles of complexes – many of which are relevant to more than one other complex. Contiguities in one plane are physically limited.

Here enter a variety of devices, depending on statement and recall (not repetition) of statement; thus on memory and more particularly on the rate of memory's fade within an implied time-lapse. When these develop into pattern, this is musical, because it implies time not space.

Of these devices of recall, one is to present a state, then to 'rhyme' it in a quite other form, without any reference to the vehicle of its first expression. Venice is assumed into a world of crystal in Cantos XXV and XXVI; at the end of the presenting of this, we have 'Wind on the lagoon, the south wind breaking roses'. It should remind us of Confucius:

> 'The blossoms of the apricot
>   blow from the east to the west,
> 'And I have tried to prevent them from falling.'

The 'same' statement (something concerning transience) has the same ambiguous effect on Confucius' immortalisms as on Venice's. These echoed emotionalities make for a binding-together. Though Pound berates Dante for his 'rudimentary' sense of structure 'by comparison with Flaubert', he none the less does point out certain details that echo: Statius and Virgil are (it is hinted by Dante) master craftsmen, technicians, which balances the *miglior fabbro* compliment to Arnaut Daniel elsewhere in the *Purgatory* (*L*, 314); Agnello and Cianfa, two monstrously metamorphosing into one, counterbalance the Bertran de

Born who is 'one in two', carrying his head under his arm (*E*, 212). And we begin to see that for Pound 'main construction' has nothing to do with charted layouts of journeys or numbers of cantos; it consists in rhymed emotionalities, and the sense of direction and ultimate coherence that they give to the whole.

This 'rhyming' may be done at much greater length, in passages with only an echo of a visual tonality; as when Zagreus feeds his panthers in Canto XVII, recalled by the air of Phoibos' land in Canto XXI. Such visualities connote emotion. Pound modulates them quite specifically; filling these with red and dark half-seen movement, for Dionysiac rite; or man-made ranked and ordered beauty, as in his ideal landscapes evoking Venice. They recall each other through their differences, aesthetic and 'moral'.

Pound tends to avoid connected narrative; but locally he can use it to restate a complex without repeating it. He can simply pick up the narrative where it was dropped, and add more facts. Carmagnola, a freelance mercenary captain like Malatesta, was invited for consultation by his employers (in Canto X) so that they might do away with him. And Giacomo Piccinino on the next page, another *condottiere*, suffered a similar deception: Sforza's daughter was the pawn, and after the marriage feast

> he fell out of a window, Count Giacomo,
> Three days after his death   (X, p. 43)

A point here: the dangers Malatesta has to survive among. Now intervene many Cantos, on many quite remote themes. Comes the Medici family, much involved with workings of power and money. Lorenzo observes that 'in Florence it is difficult to live as a rich man without controlling the state' (XXI, p. 97); example, his brother Giuliano, assassinated in 1478. Then the remark (actually Machiavelli's[15]): 'And because Piccinino controlled no state, anybody who had one had to fear him.' That both tells us something we did not yet know about the death of the unfortunate Piccinino, and, at the same time, recalls the whole narrative about him given earlier – *with* its surrounding complex of Carmagnola, Malatesta's turbulent creativity, and so on. The illumination added this time: Lorenzo's world is at least as insecure as Malatesta's. Thus:

(Canto X)   Carmagnola : Piccinino : Malatesta

(Canto XXI)   Lorenzo : Piccinino
                        (*and memory adds* Carmagnola: Malatesta . . .)

There is the simply verbal recall: by simply requoting a phrase, Pound can 'juxtapose' Jefferson at long distance with Malatesta.[16] Mere diction can recall: 'that he ply', 'seabord', 'so laid we house', 'layed in the wide plain', used for Hanno as late as Canto XL, recall the language used for Odysseus in Canto I.

In the section of the Cantos written in the prison camp at Pisa (1945) this whole mechanism is accelerated, to the point where it changes in quality. In the Pisan Cantos each line or half-line is a tag, shadowed by the ghostly complex (built up earlier in the poem) from which the author's memory has now extracted it. When these tags are so abbreviated – yet pregnant, if rightly chosen, with the original complex's full force – they can be juxtaposed and then re-ordered in their juxtapositions, suddenly and lightly. One complex goes through a dozen colourings as it passes through the light shed by different tag-clusters. In successful passages, the emotional sense remains quite precise, yet is charged with such nameless-seeming depths as ought logically to contradict that.

The ordering of the recalls, and developments, was to be musical. Whatever the reader does to it, once a book has been fully read, it re-orders itself into a straight line, in a sort of mental time-space that functions as if it were time. Now if a complex evoking certain emotions – say, Odysseus into Hades – is given, it will hang in the mind for a certain duration, in this time-space, while the next complex is being stated, and the next, and perhaps the next. Fading, it will still have effects on later subjects with which it is not in direct contact. Beyond that point, if it is to remain available as comparison in the mind, it must be restated, perhaps after a long gap. Compare what Pound has to say about Arabian music:

In especial one notes the 'extraordinary' length of the rhythm pattern units, comparable to the medieval rhyme-scheme of Provençal canzos, where, for example, one finds a rhyme pattern which begins its six-ply repeat after the seventeenth different terminal sound.

In other words: a sonnet is ABAB CDCD EFEF GG, but this canzone is ABCDEFGHIJKLMNOPQ ABCDEFGHIJKLMNOPQ ABCDEFGHIJKLMNOPQ – through six plies (stanzas). And

In this Arabian music, as in the Provençal metrical schemes, the effect of the subtler repetitions only becomes apparent in the third or fourth strophe, and then culminates in the fifth or sixth, as a sort of horizontal instead of perpendicular chord.

Thus in the Cantos: there might be a 'rhyme' of the Earthly Paradise atmosphere, which might (being subtle) pass unnoticed; but on the third or fourth encountering, in different Cantos, of such a tonality, it would make itself consciously felt, and gain added beauty through the echoes, bringing to mind earlier relations, playing them off against new material.

One might call it 'sort of' counterpoint; if one can conceive a counterpoint which plays not against a sound newly struck, but against the residuum and residua of sounds which hang in the auditory memory.[17]

With these recalls and developments a shape is to be built. For it, Pound several times gave the analogy of fugue.[18] In fugue there is the statement of a melodic idea, which is the *subject*, then the echoing of this melodic idea by a different instrumental voice, which is the *response*, and then the statement of another, separate but somehow related, melodic idea which is the *countersubject*. Pound regularly gave the Descent into Hell in Canto I (a voyage) as his subject; a response would be any following theme that 'rhymed' with that (Pound's lonely arrival in Venice in Canto III, or his descent into the hell of contemporary London in Cantos XIV–XV). The countersubject then cited by Pound was metamorphosis, as in Canto II; which quickly gets its response in IV, where the 'metamorphosis' of Peire Vidal has (in turn) *its* response in Actaeon's.

All this, with numerous further possible shape-tricks, develops (in fugue) into rhythms: creating expectations, to be manipulated as the composer thinks fit. It is not in itself satisfactory structure, because the development of these patterns is not given by the form; if it were, all fugue-works would be disastrously similar. Fugue is only a texture – or perhaps one should say a 'ribbing', as being stronger in outline than texture. From it the composer has to build total structure for himself, and (since the value of the elements is emotional), the sense of whether structure is finally achieved or not is 'no more than emotional'. But one attraction for Pound was clearly in the separation of elements. He loved clarity, demarcation, 'autarchy'. The themes are separate but affect each other; it is polyphonic and contrapuntal. He wrote in 1936: 'The basic principle of counterpoint, as distinct from any set of niggling "rules", is that a number of melodic lines carry on and, by carrying on, interact.'[19]

Now, Daniel Pearlman (in *PB*) has described how there is a 'sacred time' in the Cantos, corresponding to a perception found in various cultures by Eliade. The famous letter on fugue to Pound's father (1927) makes it clear that metamorphosis goes outside ordinary time:

> Dear Dad: [. . .] Have I ever given you outline of main scheme ::: or whatever it is?
>
> 1. Rather like, or unlike subject and response and counter subject in fugue.
>
> A. A. Live man goes down into world of Dead
>
> C. B. The 'repeat in history'
>
> B. C. The 'magic moment' or moment of metamorphosis, bust thru from quotidien into 'divine or permanent world'. Gods, etc.
>
> (*L*, 210)

The 'metamorphosis' theme implies both an ordinary time (what you 'bust out of') and a divine time, the permanent world. The 'repeat in history', in which such things as descents into hell and metamorphoses recur, itself implies a kind of durability. Thus all this links with Pound's attempt to classify observed phenomena into 'the permanent, the recurrent, the casual' (*L*, 239). Also with the great Dantescan scheme: for Hell is the casual, where 'the personnel changes' (XIV, p. 62); all is busy, yet none 'rise into significance'; the personnel of Pound's Hell Cantos XIV–XV so trivial that Pound cannot remember who they are (*L*, 293). At the opposite pole, Heaven is where the eternal bones of things are seen, and this quality of perception is (for Pound) inseparable from passion. Casual, recurrent and permanent seem to correspond more or less to Hell, Purgatory and Paradise; or, further, to the loci Zukofsky identified in the Cantos as 'hate, comprehension and worship'.[20]

Now inasmuch as these are different *planes* of existence, and inasmuch as they are not reached in an orderly sequence, but are to some extent all present from the start, they have a simultaneity which invites spatial analogies. Pound discovered the ideal one after the event, in the Schifanoia frescoes at Ferrara (see especially B*FT*, 80 n.).

Vistas of battered pale fresco encircle a large room in what was (by 1469) Borso d'Este's summer palace in Ferrara; Pound took it that they were painted by Cosmè Tura. In sequence, round the room, the sections are divided according to the twelve months. Horizontally they are divided into three strips: the top one shows the Triumphs of the various gods; the middle, the signs of the Zodiac; the bottom one, Duke Borso strutting genially among his peasants and noble fellow-hunters. The guidebook notes that 'The frescoed scenes imply a time sequence so the characters – the Duke, courtiers, peasants and others – can reoccur more than once in the same picture.' Thus, horizontally, sequences; vertically, a comparison of planes, of levels of existence. There was a conversation with Yeats in which Pound evidently brought the temporal (fugal) and spatial analogies together for the whole envisioned sequence of Cantos; Pound rejected this account (1929) as garbled, but it is of great interest:

Now at last he explains that it will, when the hundreth [sic] Canto is finished, display a structure like that of a Bach Fugue. There will be no plot, no chronicle of events, no logic of discourse, but two themes, the descent into Hades from Homer, a metamorphosis from Ovid, and mixed with these mediaeval or modern historical characters [. . .] He has scribbled on the back of an envelope certain sets of letters that represent emotions or archetypal events – I cannot find any adequate definition – A B C D and then J K L M, and then each set of letters repeated, and then A B C D inverted and this repeated, and then a new element X Y Z, then certain letters that never recur and then all sorts of combinations of X Y Z and J K L M and A B C D and D C B A and all set whirling together. He has shown me upon the wall a photograph of a Cosimo Tura decoration in three compartments, in the upper the Triumph of Love and the Triumph of Chastity, in the middle Zodiacal signs, and in the lower certain events in Cosimo Tura's day. The descent and the metamorphosis – A B C D and J K L M – his fixed elements, took the place of the Zodiac, the archetypal persons – X Y Z – that of the Triumphs, and certain modern events – his letters that do not recur – that of those events in Cosimo Tura's day.[21]

When a blueprint as complex as this is said to organise a 'matter' (historic, economic, human, tonal, visual) as dense as Pound's, then it is to be understood (*a*) that it is probably futile for critic or reader to try to follow the workings of this organisation beyond the simpler outlines, and (*b*) that the reader need not worry.

> Good old Richter, ripe with years and with wisdom, has the sense to interlard his treatise on theory, counterpoint, harmony with the caution that 'these are the laws and they have nothing to do with musical composition which is a different kind of activity.' (*GK*, 29)

At some point Pound's *nous* or instinct or *caelestis intus vigor* had to take over.

> Give your draughtsman sixty-four stencils of 'Botticelli's most usual curves'? And he will make you a masterpiece? (*ABC*, 206)

NOTES: CHAPTER 4

1 One might have said 'from *A Draft of XVI. Cantos*', but that in that collection Canto VI still had to be drastically altered.

2 'Je crois que dans ce qui suit il fait allusion à un certain examen qu'il fit autrefois de l'âme ou plutôt de son âme, pour découvrir la suite des objets auxquels il lui serait possible d'atteindre, et dont chacun une fois obtenu devait former une espèce de plateau d'où l'on pouvait apercevoir d'autres buts, d'autres projets, d'autres jouissances qui, à leur tour, devaient être surmontés.'

3 Victor Bérard, *La Résurrection d'Homère* (Paris: Bernard Grasset, 1930), pp. 147, 149. The book is condensed from his earlier studies.

4 ibid., pp. 154–5.

5 *L*, p. 323; cf. *WW*, pp. 93, 112.

6 See esp. Edward Moore, *Studies in Dante: Third Series* (Oxford: Oxford University Press, 1903), pp. 127 ff.

7 Hugh Kenner, *Ulysses*, Unwin Critical Library (London: Allen & Unwin, 1980), esp. pp. 26–7.

8 Basil Bunting has suggested that the twentieth-century world was changing too fast to be coherently reflected in an epic such as Pound's, written over a period of several decades – a problem he shared with Spenser.

9 'Note to Base Censor', *Paris Review*, no. 28 (Summer–Fall 1962), p. 17.

10 Remarks made to Daniel Cory in 1966, quoted in *SL*, pp. 586–7.

11 Such framing devices are implied in 'Lie quiet Divus' (I, p. 5); 'And we have heard' (II, p. 10); 'Or:' (III, p. 11); 'an old man seated/Speaking' (IV, p. 13); 'Look down on' (IV, p. 16); 'And we sit here.../there in the arena...' (ibid.); 'the vision:/ Down in the viae stradae' (V, p. 17); 'and from parapet looked down./To North was Egypt' (ibid.); 'the vision, flitting' (ibid.); 'Titter of sound about me' (ibid.); 'The lake of ice there below me' (V, p. 19); '(Clock-tick pierces the vision)' (V, p. 18); 'And the wind is still for a little' (VIII, p. 32); 'In the gloom, the gold gathers the light against it' (XI, p. 51); 'And we sit here/under the wall,/Arena romana' (XII, p. 53); 'Up to the open air/Over that mound of the hippodrome' (XXIX, p. 141); and perhaps in other lines.

12 *P*, p. 167; cf. *SR*, p. 129, on the order of the *Divine Comedy*, and *L*, p. 346 (29

October 1940), on the 'Ban Gumi', i.e. the set programme of plays in the Noh.

13 See also Int, p. 172, referring perhaps to a turning-point around Canto XLVI.

14 Louis Zukofsky, *Prepositions: The Collected Critical Essays of Louis Zukofsky*, expanded edn (Berkeley/Los Angeles, Calif.: University of California Press, 1981), p. 67; cf. also pp. 68, 141.

15 *Istorie fiorentine*, bk 7, ch. 7.

16 '*affatigandose*' (XXI, p. 97), refers to VIII, p. 29.

17 Ezra Pound, *Ezra Pound and Music*, ed. R. Murray Schafer (London: Faber, 1978), p. 288 (1920).

18 Pound rejected Yeats's garbled account of his fugue analogy, but not the analogy itself; see, e.g., Int, p. 172, and *L*, p. 294. Full references, and technical information about fugue, are in Kay Davis, 'Fugue and Canto LXIII', *Paideuma*, vol. 11, no. 1 (Spring–Summer 1982), pp. 16–26, my source for some of what follows.

19 *Ezra Pound and Music*, p. 403.

20 Zukofsky, *Prepositions*, p. 75.

21 W. B. Yeats, *A Packet for Ezra Pound* (Dublin: Cuala Press, 1929), pp. 2–3.

CHAPTER 5

Values, 1: Religion

Pound wrote in 1937 that the Encyclopaedists of the Enlightenment were an end:

> The Encyclopaedists have a rich culture. What is the Dictionnaire de Bayle? As an arrangement it treats topics ALPHABETICALLY. Voltaire's Dictionnaire is hardly more than a slight addendum [...] The multifarious nature of cognisance remains, but they have only the Alphabet for a filing system. (*P*, 154)

The Encyclopaedists still assumed that it was their job to tackle, and 'criticise', the whole universe; and so did Thomas Jefferson and John Adams, their heirs. But how: with what sense of direction, or purpose? The use of the alphabet as classifier suggests that they had none. One might classify things according to the order of their importance; but that would lead ultimately to the Most Important. The Encyclopaedists implicitly denied the traditional 'Most Important', and were left with no way of deciding between greater and lesser importances, except on a basis not different from what Bentham's was to be: the greatest convenience for average man.

Fielding tries to stop this value-gap with a very strong sense of generosity, humanity – of what the average man is capable of. But he seems to try to give this value universal dimensions by referring to a Supreme Being, author of the same: a Supreme Being so fulsomely and vaguely lauded (like the 'best of fathers' that his good characters generally have) that an unease, whether of guilt or vacuity, is evident.

After their era it became more apparent that there was no basis for ordering investigation, or for relating one set of discovered facts to another; nothing but an infinitely reshufflable Alp of local connections, none more 'important' than another except from some momentary angle. Thus we come to the age of specialisation and voluntary blinkers, of what Pound associated with Germanic philology, in which all poems are of equal importance, all buried in the *Zeitschriften* with equal philological ceremony (cf. *P*, 21–2).

Against that (according to this 1937 essay), before the Renaissance destroyed them, the writers of the Church had offered a criterion of importance, hence a way of relating things. The sense of this derived ultimately from patches of early Greek culture; it had woven in and out of rising and declining cultures in the West thereafter.

> Say that this civilisation lasted down to Leo the Tenth [Giovanni de' Medici (1475–1521), contemporary with Luther]. And that its clearest formulation (along my present line of measurement) is Dante's 'in una parte piu e meno altrove'.
>
> Which detached phrase I had best translate by explaining that I take it to mean *a sense of gradations*. Things neither perfect nor utterly wrong, but arranged in a cosmos, an order, stratified, having relations with one another. (*P*, 150)

But what gives precedence in this 'order'? Without such a principle of precedence, any 'order' is a sandcastle that tomorrow's ego can heap up in another arbitrary and fear-of-chaos-placating manner. The requisite principle, as described in this article, is 'the grades of divine intelligence and/or goodness or goodwill present in graduated degrees throughout this universe', a God-ness inherent in things, *in their degrees*, as in the lines from Dante that Pound has quoted:

> The glory of Him who moves all
>   penetrates through the universe, and re-glows,
>   more in one part, and less in another.
>   (*Paradiso*, 1.1–3)

– *in una parte più, e meno altrove.*

(i) OVID AND METAMORPHOSIS

If godhead was present more here, and less there, Ovid knew places where it was present most fully. In 1922 Pound wrote to Harriet Monroe: '[. . .] I consider the Writings of Confucius, and Ovid's *Metamorphoses* the only safe guides in religion [. . .] I consider the *Metamorphoses* a sacred book' (*L*, 183); in 1957 he called himself 'a follower of Confucius and Ovid'. The first short poem in the final canon, 'The Tree' (1908), is an Ovidian metamorphosis, and important Ovidian passages are scattered through the earlier Cantos. But since Pound believed quite literally that 'a great treasure of verity exists for mankind in Ovid and in the subject matter of Ovid's long poem, and that only in this form could it be registered' (*GK*, 299), he did not make extensive attempts to explain it, or to explain the phenomenon of metamorphosis in literature.

Pound visited the musician Dolmetsch, and recorded that he had seen the God Pan, 'and it was in this manner: I heard a bewildering and pervasive music moving from precision to precision within itself. Then I heard a different music, hollow and laughing. Then I looked up and saw two eyes like the eyes of a wood-creature peering at me over a brown tube of wood [...] shortly afterwards I saw and heard Mr Dolmetsch' – who, we gather, was playing the recorder (*E*, 431–2). Ford Madox Ford was, according to Pound, 'almost an *halluciné* [...] he saw quite distinctly the Venus immortal crossing the tram tracks' (*P*, 461). Pound himself recognised Venus in his lady as she came ashore from her swim:

> as by Terracina rose from the sea Zephyr behind her
> and from her manner of walking
> as had Anchises
> (LXXIV, p. 435)

'The undeniable tradition of metamorphoses teaches us that things do not remain always the same. They become other things by swift and unanalysable process' (Pound in the Dolmetsch essay, *E*, 431). Thus in Ovid men become gods, animals, plants.

The transformations are not random. 'An organisation of forms expresses a confluence of forces,' Pound wrote, describing visual and plastic forms (*VA*, 7); he might equally have been speaking of shapes in nature. Metamorphosis depends on individuation. Much of the point in Io's being transformed into a cow lies in the fact that this cow is soft-skinned, white, timorous, and capable of falling on its knees and speechlessly raising its cow-eyes to Heaven (*Metamorphoses*, 1.729 ff.). Pan 'explains' Dolmetsch. In Canto II, Eleanor of Aquitaine and the seal explain each other. There is a progression of transformations, from seal to sea-nymph, from sea-nymph to Helen of Troy who is also Eleanor of Aquitaine (ἑλέναυς, 'ship-destroyer', is a pun on Helen's name):

Seal sports in the spray-whited circles of cliff-wash,
Sleek head, daughter of Lir,
      eyes of Picasso
Under black fur-hood, lithe daughter of Ocean;
And the wave runs in the beach-groove:
'Eleanor, ἑλέναυς and ἑλέπτολις!'

Thus things only 'become other things by swift and unanalysable process' in so far as their textures are seen to be precisely individuated. 'Woman is metamorphosed into seal', or vice versa, perceived thus vaguely, would have no sense of truth. But the seal that sports in its anarchic cliff-spray (still these terms are more generalised than Pound's) readily inhabits the limbs of the Helen who stirs the old counsellors on the walls of Troy, both to desire and to unease about the future. 'Eyes of Picasso' and 'black fur-hood' are specificities of texture that can inhabit both.

Ovid can show these showings-through of full 'thisness' by mere quality of colour. Thus Pound quotes Golding's version of Atalanta's race in Ovid:

> The wynd ay whisking from her feete the labells of her socks
> Uppon her back as whyght as snowe did tosse her golden locks,
> And eke thembroydred garters that were tyde beneathe her ham.
> A redness mixt with whyght uppon her tender body cam,
> As when a scarlet curtaine streynd ageinst a playstred wall
> Dooth cast like shadowe, making it seeme ruddye therewith all.
>
>   (*E*, 236–7)

('haud aliter, quam cum super atria velum/candida purpureum simulatas inficit umbras': *Metamorphoses*, 10.595–6.) A wall that is white, but tinted with a purple light thrown on it by a hanging, is not like a wall painted purple; it seems as if it were translucent, a colour that you cannot touch. Dante wanted such an unreality in Paradise, where Cacciaguida's spirit's light 'did not leave its riband,/but coursed along the radial line/and seemed like fire behind alabaster' (*Paradiso*, 15.22–4). These lights are part of Ovid's 'subject': impalpable shadings, like Arachne's blush (as when the heavens are reddened and then turn white with the sunrise), or Diana's when she is surprised naked by Actaeon ('the colour that is in clouds tinged by the sun when it is opposite them': (*Metamorphoses*, 6.47 ff.; 3.183 ff.). The word 'tinge', 'stain' (*inficere*), recurs at such moments. *Concolor* brings together Adonis' blood and the anemone (*Metamorphoses*, 10.735).

Pound's eye went to these colorations, and he quoted them, and with
labour learned to imitate.

> Glass-glint of wave in the tide-rips against sunlight,
>   pallor of Hesperus,
> Grey peak of the wave,
>   wave, colour of grape's pulp,
>
> Olive grey in the near,
>   far, smoke grey of the rock-slide,
> Salmon-pink wings of the fish-hawk
>   cast grey shadows in water,
> The tower like a one-eyed great goose
>   cranes up out of the olive-grove,
>
> And we have heard the fauns chiding Proteus
>   in the smell of hay under the olive-trees.
> And the frogs singing against the fauns
>   in the half-light.
>
> And...   (II, p. 10)

As in Ovid, these things ought in themselves to make the air to be
sensed as god-filled, by mere subtlety of colour-grade. But also specific
colours recall specific god-stories. Dionysus, the wine-god, in Canto II
turns Acoetes' men into dolphins, leaping among the waves, and the
phrase 'wave, colour of grape's pulp'[1] has that reference to Dionysus.
At the same time, by a sharpness of Pound's eye (who had noticed that
colour in the grape?) it brings alive a scene which, in the cribs we use,
was mere mythical archaeology; and makes us understand the metamorphosis itself – the relation between sea and vine. Pound pursued
this craft from the beginning of the Cantos to the end. If one recognises
Aphrodite, wave-born, of the copper earrings, in this passage, it has
meaning because one sees the sunset making that copper across the
waves:

> had I the clouds of heaven
>   as the nautile borne ashore
> in their holocaust
>   as wistaria floating shoreward
> with the sea gone the colour of copper
>   and emerald dark in the offing
>   (LXXX, p. 500)

Exact tone or texture makes for difference, unlimitedly; textures can
be grouped, but only *ad hoc*. One texture has relations with others that

do not allow of any but arbitrary borderlines between them. If an alveolar fricative in the Tokyo dialect is different from a velar plosive in the dialect of Seine-et-Marne (supposing those sounds to exist), there are no gaps in the continuum of sound that comes between, any more than there is a line between where the colour of yesterday's sunset stops and the colour of a crab's back starts. This, along with movements along such gradients caused by time, is that which worried the philosophers of Plato's era: the world contains no fixed points, synchronically or diachronically, but only the 'Ineluctable modality of the visible' as observed by the scholastic Stephen Dedalus. What is unfixed is not complete, or fully real, they said; and they therefore invented mental worlds of fixities, Ideas, Ones, and the whole paraphernalia of abstraction and reification that has led to modern religion and philosophy.

But the fact of unfixity, which seems to lie at the root of this dualism, is what delighted Ovid. It caused him to celebrate textures, their precisions (not definable, but communicable) and their changes:

> You might see her limbs soften, her bones become subject to bending, her nails lay aside their hardness: each, too, of the smaller extremities of the whole of her body melts away; both her azure hair, her fingers, legs, and feet, *for easy is the change of small members into a cold stream.*

– 'nam brevis in gelidas membris exilibus undas/transitus est' (*Metamorphoses*, 5.433). No truly seen configuration of forces is stable; its specificity is so fine that it can hold only for a moment, before it has gone to the thing it was only a gradation away from.

Swiftness evokes this ungraspability, and at the crisis-points of his stories Ovid dwells on speed:

> For the earth closes over her legs as she speaks, and a root shoots forth obliquely through her bursting nails [. . .] (*Metamorphoses*, 10.489–91)

Modo is one of his key words: 'just now she was . . . but now. . .' Again and again a he, or a she, tries to stretch forth his/her hands, but finds them already gone; or still and bark-covered; or beast's paws.

Fluidity and precision are of the nature of things. We have neither a moral/phenomenal geometry nor an undifferentiated jelly about us. But there is relationship, and force of one kind showing through where the dull eye expects another. Between the vacuity of 'fact' and the vacuity of metaphysic – between the 'raw meat' (LXXX, p. 511) and the void – Pound tried to show meanings and hence Meaning, shapes and also Shape, immanent in things. He bypassed systems of binary opposition, mental geometry, and metaphysics, with metaphor, and metamorphosis, which depend on perception-gradients like this one, remembered in 1960 from his youth:

> Gold is simple. It is weighed, then refined and weighed again. You can tell the grade of the ore by the relative weights. But the test for silver is a cloudy solution; the accuracy of the eye in measuring the thickness of the cloud is an aesthetic perception, like the critical sense. I like the idea of the *fineness* of the metal. (*WW*, 105)

Individuation, in Ovid, is related to movement and speed. Also Ovid is attracted to movement itself, as in the leaping of dolphins; and to the powers working through creatures (such as passion), and hurtling them along like avalanches. In fact it may be that his subject is abundance and multiplicity itself, whether of movement or texture. He delights in the silliness of gods' and humans' ways, as an aspect of the general energy and variety. Pound noted that in Ovid the gods' doings had the immediacy of the doings in the parish register, but he did not often follow the drollness in Ovid that makes the gods so 'human'. Perhaps the 'nasty little Ralph Waldo Emerson',[2] the New England seriousness, that he suspected in himself, inhibited him. But he did follow this delight in abundance. Heaven and the western Mediterranean are one big gossip-shop in Ovid, and that is the nature of Ovid's literary form (Allen Tate alleged the same of Pound's[3]). As he delights in abundance of textures and powers, so he delights in abundance of invention of all kinds. Stories framed in stories flower in substories, by way of some connection of image or place, with the briefest transition: 'There is a grove of Haemonia . . .' Time stretches and compresses so that Ovid may rush to the *aperçu* that interests him. Like Pound, Ovid has no concern with long-range narrative 'justification' in Ford's sense. Like some newborn babe or Henry Miller, his delight is to gambol among the swift fertility of his perceptions of relations, sensuosities, metaphors. To get this on paper, not a symmetrical plan but rhythms of 'subject-rhymes' are needed – as in the Cantos. Only these quick echoes can catch the multiplicity of connection within the whole abundant multiverse, without clogging perception.

Abundance of textures and powers cannot be named, except by things (verse-cadence, metamorphic image) as ungraspable as itself; it cannot be controlled; it is awe-worthy. Delight (*diletto, hilaritas*) is not in conflict with this abundance, but almost a necessary concomitant. Thus it is a 'mystery', and a good part of what Pound meant by religion.[4] It arouses a desire to enact it, by music, rite, or word-music:

> undique dant saltus multaque adspergine rorant
> emerguntque iterum redeuntque sub aequora rursus
> (*Metamorphoses*, 3.683–4)

That is Acoetes' men (see Canto II), now dolphins; the metre leaps and plunges. Pound catches this in his very last book of Cantos:

> Came Neptunus
> his mind leaping
> like dolphins
> (CXVI, p. 795)

To return, then, to Dante's image of a universe in which godhead 're-glows/more in one part, and less in another'. It may be that one of the differentiators between the valuable end of this spectrum and the evil end is differentiation itself. Thus full selfhood is both a manifestation of God and a maximum self-differentiation. It is felt as active: 'The duty of being is to persevere in its being and even to augment the characteristics which specialize it' (Gourmont, quoted by Pound: N*EP*, 290); 'the more perfect a thing is the more it acts and the less it suffers' (Spinoza, quoted by Pound[5]). At the other end of the spectrum is *hyle* (Greek; cf. XXX, p. 148), uninformed, undifferentiated matter; which, in so far as it is worshipped for its own mere grossness, becomes as excrement, Pound's standard image for the Evil. (*Hyle* might correspond morally to Limbo, excrement to Hell.)

Ovid's world belongs almost entirely to the former. Though he purports to present evil states, like Whitman he has no real perception of them. For that, Pound had to turn to Dante's development out of Ovid.

(ii) EVIL AND THE NATURAL

How Pound used this Ovidian Dante may be seen particularly in an early pair of Cantos, XIV–XV, commonly known as the 'Hell Cantos'.

These show typified inhabitants of contemporary England, in a fanta-sised Dantescan Inferno, suffering for abasements and bestialities such as Pound saw among the English during his stay in London.

Pound's version of 'eternal justice' is his feeling that the universe has its harmonies, and that our being part of those harmonies – in our own in-structure – will cause our punishment if we go against them. Such a rebellion is essentially evil, not evil by decree; and indeed there can be no other proper definition of evil. Pound's Hell has no concern for flouters of Authority as such (heroic or otherwise, Satans or Baude-laires). Authority that is only authority is necessarily arbitrary. 'Mil-ton's god is a fussy old man with a hobby' (*SR*, 157), bearing no relation to the structures of the universe; to rebel against him can have no metaphysical significance, being merely an act against a particular person.

The quality of evil for Pound can only be described by using words like 'monstrous', and that leads to an important technique for present-ing it, both in the Cantos and in Dante. In subtle ways the body is a bodying-forth of the 'mind', improperly so called. Pound said that Gourmont 'does not grant the duality of body and soul, or at least suggests that this medieval duality is unsatisfactory; there is an interpenetration, and osmosis of body and soul, at least for hypothesis' (*E*, 341). And we understand all things (including bodies) in terms of other things, by a suspended half-fusion with them, that is, in metaphor. And we judge the whole ('morally') by comparison with our sense of the natural – which no writer, however structuralist, can help implying in every paragraph he writes.

In these Bunting lines, the critics are dogs *or* some other creature, simultaneously held in half-realisation:

> teeth for knots and
> each other's ankles

Now, Pound said that this was Dante's contribution to literature:

After a comparatively dull stretch, canto XXV imposes Dante's adjunct, the profounder metamorphosis of the nature (soul), agglu-tinous fluidity, and he calls specific attention to it, and to the fact that he is adding something not in Lucan or Ovid. In fact after Guido and Dante, whatever there may have been in human mind and percep-tion, literature does not again make any very serious attempt to enter

these regions of consciousness till almost our own day, in the
struggles of Henry James and of Ibsen [...] (*E*, 212)

Canto XXV of the *Inferno* is the one in which the Florentine nobleman
Cianfa appears as a serpent which fastens itself upon his peer and
fellow-thief Agnello:

> With its middle feet it clasped his belly,
>   and with the anterior it seized his arms;
>   then it fixed its teeth in both his cheeks.
> The hinder feet it stretched along his thighs,
>   and put its tail between the two,
>   and bent it upwards on his loins behind.
> Ivy was never rooted
>   to a tree so, as the horrible beast
>   entwined its members around the other's [...]
> Two arms were made of the four lists;
>   the thighs with the legs, the belly and the chest
>   became members that were never seen before.

Another reptile appears, the nobleman Francesco, and pierces the navel
of his peer, a normal human, Buoso. Side by side each transforms itself
into the form of the other, in equally horrible manner; monstrosity
reaches its peak.

Pound knew very well that such metamorphosis need not be
presented complete. In metaphor, or simile, the inner face may dissolve
through the outer ('porcine'; cf. *GK*, 300–1) face for a moment of
perception. The metaphor may be in the verb only (cf. *OS*, 1264):

> and I want you to believe for certain,
>   that under the water there are people that breathe,
>   and make this water pullulate at the surface
>   (*Inferno*, 7.117–9)

Pullulate suggests the activity of multiple generating life beneath,
obscene. The safe translation of *pullular* would be 'to bubble', which
simply deletes that incipient metamorphosis in our minds. Pound in
these Cantos uses almost precisely the same suggestion, and a paraphrase would kill it just as surely:

> beneath one
>   nothing that might not move,

> mobile earth, a dung hatching obscenities,
> inchoate error,
> boredom born out of boredom
>
> (XV, p. 65)

The verb is 'hatch'.

This bolge of Pound's Hell has elements in common with Dante's Antinferno, where people go because they did not rise to moral existence: they never chose. And thus in this kind of metamorphosis it may be that a *lack* of inner face dissolves through the outer face:

> melting like dirty wax,
> decayed candles, the bums sinking lower,
> faces submerged under hams [. . .]
> The soil a decrepitude, the ooze full of morsels,
> lost contours, erosions [. . .]
>
> liquid animals, melted ossifications,
> slow rot, foetid combustion   (XIV, pp. 62–3)

Compare Miss Birdseye in chapter 4 of *The Bostonians*:

> [. . .] the vast, fair, protuberant, candid, ungarnished brow, sur-mounting a pair of weak, kind, tired-looking eyes [. . .] She had a sad, soft, pale face, which (and it was the effect of her whole head) looked as if it had been soaked, blurred, and made vague by exposure to some slow dissolvent. The long practice of philanthropy had not given accent to her features; it had rubbed out their transitions, their meanings. The waves of sympathy, of enthusiasm, had wrought upon them in the same way in which the waves of time finally modify the surface of old marble busts, gradually washing away their sharpness, their details. In her large countenance her dim little smile scarcely showed. It was a mere sketch of a smile, a kind of instalment, or payment on account; it seemed to say that she would smile more if she had time, but that you could see, without this, that she was gentle and easy to beguile.

This is quite as definitely a metamorphosis as the 'decayed candles' in Pound, though what Miss Birdseye is transformed into is not specified and thus not limited. It is the very namelessness of half-dissolved objects that float in factory slime that gives them their horror. James puts together the inner, the outer, and the fusion of the inner and outer in metaphor, specifying its (monstrous) 'isness'.

Thus Churchill in Pound's Canto XV, 'like a swollen foetus', and Adam of Brescia in *Inferno*, 30.49, 'shaped like a lute', and those half-egg creatures in Hieronymus Bosch, and the 'medieval' (and most durable) part of *Macbeth*, all depend on our inherent sense of the monstrous, and conversely of the natural. From these comes the actual moral effect of those presentations; which may be contrasted with the actual moral effect of the picture of Paolo and Francesca in the *Inferno*, which has never persuaded anyone that those two are evil except by decree.

(iii) ELEUSIS

Glaucus' story in Dante seems to incorporate a great part of Pound's sense of religion. At the peak of Mount Purgatory, in the Earthly Paradise, Dante has just tasted of the River Eunoë. Then, as Beatrice gazes fixedly at the sun, he, Dante, gazes into her eyes; and changes, he says, as Glaucus did.

> Gazing on her, such I became within myself
> as did Glaucus, in the tasting of the grass
> that made him sea-fellow of the other gods.
> (*Paradiso*, 1.67–9)

Dante is 'transhumanated', he says, taken beyond the human, wholly re-created by the Love that rules the heavens, and winged, without knowing it, towards the heavenly spheres.

Words will not make you understand this, Dante says, so let the example suffice to indicate what I mean to those who have had the experience. He takes the example from Ovid (*Metamorphoses*, 13.924) where Glaucus sees how a certain grass revives his fish, tastes it, and is transformed into a sea-god, leaping beneath the waves. Of the Dante passage Pound wrote in 1910:

> The disciples of Whitman cry out concerning the 'cosmic sense', but Whitman, with all his catalogues and flounderings, has never so perfectly expressed the perception of cosmic consciousness as does Dante [here]. (*SR*, 155)

Dante is transformed by gazing on Beatrice. Here the beloved is goddess, and the poem her icon, as (Pound thought) in the troubadour lyric. But she is also relaying a somewhat Neoplatonic light. She is

gazing on the sun, whose light is often used by Dante to figure that of
God, the original and pouring-forth source of all Forms, including
souls. (We shall look further at this Neoplatonic concept in comment-
ing on Canto XXXVI.) Dante's Glaucus also carries an Ovidian
meaning, for in this moment he is transformed, and enters a world of
transformations, thereby acquiring a new religious awareness. Lastly
there is what I shall call an Eleusinian meaning, for Glaucus (and hence
Dante) is transformed by a plunge, a kind of ecstasy.

In Pound, seeing the transformed world, when it takes on its 'true'
strangeness, is constantly associated with sexual desire and ecstasy,
which in turn are seen as standing outside ratiocination, and also
casting caution aside. It is Niccolò d'Este, bullnecked begetter of
thousands, who has the mad dream which is Canto XX. 'La copulation
complète et profonde' is literally supposed to extend the cerebellum, in
Pound and in Gourmont (*NPL*, vii) – the 'profonde' is important. Peire
Vidal's passion shows him his lady as a she-wolf, so that he himself
enters the wolf-world (IV, p. 14). In Pound's understanding of the
Provençal troubadours, both desire and fulfilment clarify sight. The
alba is verse of the morning after love, and was Pound's first favourite among the Provençal genres. To the lovers in the dawn comes
clarity:

> [. . .] the drowsy watcher cryeth,
>   'Arise!' [. . .]
>
> O'ver cliff and ocean white dawn appeareth,
> Passeth vigil, and the shadows cleareth.[6]

This is the old Romantic idea of ecstasy. Pound had defined ecstasy in
1907, in a letter full of Blake and Coleridge, as 'the sensation of the soul
in ascent'.[7] Or more particularly it is as the dawn in Thoreau.[8] Pound
singled out lines by the troubadour Arnaut Daniel, which he translated:
'with laughter and caresses, she shall disclose to me her fair body, with
the glamor of the lamplight about it'. He commented on this in 1912:
'the ecstasy is not a whirl or a madness of the senses, but a glow arising
from the exact nature of the perception' (*SR*, 34, 91). (Exactly not
Wagner.)

He saw that it was connected in the troubadours with spring; the
spring opening of their songs (to the critical historian merely a
convention) being to him 'an interpretation of the mood; an equation,
in other terms, or a "metaphor by sympathy" for the mood of the

poem' (*SR*, 31). How a metaphor for it? That 'mood' is a stepping-beyond, an ecstatic seeing; Arnaut sees by a religious light:

> So clear was my first light in choosing her whose eyes my heart feareth [. . .] (*SR*, 29)

In physiological rhythm, spring bears the same relation to the year as does dawn to the day. It is not only young men that fall in love in the spring, but young beasts also; the Shakespearian convention, like all conventions that work, has a sounder basis. Passions originate in spring; spring is sensed as a time of new seeing. Also of turbulence, the breaking of laws, and adultery – like that of the Provençal 'April-like queen'.

Now various anthropologists in the late nineteenth century were noticing cultural connections between 'spiritual' and natural fertilities. And Pound became interested in these matters quite early in his career. Already in 1910 he was putting together the 'Aprilish Queen', who in a Provençal ditty challenges her lover to defy the jealous one, with 'such fragments of the worship of Flora and Venus as survived in the spring merrymakings' (*SR*, 39); by 1912 he was asserting that 'the birth of Provençal song hovers about the Pagan rites of May-day' (*SR*, 90). He considered, 'Psychology and Troubadours' (1912) makes clear, that the troubadours used some sort of disciplining and delaying of the sexual impulse to heighten general sensitivity. Of this the song itself consti- tuted an emotional organising, that is to say ritual, and at the same time it alluded to secret cult practices[9] that further emotionally organised (ritualised) that impulse. The resulting sensitivity, extending to the troubadours' perception in general, then made possible the particular perceptions of nature, and so on, that were registered in the fine interstices of the song itself.

There was thus a secret cult. It was not a cult only of sexual delay (the 'psychic function' that Pound said Ovid ignored: *SR*, 97), but included sexual fulfilment. And Pound had already by 1912 long known the ancient myth-and-ritual that would fit this: the Greek mysteries at Eleusis. This is clear from his veiled remarks: that in order to understand the sensitivity observable in Provençal verse we must

> consider carefully the history of the various cults or religions of orgy and of ecstasy, from the simpler Bacchanalia to the more complicated rites of Isis or Dionysus – sudden rise and equally sudden decline.

The corruptions of their priesthoods follow, probably, the admission thereto of one neophyte who was not properly '*sacerdos*'. (*SR*, 95)

And we must consider a line that goes from 'the ancient ideas of union with the god, or with Queen Isis' – that is, evidently, the worshipper's union with that god or that goddess – to Peire Vidal's 'Good Lady, I think I see God when I gaze on your delicate body'.

Eleusis: in Pound's usage, a rite enacting several related, overlapping myths. They each have a plunge into another world. In each case it follows a mating.

The key was Frazer's simple formula: having perceived a resemblance between procreation in nature and procreation in man, primitive tribesmen concluded that enacting the one would stimulate the other. In *The Golden Bough* (1890–1915), Frazer suggested that the first stage was simple animism: every kind of plant, even every plant, was inhabited by its spirit. These spirits had a kind of consciousness, but their life-cycles were precisely those of the things whose spirits they were: the corn-spirit would die when the corn died. Now, to act is to encourage analogous action: that is the principle of 'sympathetic magic', the central discovery of Frazer's school. If there are beings there in the corn and rain, going through their procreative action, the thing to do is to help them: to enact what they are doing. Someone will perform the human act of fertilisation – in the earth's furrow, which is thus affected by the analogy with the woman's; and he will 'be' the spirit of the rain for the time, and she the corn's. Thus, according to Frazer, the begetting of Plutus by Iasion and Demeter in the thrice-ploughed field, in the story that crops up in book 5 of the *Odyssey*, suggests

an older practice of performing, among the sprouting crops in spring or the stubble in autumn, one of those real or mimic acts of procreation by which, as we have seen, primitive man often seeks to infuse his own vigorous life into the languid or decaying energies of nature.[10]

But there now enters an anthropomorphism: the putting of human attributes into the spirits, giving them biographies. The process is already complete in Demeter and her daughter Persephone, whom we must look at closely because they are so important in the Cantos.

Pound more or less follows their biography as given in the Homeric

Hymn to Demeter.[11] Persephone (or Kore, 'Virgin') plays in her perpetual springtime, till 'Dis caught her up' (XXI, p. 100). Dis (Hades) carries her off to the underworld, where he is king. Her mother Demeter, the grain-goddess, searches for her. She is informed that Persephone is now Queen of the Underworld, no unworthy rank; still Demeter is not satisfied. In her grief (or, says Ovid, in her anger against the earth for permitting the rape) she blasts all crops: 'the ground would not make the seed sprout, for rich-crowned Demeter kept it hid'. On behalf of the anxious Zeus, Hermes persuades Hades to give the girl up. But Hades makes sure that she has tasted of something before she goes – a pomegranate – with the result that she is condemned to spend with him, in perpetuity, one-third of each year.

> But when the earth shall bloom with the fragrant flowers of spring in every kind, then from the realm of darkness and gloom thou shalt come up

– says Demeter. Satisfied, Demeter flies back to Rharus' plain, where lies Eleusis; the plain

> was soon to be waving with long ears of corn, and its rich furrows to be loaded with grain upon the ground, while others would already be bound in sheaves.

Then

> to the kings [of Eleusis] who deal justice, Triptolemus and Diocles, the horse-driver, and to doughty Eumolpus and Celeus, leader of the people, she showed the conduct of her rites and taught them all her mysteries [...] awful mysteries which no one may in any way transgress or pry into or utter, for deep awe of the gods checks the voice. Happy is he among men upon earth who has seen these mysteries; but he who is uninitiate and who has no part in them, never has lot of like good things once he is dead, down in the darkness and gloom.

At the stage of animism there is much logic. Persephone the young girl would be the seed-corn; her descent into Hades the sowing; her reappearance in spring the corn's sprouting. 'In this way the Persephone of one year becomes the Demeter of the next, and this may very well have been the original form of the myth.'[12] But·if you take these spirits away from the cycle that they represent, and give Persephone a biography, and the mother-stage (Demeter), too, a biography, then Persephone clearly cannot grow up and 'become' Demeter. They must now be forever separate persons. So when Persephone grows up with the year, what do you do about the biography of Demeter – what is there for her to do? Her part is reduced to a bit-part: simply to weep for her daughter lost under the earth, so that all the plants shrivel.

The spirit with a biography is a goddess; obviously more 'sympathique', more appealable-to 'by sacrifice, prayer or praise',[13] more conveniently manipulable by a priesthood (the class that has thus anthropomorphised her) by adjustments of the story to have her visiting the local temple, and so on. But by that process she has become less closely involved with the vegetation she first represented. She is on her way to being part of that long-running family comedy that fills the less significant part of Ovid; or (to Pound, worse) an agent in the megalomania of the supergod, Zeus, or his equivalents, generally magnified reflections of the self-image of the powers and hierarchies that be.

But it all began with a *sympatheia*[14] between processes. And Pound selected from the whole mass given him by his classical reading and by Frazer, of whatever date, to re-create a myth-stage roughly equivalent to the pre-Homeric. He picked out those parts of the lives of the gods and goddesses that were most clearly sympathetic parallels with the processes that they started out by representing. As god's life-shape was still for him the shape of the natural process, so the shape of the rite must enact the shape in the god's life, in order to encourage him properly to affect that process. So the rites Pound shows are those that Frazer says are found at an animist stage; not mere payments, of oxen with gilded horns, etc., but ceremonies that 'are believed to influence the course of nature directly through a physical sympathy or resemblance between the rite and the effect which it is the intention of the rite to produce.'[15] Pound is really not interested in what Juno had for her tea.

Most of this presupposes representative enactment: that not everyone need perform the sympathetic act, but that the community·wants it performed, and that it should be performed by the most suitable representative. The archetypal male task is to imitate the fertilisation in nature: the sky's rain, the seed's sowing, the beasts' insemination, perhaps the flowing of sap in tree or vine. Since the whole sense of whether this job is done well, or done badly, is an emotional sympathetic sense in the human, everything depends on the vigour that is sensed by the populace in the actor. He must be selected. The same selection processes that prove his fitness for this task (chiefly, combat) will tend to select him to rule over others; priest's job is identified with king's. Mussolini, 'male of the species' (*E*, 83) was no doubt the erection (*rex*) of the body politic, as John Adams had been before him (in Canto LXVII).[16]

The human mind transfers: the king who at certain times enacts the movements of a raining or a sowing retains the specialness that that job gives him; the divinity inheres in him; his body and processes are felt to contain in themselves the spirits of fertility they imitated. They must be fed to the soil; he must be sacrificed. He may be torn apart and eaten, to distribute his strength; thus the followers of Dionysus, eating blood-dripping flesh, are consuming the god's strength by imitation. He may simply be sacrificed and replaced; or the combat that tests whether his strength is still there is itself ritualised, and becomes an earth-fertilisation if he is killed. Dionysus' story and Osiris' and Adonis' all seem to have elements of the life of an imagined fertility-god, the shedding of whose blood echoes the deaths of earthly fertility-kings of whom they may be the divinised memories.

In a classical education such as Pound received in college, the gods would have been fixed and other, apart. Any variations, such as a Virgil introduced into his stories, would have been considered (as they probably were by Augustans) as poetic decoration. But in Pound's writings it is all fluid; there is endless movement between the planes of god, man, and flora/fauna – as is natural where the priest-heroes and the gods take their life contemporaneously from 'the force that through the green fuse drives the flower' (in Dylan Thomas's phrase), and vice versa. Men are constantly making gods ('His rod hath made god in my belly': XXXIX, p. 196) or becoming gods ('with a mind like that he is one of us', says Zeus of Odysseus: LXXX, p. 512; cf. *L*, 270).

With superior vigour, superior insight, because intelligence (Pound's word is not 'intellect'[17]) is intimately involved with the organism as a whole. *Contemplatio* is for him defined as a movement, multi-directional like Neptunus' leaping.[18] His phallus-mind *drives* an idea into 'the great passive vulva of London' (*PD*, 204); Wyndham Lewis's mind is '*The* fecund mind with any amount of form-organizations fermenting in it' (*VA*, 239), waiting to inform the hitherto formless. This is a 'light fighting for speed' (XCI, p. 616); as the dawn (in 'Battle Dawn', a very

early poem) comes 'as a man against the night' and is called on to
'Unsheathe the sun-blade brand'. Energy of the intelligence is itself
both part of the god and the way to perceive and participate in the god;
Pound quotes Ovid to the effect that 'there is a god in us; when he stirs
we warm' (*P*, 72). Therefore this vigour is not 'mere dynamic' (XCII,
p. 620; cf. *E*, 154); Pound was never interested in undirected momentum. The true priest-king was 'the antenna of the race', like the artist;
as in Allen Upward's account:

> The Genius of the Thunder who revealed himself to me could not call
> the thunder, but he could be called by it. He was more quick than
> other men to feel the changes of the atmosphere; perhaps he had
> rendered his nervous system more sensitive still by fasting or mental
> abstraction; and he had learned to read his own symptoms as we read
> a barometer. So, when he felt the storm gathering round his head, he
> put on his symbolical vestment, and marched forth to be its Word,
> the archetype of all Heroes in all Mysteries. (*P*, 403)

In the prewar Cantos, Persephone is at the moment of explosion of
awareness in coition. She is the mistress of the dark regions: it is she
who grants his whole mind to Tiresias, though he is dead, and she who,
being praised (in Canto I), permits the shades to speak to Odysseus.
Coition brings light out of darkness, and the governing image for this is
not an image but a light, a light-in-darkness: that of the translucent
pomegranate, and what it shares with fire, blood and wine. The
pomegranate is blood-coloured, thus the blood of Adonis/Tamuz/
[Dionysus] that is poured forth when he is sacrificed as vegetation-god
in Canto XLVII. (Pomegranates sprang from the blood of Dionysus.[19])
Evidently the hero's coition is his death.[20] Persephone eats the
pomegranate, 'acquiring' this carrier of passion and understanding, fire
and light (the 'red flame' of the lamps annually set in the sea in
the ceremony in Canto XLVI, understood there as Adonis' blood),
when she is impregnated by the vegetation-god; it now glows through
her:

> Wine in the smoke-faint throat,
> Fire gleam under smoke of the mountain,
> Even there by meadows of Phlegethon
>   (XXV, p. 118)

For she is also 'Queen over Phlegethon' (CVI, p. 752), the river of

Hades, and 'phlegethon' means 'burning'. But the wine-god Dionysus
is thereby also made in her belly; as, at Eleusis, Iacchus is an infant
Dionysus, possibly the product of the rite. Cats are Dionysus' animals:

> Thus made the spring,
> Can see but their eyes in the dark
> > not the bough that he walked on.
> Beaten from flesh into light
> Hath swallowed the fire-ball
> A traverso le foglie [through the leaves]
> His rod hath made god in my belly
> > (XXXIX, pp. 195–6)

Thus the pomegranate, fire-blood-wine-coloured, is the bridge between
Persephone and Dionysus, god of lynxes, even in late Cantos (e.g.
LXXIX, p. 490).[21]

Dionysus at first sight has no place in the Eleusis myth; but he (and
his other manifestations, Zagreus and Iacchus) are found in various
points of what is known of the Eleusinian rite. He is the god of the vine,
and thus a vegetation-god, a god of abundance, the 'god of abundant
grape-clusters' as the Homeric Hymn describes him. For his worship-
pers, wrote Pater in 1876, Dionysus had the same relation to the vine as
did Demeter to the grain: he 'is the life of the earth through the grape as
she through the grain'.[22] But his fruition is the grape, and Pater
explains this as light and fluid combined: the sun shrivels the earth, as
Zeus shrivelled Semele in the conceiving of Dionysus, and the result is
the fluid globe whose freshness seems to contrast with the scorched
Mediterranean earth around it. (Pound stresses the translucence of the
'grape-pulp'.) Pater goes on: 'He is πυριγενής, then, fire-born, the
son of lightning, lightning being to light, as regards concentration,
what wine is to the other strengths of the earth.' Wine concentrates
earth-strengths, as blood concentrates body-strengths (Pater's picture
of Dionysus coincides remarkably with Dodds's in 1944[23]).

For the purpose of understanding Pound's cult, it hardly matters
what exactly the rite at Eleusis was, or what Pound thought it was.
Indirectly it is indicated that Pound thought the priestess and the priest
enacted the copulation of god and goddess. The meaning of the cult is
clear; but what worries some is the lack of a theology, an Eleusinian
god-theory, which would give fixity of meaning to the various elements
of the various stories. Conjectures as to the date of origin of the
Eleusinian Mysteries vary from 1580 to 700 BC, but they lasted until

Alaric the Hun invaded Greece in AD 396, thus for more than a
thousand years. They are of great importance to the understanding of
Greece; but the Athenian state was strongly interested in them, and
severely punished sacrilege, and the chief sacrilege was the breaking of
silence about them. Things may be inferred from the *Hymn to Demeter*,
statuary, reference to public elements of the festivals, and so on. As for
the central Mysteries, our chief source is the Christian Fathers, who
were concerned to destroy them as expeditiously as possible. What
weight is to be put on their evidence depends entirely upon the effects
such an aim might be considered by the student to have had on
it.[24]

Pound wrote in 1931 that 'The so called difficulties of penetrating the
Eleusinian cult or of getting at the meaning of a "religion" are due to
the cult's indifference to empire.' Christianity by contrast became a
state religion, and 'Out of a need to administer arises or arose theology'.
To understand a religious mystery is not the same as to be able to talk
about it; in fact the ancient wisdom died 'when the mysteries entered
the vain space of Christian theological discussion'.

One can, he says, say vaguely and comprehensively what the whole
Eleusinian business is about: 'The modern author can write "aim the
union with nature" or "consciousness of the unity with nature". This is
at the root of any mystery [. . .]' That is where we started, with Glaucus
and Whitman. From the point of that statement onwards, he says, it is
almost impossible to judge what any other individual understands of
the matter; and so creeds are not to the point. But Pound goes on to
make it perfectly clear that the rite, in his opinion, was copulation. Or
as he wrote, concerning Eleusis, in his notebooks for the Cantos: 'The
secretum/secretum est coitus'.[25]

From there onwards, according to Pound's essay (*P*, 54–60), it is a
question of religious history; mainly a matter of Christianity's having
absorbed the fascination with darkness, evil and sacrifice that character-
ised cults (like Mithra's) then prevalent in Imperial Rome – '"The
celebrant immolated victims" would seem to be the main theme.' (In
later years Pound would decide that Mithra, Manes and Zoroaster had
not been guilty of this 'manichean' dualism.[26]) Meanwhile Christianity
ignored what was offered by the cult of Eleusis. The cult survived,
Pound hints, underground, and can be connected with the Albigensian
'heretics' who were burned at Montségur when the Provençal troubadour culture was destroyed by the Church and the French; and with the
beauties of ecstatic illumination in Arnaut Daniel and Cavalcanti.

NOTES: CHAPTER 5

1 Glaucus' name also means that colour (*'bright, sparkling, gleaming, grayish ... so of water'* – Lewis and Short, *A Latin Dictionary*), and thus connects him with Pound's dealings with the words *glaux* and *glaukopis* for the owl and Athena's eyes (see esp. *KPE*, p. 45 and LXXIV, p. 438).

2 The quotation is approximate; I cannot now trace the remark.

3 See Allen Tate, *The Man of Letters in the Modern World: Selected Essays 1928–1955* (London: Thames & Hudson, 1957), esp. p. 258.

4 'Religion is not only dejection, grief, sufferance – it is the eternal energy; it is even exuberance of energy ...' (Pound in 1934, quoted in B*FT*, pp. 332–3).

5 'Gists from uncollected prose', chosen by William Cookson, *Agenda*, vol. 17, no. 3–4, and vol. 18, no. 1 (Autumn–Winter–Spring 1979–80), p. 74.

6 'Belangal Alba', *Hamilton Literary Magazine*, vol. 39, no. 9 (May 1905), p. 324 (see 'Alba Belingalis' in *Collected Early Poems*). This is Pound's second published poem.

7 'Letters to Viola Baxter Jordan', ed. Donald Gallup, *Paideuma*, vol. 1, no. 1 (Spring–Summer 1972), pp. 109–10.

8 *Walden*, 'Where I Lived, and What I Lived For'.

9 Perhaps (in Pound's opinion) in the Arnaut lines already quoted; see also *SR*, p. 30 (on 'the shadowy suggestion of mediaeval ceremonies'); *SR*, p. 89, and *E*, p. 180 (on the 'mantle of indigo' and the castle); *MPP*, pp. 241, 244, 381–2; and below, p. 297.

10 Sir J. G. Frazer, *Spirits of the Corn and the Wild* (*The Golden Bough*, Pt 5), Vol. 1 (London: Macmillan, 1933), p. 209.

11 The following quotations are from *Hesiod, the Homeric Hymns and Homerica*, ed. and trans. Hugh G. Evelyn-White (Cambridge, Mass. London: Harvard University Press/Heinemann, 1977), pp. 289–325.

12 Frazer, *Spirits*, Vol. 1, p. 210.

13 ibid., p. 169.

14 I have borrowed this term from a Neoplatonist context, where it refers to a harmony that 'binds the whole universe together, the sensibles to the intelligibles and the intelligibles to the gods' (*The Cambridge History of Later Greek and Early Medieval Philosophy*, ed. A. H. Armstrong (Cambridge: Cambridge University Press, 1980), p. 458; cf. p. 432). It will be seen from what follows that Pound, like Pater, reads anthropology to some extent with a Neoplatonist eye.

15 Frazer, *Spirits*, Vol. 1, p. 169.

16 In LXVII, p. 393, Pound has 'erected' where the source has 'elevated by the popular voice to the chief offices of the state' (see Frederick K. Sanders, *John Adams Speaking: Pound's Sources for the Adams Cantos* (Orono, Me: University of Maine Press, 1975), p. 341). 'Erected' is not an error: see *L*, p. 329. Norman O. Brown, I believe, makes the connection between *rex* and 'erection'.

17 See N*EP*, pp. 372–3: intellect is 'the mental scaffolding men erect to deal with what they don't understand. Belief is from intelligence.'

18 See Pound's 'Excerpt from "*Benjamin Major*"': Cogitatio, Meditatio, Contemplatio', *Gnomon*, no. 2 (Spring 1967), esp. p. 38. Contemplation is 'an unlimited clarity of the mind', when 'with wonderous agility, it is borne almost instantly through a world of things without number'.

19 Frazer, *Spirits*, Vol. 1. p. 14.

20 In the Cantos, the fertilising of Persephone is associated with the eating of the pomegranate, the drinking of Dionysus' blood, wine and smoke and fire in the throat, Phlegethon, blood-spilling, the descent of Odysseus, Adonis, etc., to the underworld, ploughing, body as seed for new grass, and so on, perhaps more than with Persephone's own descent to the underworld. See XXI, p. 100; XXV, p. 118; XXXIX passim; XLVII passim; LXXIX, pp. 488 ff.

21 In *Thrones*, especially in CVI, the rite seems to lose its tincture of blood, emphasising the white light from the eyes of Persephone-as-grain (cf. Sir J. G. Frazer, *Adonis, Attis, Osiris (The Golden Bough*, Pt 4), Vol. 2 (London: Macmillan, 1951), p. 90, on the revelation of the reaped ear of corn in the Eleusinian Mysteries).

22 Walter Pater, *Greek Studies: A Series of Essays* (London: Macmillan, 1922), p. 18.

23 For Dodds's, of which Pound approved strongly, see letter to the editor from Lester Littlefield in *Paideuma*, vol. 1, no. 1 (Spring–Summer 1972), pp. 131–2.

24 See, for example, discussions in Jane E. Harrison, *Prolegomena to the Study of Greek Religion* (Cambridge: Cambridge University Press, 1922), K. Kerenyi, *Eleusis: Archetypal Image of Mother and Daughter* (London: Routledge & Kegan Paul, 1967); and George E. Mylonas, *Eleusis and the Eleusinian Mysteries* (Princeton, NJ: Princeton University Press, 1962).

25 Quoted in John Driscoll, *The China Cantos of Ezra Pound* (Uppsala: Uppsala University, 1983), p. 60; the lines were intended for LIII, p. 272.

26 The one view (which Pound consistently associated with elements in Christianity) insists on the domination of evil in man and the world, which are therefore to be spurned as far as possible; the other (which he always associated with Eleusis) assumes abundance of good, and sets out to encourage it. The 1931 essay clearly puts Mithra on the side of the former, and Manicheism likewise. But (*contra* my opinion in *MPP*, pp. 217–21) references to Mithra, Manes and Zarathustra (Zoroaster) in the Pisan Cantos show that they have been shifted over to the side of love, illumination and abundance. (A clue to the shift is in a wartime broadcast, in *EPS*, pp. 410–11.) This does not affect the point that Pound absolutely rejected the idea of any similarity between the ethics and world-view of the Provençal troubadours (and heretics associated with them) and those of Manicheism as it is usually conceived.

CHAPTER 6

Values, 2: History

(i) HISTORY AND MONEY

A number of traits in Pound, put together and produced back, suggest an Emersonian atmosphere in his immediate background (though the Cantos scorn Emerson: XXVIII, p. 134). One of them is his moral urge. The letter he wrote to his mother in 1905, already quoted, offers the *Divine Comedy* as a measuring-rod, evidently of a moral nature, for all phenomena 'in the lives of men and nations'. Pound always felt that the artist had social responsibilities. Perhaps the Nineties sense of the artist as priest at first led him to think that he could fulfil them by heading straight for the plane of the eternal. It was the shock administered by Ford in 1911 that made Pound see he was missing certain realities that might be important. The quality of these is perhaps hard to define except by saying, for example, that they feel like bricks; that high passion does not intervene between them and the perception; that they are quite commonly not attractive. And Pound was quite definitely not attracted to them; but he knew his duty; he 'schooled' himself to study the human hell, as he later put it.

Getting to grips with history, the steely, ordinary, mundane, was difficult; five years after his epic had officially started with the 'Ur-Cantos', Pound's Canto material was still drawing from Ford the opinion that he was a 'mediaeval gargoyle, Idaho or no!' (*PF*, 64). Success waited until Pound had discovered his documentary method, a method which is thus of considerable importance in the Cantos.

Pound seems to have discovered this method quite suddenly in 1922–3, simultaneously with his discovery of the Renaissance *condottiere* Sigismondo Malatesta as a suitable hero for a segment of the Cantos, and the necessity of piecing him together from the archives.[1] Earlier Cantos had been full of quotations, but these had been transmuted and given certain common colorations by being, as it were, oral quotation digested by memory. Suddenly in the Malatesta Cantos (VIII–XI), not only are large numbers of lines verbally close to a particular printed or manuscript document as source, but this fact is also flaunted before the reader:

> 'ILLUSTRIOUS PRINCE:
>   'Unfitting as it is that I should offer counsels to Hannibal ...'
>
> '   *Magnifice ac potens domine, domini mi singularissime,*
> '*humili recomendatione permissa* etc. This to advise your
> 'M^{gt} Ld^{shp} how the second load of Veronese marble has finally
> 'got here [...]'   (IX, p. 40)

The snippets and scraps are very obviously the product of Research, of drudgery in archives and libraries. Bibliographical references are given; manuscript lacunae are noted; scribal idioms are kept, suggested or heightened; there is no attempt to rework into homogeneous prose. Indeed, the scraps are merely placed together.

The procedure gives that sense of suggestive concreteness that the 'Ideogramic Method' demands. The fact that it is *this* document-fragment, with all the fusty smell of *its* decaying binding (as it were), and quirkiness of *its* period's style, gives depth to our understanding of its relation with the adjoining fragment. By the same token the procedure removes the homogenising point of view of a presenting author's prose, and (an equivalent process) the abstract term stating the proposed relation between the two phenomena.

The method makes the reader more aware than in any previous poetry of textual/documentary sources (more, even, than in *The Waste Land*, which has a supple homogeneity). Yet at the stage of the Malatesta Cantos there is still a strong sense of the open air and of the sensory range in the life of a man like Pound. These leave a trace in turns of phrase in translation, in choice of documentary scraps (bills of lading for marble, of specified grades), and in the frequent authorial insertions. And the group of Cantos itself is the product of very wide-ranging reading. The variety of documentary sight-lines on a given event gives a sense of depth; and the sources here fortunately include not only various antagonistic histories, but also a bundle of Malatesta's letters (captured in a skirmish), in very varied Italian. Pound gives his ear for English full scope in rendering these, and the result is that the collage-text of the Canto (IX) appears as a window to *voices*. Thus Pound gives the effect of having gone one better than the academic historians, by having penetrated the source of their magisterial scholarly authority (the archives, the difficult palaeography, the awkward dialects, the piled volumes) to produce a self-declaratory and incontrovertible human sense. And this result, more often than not, controverts the conclusions (in the given case) of the historians, whose interpretations he feels always tend to empty history of meaning.

Thus, in this documentary method, a certain type of authenticity is aimed at. There are also inauthenticities: in the quality of the source-material, in the handling of it, and in the fictions constructed about how the writer has handled it. Pound was quite content with romances, college anthologies of documents, and a variety of sources that did not have the modern historian's sense of 'fact', if he felt they told the truth (a matter more of wholes than of details).[2] And, while playing fast and loose with fact in this way, he also erected certain fictions, within the poem, as to his method. One was the fiction of a greater scholarliness than it really possessed; as here:

> *Florence, Archivio Storico, 4th Series t. iii, e*
> *'La Guerra dei Senesi col conte di Pitigliano'.*
> (X, p. 42)

When we read this, we naturally imagine that this was Pound's source for the preceding detail; and so the book is listed in commentaries as a Pound source. But Pound probably took both the detail and the reference from Yriarte, a very secondary source.[3] Conversely, certain sections of the Cantos deliberately suggest a greater ignorance than was Pound's. For example, in the Cantos about the Bank in Siena (XLII ff.), Pound takes care to leave in his poem traces of labours and difficulties with the manuscripts. He, it seems, is the plain untrained researcher; arduous, independent, unauthorised (and therefore Odyssean) burrowing, it seems, is a natural part of the process. However, Pound in fact went to the book first (*Il Monte dei Paschi* . . . , 9 volumes, 1891–1925), and then to the manuscripts. Coming to the manuscripts, he put in misreadings where he had read the book rightly before, and took care not to go back to the book to sort out new puzzles.[4] Thus the traces of Pound's palaeographical difficulties are an essential part of his fiction, but irrelevant (at least in this case) to the process by which he actually found out about Siena.

Even had there been no unreliability in Pound's sources and no distorting fictions as to his method, his way of making verse out of the documents would have been fatal to 'fact'. It was an oral way. He sought the 'essential cadence' of his source, hoping that the texts would rearrange themselves in his mind, without important loss, to fit it. (See further on this question, in Chapter 16.) And for him a wrong date, a wrong speaker or a wrong reference might well not constitute important loss.

Pound challenged the critic of his historiography to find any error in his Malatesta Cantos. The critic, my experience suggests, could find a great many. Pound would certainly have replied that this was the kind of academic idiocy that cannot see the wood for the trees, and I think he would be right. The literary critics who have cried 'Ahistorical!' over Pound's Cantos do not have a monopoly of historical evidence; the odd thing is that they rarely touch it, relying instead on the authority of the classic historians whose views Pound is often consciously trying to overturn. We are still in the grip of a literary materialism, coming from the Biblical Higher Criticism down through classical scholarship of the A. E. Housman era, for which failure to revere the dot and the comma is in itself sign of incapacity. But the studies of Pound's historical analyses that bother to go back to good sources have recently tended to find them of considerable value in their sense of total situation.[5] Pound's documentary method does not have the authenticity (which has sometimes been claimed for it) of factual accuracy coming from the sources closest to the events – at least, not consistently. It has the authenticity of a multifarious concreteness, which the reader 'reads' like flotsam on a beach or like a group of exhibits in a museum, for the tones of life or mechanisms behind it. In it, items like dates and names, normally the essential of a historian's message, may be semiotically quite redundant.

The documentary method was developed by Pound to handle history, which was always a special and separate subject in his mind. The purpose in bringing history into the poem was to show that divinity and beauty – or the 'timeless' – were not defeated by an awareness of fact and time; ultimately, to show how the timeless was attainable within time, the beauty of Malatesta and his constructs within the facts of Renaissance history. Now, it appears to me that Pound's attitude towards documentation develops in parallel with his attitude towards history, with some very important results in his political actions during and after the Second World War. We must therefore take a close look at his historical investigations.

The historical material in the Cantos as a whole offers a thesis about history, which of course Pound did not arrive at at the outset. Emersonian predispositions would have suggested to him that spiritual enlightenment was not compatible with inhumanity towards one's fellows; but Pound's own social and economic position seems to have appeared to him, at first, essentially normal.

In the same year that Ford shook up his ideas about over-evanescent verse, Pound became a contributor on literary subjects to the *New Age*, edited by A. R. Orage. This was one of the few journals in British cultural history to incorporate successfully both political and artistic concerns.[6] It 'took in' debates about literary realism (between such contributors as Shaw, Bennett, Wells and Chesterton); about Imagism and Vorticism, and socialism; it reproduced painting by Sickert, and the cartoon for Jacob Epstein's 'Rock Drill'; Lawrence, Ford, Harold Monro, Wyndham Lewis, T. S. Eliot read it. After the war had started, one of the signs of a new restlessness was an intensified debate in the *New Age* about socialism. Certain contributors began to attack what they called 'Collectivist Socialism', fearing that it would merely replace capitalist despotism with bureaucratic despotism. Socialists seemed to conceive a perpetuation of the worker-as-herd, directed in mass towards tasks in themselves of merely wealth-producing significance, and given no direct responsibility for the choice or development of their particular functions. The only change under this socialism was to be a reapportionment of wealth. The result would be non-responsibility in attitude both towards the object produced and towards society. Like William Morris and like Marx, these *New Age* writers conceived that alienation in the process of production was the root problem. Like both of these predecessors they turned to the Middle Ages for a model of non-alienation. Unlike Morris, they did not fantasise a return to cottage industry, but 'Guild Socialism', which amounted to monopoly control of a given industry by its workers, chartered by the government. Guild Socialism became a political movement between 1913 and 1915. The idea attracted Pound very strongly; he was to believe eventually that it had been made a reality in Italy's professional corporations under Mussolini. Images of it crop up in very late Cantos projecting spiritual and economic Paradise (for example in XCI, p. 613, and CIV, p. 741).

When the First World War began, Pound already feared it was merely the collision of an atavism with a corrupt mediocrity (*L*, 46). His eyes were opened to its realities the sooner because he was in contact with *New Age* circles. Then in 1919 occurred an important encounter in the *New Age* office: Pound met C. H. Douglas, who in that year published in the journal his new analysis of the economic problem.[7] Douglas wished to foster the fluidity and independence found in small-scale capitalism. He proposed that the seed of friction and war was not the capitalist mode of production, but systems of accountancy, and, above all, credit. He argued that there were certain inbuilt leaks in the production–consumption cycle – one of them being the cost of credit. These drained away purchasing-power, so that there was never sufficient demand for goods produced at the time of their production. Demand was often made up by finding new markets: hence colonialism, fierce competition, and conflict. Meanwhile the sources of credit controlled the producers. Hence centralisation, the enslavement of the whole of society to high-speed turnover, and industrial sabotage. Decentralised local authorities should take away the administering of credit from private interests; and the state should create and distribute purchasing-power to make up inevitable deficiencies.

These theories gave Pound a distinction between social health and unhealth, around which he could organise a fundamental dissociation and grouping of values; for they so evidently went back to personal, emotional, 'spiritual' values. The distinction was: the leech, parasite and distorter of values versus the responsible maker. And these theories gave him a programme for action, with, as corollary, the sense of present resistance to it; he probably needed these to generate enough emotional pressure in himself to clarify and present those values. But there was lacking one important ingredient: the sense of crime. In Orage's writing, and Douglas's, there is no strong sense that any particular group of persons is criminally responsible for having arranged past or present injustices; it is felt, rather, that the system is in error (though many have profited from the fact), and must be changed. Pound, however, paid more and more attention to investigators who laid bare particular riggings of the system for the benefit of private interests. After the Wall Street Crash of 1929 and the coming of the Depression, these writers multiplied. Pound was most impressed by writers like Christopher Hollis, who sought out more ancient roots for the evil. Hollis's *Two Nations* (1935) took the present crime inherent in the credit-creating system back to a source at a particular historical moment (the founding of the Bank of England in 1694), and tried to show that there had existed throughout the subsequent centuries a hidden party or interest-group, persistently at work corrupting the nation economically and politically.

In an interview broadcast in 1959, Pound said of the Cantos

There is a turning point in the poem toward the middle. Up to that

point it is a sort of detective story, and one is looking for the crime.
(Int., 172)

Canto XLVI in particular (published in November 1936) has the
rhetorical form of a prosecutor's address: it gives the damage inflicted
by the economic crime (fetid brickwork; mass unemployment), the
steps by which the investigator was led to track the crime down, and the
documentation as to the time and the place where it was perpetrated.
Said the founder of the Bank of England in 1694 (according to Hollis):
the Bank

> <u>Hath benefit of interest on all</u>
> the moneys which it, the bank, creates out of nothing.
> (XLVI, p. 233)

And similarly

> Said Mr RothSchild, hell knows which Roth-schild
> 1861, '64 or there sometime, 'Very few people
> 'will understand this. Those who do will be occupied
> 'getting profits. The general public will probably not
> 'see it's against their interest.'
> Seventeen years on the case; here
> Gents, is/are the confession.   (XLVI, p. 233)

The prospectus of the Bank of England (then a private company)
announced to shareholders that it, the Bank, would create money from
nothing, and draw interest on it. This seemed to Pound the key to all
later banking.

The historical thesis could thus be presented as formula by the
mid-1930s. Pound had come to believe that the reason for starvation,
gross inequality of wealth, and resultant conflict was a permanent
undeclared tax on most economic activity. This tax concentrated power
where it was used to bring about destructive decisions. The taxing
occurred in the creation of money; and money was created (increases in
the money-supply were brought about) in bank lending.

When a bank lends, it lends what John Thrifty has deposited with it.
(I owe both the name and the little parable to James P. Warburg, the
banker and adviser to Roosevelt, with whom Pound corresponded.[8]) It
does not ask John Thrifty; the fiction, as far as he is concerned, is that
the money is there in his account, waiting to be given to him the instant

he presents himself at the counter. There is no harm to him, because he knows that in fact his money is lent out, and that unless it were, he could receive no interest. But, for the purposes of the bank, the money he has deposited with it suddenly has two functions. It figures as John Thrifty's spendable money, ready for him to use, for example, to pay another man who has an account at the same bank; and it figures as money out on loan to someone else. The bank has thus doubled it, for the duration of the loan. Since the bank never ceases to loan, a large body of money is thus created by it, on which it receives interest which will eventually amount to further capital.

Suppose now that the government wants to spend more money than it possesses. It may borrow for the short term by issuing Treasury bills. Thus each week the United Kingdom government offers at auction a certain number of these bills. Overseas central banks, overseas commercial banks, and big commercial and industrial firms bid for these bills; the rest are taken up by the twelve London discount houses, acting as a syndicate. Thus these institutions loan to the government the money it wants, in return for bits of paper that entitle them to get the same money back in a few months, plus interest, all to be paid by the taxpayer.

Surely this 'new money' is merely old money, already possessed by these institutions, and now transferred to the government?

The banks, at least, did not possess it; it was John Thrifty's money, whose phantom double was still held by them in his account. Every time the banks extend a loan, it is on the strength of the money (it is the money) that John has deposited with them. In present British banking practice, only 8 per cent of his money need be kept in the bank ready for repayment to him should he ask for it. The other 92 per cent is doubled by being fictionally present, and factually out on loan, earning interest for the bank's shareholders.

The same operation takes place when government bonds are sold to the banks. These mature after a long period or never, so that for a long period the taxpayer is paying interest to the banks for money that they have created.

The banks' debts, to put it another way, are used as money; and they are the only institutions that can do this. Governments cannot increase the money-supply except by asking the banks to create it.[9] 'Whether it be not a mighty privilege for a private person to be able to create a hundred pounds with a dash of his pen?' – Bishop Berkeley, in the 1730s, quoted by Christopher Hollis.[10]

It is not unnatural, unjust, that money should be created from nothing. It leads to the creation of real (non-monetary) wealth. But there is no clear reason why private interests should profit from this process, rather than the public. It is said that banks, not governments, must create money, because banks are restrained: they at least create 'on the basis of' real money, whereas governments would certainly print money unlimitedly. But if governments are so untrustworthy, why do these trustworthy banks lend to them? The reason why banks lend to governments is that governments have absolute power to tax, to find the future money to repay the loans. The same power could be the basis of government creations of credit, and therefore of money.

And what is the trustworthiness of banks, when any bank balance-sheet shows that if the John Thrifties withdrew their deposits more rapidly than usual only some 8 per cent of their money would be available and the banks must collapse? '"You exaggerate," says the objector. "The financial system does not collapse, because the Government steps in with special measures to prevent the final calamity." "Exactly,"' answers Bishop Berkeley in effect, '"and do you not see what that proves? It proves that the bank is lending money to the community not, as is pretended, on the credit of the bank but rather on the credit of the community itself."'[11]

As C. H. Douglas wrote, 'The modern State is an unlimited liability corporation, of which the citizens are the workers and guarantors, and the financial system, the beneficiary.'[12]

So far the citizen is merely paying a tax to private interests on new money-supply. But governments do not normally pay off their borrowings except by further borrowing; hence the National Debt. ('The earth belongs to the living,' said Thomas Jefferson as quoted by Pound (*P*, 256), but the living inherit this burden.) The interest payments are a massive continuous transfer of wealth from the taxpayer to banks and bondholders.

Once monetary wealth is accumulated, it can be 'played' against real wealth. It could not be played unless it had a value – unless, that is, someone wanted it badly; and it is wanted by you and me, as a means of exchange. The game consists of betraying this need, of making money unstable as a means of exchange, by affecting its value as against real (non-monetary) wealth. The holder contrives to find the moment when it will profit him to sell his accumulated pounds sterling for gold, or aluminium futures, or real estate, or Deutschmarks; and his selling affects the value of the pound. Or, says Pound, if he is a big enough

fish, he may be able to influence, for his own purposes, national
decisions that affect the currency. Canto XXXIII describes such a case.
The Federal Reserve System is one of the two central monetary control
institutions of the United States, but it judiciously interweaves public
with private interests. The Federal Reserve Banks' loans to the
(private) member banks affect general interest rates and money supply,
and hence inflation and deflation. In May 1920, according to a Senate
speech by Senator Brookhart, there was a secret meeting of the Federal
Reserve Board, the Class A directors of the Federal Reserve Banks
(who are also private bankers), and the advisory council. It was decided
to restrict loans to the member banks.[13] The Governor of the Board,
says Canto XXXIII, even

> put into the mouths of the directors of the Federal Reserve banks the words
> that they should say ... 'You have got more than your share, we want you to
> reduce, we can not let you have any more.'

He also

> said to them: wd. suggest, gentlemen, you be careful not to give out any-
> thing about any discussion of discount rates disturbs everybody immediate
> rush never discuss in the newspapers .....

What, for the unsuspecting man in the street, is an imminent change in
the value of his means of exchange, is a chance of profit for those who
know:

> .... & Company's banker was in that meeting, and next day he was out
> after a loan of 60 millions, and got it. Swiftamoursinclair but the country at
> large did not know it. The meeting decided we were over inflated. (XXXIII,
> p. 164)

Pound became more obsessively concerned with these value-
manipulations as the war threatened, and then destroyed, what he saw
as Mussolini's attempt to create the ideal society. 'The elements remain
the same: debts, altering the value of monetary units, and the attempts,
and triumphs of usury, due to monopolies, or to a "Corner"' (*P*, 170).
The sleight of hand, the falsification whereby the unit of exchange was
invisibly transmuted, was the particular aspect of monetary economics

that became the substance of the historical part of the Cantos after the Second World War.

Pound was probably not overworried by parasitism in itself, or what Lenin, according to Pound, called 'a class, or rather a stratum, of *rentiers*, i.e. persons who live by "clipping coupons", who take absolutely no part in any enterprise' (*P*, 299). But he was worried by the effects of such groups as a force.

> 'and having got 'em (advantages, privilege)
> there is nothing, italics *nothing*, they will not do
> to retain 'em'
> yrs truly   Kungfutseu   (LXXVII, p. 464)

If a reformist government appears in some banana republic, there are ways in which it can be unsettled very quickly. And Italy in the 1930s, as Pound saw her, was trying to emerge from the position of a banana republic. Mussolini asserted his country's independence from the international financial web, and the result, Pound believed, was the League of Nations Sanctions of 1933, an attempt at economic strangulation, on the excuse that Italy was building an empire in Africa. Pound compared this to British attempts to strangle the American colonies ('le sanzioni inglesi') before 1776 (*OS*, 1360).

There was also the question of stifled human creativity, debased products, and the consequent debasement of body, mind and environment. The money market requires rapid and continuous profit; a bank manager does not favour a low-interest project over a high-interest project merely because the former produces more wealth for the community in the long run. If you want a loan, open a newsagent's (cigarettes, Coca-Cola and the *Sunday Express*). Produce cars that require leaded petrol. The child's vital strength is sapped before he can defend himself.

> *With Usura* [. . .]
>
> no picture is made to endure nor to live with
> but it is made to sell and sell quickly
> with usura, sin against nature,
> is thy bread ever more of stale rags [. . .]
>
> Usura slayeth the child in the womb
> It stayeth the young man's courting

It hath brought palsey to bed, lyeth
between the young bride and her bridegroom
CONTRA NATURAM
(XLV, pp. 229–30)

And so, as Marx records in Canto XXXIII,

report of '42 was merely chucked into the archives and
remained there while these boys were ruined and became
fathers of this generation . . .   (XXXIII, p. 162)

The proposals scattered in Pound's writing might, then, be summarised as follows. Governments should themselves create new money
when they need it (Jefferson had proposed this in slightly different
terms: *P*, 296). New issue should be limited to the amount of real
wealth that the government expects to be created nationally during the
period of the loan. Governments should index the values of important
necessities and, by regulating money-supply, hold the value of the
currency steady against them (creating a 'commodity dollar'). (The
United States Constitution, Pound held, required the government to
control the purchasing-power of the currency.) Private interests should
be allowed to lend only that money they possessed; and interest rates
should be strictly controlled.

These are more or less practical and rational ideas. But two aspects of
his language baffled and alienated Pound's contemporaries. One was his
insistent repetition of simple and obscure conundrums: 'Money is not a
commodity', 'Money does not create wealth'. The other was the
Freudian concreteness of his images, strangely mixed up with a
theological tone. His insistence on these simple distinctions was loaded
with a certain anger because his contemporaries – Christians in
particular – had abdicated the duty of relating mental clarity to moral
implications. A share, he insisted, is not a bond. With shares, the
lender participates in the risk of the enterprise: if it fails, his money is
gone; if it does badly, there is no dividend. With bonds, whatever
happens to the enterprise the lender has legal right to capital and
interest. That in particular is the bearing of the word 'Usury', as Pound
defined it (XLV, p. 230), and part of the reason why the word became
like a malediction to him. The Church had once cared about these
crimes, and now understood no such distinctions (cf. LII, p. 258).

Design, whether of earthenware bowls or carbon fibres, works with three things: present human wit and labour; a heritage of knowledge; and the integrity (coherence) of nature's structures. Finance denies the awe or reverence which is due to the latter two, and transfers that due to the former into money. It thus invests money with powers we associate with the result of all human creativity; hence with a mystique, seen in its language ('creative finance', 'Watch your money grow!', 'Does your money work as hard as you?'). The people who handle it become high priests, which is their function in present society. It is so because the public is willing to 'buy' their metaphors. In a man like Pound, to whom the natural *is* God, both his perception of this behaviour and his emotional response to it will necessarily express themselves in language which is at once concerned with nature (including the sexual and scatological) and theological:

Mill defined capital 'as the accumulated stock of human labour'.
And Marx, or his Italian translator (U.T.–E.T. edition): 'commodities, in so far as they are values, are *materialised* labour,'

so denying both God and nature.

With the falsification of the word everything else is betrayed.

Commodities (considered as values, surplus values, food, clothes, or whatever) are manufactured raw materials.
Only spoken poetry and unwritten music are composed without any material basis, nor do they become 'materialised'.
The usurers, in their obscene and pitch-dark century, created this satanic transubstantiation, their Black Mass of money, and in so doing deceived Brooks Adams himself, who was fighting for the peasant and humanity against the monopolists.
'. . . money alone is capable of being transmuted immediately into any form of activity.' – This is the idiom of the black myth!
One sees well enough what he was trying to say, as one understands what Mill and Marx were trying to say. But the betrayal of the word begins with the use of words that do not fit the truth, that do not say what the author wants them to say.
Money does not contain energy. The half-lira piece cannot *create* the platform ticket, the cigarettes, or piece of chocolate that issues from the slot-machine.
But it is by this piece of legerdemain that humanity has been thoroughly trussed up, and it has not yet got free. (*P*, 307–8)

An interviewer asked Allen Ginsberg about Pound's 'obsession' with money. Ginsberg held that it was a service to humanity: Pound had demystified the banks. Like John Adams more than a hundred years before him:

> Every bank of discount is downright corruption
> taxing the public for private individuals' gain.
>   and if I say this in my will
> the American people wd//pronounce I died crazy.
>   (LXXI, p. 416)

(ii) FACT AND HYSTERIA

But this is the same Pound who strongly supported Mussolini's regime even when it became Hitler's ally (immediately before the Second World War). The Pisan Cantos, written immediately after the war, do not recant, though this fact was somewhat obscured at the time of publication by certain obscurities of reference and by publishers' deletions. During the war years, though not before, Pound seems to have come to admire Hitler, and Cantos written much later seem to turn him into a kind of misguided saint (XC, p. 606; CIV, p. 741). And Pound is held to have been anti-Semitic.

People in Italy during the war did not know what was happening to the Jews in Germany; Pound cannot be held responsible in that sense for the death-camps. From the earliest days of his concern with usury, Pound had used 'Jews' as a shorthand term for usurers – a symptom of a prejudice then widespread among the Anglo-Saxon middle classes; but whenever his attention was brought to the question of race he would carefully distinguish between Jewish financiers and those blamed by association. But it seems to me clear enough that by the time of his wartime broadcasts for the Mussolini regime he conceived of evil Jewish racial qualities, among which the presence of the good was generally secondary. He had in fact swallowed the whole nineteenth-century Jewish Conspiracy theory, with its imagery and antecedents stretching back to the popular persecutions of the Middle Ages.[14] His language on the subject of money was medieval, a sort of chant of lexical nastiness, filled with the suggestion of exotic and ancient tongues, much as Poe filled his artificial excitements with the Inquisition and dark jargon. The Hebrew word *neschek* ('usury') recurs. This piece was written 'Circa 1941':

The Evil is Usury, *neschek*
the serpent
neschek whose name is known, the defiler,
beyond race and against race
the defiler
Τόχος   hic mali medium est   [Poison   here is the centre of evil]
Here is the core of evil, the burning hell without let-up,
The canker corrupting all things, Fafnir the worm,
Syphilis of the State, of all kingdoms,
Wart of the common-weal,
Wenn-maker, corrupter of all things.
Darkness the defiler

This serpentine darkness makes 'wens' in much the same manner as, among Hardy's peasants, the presence of lovers stops the butter from turning. The conspiracy, once discerned, transforms the meaning of all things; which is a defining characteristic of paranoia.

> *Sero, sero*! [Late, late!] learned that Spain is mercury;
> that Finland is nickel. Late learning!
> S[assoon] doing evil in place of the R[othschild]
> (Addendum for C, pp. 798–9)

The antecedents for this state, in Pound's own work, seem to lie in his handling of a sense of social responsibility in which he identified with John Adams, and in the documentary/historical method through which he expressed this. Adams, and American material in general, drew from Pound an excessive desire for order, which led to a need for dogmatic and clear-cut statement. 'The evidence', preferably on producible documents, had to be marshalled to support this. Perception of tones, contemplation and the unspoken kinds of knowledge, Dionysian impulse, went out of the window. (Ovid more or less disappears from the Cantos between XXVII (1928) and XCVIII (1958).) But documents offer no security; the 'facts' on them are merely pawns or switching diodes among which a thousand possible patterns may spring up at the observer's suggestion; patterns which branch endlessly off the page into the fact-hoards of other documents. The conspiracy theory, replete with footnotes proving the case conclusively, seems to be a phenomenon of our time. Meanwhile the restless researcher is back at his desk in the British Museum, digging out the proofs to clinch his footnotes. So Pound's mind seemed to explode into a mad fragmentation of documents during and after the war.

The earlier Cantos are full of turbulence, of 'Mediterranean gods; startling, sudden [. . .] Gods tricky as nature' (*L*, 273), of Ovid. The sea is one of the governing metaphors of the first three; sudden change is celebrated. Pentheus is the fool: the man who would try to hold Dionysus and ecstasy in bonds. And even in the first American material, concerning Thomas Jefferson (Cantos XXXI–XXXIII), Pound tries to show the value of instinct as a political quality. (There is a connection between Jefferson and Mussolini the Dionysian.) But Jefferson is rather intractable material for this. There is no 'Eleusis' in him: no song, sensual knowledge, religion-and-rite-as-mystery. Canto XXXIV deals with John Quincy Adams, son of Jefferson's friend John, and he is made Eleusinian by texture:

> Oils, beasts, grasses, petrifactions, birds, incrustations,
> Dr Mitchell's conversation was various . . . . .

That opens the Canto, and it closes with ecstatic popular celebration:

> The firemen's torchlight processsion,
> Firemen's torchlight procession,
> Science as a principle of political action
>
> Firemen's torchlight procession!

But a check of the sources makes this presentation seem a little factitious.[15] And in between this opening and this close all shows a mind of eighteenth-century American (still Puritan and classical) limitations. (John Quincy died in 1848.)

And the Jefferson group is the last Cantos section in which Pound holds up instinct as a political ideal. In his prose he is soon forcefully rejecting Jefferson in favour of John Adams, who with his descendants is 'our norm of spirit' (LXXXIV, p. 540). Now Adams, as Pound presents him, is the principle of stability, of immovable conscience – indeed, of the Puritan 'plymouth-rock conscience' that Pound ironically prided himself in, in a letter to Harriet Monroe in 1912 (*L*, 12). One of Adams's chief political functions in the Cantos is to warn against the hidden, insidious usurpations of money-power that work through, and manipulate, democracy – by, for example, corrupting terminology.

The China Cantos, published simultaneously with the John Adams Cantos in 1940, pull history towards the two poles of softness, obfuscation, intrigue (associated with women and Buddhists), and social order, on which the verbal tone insists more and more excessively and irritably. This anger returns in full force in the *Rock-Drill* (1955) and *Thrones* (1959) sections, which betray a hysterical fear of all that is unknown and amorphous. In the Chinese parts of *Thrones*, the ideal is discipline and again discipline, inner and outer. Meanwhile the emotional coherence of this poem's sensibility has collapsed: it moves endlessly between the two poles of Erebus and the Empyrean, grasping at fragments of cleanness and light, while the black void gapes.

Now this move towards a hysteric sense of order goes together with a move towards documentation felt as documentation (assemblage of hard written matter), rather than, for example, as voices. Already in the Jefferson Cantos (the first documentary section after the Malatesta), there is much less voice-differentiation. Only the two men Jefferson and Adams 'speak' (to each other, in their letters), for the most part; and they are much less oral men. The prewar culmination of the documentary method is seen in the Adams Cantos, where Pound strives to bring to life a uniform surface, which is the voice of John Adams himself, as registered in his *Works* (almost the sole source). Like a recording engineer reprocessing an early disc, Pound can do no more than heighten certain contrasts of tone. But by this time Pound is in any case not so much concerned with the emotional depth communicated in such ways. He is now much less interested in the qualitative Fact of an era; much more interested in the atomic, material facts, and formulae, and distinct rational decisions. And that is part of the problem I am approaching.

But there is a contradictory tendency. Adams is the legal researcher, hunting for the truth in the hidden texts (thus the archetypal Protestant act: translating the Bible). But the ancient terms from the ancient legal authorities, alien and exotic in distance and tongue, come to seem in themselves the fount of the mystic law. Pound heightens this effect, seeming to prefer Adams snippets that have bits of Latin in them to those without. These phrases, chanted, are emblems of the Mystic Books:

> Whereof memory of man runneth not to the contrary
> Dome Book, Ina, Offa and Aethelbert, folcright
> for a thousand years   (LXVII, p. 387)

The Pisan Cantos in many ways set themselves apart from this progression. But thereafter Pound develops a way of coming at documents so that they render up this dislocated mystic authority instantly (and without the intervention of memory, which in the Pisan Cantos has a quite different effect). Plunging into a sea of arcane documentation, omitting (as so often) the syntactic connections that give the phrase its meaning in context, he places on his page a detail that has become not historically 'luminous' (a term from his *New Age* articles of 1911: *P*, 21–2), but numinous: '2 doigts to a boodle, one bawbee: one sixty doigts' (XCVII, p. 671). Chinese characters in particular have this role. They are both world-shattering and perfectly private, because they are clues to hidden patterns of force that only this researcher can understand: 'Wang's middle name not in Mathews 樂' (XCVI, p. 653).

The typical source for one of these Clues is an academic footnote. And the form of many of these late Cantos is an arrangement of footnotes, to which footnotes will be found in such parallel publications as *Versi Prosaici*, and in Pound's enormous outpouring of fragmentary correspondence, communications to scattered journals, and written marginal annotations in printed volumes in this period.

It is possible that both prose (documentation) and history were a mistake for Pound. Ford may have put his finger on the problem when he accused Pound of hating literary decoration in prose, and loving the 'STRONG STORY', both because he disliked prose itself and because of a Puritan bent. And 'you *might* harden into the Puritanism of the Plymouth Rock variety – which would be a disaster . . .' (*PF*, 45). It is possible that Pound was fundamentally unsuited to prose reality, and that what he called (*P*, 167) the forty-year effort of 'schooling' himself to deal with the grim, the hard, with human fallibility and error – in a word, the 'Dark Forest' – was unnatural for a writer who was essentially Ovidian; and that a hysterical exaggeration of a New England heritage was the result.

Still it seems to me that until the war years Pound's sense of history was not yet irrational. To give an analogy: any Latin American with a sense of social justice might be justified in seeing, in one sense, a conspiracy between the American corporations, the State Department, the International Monetary Fund, the large banks, and the wealthier groups in his own country. That is, effectively, collusion exists. But it is merely instinctive, shifting and temporary, and the various conspiracies, transient and amorphous, are a product and not a cause. I think Pound was at such a mental position in about 1939, as far as usury was concerned. As far as the Jews were concerned, he thought that too many Jews were prominent in usury, but demanded (reasonably enough if that were true) that Jews seek out their economic criminals and disown them, and dissociate themselves from usury by attacking the many very visible non-Jewish financiers (*P*, 299–300; *PF*, 165).

With the steady tightening of Pound's mental processes, and with the coming of the war, both positions were fatally modified. Instinctive collusion in financial and governmental circles became, in Pound's mind, grand conspiracy; the presence of Jewish figures in high finance became, to Pound, Jewish control of high finance.

By about 1939 he was tending in the direction of a general theoretical anti-Hebraism on the level of cultural roots (cf. e.g. *L*, 331–2). But what he thought of as Hebraic on this level was what he also identified with Protestantism (in particular Calvinism): materialist and Man-ichean attitudes, destructive of the sense of immanent godhead in the world and in rite. And finally there is Pound's dislike of the 'Middle-European', the cosmopolitan, the culturally fluid. Here the approved image is of a small-town republican stability, such as we find it in John Adams or in Dante (note the ideal of Cincinnatus in both):

> Sempre la confusion delle persone
> principio fu del mal della cittade,
> come del corpo il cibo che s' appone.

> Ever was mingling of persons
> the source of the city's woes,
> as piled-on food is of the body's.
> (*Paradiso*, 16.67–9)

But it is most likely that Pound would have latched on to quite other archetypes for these tendencies than the Jews, had not both history and his own development created in him the kind of dualism that needs a strong single focus for its animus, and provided that focus in inherited images of the Jewish race.

The Jews were a traditional scapegoat, ready for Pound to latch on to. One factor in this was a vicious circle of primitive fear and convenient hypocrisy. Thus the fact that particular Jewish families have been prominent for some centuries as money lenders seems partly traceable to the fact that Christendom forbade Jews most occupations except the occupation of money-lending – which was forbidden to Christians as being sinful. This itself was partly a manifestation of those

dark medieval feelings about Jewry that stemmed merely from their
position as an unabsorbed cultural Other. But in turn it gave Jewish
moneylenders a vulnerability that kings were not slow to exploit; and
intensified suspicion and hatred of Jews. These welled over into
pogroms in times of social unrest. Prejudices still hardly developed
from these ancient origins were common currency in the American
Populism of Pound's youth, as among middle-class intellectuals in the
Edwardian London to which he migrated in 1908.

Jung has described how fears of conspiracy are fostered by an
abnormally heightened, simplified sense of good/evil dualism, which in
turn tends to appear in times of social disturbance. And if we seek to
explain why Pound shifted, from about 1939 onwards, towards witch-
hunting it seems to me necessary to remember his position of isolation
in a country at war. War hysteria is powerful and takes many forms,
and at any point during the present century one can find actions by
otherwise reasonable men and women that have no other explanation.

Some find such moral attitudes irrelevant to the value of verse, even
when they are present in the verse. But the profundity or otherwise of
the moral understanding in a poem is a considerable factor in the
interest (or otherwise) of the poem. I should like to persuade the reader
that the breakdown in Pound's moral values in a certain area at a certain
time does not necessarily affect those elsewhere.

NOTES: CHAPTER 6

1 A crucial shift, from a dramatic to a documentary handling of Malatesta, may be seen
   in Pound's drafts, between January and July 1923. See Peter D'Epiro, *A Touch of
   Rhetoric: Ezra Pound's Malatesta Cantos* (Ann Arbor, Mich.: UMI Research Press,
   1983), pp. 41, 51.
2 See below, p. 307, concerning Canto VI; also note how XX, p. 90, 'He was playing
   there at the palla', is (typically) taken from a romancing chronicler cited in Alfonso
   Lazzari, 'Ugo e Parisina nella realtà storica', pt IV, in *Rassegna Nazionale*, vol. 37,
   no. 202 (1 April 1915), p. 248.
3 Charles Yriarte, *Un condottiere au XV siècle* (Paris: Rothschild, 1882), p. 282.
4 Ben Kimpel and T. C. Duncan Eaves, 'The sources of Cantos XLII and XLIII',
   Paideuma, vol. 6, no. 3 (Winter 1977), p. 515; and 'The sources of the Leopoldine
   Cantos', *Paideuma*, vol. 7, no. 1–2 (Spring–Fall 1978), p. 249.
5 See, e.g., Michael F. Harper, 'Truth and Calliope: Ezra Pound's Malatesta', *PMLA*,
   vol. 96, no. 1 (January 1981), pp. 86–103, and D'Epiro, *Touch of Rhetoric*, p. xxii.
6 This paragraph is based on Wallace Martin, *'The New Age' under Orage* (Man-
   chester/New York: Manchester University Press/Barnes & Noble, 1967).
7 *Economic Democracy* (published as a book in 1920) was serialised in *New Age* from
   June 1919. See reviews by Pound in *P*, 207–12.
8 James P. Warburg, *The Money Muddle* (New York: Knopf, 1934).

9   For Treasury bills, cf. A. C. L. Day, *The Economics of Money* (London: Oxford University Press, 1968), pp. 77 ff., and Herbert V. Prochnow (ed.), *The Federal Reserve System* (New York: Harper & Row, 1960), p. 59; for rediscounting as cover for note issue, cf. Warburg, *Money Muddle*, pp. 35–6, and Prochnow, *Federal Reserve System*, p. 97.

10   Christopher Hollis, *The Two Nations* (London: Routledge, 1935), p. 60.

11   ibid., p. 59.

12   C. H. Douglas, *The Monopoly of Credit* (London: Chapman & Hall, 1931), p. 14.

13   See William Chace, 'The Canto as cento: a reading of Canto XXXIII', *Paideuma*, vol. 1, no. 1 (Spring–Summer 1972), pp. 89–100.

14   *EPS*, p. 60; cf. pp. 62, 97–8, 110, 114, 177–9 and passim; *P*, p. 340. On the 'Protocols of the Elders of Zion', cf. *EPS*, p. 115.

15   In the source, Adams is complaining about these processions, and saying that one should follow the political principle of acting as patron to scientific studies. See *The Diary of John Quincy Adams 1794–1845*, ed. Allan Nevins (New York: Charles Scribner's Sons, 1951), p. 559.

CHAPTER 7

Commentary:
Cantos I–XVI
(*A Draft of XVI. Cantos*)

In March 1917 the first three 'Ur-Cantos' were sent to *Poetry*; in spring 1924 Pound seems to have had the revised and almost-final version of I–XVI ready. The intervening period was difficult for Pound. In 1917 there was the shock of his friends' reception of the 'Ur-Cantos', which Pound clearly realised he could defend only half-heartedly. Between then and spring 1922, there was not a growing body of work and a growing confidence, but a long period of great doubt. After much fruitless revision of various versions, Pound actually came to a dead halt between late 1920 (completion of versions of the present Cantos V, VI, VII) and early 1922. But even the writing in early 1922 of what he called Canto VIII, which was to become the present Canto II, still offered no standpoint from which to judge from the outside, and thus set in proper relation, Pound's gods and medieval passions in the other pieces. By 14 July 1922 he had 'blocked in five more [Am?] Cantos', namely (it seems) what he then called IX, X, XI, XII and XIII.[1] But 'XI' in this series was about Sigismondo Malatesta, and this took the best part of a year to develop into the four present Malatesta Cantos (VIII–XI). That group completed, Pound at last had the confidence to ditch what was weak in the earlier glamours and phantasms. By 28 January 1925, Myles Slatin tells us, 'the passage from the Nekuia [in the *Odyssey*], which had come at the end of Canto III in August, 1917, was moved to the place of honor in Canto I. The Canto which had been published in May, 1922, as Canto VIII was moved into position as Canto II; the [Confucius] Canto was given its number, XIII, and lines 3–6 of the present text added; line 38 was added to Canto XII and the story of the Honest Sailor given its rightful place alongside Baldy Bacon; the war and hell Cantos were put into place. In other words, between the summer of 1923 and the spring of 1924, the scattered pieces of the Cantos fell into order [. . .]'

The intervening period spans the production of the separate chapters of *Ulysses* (received by Pound from December 1917 onwards), and of *The Waste Land* (draft shown to Pound in Paris in January 1922). 'Resolute though in doubt', to borrow Bunting's phrase, Pound had not slacked at all in his striving. In 1917 he had published the important series of essays 'Elizabethan Classicists'; in 1918 the series of Provençal versions called 'Homage à la langue d'oc', and the 'Early Translators of Homer' essays. Pieces of *Homage to Sextus Propertius* had appeared in *Poetry* in 1919, and between 1919 and 1920 Pound completed *Hugh Selwyn Mauberley* in manuscript. But Pound was no longer the aesthete who had fitted so easily into literary London in 1909. And Orage of the *New Age* was to note that his 'exhilarating influence' on culture had made him 'more enemies than friends, and far more powerful enemies than friends. Much of the Press has been deliberately closed by cabal to him [. . .]' (*SL*, 295). He lost his column in the *Athenaeum*, which had provided a much-needed £10 a month. Staying on in London came to seem a mere masochism; and New York, he wrote to William Carlos Williams, 'wants me as little now as it did ten and fifteen years ago' (*L*, 158, September 1920). Paris suggested itself, and by Christmas 1920 the Pounds were well settled there.

He found interesting company:

Brancusi, Picabia, Cocteau all more free and flightful than the moulting vultures of W.C.2.

I daily ask myself why the hell I stayed in Eng. so long [. . .] It is ridiculous after so short an immersion here, that one shd. suspect oneself of being about to feel about english visitors here, as one did about Americans in London. (*PF*, 58)

Ford moved to Paris. Pound met and helped Hemingway, and published pieces in Dada magazines edited by Francis Picabia and Tristan Tzara. But the Paris period, it has been noted, made rather little impression on Pound. The 'public' continued to drift away from him: in early 1923 he was fired from his well-paid connection with the New York *Dial*, in the usual somewhat treacherous manner. Perhaps he did not fight with much conviction to remain involved in literary life. Whatever marginal addition to his understanding could come from the

Paris milieu in no way compared with what, as an aesthete from
suburban Pennsylvania, he had learned in a few short years from Ford,
Lewis and Gaudier-Brzeska in London before the war. And so, more or
less simultaneously with his discovery of Malatesta and (apparently) the
right form for the Cantos, came the realisation in about 1923 that his
true country was not Paris but Rapallo, in provincial Italy.

   The completion by early 1924 of a finished draft of Cantos I–XVI
(with only one important piece, Canto VI, yet to be put right) is a
watershed for Pound, as the 'Ur-Cantos' of 1917 were not. Before 1924
was out, his plans and sketches had rushed ahead as far as Canto XX.
And after the publication (June 1925) of *A Draft of XVI. Cantos* he made
the gesture that terminated his career as a writer of short poems: he
established the canon of his short verse in *Personae* (1926), a text that he
never saw reason to alter, or add to, during the rest of his life. From
now on, all original verse was either a significant enough part of him to
find its way, eventually, into the 'long poem' of the Cantos, or it was not
worth keeping.

   The following pages, then, will comment on the Cantos I–XVI of the
current editions. (The separate identification of this group disappeared
in 1930, and the following group, XVII–XXX, never was identified
independently; yet there is still a distinct change of direction between
them.) First, I shall offer a somewhat detailed reading of Cantos I–IV.
Then I shall pick out two particularly important sets of Cantos (the
Malatesta and 'Hell' groups) from those that follow; and conclude with
a thumbnail sketch of I–XVI as a whole.

(i)   CANTO I

The first four Cantos contain the central motifs of the whole work.
   In book 10 of the *Odyssey*, Odysseus is instructed by Circe that he
must sail to Hades, to consult the shade of Tiresias, before he can
journey home. The first line of Pound's Canto I catches this sailor in
mid-utterance:

> And then went down to the ship,
> Set keel to breakers

It seems that he is intent on his action: our attention is not drawn to his
person or his personality. Also he has a religious bent, but the word
'godly' does not obstruct his narrative:

> Set keel to breakers, forth on the godly sea, and
> We set up mast and sail on that swart ship,
> Bore sheep aboard her, and our bodies also
> Heavy with weeping, so winds from sternward
> Bore us out onward with bellying canvas,
> Circe's this craft, the trim-coifed goddess.

Stresses bear heavily on short words that start with hard or shaggy consonants, and these soon begin to alliterate: 'Bore sheep aboard her, and our bodies also'. 'Thing is a MARCH', as Bunting said of Pound's 'Seafarer', an utterance suggesting the state of one who has to get on with it. He does not tell us till the middle of his sentence that he and his men are 'Heavy with weeping'.

In this narrative, winds arranged by goddesses and dark cities of the sunless Kimmerians are wonders taken for granted. But, arrived at the edge of Hades, there is pause for more technical detail, of a religious kind:

> Here did they rites, Perimedes and Eurylochus,
> And drawing sword from my hip
> I dug the ell-square pitkin;
> Poured we libations unto each the dead,
> First mead and then sweet wine, water mixed with white flour.

The best beasts are sacrificed:

> A sheep to Tiresias only, black and a bell-sheep.
> Dark blood flowed in the fosse

– and the gibbering dead crowd forth, to be kept off by a pale Odysseus, at sword-point, while he hastily prays and sacrifices more till Tiresias shall present himself. Elpenor appears and relates his untimely end, and demands that rites be performed for him later, that his shade may rest. Then Odysseus' mother, 'whom I beat off', and at last Tiresias, who demands his blood-drink:

> 'Stand from the fosse, leave me my bloody bever
> 'For soothsay.'
>   And I stepped back,
> And he strong with the blood, said then: 'Odysseus
> 'Shalt return through spiteful Neptune, over dark seas,
> 'Lose all companions.'

So we start this great re-sorting of our culture with a return to Greece. Now, Greece of course is the treasure-house of the values of Arnold and (later) many a muscular Christian, and still of a thousand schoolgirls trooping through the British Museum and the Louvre. These are among the values that Lord Clark meant, when he said Western civilisation was 'saved' when the Moors were turned back at Poitiers in 732. This Odysseus, however, is rather 'unsivilized', as Huckleberry Finn might have said. He has more in common with Roland, who legend says was slain at Roncevaux in 778, and who was no doubt a hairy barbarian compared to the Moors he might have fought; or with the warriors of Benin, whose 'primitive' sculptured forms were carried off to the British Museum by a culture whose superiority was proved, it thought, by Praxiteles and the Venus de Milo.

'Dark blood flowed in the fosse': Odysseus is feeding blood to the shades (not the spirits, a Christian concept). Without it they cannot speak, and without the potion, a ritual drink compounded of Demeter's flour and Dionysus' wine. This is a religion in which force is immanent in the particular, in which bull and bell-sheep contain powers that can induce similar powers in man, in which each has its 'blood' pumping through it, so that to offer one is to invoke another.

> And he strong with the blood, said then: 'Odysseus
> 'Shalt return [. . .]'

This is at a great remove from the cult of purity (ideality) that produced the smooth Praxiteles, and that was finally reflected, through many byways, in a Christianity of whose God nothing might be predicated. Strength comes to the throat with blood, and thence the voice. The rhythms of the voice are as feeble or strong as those of the heart. It follows that all this ritual cannot be recalled in the voice of a man standing at a lectern; strong rhythms must enact the behaviour of whole man involved in earth-rite. As Zukofsky has noted, 'the cadence carries the picture [. . .] the imagism of the Cantos is not a static brittleness, a fragility of bits. The feelings of painting and sculpture travel with the movement; the body of what is seen is in the music.'[2]

Dead connectors, subject pronouns, articles are trimmed away to leave force in verbs and nouns:

> Slaughtered the herds, sheep slain of bronze

These then group into series of strong stresses ('herds, sheep slain'), which can then form a patterning or dance with groups of weak stresses ('slaughtered the'), heightening vigour. Given these elements, it only remains that they should be articulated with invention, and that the resultant cadence should unfold in step with content, in a cogent emotional logic. The whole is then seen to have a completeness, such that it will seem a truncation and a false ending when anything less is quoted than the whole. Pound thus vindicates a new metric, made from his labours over the Anglo-Saxon 'Seafarer' and Andreas Divus' Latin version of Homer.

To whom he now does homage:

> Then Anticlea came.
> Lie quiet Divus. I mean, that is Andreas Divus,
> In officina Wecheli, 1538, out of Homer.

Pound owes a good deal of his success to Andreas, whose version has perhaps none of the flavour of its era, the Latinate high Italian Renaissance. It is a bastard Latin created by forcing the language closer to Homer's Greek than it will properly allow, thus creating an exotic syntax and rarities of vocabulary formed on Homer: 'Insulam in Aeaeam impellens benefabricatam navim' (see the text in *E*, 259–62). This aspect of the Italian Renaissance was a bridge to the past because the classic texts were still alive for it, and it 'naïvely' and shamelessly tried to re-create that life in Latin cribs (as Botticelli 'translated' Venus). This one enabled Pound, who knew his Homer well but not so well as his Latin, to fabricate something that he felt gave the force of the Homeric original; and hence his homage to that era.

Finally the Canto turns to the Aphrodite of the Homeric Hymn, as rendered by another Renaissance Latinist, Georgius Cretensis:

> Venerandam,
> In the Cretan's phrase, with the golden crown, Aphrodite,
> Cypri munimenta sortita est, mirthful, oricalchi, with golden
> Girdles and breast bands, thou with dark eyelids
> Bearing the golden bough of Argicida.

Here is suggested a close relation between Venus and Circe, previously mentioned; and also Venus' power and mystery. And 'bearing the golden bough of Argicida' seems to suggest a whole sequence of matings of priests, priest-heroes and gods with goddesses, colleagues of

Aphrodite[3] – as Odysseus had been mated with Circe. These suggestions of power lead the poem on, to the last words of the Canto:

> So that:

(ii)   CANTO II

'So that' means 'The things already mentioned are so; with the result
that these other things are so.' That is the connection we expect in
continuous writing, and the Cantos make a joke of it, as who should say
'The Sphinx; and therefore la Gioconda'. There are causations, but it
will take a great deal of tracing-out of apparently divergent branches
before they will begin to show themselves.

Canto II offers textures and transformations. But, first, a statement
of intentions concerning the epic now under way. It was begun in
earlier drafts as a development from Browning's *Sordello*, in which
poem a blank outline, that of the troubadour Sordello, was taken from
the historical cupboard and made to move with Browning's own self's
musculation and struggles. Is Pound to do the same with his figures, the
many ghosts who will walk in these pages? Is he to use them merely as
excuses for self-projection? What is the relation, Browning, between
your *Sordello*, and Sordello the troubadour, and the Sordello who will
walk in my poem?

> Hang it all, Robert Browning,
>   there can be but the one 'Sordello'.
> But Sordello, and my Sordello?

The answer: Sordello has his own locus, and it will breathe through his
own language in my poem:

> Lo Sordels si fo di Mantovana.

'Sordello was from Mantua', as it says in his Provençal biography. 'It
can't be all in one language' (LXXXVI, p. 563); local conditions mould
ways of being and of breathing, and hence utterance: 'Earth and water
dye the wind in your valley' (XCVIII, p. 689). The texture of the
language defines the man, and the culture he helps to make. The
Sordellos, Odysseuses, Confuciuses who walk in this poem will not be
homogenised masks for the all-conquering ego of the poet.

As I have said, Ovid and Pound both celebrate texture, which means differentiation, and change along a gradient of differences. The sea is the locus *par excellence* of change, and water is found everywhere in these first Cantos. So-shu (whose identity is doubtful[4]) has a drunken seer's delight in it:

> So-shu churned in the sea

– or as the same Canto tells us three pages later:

> So-shu churned in the sea, So-shu also,
>   using the long moon for a churn-stick . . .

The latter lines are in the middle of things 'seen, and half seen', muscle merging into wave. Here, at the beginning of Canto II, 'So-shu churned in the sea' leads into a graded sequence of transformations, starting with seals and passing via sea-nymphs to Helen of Troy, who so disturbs the old Trojan counsellors as they sit gossiping on the walls of the city and watching her (*Iliad*, 3).

And so this Canto, like Ovid's *Metamorphoses*, is full of exactnesses of texture. Texture of sound, of the 'murmur of old men's voices' (grasshopper-like, in Homer, as the remains of desire trickle through their limbs, stirring only to gossip), fretting, and wishing this dangerous female (emblem of the threat and renewal in change) would go home. Texture of the grace of her movement:

> Moves, yes she moves like a goddess
> And has the face of a god
>   and the voice of Schoeney's daughters

– where 'the body of what is seen is in the music', and we do not have to be told what Schoeneus' daughters looked or sounded like. Or the exact sense of fluid strength that is seen in an arching breaker and the male embrace; here, in the rape of Tyro by Poseidon:

> That by the beach-run, Tyro,
>   Twisted arms of the sea-god,
> Lithe sinews of water, gripping her, cross-hold,
> And the blue-gray glass of the wave tents them,
> Glare azure of water, cold-welter, close cover.

The forces implied here are both those that are visible only to the alert and intuitive eye, and those that govern us most irresistibly. The rational faculties are powerless either to perceive or to withstand them. Whence follows a moral tale in Canto II. Acoetes is a plain man and craftsman of navigation, in Ovid's *Metamorphoses*, owning nothing but his art. (He recounts of his father, wryly, in *Metamorphoses*, 3.588–91:

> ars illi sua census erat; cum traderet artem,
> 'Accipe, quas habeo, studii successor et heres,'
> dixit 'opes!' moriensque mihi nihil ille reliquit
> praeter aquas.)

Picking up water on Scios he is confronted with a graceful boy whom his men have encountered; he knows him to be a god –

> 'He has a god in him,
>   though I do not know which god.'
>   (II, p. 9)

– and he does homage, offering to take the boy to Naxos. His men, of criminal backgrounds and seeing in the boy a chance for slave-money, plot to sell him; they overpower Acoetes and set another course. The boy appears to come out of a stupor, as of wine, and accuses them of deceit. They laugh at him. He transforms them into dolphins and the ship into a rock, as it says in Canto II:

> Aye, I, Acœtes, stood there,
>   and the god stood by me,
> Water cutting under the keel,
> Sea-break from stern forrards,
>   wake running off from the bow,
> And where was gunwale, there now was vine-trunk

For the boy was Dionysus, wine-god. His kingdom of grapes and of leopards asserts itself:

> And the ship like a keel in ship-yard,
>   slung like an ox in smith's sling,
> Ribs stuck fast in the ways,
>   grape-cluster over pin-rack,
>   void air taking pelt.

And the moral is given by Acoetes as he tells the story to King Pentheus, who would like to eradicate Dionysus' worship from his kingdom:

> And you, Pentheus,
> Had as well listen to Tiresias, and to Cadmus,
> or your luck will go out of you.

Which it does, in the Ovid: Pentheus is torn apart by Dionysus' (Bacchus') revellers.

Pound introduces his own transformation: a fleeing seaborne Daphne turned into coral. Then Tyro, with the seagulls that were present at her rape, and a wave of Dionysus' colouring run together:

> Lithe turning of water,
>   sinews of Poseidon,
> Black azure and hyaline,
>   glass wave over Tyro [. . .]
>
> Sea-fowl stretching wing-joints [. . .]
>
> Grey peak of the wave,
>   wave, colour of grape's pulp

Sea, creator of forms, ever changing. And the Canto closes with a scene that belongs either to the world of the usual 'real' or to a god-world; but, if the one, obviously tending towards the other:

> The tower like a one-eyed great goose
>   cranes up out of the olive-grove

– and a scene in which frogs, fauns and Proteus all inhabit the same plane of reality.

All this is not a proof to any Pentheus that (*E*, 431) things 'become other things by swift and unanalysable process', but a statement that 'I have seen what I have seen' (Acoetes to Pentheus), whose force depends on the exactness of the textures rendered by metaphor and like means. If the Canto has a weakness, it is that these are too *rarissime* and rendered at too great length. More delicate and yet more ordinary shades, in much lesser compass, will do an even better job in later Cantos.

(iii) CANTO III

After Odysseus, telling his story, and Acoetes telling his, there enters
another narrator, who bears a close relationship to a historical Pound:

> I sat on the Dogana's steps
> For the gondolas cost too much, that year

Canto XXVII will tell us (pp. 129–30) that 'that year' was 1908, 1909
or 1910. It will speak of the moment of its own writing, 'this year, '27'.
A narrator is thus giving us his autobiography, and relating it to the
biography of the poem.

Arrival at the Dogana's steps in Venice is the first stage in an Odyssey
that started (as we may later piece together from the poem) from Idaho,
Pennsylvania and New York. Here the hero wishes to tell us of the
vision experienced at this youthful stage, a girl carried in his mind,
which grades into the presence before him of the gods. In his mind were
not 'those girls' that Browning saw before him in *Sordello*:

> And there were not 'those girls', there was one face,
> And the Buccentoro twenty yards off, howling 'Stretti',
> And the lit cross-beams, that year, in the Morosini,
> And peacocks in Koré's house, or there may have been.

The girl's vision leads to the gods' presence because intensity of passion
makes full awareness, and vice versa. But here there are only flat verbs:
'sat', 'cost (too much)'. Emotion is hidden behind denotation, in
particular this one:

> there was one face

which is thrown in as afterthought, syntactically loose. It is ironised
immediately by the presence of a gathering of Venetian oarsmen,
twenty yards 'off' (not 'away'), 'howling' the new hit: 'Locked in Our
Embrace'. And the voice does not dwell thereon, but moves to other
memories:

> And the lit cross-beams, that year, in the Morosini,
> And peacocks in Koré's house, or there may have been.

The 'one face' floated in the mind like the gilded beams of the Morosini palace, defying perhaps time and space; gold in the gloom. And somehow we find ourselves in a Venice where the gods have their houses, like Koré's, in which peacocks apparently walk, and whether Koré is now a godly name for a woman who has gone beyond her fleshly state and attained godhead, or the name of the goddess herself who here lives in Venice – and whether Pound arrived at the knowledge of this being via a poem of D'Annunzio – affects little. Even this presence is stated as if the narrator were not greatly moved, for the subject of the clause is peacocks, not Koré. This is the experience of a 23-year-old man, that the language so far laboriously acquired by the 23-year-old man ('the backwash of Lionel Johnson, Fred Manning [...] and the rest of 'em': *P*, 462) had been inadequate to sustain, and that is now given adequately in the 'laconism' fought through to by the man of 40.

By this series of steps in Canto III we have come to a crucial presenting – one that in the draft Cantos had cost Pound so much fretting and awkwardness of preparatory rationalisation.

> Gods float in the azure air,
> Bright gods and Tuscan, back before dew was shed.
> Light: and the first light, before ever dew was fallen.
> Panisks, and from the oak, dryas,
> And from the apple, mælid,
> Through all the wood, and the leaves are full of voices,
> A-whisper, and the clouds bowe over the lake,
> And there are gods upon them,
> And in the water, the almond-white swimmers,
> The silvery water glazes the upturned nipple,
> As Poggio has remarkèd.

'Gods float', and so does the verse, lightly. But it is important to allow the words the space that their syllable-lengths and consonant-groupings make for them, in deliberately paced utterance; in which the line naturally comes out something like this, not crowded to a gabble as in casual reading:

> Gods   float   in the   a   zure   air.

In such deliberate reading of this passage, a pattern soon offers itself: /× ×/×/: 'float in the azure air', 'back before dew was shed', '-fore ever dew was fall-', 'wood, and the leaves are full'. It occurs perhaps eight times. It is a rhythmic shape found in Sappho, and the demigods, panisk and dryas, are of a Hellenic era.

The air is full of movement, seen: implied in a preposition, '*through*
all the wood' (not 'in'); in a verb suggesting an action (not a state) of the
clouds – 'bowe', curve down like a bow; in a verb describing what
happens for an instant:

> The silvery water glazes the upturned nipple

The gods, and the seeings and guessings of them, are multiple, behind
leaves and clouds, in apple and oak. And the knowing of their presence
is somehow consonant with a preternatural visual sharpness, as before
dawn, or as when one whiteness ('almond-white') makes itself clear
through another:

> The silvery water glazes the upturned nipple

It is all anachronistic: Poggio made his observation (1416) in the age
of Cosimo de' Medici, or some 116 years after the death of Cavalcanti,
interpreter of those 'Tuscan' gods of whom the passage no doubt
speaks; and, say, 2,000 years after the last Greeks to speak convincingly
of their gods and dryads. This god-vision is not limited by period;
Pound is trying to evoke, by image and sound, an experience evoked
'undeniably' by Homer, Ovid, Botticelli, Golding, Gaudier-Brzeska,
Matisse, the precision and self-consistency of whose art is the only
'proof' that they saw anything.

Now there is a break in the Canto.

> My Cid rode up to Burgos,
> Up to the studded gate between two towers,
> Beat with his lance butt, and the child came out,
> Una niña de nueve años,
> To the little gallery over the gate, between two towers,
> Reading the writ, voce tinnula

We are in the world of *geste*. The *chanson de geste*, medieval relative of
the epic, is a song of 'thing done' or 'deed'; Pound in *The Spirit of
Romance* calls it song of 'gesture', and it is always of a *coup d'esprit*, the
brilliant conception carried into action with a slightly mad courage
about it. This section is taken from the *Cantar de myo Cid* (*c*.1140).
The Cid is exiled, unjustly. All are forbidden to have contact with him.
The terrors of the writ are braved, coolly, by a reed-voiced girl, who
calmly and with the dignity of nine years reads to him the writ: that she

or anyone else who speaks to him will have his heart cut out. There is a touching contrast between her taking on the dignity of the official language and her awe of its embodiment, in the 'big seals' and 'the writing'. It is a deed to be treasured by the hearer of *gestes*.

This Odysseus uses his wits to swindle money out of the pawn-brokers, much as his prototype would have done in a similar tight spot; and his subsequent campaign is given with a vigour and directness that Homer's audience would also have appreciated, in one line:

> Breaking his way to Valencia.

A parallel with the first hero of the Cantos is established. But a difference is suggested by the Canto's end:

> Ignez da Castro murdered, and a wall
> Here stripped, here made to stand.
> Drear waste, the pigment flakes from the stone,
> Or plaster flakes, Mantegna painted the wall.
> Silk tatters, 'Nec Spe Nec Metu'.

Ignez da Castro is murdered by jealous courtiers, and when her lover becomes king he has them do homage to her corpse. These are deeds of murk and *bravura*, where there is always a slight reaching for effect; not the daylight dodges of Odysseus, among sea-waves and islands, but among galleries, lances, courts. This element, a rhetoric of action, endures in Renaissance art, in Uccello's Sir John Hawkwood, as it were strutting on his horse; in Mantegna's fresco of the Gonzaga princes strutting in a frozen ballet; or in Malatesta's Tempio in Canto IX, with its 'touch of rhetoric in the whole' (p. 41). The art holds their image of themselves, and hence the theme of transience in these last lines of the Canto, as the peeling plaster mocks that brave gesture at eternity, 'braving time' (*Mauberley*), *Nec spe nec metu*, the Gonzaga motto: Neither with hope nor with fear.

The Canto perhaps comes to a circle. At the beginning the narrator moves back from his position on the Dogana's steps, among the splendid traces of Venice, through visions into a Greek–Italian world of gods. At the end of the Canto, the movement of the mind is back through fading traces in art to the splendid *gestes* of the Middle Ages that were their prototype. These are worlds that are alleged to be lost to modern man, wherefore Pound had once asked: should he 'sulk and leave the word to novelists'?[5]

(iv) CANTO IV

First there is invocation of past visions of intense splendour and
wreckage, passion-caused endings of godly cities – Troy abandoned by
Aeneas, whose wanderings led to the founding of Rome – and
foundings of godly cities, as Thebes by Cadmus. There is a presentation
of a state that is a door into seeing these things: 'our waking' in the
'dawn', after love. Soon an old man speaks, narrating ancient visions,
which begin to double each other. Thus Actaeon was hunted by his own
dogs because he saw Diana naked; Peire Vidal the troubadour ran wild
dressed as a wolf, for the sake of his lady whose name was 'She-Wolf',
and was hunted almost to death. The clarity in this double moment is
overcharged; sunlight floods and reglitters from the tops of the trees,
but none of it reaches down to Diana's pool, which is suffused with her
own light.

Among further visions comes another doubling that gives a different
tone to this medium. Ecbatan is the city whose terraces are planned in
harmony with the order of the cosmos. Pound fittingly makes it the
place where the god's radiance comes to earth, in the story in which
Zeus visited Danaë ('the god's bride') in a golden shower. The
fertilising (raining) light of the male principle is drawn to earth by that
magnet: as it were Venus, her power focused by the mystic layout of the
Celestial City. That encapsulates a great deal of the religious anthropology that will be found elsewhere in the Cantos.

The structure of the kernel constituted by these first four Cantos is
tripartite, following the formulation in that letter to Pound's father
(1927):

Live man goes down into world of Dead.
[. . .] The 'repeat in history'
[. . .] The 'magic moment' or moment of metamorphosis, bust thru
from quotidien into 'divine or permanent world'. Gods, etc. (*L*,
210)

Canto I clearly shows the first of these. The meaning of it is not stated,
and in a sense is nonexistent, like the 'meaning' of the going down of
the sun, or of the assassination of President Kennedy. It is a complicated action, and in it are certain patterns, which will be shown to
appear in other actions; and the showing of these parallels (later) is the

bringing out of the 'meaning'. To state them briefly here: a contrast between vigour (the 'live man') and the half-living in their 'hell'; continuity with the past; a warner (Tiresias) from that past; the way 'outa here' and home to the Earthly Paradise; some kind of accomodation with dark pre-rational chthonic forces.

Canto II shows the third element in Pound's list: metamorphosis. Meanings: 'that' is in and around us; 'it' is not a separable state, attained and held, but has to do with the grain and texture of the here and now, which is not static, but full individuation of which tends towards godhead.

Both these Cantos contain bridges towards the god-worlds; the difference seems to be that the first locates impetus more in the intelligent choice of the man of sensibility, and the second more in the confluence of the fluid force that his sensibility (as passion) may trigger.

The status of the 'repeat in history' is more difficult. If we consider history to be specifically that which is *not* outside time, then this corresponds to the 'mediaeval or modern historical characters' of Pound's remarks to Yeats – the local, 'quotidien' level of the Schifanoia frescoes – and is found in Canto III, which 'repeats' the *Odyssey* through the actions of the young Pound, of the Cid, etc. But it will be noted that these actions themselves, like Odysseus', impinge on the world of the gods. And in a letter of 1937, in a position apparently corresponding to his 'repeat in history', Pound referred to 'parallel (Vidal-Actaeon)' (*L*, 294). So these 'repeats' may occur either 'inside' or 'outside time' – or halfway between – and Canto IV is a primary example of them.

(v) CANTOS VIII–XI: MALATESTA

Who was this Malatesta? 'Cette nature de fer [. . .] cet époux sanglant [. . .] ce capitaine farouche',[6] etc., is one pre-Pound way of looking at him; height 1.70 metres, dolichocephalic cranium, with a capacity of 1,500 cubic centimetres (as ascertained from his remains),[7] is another. But Pound's interest is neither Romantic nor determinist. 'The name of the Fascist era is *Voluntas*' (*P*, 312), he wrote in 1942. Sigismondo Malatesta is an Odysseus with a constructive element superadded.

Am reading up historic background [. . .] shall probably only get more bewildered; but may avoid a few historic idiocies, or impossibilities.

Authorities differ as to whether Sigismund Malatesta raped a german girl in Verona, with such vigour that she 'passed on' [. . .] in fact all the *minor* points that might aid one in forming an historic rather than a fanciful idea of his character seem 'shrouded in mystery' or rather lies.

I suppose one has to 'select'. If I find he was TOO bloody quiet and orderly it will ruin the canto. Which needs a certain boisterousness and disorder to contrast with his constructive work.

(PB, 302)

Pound is interested in the capacity to decide; he wishes to have a test case, to demonstrate this capacity to decide constructively. This requires that the subject shall *not* find that as soon as he waves his wand the path is made straight for him, or even that his capacity for decision be explainable by some less-than-full emotionality (say, an officer-class blinkeredness). He must, along with his constructivity, have a completeness of vigour and faculties, and exist in a disorder (created by himself and villains) that will test his capacity for ordered action.

Sigismondo Pandolfo Malatesta was born on 19 June 1417, illegitimate son of Pandolfo Malatesta, a celebrated captain-general and descendant of a line of the same in the Romagna.[8] By the age of 13, Sigismondo was effective head of his states and had conducted his first victorious assault on its enemies. He allied himself by marriage with Niccolò d'Este, who remained his only constant friend, and at the age of 16 was captain-general in charge of the Pope's armies in the Romagna, and had already won glory against the two most illustrious captains-general (mercenary leaders, *condottieri*) of his day, Francesco Sforza and Giacomo Piccinino.

Sigismondo's career as a hired captain-general, in charge of his couple of thousand lances, is complicated and of interest only in certain key mechanisms. The struggles for power between the Visconti of Milan, Francesco Sforza, Alfonso of Aragon, and the Papacy were very fluid, and over the years Malatesta showed poor political judgement. By 1454 he had made an enviable name for himself as a captain-general, but had acquired enough implacable personal enemies to make it almost certain that he would never be profitably employed in that capacity. For in all this politico-military anarchy there is a kind of code: A will happily employ B, who once fought against him with all his power, *provided* that B have never broken a contract with him.

By contract-breaking and ill-chosen alliances, Malatesta had given aid and comfort to his neighbour Federigo da Montefeltro, lost the strategic town of Pesaro –

> And this cut us off from our south half
> and finished our game, thus, in the beginning
> (IX, p. 35)

– and found himself excluded from all useful association. One more broken contract (with Siena), and Malatesta had made the enemy who would finally bring him down: the future Pope Pius II, Aeneas Silvius Piccolomini, who was a Sienese. For further errors Malatesta was finally anathematised. The charges listed in the solemn Consistory, on 16 January 1461, were of awesome dimensions; he was burned in effigy and excommunicated, despite the pleadings of Venice and Sforza, and the Pope's armies invaded his remaining territories, leaving him in charge of Rimini and a small patch of land. A melancholy appeared in his letters. Miserable employ in the far-off Peleponnesus was followed by new insults from Pius' successor. Exhausted, ill, embittered by his son's ambitions against his bastard Sallustio, he died in 1468 at the age of 51.

He left a temple (unfinished), which is the chief cause of these four Cantos. Inscriptions on the flanks of the building (which remains in the Church's eyes the Church of St Francis, as it was before Malatesta's architect Alberti covered it with marble) say that it is dedicated to immortal God. But the words are in Greek, the somewhat suspect language of the new (heretical?) Platonisers, and of the schismatical and Platonistically mystical Eastern Church. When the humanist Platina was interrogated under torture in 1465 by Pius II's successor about his relations with Sigismondo, the arrest had come, as Pound puts it,

> For singing to Zeus in the catacombs
> (XI, p. 50)

– alleged. Sigismondo 'built a temple so full of pagan works' (IX, p. 41), as Pius II charged. Diana and Venus and the Sibyl of Cumae figure equally with St Luke; very naked *putti* gambol more abundantly than angels. Water is shown everywhere. Pound ascribes this (LXXXIII, p. 528; *GK*, 224) to Sigismondo's connection with Gemisthus Plethon, Byzantine Platonist, met at the great Council in 1438, his ashes eventually brought back by Sigismondo for the third sarcophagus in the south flank of the Temple. Gemisthus wished to make the Greek gods live again as Neoplatonist emanations from pure Being (= Zeus), and the first of these emanations[9] was

POSEIDON, *concret Allgemeine*
(VIII, p. 31)

– Neptune, qualified as 'concrete Universal' by Gemisthus' German commentator.

A recent iconographic analysis finds a main theme of the decorations of the Temple to be the glorification of Sigismondo.[10] His phallic and stern bas-relief, a representation of settled power reminiscent of Assyria, meets the visitor at eye-level, cut in a solid pediment that rests on two elephants, Malatesta's personal emblems. Romance has always found his mistress to be the goddess of the place. Isotta degli Atti is not known to us other than by Sigismondo's glorification of her, her protestation in writing against his infidelity, and her wise rule over his states in later years. Sigismondo conquered her love in the year 1446, and that date is therefore carved on monuments within the temple that were not even thought of in that year.[11] Her sarcophagus is inscribed 'D. ISOTTAE. ARIMINENSI. B.M. SACRUM. MCCCCL', which Pius II promptly interpreted to mean 'to the goddess Isotta'.[12] And throughout the church is found an S intertwined with an I, (though modern criticism prefers to see this as the first two letters of Sigismundus'). Malatesta would have been familiar with Dante's similar apotheosis of Cunizza, the celebrated concubine, in the *Divine Comedy*, for that poem was partly a Malatesta family history (*Inferno*, 5.74 ff.; 27.46; 28.81, 85).[13]

Celebrating strength and grace, the building coheres. Inside, Alberti's rectilinear volumes are at peace with the carvings of Agostino that modulate their surfaces. Outside it is saved from Alberti's grandiose tendencies by not having his usual curves. The cupola was never built, and the letter survives that changed, with a little scratch of a sketch, the curves at the top of the façade to diagonals. Above the door, instead of the planned cupola, there is a gap. 'The Tempio was stopped by a fluke? or Sigismundo had the flair when to stop it?' queried Pound (*GK*, 159). Pound did not know of the little sketch in Alberti's letter,[14] which seems to support his idea: Sigismondo demanded changes, which halted everything, and then his troubles brought an end to the works. The whole rebuilding is the work of a sort of committee, brilliantly assembled by Malatesta (another man would certainly have brought in some Donatello), literati and technicians known and unknown. And all done without leisure, or the kind of established power that would know what reserves and surplus it could call upon: as Pound wrote, 'All that a single man could, Malatesta managed *against* the current of power [...] You can contrast it with ANY great summit done WITH the current of power' (*GK*, 159–60).

The whole organisation of the Malatesta Cantos is to present *difficulty*. The world is a multiplicity of circumstance, each circumstance impinging on a direction. That is another way of saying: chaos. Pound had concluded that prose was pathology, diagnosing the causes of particular states. 'Counterparts' in Joyce's *Dubliners* gives a result (a child-beating) preceded by a set of causes (a large man; a stifling way of life; whence 'heavy dirty eyes'; then humiliation as underling, humiliation *vis-à-vis* the female). In such prose, one element is missing: the exercise of choice. Leopold Bloom floats buoyed up by his amniotic benevolence; Stephen Dedalus floats buoyed up by grandiose self-images supplied to him from a highly explicable tradition. The prose-writer diagnosed local networks of causes, within a great web of causality, as infinite in its interconnections as a Faulkner Yoknapatawpha-map on which are imposed the ghostly traces of passings and meetings in all the layerings of time. But having opened it up with his scalpel to display one such local network, the prose-writer could only allow the web to close and re–ply its filiations again; there could be no suggestion that anything (any free choice) could significantly *change* the tissuings of causalities in the combinations in which preceding causalities had destined them to occur. And that is another way of describing what is for us chaos: complexity, in which nothing offers choice.

To assert the possibility of choice by falsely simplifying actuality is sentiment. And by the 1910s enough had been learned about what causes what, in the universe and in man, for any intelligent person (but not lyric poets) to feel somewhat tied down by causal complexity. Now choice cannot be described: neither literature nor any other form of communication can show a man at a certain moment exercising free will to the exclusion of the influence of material fact upon him. Perhaps that is why Pound believed that only poetry could present the constructive element in human life (*E*, 324 n.); the means available to poetry, working at a deeper level than our cogitative capacity, can persuade our intuitions that someone has made significant choice.

So the Malatesta Cantos present a chaos of diversions, obstructions,

versus *Voluntas*, will, in a perpetual struggle. There is not a happy and
predictable movement towards the note triumphant, nor a mere yo-yo.
Pound's sense of the case Malatesta is that there are, among attempts,
failures, half-successes, *moments* when the thing as nobly conceived
emerges and marks itself on the visible environment for some centuries.
And also, that part of the interest of this visible trace is the very
indomitability of the man who made it, inevitably marked in it. This
sense of the final meaning of Malatesta's life requires Pound to work
these four Cantos to a shape, suggesting resolution (the sad inmixed in
the triumphant), such as Malatesta himself would not have felt in his
lifetime. Later, as the tone of the Cantos as a whole changes, the sad
note will be picked out alone: *olim de Malatestis*, the description of the
palaces at Fano 'that once belonged to the Malatesta' (XI, p. 50;
LXXX, p. 501).

The first of these Cantos is of uninterrupted vigour, passion and
achieved beauty, but for this ominous note:

> with the game lost in mid-channel,
> And never quite lost till '50,
> and never quite lost till the end, in Romagna
> (VIII, p. 32)

The last of them is of humiliation and fatigue, mitigated by defiance *and*
by the note that recalls youth's gaiety:

> And he said in his young youth:
> Vogliamo,
> *che le donne*, we will that they, *le donne*, go ornate,
> As be their pleasure, for the city's glory thereby.
> (XI, p. 50)

Not, as I have said, letting these poles alternate like a yo-yo, the whole
group instead begins by stating chaos, constructivity, and their upshot,
timeless achievement (VIII); develops the intensity of this conflict
between chaos and constructivity, multiplying slings and arrows, and
states the timeless achievement, as culmination of the first movement
(IX); shows an unrelieved movement towards defeat, intensifying
grimness (X); brings grimness and humiliation to a climax, with a recall
of that early hope that (in this context) evokes pathos (XI). The note of
achievement is half-transmuted to mute loss:

> In the gloom, the gold gathers the light against it. (XI, p. 51)

The texture of this section shows a sea of the particular. We come at the action through torn letters:

> *Frater tamquam*
> *Et compater carissime: tergo*
> > . . . *hanni de*
> > . . . *dicis*
> > . . . *entia*
> (VIII, p. 28)

Contracts, bills of sale, verses, architectural memos, a letter from the slighted Isotta, a formal complaint concerning the theft of marble, a receipt for damages incurred in the same, letters proposing treachery, letters between third parties, formal denunciations: *documents*. This batch of Cantos is the first in which is thrust at the reader a sheaf of documents, of non-homogenised history – not the magisterial unifying voice of Gibbon, Ramsay, Luchaire, but scraps that flaunt their heterogeneity, with the archive labels dangling off them:

> As Filippo Strozzi wrote to Zan Lottieri, then in Naples,
> 'I think they'll let him through at Campiglia'
>
> *Florence, Archivio Storico, 4th Series t. iii, e*
> '*La Guerra dei Senesi col conte di Pitigliano.*'
> > (X, p. 42)

Yet at the same time the voice is part of the documentary artefact. And in this section a main device is the babble of English voices, improvised equivalents for the Italian voices that are sometimes left showing: legal ('by the said'), Chicago gangster ('If we split with Francesco'), English peasant, and an equivalent of Renaissance high-Latin rhetorical flourish – which, at need, can co-exist in the same person with Brooklyn Irish: 'Siggy, darlint, wd you not stop making war on insensible objects'.

All these are 'in time'. But there is another kind of speech in these Cantos that belongs elsewhere:

> From the forked rocks of Penna and Billi, on Carpegna
> with the road leading under the cliff,
> > in the wind-shelter into Tuscany
> > (VIII, p. 30)

These passages show the significant result ('And the wind is still for a little/And the dusk rolled/to one side a little') of the whole struggle of will, directed desire, with chaos; they show that without which Pound would consider all the data trivial. They have the hyphenated doubles ('mud-stretch') of which William Carlos Williams complained (see below, p. 312), along with a dropping of the article. There is an odd exotic-seeming use of prepositions ('on Carpegna', 'by San Vitale'), and an abbreviating of 'from' and 'of' phrases ('creek's mouth', 'wind-shelter'). There is a pregnant but uncompleted sense of direction ('From the forked rocks' – no verb) and an archaic appending of a second subject after the verb ('For this tribe paid always, and the house/Called also Atreides''). There is the parallelism ('Under the plumes, with the flakes [. . .]/With the sheets spread [. . .]/with leaves [. . .]/out of the dust'), which is found later in consciously ritual passages in the Pisan Cantos and in *Rock-Drill*: 'from under the rubble heap/m'elevasti/from the dulled edge beyond pain' (XC, p. 606). There is a particular quality of colour used in passages concerning those who desire clearly: 'Boats drawn on the sand, red-orange sails in the creek's mouth' recalls Bernart de Ventadorn in Canto VI speaking of his lady to Eleanor:

> Nor the glare-wing'd flies alight in the creek's edge

And chiefly perhaps there is sound:

> The filagree hiding the gothic,
>> with a tOUch of rhetoric in the whOle,
> And the Old sarcophagI,
>> such as lIE, smOthered in grAss, by San VitAle.

All these take language out of the specificity of daily usage in any time or place; they are an 'illustrious' aulic use, paralleling the one Dante strove for,[15] compounding and extrapolating from the decencies of the best normal usages, to carry the 'beauty' Pound inherited from Rossetti as a goal that Rossetti's language denied him. They are the delicate centre that the Hemingway toughness of Sigismondo's ordinary dialect (in Pound) is armour for.

(vi) CANTOS XIV–XV: 'HELL'

These two Cantos are a projection of some of the states that Pound had seen around him at the time of writing. He found these particular ones chiefly among 'the English', chiefly in London; and in the verse the English and London function as symbols. Using Dante's own critical scheme, Pound wrote that in the *Divine Comedy*

> ... Dante or Dante's intelligence may come to mean 'Everyman' or 'Mankind', whereat his journey becomes a symbol of mankind's struggle upward out of ignorance into the clear light of philosophy [...] In a fourth sense, the *Commedia* is an expression of the laws of eternal justice [...] the law of Karma, if we are to use an Oriental term. (*SR*, 127)

Thus Cantos XIV and XV are a fantasy-image for the mental punishment that men make for themselves with their crimes. Let us suppose that each act of lust, gluttony or avarice grabs after some quick satisfaction to the denial of the individual's own inclination towards a deeper kind of satisfaction, which he himself is in some way aware of. Extended, it becomes a habit, a twitch, or a tension; we recognise these states in others, and they are the opposite of a contentment. Such quick satisfactions are afforded by the little treacheries of professional life; here we enter the mental world of Canto XV:

> et nulla fidentia inter eos,   [and no trust between them,]
>   all with their twitching backs,
>   with daggers, and bottle ends, waiting an
>   unguarded moment

The sign of this bolge of Hell, as Pound said, is unrest, busyness, professors

>   sitting on piles of stone books,
>   obscuring the texts with philology,
>   hiding them under their persons,
>   the air without refuge of silence,
>   the drift of lice, teething,
>   and above it the mouthing of orators
>   (XIV, p. 63)

(Similarly in Dante, Pound said, the only escape from this 'aimless turmoil and restlessness of humanity' was in the lowest bolge, 'in the still malignity of the traitor's wallow': *SR*, 133–4). The association of light with serenity seems basic to humanity, perhaps because we

recognise a connection of serenity with understanding. And to 'shut out
the light', God's light, which is the primal sin in Pound, is taken as the
same thing as choosing these multiplex miseries that were grabbed as
satisfactions.

Some understanding that the crime makes its own inner punishment,
even in this life, perhaps helped Dante to decide to make his fantasised
hell-punishments so often fit the crime:

> Fitti nel limo dicon: 'Tristi fummo
>   nell' aer dolce che dal sol s'allegra,
>   portando dentro accidioso fummo;
> or ci attristiam nella belletta negra.'

> Stuck in the slime they say: 'We were sad
>   in the sweet air that delights in the sun,
>   carrying the fume of *accidie* within ourselves;
> now we sadden in the black mire here.'
>   (*Inferno*, 7.121–4)

Darkness and endless harassment punish lust, gluttony, and both
avarice and prodigality. But, conversely, Pound takes Dante's fantasy
of a punishment in the afterlife to project his own sense that hellish
states are here and now, because it objectifies those states *as misery* (an
aspect we do not usually recognise) while still dramatising them as
crime.

Much of the projection in Cantos XIV and XV done by the old
satirical device: let the person keep his usual gestures, and a few of his
usual props, but let the environment that provides rationale and
psychological support for these things be taken away. Eliot:

> O dark dark dark. They all go into the dark [. . .]
> The captains, merchant bankers, eminent men of letters
>   ('East Coker')

– and the dark is unimpressed by them, and by

> De Bailhache, Fresca, Mrs Cammel, whirled
> Beyond the circuit of the shuddering Bear
>   ('Gerontion')

The dignity, which is borrowed from trappings and gestures, here
mocks itself by its irrelevance:

         ......r,
        a scrupulously clean table-napkin
    Tucked under his penis,
         and .... m
    Who disliked colloquial language,
    Stiff-starched, but soiled, collars
        circumscribing his legs
                    (XIV, p. 61)

Thus the prurient vice-crusaders of their day,

                fahrting through silk,
            waving the Christian symbols,
        .... frigging a tin penny whistle
                    (XIV, p. 63)

But T. S. Eliot, in a passage which has become almost an indissociable critical appendix to these Cantos, accused Pound of moral/theolog-
ical superficiality in them.

With satiric intent, he listed the population of the 'Hell Cantos' quite
accurately. 'It consists (I may have overlooked one or two species) of
politicians, profiteers, financiers, newspaper proprietors and their hired
men, *agents provocateurs*, Calvin, St Clement of Alexandria, the English,
vice-crusaders, liars, the stupid, pedants, preachers, those who do not
believe in Social Credit, bishops, lady golfers, Fabians, conservatives
and imperialists; and all "those who have set money-lust before the
pleasures of the senses".' 'From this list, Eliot did Pound the justice to
draw the three principles of selection: '(1) the aesthetic, (2) the
humanitarian, (3) the Protestant.'[16] That is to say, these individuals are
in Hell because they are (*a*) nasty, (*b*) inhumane, (*c*) connected with
institutions and hence necessarily more or less obscurantist.

Eliot then went on to suggest that Pound had failed to present the
inner spiritual struggles of any of the inhabitants of this Hell; thus
failed to show how they entered their hellish state; thus had intimated
that their being in a hellish state was something that had just happened,
and was of equal significance whether the result of an inner struggle or
not; and thus had failed entirely to consider whether such struggles
might be necessary in *oneself*, i.e. in the author and his peers. 'Mr
Pound's Hell [. . .] is a perfectly comfortable one for the modern mind
to contemplate, and disturbing to no one's complacency: it is a Hell for
the *other people* [. . .]' The people in it are trivial, because their struggles

are not shown to be of significance; equally, then, the people in Pound's Heaven must be trivial, since their triumph in such struggles cannot be shown to have been of significance.

But Eliot ignored the implications of Pound's, and Dante's, 'metamorphic' method – their development out of Ovid. Eliot's writings on Dante's Hell show him most interested in the figures who, justice tells us, should not be there. Farinata is punished because he did not believe in God; Brunetto Latini for sodomy; Francesca for her desire. Eliot celebrates Dante's wisdom: Dante refused to make these people any the less admirable just because they were damned. Eliot returns to Ulysses' words: 'as it pleased Another'. That seems to be the core of Dante's theological understanding. Indeed, the line 'His will is our peace' (*Paradiso*, 3.58) is, for Eliot, one of the chief beauties of the poem. This fits with Eliot's tendency in all his writings to celebrate surrender, renunciation, in all its forms: here we renounce our sense of what is just, in favour of a higher decree of order. But the result is that people can be in Hell without – as generations of readers have felt – being evil. By contrast, when in the hellish transformations of Pound's Canto XIV we find figures

> melting like dirty wax,
> decayed candles

the sense of crime against an order of things is forceful, for it is an inherent, not an arbitrarily asserted order.

The claim that Pound's poem views complacently the otherness of its Hell/London seems valid only in so far as Pound has failed to present the states of his hell-denizens fully. It is not required that a writer identify overtly with his sinners; Dante does not identify with Adam of Brescia explicitly, and almost spits at some of the slime-swimmers he meets. But a sensitive reader finds Eliot participating in the tortures of his hell – and not because Tiresias is bleating in the background. The weakness of Pound's Hell Cantos is that some states are not fully articulated:

> and the fabians crying for the petrifaction of putrefaction,
> for a new dung-flow cut in lozenges
>
> (XV, p. 64)

is not *quite* mere jibe. It is intended to suggest to us that the Fabians wanted to take over a diseased social system (in which working men had no responsibility) and perpetuate it with trimmings. But it articulates so sketchily the psychological movements that led to that position that it is effectively about 'other people' – like, indeed Eliot's passages about small house-agents' clerks. It should be remembered that XIV and XV are only one bolge of Pound's Hell, as the house-agent's clerk's passage is of Eliot's.

In the last page and a half of Canto XV, light becomes available to the hero (here referred to specifically for the first time since the opening of XIV), and at the same time we learn that he has a 'guide', who is Plotinus, the Neoplatonist. Pound's fantasy attributes to this guide a technical knowledge in the defeating of malignant stupidity. The trick is to borrow the shield that bears the active image of the chief Gorgon (Medusa), whose glance turns creatures to stone, and to point it downwards at the evil maggots in the sewage, thus hardening the whole stew to the width of a narrow track, enough to escape over. Thus the psyche seems indebted to grace coming from outside, for the ability to steel itself against over-awareness of these bestialities; but the path is a narrow one, requiring much self-control. Having passed over, the hero faints, wakes, finds Plotinus gone, staggers out of Hell's gate, purifies himself in acid (again the psychic antisepsis; cf. XCIV, p. 635), and finds himself in divinity's o'erpowering grace, the sunlight, which knocks him unconscious.

The place of I–IV and the Malatesta and Hell groups within the whole sequence so far may be indicated by a brief sketch; the form of the whole will be discussed further with that of the next sequence, XVII–XXX.

    I   Odysseus' descent into Hell, sacrifice to the shades and consultation of Tiresias. Matings of gods and heroes.

   II   Dionysus; metamorphosis; the sea.

  III   The poet's journey, in Venice; 'gods float'; El Cid; chivalry and its traces.

  IV   Passion and vision; transformations; Actaeon/Vidal: the 'repeat'.

   V   Late-Renaissance murkiness; people half-living; 'in time'; the past; hellish (cf. I).

  VI   Eleanor of Aquitaine and the troubadour period: vigour, conducive to spiritual 'bust thru' to light; goddess; sense of dawn (cf. III and IV).

 VII   The nineteenth century and Twenties Paris: furniture and flimflam; prose, the craft of delineating unilluminate matter. James as Tiresias (cf. I).

VIII–XI   Malatesta: one man's effort to survive and record his passion; temporal failures, momentary 'bust thru's (cf. Odysseus, Cid; Isotta his goddess/Eleanor).

    XII   Baldy Bacon and wheeler-dealers; mock Odysseus, but fun. Bankers: hellish modern state: greed, defensive (cf. I).

    XIII   Confucius: activity of socially constructive mind, grading into awareness of inclusive godhead, not announced as such.

XIV–XV   London: an area of modern world as part of hell; analysis of what that means, by metaphor (cf. I).

    XVI   Purgatory: serene air, with sense of escape from foregoing. Relapse into Hell of twentieth century, with historical analysis thereof.

NOTES: CHAPTER 7

1 For all this, see Myles Slatin, 'A history of Pound's *Cantos* I–XVI, 1915–1925', *American Literature*, vol. 35, no. 2 (May 1963), pp. 183–95.

2 Louis Zukofsky, *Prepositions: The Collected Critical Essays of Louis Zukofsky*, expanded edn (Berkeley/Los Angeles, Calif.: University of California Press, 1981), p. 81.

3 The priest, bearing the golden bough, is wedded to Diana at Aricia (see Frazer); Hermes ('Argicida') carries a golden wand when he visits Dis to persuade him to give up Persephone (Homeric *Hymn to Demeter*); Aeneas must find a golden bough to take to Proserpine (Persephone) when he visits Hades (*Aeneid*, bk 6); and the fact that the 'thou with dark eyelids' (Aphrodite: Georgius' version of the Homeric *Hymn to Aphrodite*) here seems to be bearing Hermes' golden wand suggests another connection.

4 On this controversy, see *TC*, p. 5, and also Akiko Miyake, 'A note on So-shu', *Paideuma*, vol. 6, no. 3 (Winter 1977), pp. 325–8.

5 'Three Cantos: I', *Poetry*, vol. 10, no. 3 (June 1917), p. 118.

6 C. Yriarte, *Un condottiere au XV siècle* (Paris, 1882), p. 139.

7 Corrado Ricci, *Il Tempio Malatestiano* (Rimini: Bruno Ghigi, 1974), pp. 354–5.

8 For the life, cf. F. Arduini and others (eds), *Sigismondo Pandolfo Malatesta e il suo Tempo* (Vicenza: Neri Pozza, 1970), pp. 3 ff.

9 F. Masai, *Pléthon et le Platonisme de Mistra* (Paris: 'Les Belles Lettres', 1956), p. 224.

10 In Ricci, *Il Tempio*, appendice, p. xviii.

11 Arduini, *Sigismondo*, p. 128.

12 Ricci, *Il Tempio*, pp. 437, 435.

13 Malatesta possessed Benvenuto da Imola's commentary on Dante; for Benvenuto's remarks on Cunizza, see *MPP*, pp. 199, 361.

14 The letter was lost between 1779 and 1956, and only a printed version (without the sketch) was available to Ricci; see Arduini, *Sigismondo*, pp. 141–2.

15 *De Vulgari Eloquentia*, bk 1, chs 16–19.

16 T. S. Eliot, *After Strange Gods* (London: Faber, 1934), pp. 42–3.

CHAPTER 8

Commentary:
Cantos XVII–XXX

In October 1924 the Pounds moved to Rapallo, a small seaside resort near Genoa. They stayed there for the next twenty years, living at first in hotels, then in a small fifth-floor flat on the seafront. The economics of being a poet remained very difficult; in May 1924 Pound had calculated his earnings for the past five months at 'ZERO' (*PF*, 77). Italy was cheap. Pound stayed in contact with Paris, visiting in 1926 not only for the birth of his son Omar, but also for the first performances of the *Ballet mécanique* by George Antheil (whom Pound was energetically promoting) and of Pound's opera *Le Testament*, whose libretto was taken entirely from the words of François Villon. The violinist Olga Rudge had borne him a daughter, Mary, in July 1925. Pound was becoming interested in the politics of Mussolini, and in 1927 Olga was able to arrange to meet him, following an Antheil concert attended by the dictator. The new outlet for Pound's political emotions, and his love of the Mediterranean world in general, conspired with his rejection by the Anglo-Saxon world to foster anger in him against the latter, and overidentification with the former. Thus, for instance, when Ford began to suggest American lecture-tours for Pound as a money-spinner, Pound foresaw, no doubt rightly, that he would be used over there as expendable material: 'As for interrupting "my work", or if you prefer the term "the even tenor of my life" for bare expenses dubiously guaranteed, fees not down in writing, the breakable invitations of editors who reserve right to reject stuff they consider "unsuitable" etc. TO HELL WITH IT' (*PF*, 90).

Such stresses had no harmful effect on his literary work: the translation of the Confucian *Ta Hio* (finished in 1927), important articles on Guido Cavalcanti in 1928, in preparation for Pound's edition of Cavalcanti, and studies of the German anthropologist Leo Frobenius (begun in about 1929). *A Draft of the Cantos 17–27* was published in an expensive edition of one hundred copies in September 1928; *A Draft of*

XXX Cantos came out from Nancy Cunard's Hours Press in August 1930, in an edition of 210 copies.

It will simplify consideration of the XVII–XXX group to select three core states-of-being (compare, once more, the Schifanoia frescoes). There is (1) the earthly paradise which is serenity, to be distinguished from various kinds of ecstatic vision presented here and earlier. It is projected as vision in unreal lights. With it are placed (2) modes of existence that favour its coming to be, chiefly taken from the Italian fifteenth century; and (3) states that make unlikely its coming to be, chiefly taken from the early twentieth century. I shall exemplify them respectively from Cantos XVII; XXI and XXV; and XIX.

(i) CANTO XVII

It appears that this Canto has a protagonist (the speaker, Zagreus/Pound, or perhaps 'noman'). (In the *Odyssey* that is what Odysseus calls himself, in a pun, and Pound picks up the pun to help make the epic's speaker merely the mouthpiece of his 'tribe's' experience.) But the protagonist merely moves and sees or makes love by creek, palace, cliff or almond-tree. Means of locomotion and reason for locomotion are faded out. The geography does not appear to be traceable, and there is not the profusion of specifics about place and time that, in the Malatesta Cantos, suggests traceability even where no reader is likely to be able to follow it all. We are told that one of these settings is a little farther on than the previous one, or 'To the left'. The plot is a shift between seen dream-actions, sketchily located in a single dream-world: Diana moving with her hounds, a sea-progress by a Botticellian goddess, 'Zagreus, feeding his panthers', a vibrant stone forest at which craftsmen and heroes arrive, enigmatic encounters with goddesses, the dancing of nymphs. Thus:

> With the first pale-clear of the heaven
> And the cities set in their hills,
> And the goddess of the fair knees
> Moving there, with the oak-wood behind her,
> The green slope, with white hounds
>   leaping about her;
> And thence down to the creek's mouth, until evening,
> Flat water before me,
>   and the trees growing in water,
> Marble trunks out of stillness,

On past the palazzi,
                    in the stillness,
The light now, not of the sun.
                    Chrysophrase,
And the water green clear, and blue clear;
On, to the great cliffs of amber.
                              Between them,
Cave of Nerea,
        she like a great shell curved,
And the boat drawn without sound,
Without odour of ship-work,
Nor bird-cry, nor any noise of wave moving,
Nor splash of porpoise, nor any noise of wave moving,
Within her cave, Nerea,
                        she like a great shell curved
In the suavity of the rock [. . .]

Zagreus, feeding his panthers,
            the turf clear as on hills under light.
And under the almond-trees, gods,
            with them, *choros nympharum*. Gods,
Hermes and Athene,
                    As shaft of compass,
Between them, trembled

Certain lightings make it cohere. One is a visual sharpness beyond
the usual, made more strange by aural quality ('No gull-cry'):

            the turf clear as on hills under light

– where the light is apparently a non-light that emanates from
everywhere. In passages where the light is described as non-natural
('The light now, not of the sun'), the Canto reaches an effect perhaps
like that in Douanier Rousseau's *Snake Charmer*. But while this effect
is 'super-real', it is no more so than that in those other passages where
the light is described as being of a natural first-light:

            With the first pale-clear of the heaven
            And the cities set in their hills

For while these are all parts of iconographic traditions, they also have
relatives in what oneself can experience with one's own two eyes,
walking on one's own feet. Even prose-writers notice the super-reality
of real dawn lights:

The gray half-tones of daybreak are not the gray half-tones of the day's close, though the degree of their shade may be the same. In the twilight of the morning light seems active, darkness passive [...]

Being so often – possibly not always by chance – the first two persons to get up at the dairy-house, they seemed to themselves the first two persons up of all the world [...] The spectral, half-compounded, aqueous light which pervaded the open mead, impressed them with a feeling of isolation, as if they were Adam and Eve. At this dim inceptive stage of the day Tess seemed to Clare to exhibit a dignified largeness both of disposition and physique, an almost regnant power [...] (*Tess of the d'Urbervilles*, ch. 20)

And as, seen in such lights, things have a more-than-selfness, so they also seem to participate in some deeper common substance. This perhaps gives rise to that sense of an inbinding, one-making force, which is the trigger of famous passages in Emerson. And long before Emerson it may have led Neoplatonists to conceive of an emanating, one-making Source from which the multiple reality of the universe streamed in fading stages.

Second, these lights are Eleusinian, or of Pound's version of the Eleusinian cult. This appears to be Dis's kingdom, inhabited by Persephone (Koré):

> Koré through the bright meadow

Here Zagreus presides, god of the ecstasy that is both the door to this vision-underworld, and the result of ritual union between various goddesses and various gods or heroes. The light is therefore thus strange because this is an equivalent to Dis's Hades; but it is a new kind of 'underworld', obviously identifiable with the Earthly Paradise that Dante sets at the top of the Mount of Purgatory – as Pound announced (*TC*, 73).

Dante makes us think of the Queen of Hades when we see Matilda in his Earthly Paradise:

> '[...] Tu mi fai rimembrar, dove e qual era
> Proserpina nel tempo che perdette
> la madre lei, ed ella primavera'
> (*Purgatorio*, 28.49–51)

'You make me recall where, and of what kind, was Proserpina, [future

Queen of Hell,] when her mother lost her, and she the spring.' That
'where', Enna, is recalled by the flowerets of Dante's Earthly Paradise,
and the grassy margin of the stream; but the unreal breeze and the
strange light fuse the Paradise with Hades:

> [that water] hideth nought,
> although it moves dark, dark,
>   under the unchanging shade, that never
>   lets sun shine there, or moon.
>   (*Purgatorio*, 28.30–3)

Other elements in Canto XVII have different origins. Landscape:
slopes, creeks, 'Marble trunks', palazzi, 'cliffs of amber', caves, cuts in
hills, 'the great alley of Memnons', shores, again 'the great forest of
marble', with 'silver beaks rising and crossing', caves by the sea,
meadow. Some of it may have been suggested by Pier della Francesca or
Ghirlandaio. Some is Venice heightened:

> Marble trunks out of stillness,
> On past the palazzi

The metaphor of a forest for Venice's thick multiplicity of pillars is here
developed into a full metamorphosis of trunk into marble:

> ' the stone trees – out of water –
> ' the arbours of stone –
> ' marble leaf, over leaf

As in Rousseau, this sense of sap and growth is made by rhythm of
trunks, seeming too many to be grasped; this visual multiplicity is then
added to by others of different kinds, also having their origins in Venice
memories of Pound's youth:

> ' silver, steel over steel,
> ' silver beaks rising and crossing,
> ' prow set against prow,
> ' stone, ply over ply,
> ' the gilt beams flare of an evening'

Gondolas on the canals; and 'the lit cross-beams, that year', in the
Morosini palace,[1] which we may remember from Canto III; and also the
gondola-workshops opposite Pound's garret:[2]

> Bronze gold, the blaze over the silver,
> Dye-pots in the torch-light

Between these landscapes and the fauna that inhabit them there is a sympathy. Koré's 'bright meadow' in this Canto might have come out of Ovid; from Ovid, Pound seems to see a line of descent in such scenes to Arnaut Daniel and writers of Provençal *pastorelas*, thence to the ballads of Cavalcanti and to Dante; by another route to the *trouvères* and the *Roman de la Rose*, whence to a pictorial tradition eventually including Pisanello's settings, out of tapestries like the *Dame à la Licorne* in the Musée de Cluny. And often in these there are representatives of the beast tribes behaving in sympathy with the more-than-ordinary landscape and with the serene and emotionally charged behaviour of the human beings walking there. Ovid's swans on Lake Pergus, 'near Enna' as CVI, p. 753, says, where Persephone was plucked away, emit sounds that (the phoneme-sequence and cadence suggest) harmonise with the falling waters:

> Haud procul Hennaeis lacus est a moenibus altae,
> nomine Pergus, aquae; non illo plura Caystros
> carmina cygnorum labentibus edit in undis.
> (*Metamorphoses*, 5.385–7)

Human beings in various eras have offered images of beasts for their separated powers. The Italian fifteenth century, around which this section centres, is commonly called the 'Age of Humanism' – meaning, generally, an anthropocentrism in which Greek rationalism played a large part. The label is misleading,[3] for these medieval, 'primitive', perhaps pantheist senses gave the age's art much of its force. It was so in perhaps all the cultural eras that Pound was interested in, except those connected with New England and with Chinese social ethics. Thus the 'small lions' beside St Mark's in Venice, Pound suggests, are a throwback to Ovid of Sulmona, and the execution of such images (on coins or anywhere) is a sign of that *ling*, 'sensibility', that is both godly and anti-usurious (XCVII, p. 675; CIII, p. 736). And thus heroes in the present section have their 'ferae familiares', familiar creatures.[4] In Canto XX, Isotta degli Atti, Sigismondo's mistress, moves in a procession recalling the Triumphs in the Schifanoia frescoes:

> The Khan's hunting leopard, and young Salustio
> And Ixotta; the suave turf

> Ac ferae familiares, and the cars slowly,
> And the panthers, soft-footed.   (XX, p. 94)

And Niccolò d'Este, the 'bullnecked', brings back from the East a leopard, falcons, greyhounds (XXIV, p. 112).

The new pastoralism, full of fauns and satyrs (goat-heels), bridged from Mallarmé and Debussy and Gourmont to Matisse and Stravinsky, changing towards the primitive. Epstein, Brancusi and Gaudier-Brzeska thought it sufficient to carve birds (*Doves III*, 1913; *Maiastra*, 1912; *Birds Erect*, 1914) without story or programme notes. In 1921 D. H. Lawrence wrote 'The Ladybird', in which the hero is called Dionys and preaches totemism to a girl with 'wild-cat' eyes. Pound was part of this movement. Massimo Bacigalupo has noted how the crisis of confidence in about 1920–2 was partly overcome by Pound's reincarnating himself as Dionysus (B*FT*, 34–9). Pound's difficulties with composing the latter part of I–XVI, and with the weaker first Cantos, as we have seen, coincided with the great achievement of *The Waste Land*, which Pound saw in draft at the beginning of January 1922. Perhaps the cultural horrors perfectly caught by that poem proved Pound's intuition: that no half-measures were of use in our present condition. Velleities might have value as linguistic equipment for diagnosis, but a religion based on them would change nothing. It was time to declare one's own religion. Soon Pound had written the Dionysian 'eighth canto', now Canto II; and the present Canto, XVII, seems to have been written very soon after. So the new group begins (after the purgatory of the end of I–XVI) with the bursting of vines from *my* fingers, by way of a resurrection – that of a cat-like priest-king:

> So that the vines burst from my fingers
> And the bees weighted with pollen
> Move heavily in the vine-shoots:
>   chirr – chirr – chir-rikk – a purring sound,
> And the birds sleepily in the branches.
>   ZAGREUS! IO ZAGREUS!
>   (XVII, p. 76)

And so in Canto XVII one may find elements that are Neoplatonic and Eleusinian, as well as stemming from complicated iconographic lineages; but none of these would make this earthly paradise cohere, without the writer's eye for sharp form, cool colour, non-location, and differentiated lights.

(ii)   CANTOS XXI AND XXV

In XVII–XXX, as I have noted, a second layer is largely taken from the
Italian Renaissance: modes of being that favour the manifestation of the
Earthly Paradise. The constructive and godly part of that Renaissance,
as far as these Cantos are concerned, is quite strictly the fifteenth
century: from about 1410 to about 1503. This covers the youth and
manhood of Niccolò III d'Este (d.1441); the 'reigns' of Cosimo de'
Medici (1428–64) and his grandson Lorenzo (1469–92); and the fullest
vigour of Venice. It is what might be called Pound's classic period,
when Este, Medici and Malatesta all had dealings with Venice, and each
of these powers was patron to artists of the level of Bellini (Giovanni),
Pier della Francesca, Carpaccio, Agostino di Duccio and Botticelli;
each of whom is referred to directly or indirectly in this section of the
Cantos.

There is, indeed, here an ur-phase to this renaissance: the origins of
the Doge's Palace in Venice, and its rebuilding from 1340 on. But there
is no reaching forward from the fifteenth century of the constructive
impulse. Titian appears here only for having sat on a painting for
twenty years while he drew his salary, thus making himself victim (in
1522) to a squalid little termination of contract. The sixteenth-century
Medici appear in the person of Lorenzino, murdered 1547 (in revenge
for what he did in Canto V); here certain murky powers are arranging
the assassins' escape. The sixteenth-century Este are present only in the
person of Alfonso I, who married Lucrezia Borgia for the money, took
one look at his new wife and went home. And these Borgias terminate
the section, in the death of Alessandro VI, the second Borgia Pope,
whose son John (Giovanni) was found murdered in the Tiber among the
dramatically lit squalors of Canto V. The whole *Draft of XXX Cantos*
ends with 'Il Papa morì', 'the Pope died', and the unusual 'Ends canto
XXX'. The end of the Italian fifteenth century was certainly in this
poem's view 'the end of something'; of what, exactly, will be shown by
a close look at Cantos XXI and XXV.

The Este and the Medici are the first social constructors in the
Cantos. Like Sigismondo Malatesta they cut their way through circumstance, as through 'chopped seas' (*Mauberley*); they have that
Odyssean element, to which Sigismondo has already added another
element – the desire ('goddess'-stimulated) to execute a Work that shall
lastingly register his perception. But the Odyssean and the Malatestan
do not encompass (except marginally) the aim of building a peace for

the commonweal, of leaving the memory of good government as a trace
of higher value than monuments. That is a new element found in the
Este and the Medici. Also new are the large-scale operations of finance
used for peace. Sigismondo was brief in time, and marginal in the
economy of Europe. With his aims he had no need to find methods that
would connect him lastingly and fruitfully into the systems that
surrounded him. If money were required, another campaign would
bring it; in whose service, it did not signify.

Pound was to write that he and his fellow literary revolutionaries in
the early days had found it sufficient to rebel against all non-private
emotion (*GK*, 291) (the non-private corresponded to the false). The
Malatesta Cantos had been written partly under the influence of
Hemingway:[5] individual vigour, and understated sense of private
vulnerability, were enough. Now, before the Depression made it
fashionable, Pound was looking for durable modes of social being.
Canto XXI starts with the popular cry to Borso d'Este, the illegitimate
son of Niccolò, to keep on with his peacemaking. The voice of Giovanni
di Bicci, founder of the Medici dynasty, takes up in the second line,
with a fact that was the basis of a hundred years of his family's rule in
Florence: dignity, race and electioneering have no power in the face of
money:

> Keep the peace, Borso!' Where are we?
> 'Keep on with the business,
>   That's made me,
> 'And the res publica didn't.
> 'When I was broke, and a poor kid,
> 'They all knew me, all of these *cittadini*,
> 'And they all of them cut me dead, della gloria.'
>   (XXI, p. 96)

States have economic needs, as do persons, that may cut across their
other interests. Geryon (the monster of fraud) *rompe muri ed armi* –
breaks through walls and weapons – as Pound observed in relation to
the suicide of a friend (*P*, 329; cf. *Inferno*, 17.2). Cosimo de' Medici
demonstrated this power constructively:

> And 'with his credit emptied Venice of money' –
> That was Cosimo –
> 'And Naples, and made them accept his peace.'[6]
>   (XXI, p. 96)

And Piero his son nearly ended the dynasty when, on the interested
advice of Diotisalvi Neroni, he

> called in the credits,
> (Diotisalvi was back of that)
> And firms failed as far off as Avignon,
> And Piero was like to be murdered

For that reason, book-keeping (which for Pound, in this period of his
life, was almost *the* reality) punctuates this passage. The memoirs of
Lorenzo de' Medici note that Giovanni died

> Intestate, 1429, leaving 178,221 florins *di sugello*,
> As is said in Cosimo's red leather note book. Di sugello.

The accountant in Lorenzo automatically records which currency we
are dealing with ('di sugello'); as a joiner speaks, not of plywood, but of
'three-ply Gabon'. This dry precision is found generally in Lorenzo's
Ricordi, where he adds up the family's wealth after each decease, and
tells the future reader where he may check. As rhetoric, Lorenzo's
narrative is simple; but it has Machiavelli's flair for the true locus of
self-interest – source of action – without his fascination with the horrors
that result. Lorenzo's flat wryness is as Machiavelli's. Pound renders
it:

> And in July I went up to Milan for Duke Galeaz
> To sponsor his infant in baptism,
> Albeit were others more worthy,
> And took his wife a gold collar holding a diamond
> That cost about 3000 ducats, on which account
> That signor Galeaz Sforza Visconti has wished me
> To stand sponsor to all of his children.
>   (XXI, p. 98)

But the key to the Medici regime was not barefaced money; it was a
highly refined and laborious combination of patronage with semi-
democratic process, and neither was safe without the other.[7] Lorenzo
puts his finger on this exactly as Machiavelli might have. Pound
compresses a history of conspiracies against the family, and then quotes
what Lorenzo says he said when the leading citizens came to him after
his father's death to ask him to take over:

> E difficile,
> A Firenze difficile viver ricco
> Senza aver lo stato.
>
> (XXXI, p. 97)

Green in politics and reluctant, Lorenzo says, he consented because the interests of his family's party (his 'friends') must be protected; now 'in Florence it is difficult to live as a rich man without controlling the government'.[8]

Pound is attempting to make an analysis of Renaissance realities that will stand with the observation of forces creeping into Europe's power-struggles since the Franco-Prussian War, and hence underlying the Russian Revolution, at the end of the previous set of Cantos. Justification: that the social forms offered by the twentieth century need not be assumed to be the best that history has known — we must consider others, in whole or in part. Requirement: that the analysis be equally steady-eyed and sophisticated. Pound felt that observers like Lorenzo and Machiavelli could provide the materials for this: Machiavelli, whose disgust for the pusillanimous bickering surrounding the Medici is quoted by this Canto:

> Another war without glory, and another peace without quiet.[9]

Medici and Este in these Cantos add social constructivity and economic/political *savoir-faire*, to the ideogram of the achieving man already set up in Odysseus, the tempter of fate, and Malatesta, the temple-builder. Venice adds the 'assumption' of the temple. In the same passage with Lorenzo's deeds comes this:

> And there was grass on the floor of the temple,
> Or where the floor of it might have been;
> > Gold fades in the gloom,
> > Under the blue-black roof, Placidia's,
> Of the exarchate; and we sit here
> By the arena, *les gradins* ...
> And the palazzo, baseless, hangs there in the dawn
> With low mist over the tide-mark;
> And floats there nel tramonto
> With gold mist over the tide-mark.
> The tesserae of the floor, and the patterns.
>
> (XXI, p. 98)

The poem's gaze unfocuses from what seems brief-lasting – Lorenzo's individual political successes – and takes a longer view. The locus of rite had been unused; Lorenzo, the passage perhaps says, brought it back into use, in the form of Botticelli's paintings, for example. One of the manifestations of this recurrent and immaterial temple is the mausoleum at Ravenna, built for the Empress Galla Placidia (388–450) when that place was under the Byzantine Exarchate. It waits, forgotten and hoarding the light in its mosaic: 'Gold fades in the gloom', from Galla's century to Lorenzo's. In the eye of such stretches of time, change of epoch seems instantaneous, and we revert once more to Pound's device of the scene-shift or change of spectacle before the speaker's eyes, as he sits in some Ideal Amphitheatre of History, ancient as the Roman one at Verona: 'and we sit here'. The spectacle we shift to is at Venice. As you come in on the boat, the Canto says, the Doge's Palace is suspended:

> And the palazzo, baseless, hangs there in the dawn

It is a trick of craft, a matter of its great upper mass hanging over a continuous open arcade, and of a relation with invisible waterline. This craft can take one into the double and multiple realities that give a 'sense of sudden liberation [...] from time limits and space limits', as the old definition of the Imagist image said, and that was the feat of the Venetian craftsmen, builders of marble forests.

This building is not in the dualist part of the Romantic tradition, not a Swinburnian 'House of Splendour', woven of light, or a House of Usher, whose cellars are built from no material that one might encounter. This Doge's Palace must have foundations and masses; its being must seem immanent in them. The Palazzo Ducale as seen here has aetiologies, though that is not to say that these exhaust it. Canto XXV traces antecedents, recorded in the Venetian archives. The town council has the usual problems, but there is a certain vigour in the enforcement of regulations: 'if they wont pay/they are to be chucked in the water'. There is this delightful passage concerning certain lions imported as town mascots:

> the said lioness as is the nature of animals
> whelped per naturam three lion cubs vivos et pilosos
> living and hairy which born at once began life and motion
> and to go gyring about their mother throughout the
> aforesaid room as saw the aforesaid Lord Doge

(The notary tries vainly to distance himself from his own naïvety: 'as it were', 'as it were'.) These notes suggest the mental tone of the period. As the foregoing links sunrise with the lioness's whelping, so an edict about an imprisoned Doge casually links the Sacrificial Lamb's lifespan with that of the sun and the year (it is Ascension Day):

> and when first sees the
> Christblood go at once up into the Palace and may
> stay in the Palace VIII days to visit the Doge her
> father

As to more immediate causes: building involves costs, and costs require votes, duly noted here. And, whether the visions of men's minds be great and up-leaping or not, the decision to act on them may arise proximately from something quite trivial: like an overpowering smell. (Pound is often at pains to make us see real splendour cohabiting with a homely stink: useful ammunition against the suburban conception that art, Ideal, arises from subsidised ease and abhors unsmooth surfaces.) So that at last a three-man committee is appointed:

> 1340. Council of the lords noble, Marc Erizio
> Nic. Speranzo, Tomasso Gradonico:
> that the hall
> be new built over the room of the night watch
> and over the columns toward the canal where the walk is ...
>
> ... because of the stink of the dungeons. 1344.
> 1409 ... since the most serene Doge can scarce
> stand upright in his bedroom ...
> vadit pars [agreed], two gross lire
> stone stair, 1415, for pulchritude of the palace
> 254 da parte [254 ayes]
> de non 23 [23 noes]
> 4 non sincere [4 not clear]
>
> Which is to say: they built out over the arches
> and the palace hangs there in the dawn, the mist,
> in that dimness,
> or as one rows in from past the murazzi
> the barge slow after moon-rise
> and the voice sounding under the sail.
>
> (XXV, p. 117)

With this we have penetrated the territory of what is more real than the ordinary. Canto XXV does not offer a formula for doing so, but received aesthetics would not have put together these conditions and this result.

The result (the Palazzo Ducale that people visit and scratch their names on) is located in that territory more firmly still, in what follows. Sulpicia, metamorphosed into a tree, enters that world because she was bold: 'Put aside fear, Cerinthus! God does not harm lovers.' And then is given one of the Cantos' recurrent summaries of the nature of metamorphosis: Anchises lies with Venus, and there arises a transformation of waves to crystal, like the form as foreseen by the sculptor (XXV, pp. 117–18; cf. p. 119, and XXIII, p. 109).

(iii) CANTO XIX

The third element I wish to show in Cantos XVII–XXX is of states, as I have said, that make it unlikely that any earthly paradise will show itself. These are taken almost entirely from our century. They are of the Dantean 'Dark Forest' and the 'Purgatory of human error' that Pound in 1944 said he had schooled himself to traverse in his poem.

'Pound's economics' (his variant of the Social Credit doctrines of C. H. Douglas) occupy only one-fifth of Canto XIX. They might be quite wrong and still leave significant results here, for the same reason that Marx's formulae governing economic futurity might be wrong and still leave a mass of usefully connected historical observation; or Hardy's claims about Inevitability, and still leave the chapters on Tess among the meadows. Pound gets rid of his formulae in the first page of the five-page Canto, with the rest left for grist.

The Douglas doctrines include the point that manipulation of credit breaks enterprises, and channels and thwarts energies. The banks and the great corporations can handle any man who needs credit. When one company can control another, one result is sabotage: if a new invention threatens profits, it may be suppressed. If a man has his own money, rivals can do nothing – except perhaps pay him to retire; in which case the result is the same for the public, a possible benefit dug under:

> And he said: I gawt ten thousand dollars tew mak 'em,
> And I am a goin' tew mak 'em [. . .]
> So he settled for one-half of one million.
> And he has a very nice place on the Hudson,
> And that invention, patent, is still in their desk.
> And the answer to that is: Wa'al he had the ten thousand.

And the next anecdote shows the businessman who wanted to discuss theoretical Marx, till Pound made him see the governing fact: that he, the businessman, was only there in Paris, safe from takeover at home, because he did not need any credit. That, with three vestigial lines of a third story, concludes the doctrinal Douglasism. The rest of the Canto is a bundle of historical observations about wars, finance and revolutions, each in its context essential for the man involved, and perhaps bearing only one common moral: that power is never located where it appears to be.

Thus the truth, Canto XIX says, is not the shining sword it is taken for; it may have no effect at all:

> 'Perfectly true,
> 'But it's a question of feeling,
> 'Can't move 'em with a cold thing like economics.'

And Prishnip, the Princip who started the First World War with an assassination, has none of the qualities we associate with power to move things. And there is that complicated mix of nationalism with ideology that goes into revolutions, rationalised away by academics because it does not fit schemes. The Russian soldiers shoot enemy would-be deserters until the deserters start singing songs of Slav patriotism. Meanwhile there was the war, in which the Austrian financier managed to stay on in London right through, 'and enjoying every Boche victory', because the supra-national military – financial complex required his services there to supply British fleets.

The Canto then goes back to the theme that ended the *Draft of I–XVI*: the shift of power from supra-national aristocratic connections to mass fervours and nationalisms, and to networks of other kinds. The ambassador of Austria-Hungary, Mensdorf, and the Russian ambassador, Benckendorff, and a number of their mutual relatives are in family/political conference in London. Mensdorf, from habit, is on the point of sharing the contents of his dispatches. But war has been declared; those present will be on opposing sides. The old aristocratic network no longer binds: 'No you don't, Albert'[10] – information must no longer be shared:

> Those days are gone by for ever   (XIX, p. 87)

– 'like the cake shops in the Nevsky'.

Much attention is required to grasp the point of these anecdotes. In some cases it seems clear that attention is not enough; for a look at the given passage's source yields a point that is far more significant than what the passage could be taken to mean – more significant in terms of Pound's own doctrines.[11] Pound seems to have abbreviated until the story was incomprehensible apparently because he felt defensive about this material. The new Joyce–Stein aestheticism ruled Paris, and literature about politics was the height of naïvety. Pound goes into his tough-guy voice, and the diction of the 'I' ('Waal haow is it you're over here [...]?') becomes identical with the diction given to Pound's informant, the journalist Lincoln Steffens, laboriously casual:

> Governed. Governed the place from a train   (XIX, p. 86)

But chiefly Pound seems to react with abbreviation and speed, from fear of being obvious. There is a certain tic of sweeping on to another subject before the first can have been around long enough to be thought banal. In economic/political matters Pound very rarely uses paragraphs to show shift in subject, and conversely hides subject-shift in mid-paragraph. A break between lines is merely a pause *before* the punchline. The punchline comes and the verse hurries on, without break, to the next subject. ('And' does not necessarily denote connection; 'he' is probably not the person who was last referred to.) The spacing thus perfectly supports the rhythm of meaning *if* one has previously grasped the stories, but makes stories (whence must derive meaning-rhythm) very hard to grasp in the first place.

Also this stuff has rather slight human density. The whole point of literature about politics – as opposed to pamphlet-logic about politics – is the linking of politics into the realities of human beings as they function and differentiate themselves. The stench of the regime ought to be shown to perspire from the pores of its citizens – who should none the less still be smelled to be themselves. Pound may succeed on the former count, but on the latter he is also in competition with Joyce in 'Counterparts':

> Then he imitated Farrington, saying *And here was my nabs, as cool as you please*, while Farrington looked at the company out of his heavy dirty eyes, smiling and at times drawing forth stray drops of liquor from his moustache with the aid of his lower lip.

Or with Hemingway in 'The Light of the World':

'I wouldn't hurt his career,' the peroxide blonde said.

'I wouldn't be a drawback to him. A wife wasn't what he needed. Oh, my God, what a man he was.'

'That was a fine way to look at it,' the cook said. 'Didn't Jack Johnson knock him out though?'

'It was a trick,' Peroxide said. 'That big dinge took him by surprise. He'd just knocked Jack Johnson down, the big black bastard. That nigger beat him by a fluke.'

The ticket window went up and the three Indians went over to it.

'Steve knocked him down,' Peroxide said. 'He turned to smile at me.'

'I thought you said you weren't on the coast,' someone said.

'I went out just for that fight. Steve turned to smile at me and that black son of a bitch from hell jumped up and hit him by surprise. Steve could lick a hundred like that black bastard.'

'He was a great fighter,' the lumberjack said.

'I hope to God he was,' Peroxide said. 'I hope to God they don't have fighters like that now. He was like a god, he was. So white and clean and beautiful and smooth and fast and like a tiger or like lightning.'

'I saw him in the moving pictures of the fight,' Tom said. We were all very moved. Alice was shaking all over and I looked and saw she was crying. The Indians had gone outside on the platform.

Pound's coda for Canto XIX (tales of the British Raj) hardly stands up to this as exact social recording:

> '[. . .] That was something, 14 girls in a fortnight.'
> 'Healthy but verminous?' 'That's it, healthy but verminous.
>   And one time in Kashmir,
> In the houseboats, with the turquoise,
> A pile three feet high on the boat floor,
> And they'd be there all day at a bargain
> For ten bobs' worth of turquoise.'

(iv) THE SHAPE OF *A DRAFT OF XXX CANTOS*

The divisions so far considered in this chapter have been by theme. But before I consider the patterns that are built from them, in both groups of the book (I–XVI, XVII–XXX), it may be useful to look at the patterns that are built from time-categories in the two groups. In chronology, I–XVI begins with Homer, a starting-point for our culture, and ends with the Russian Revolution and the First World War – a watershed, as Hugh Kenner has noted.[12] XVII–XXX begins with a rather more timeless beginning, when the fertility-god becomes the vine; and ends with the watershed that is the decline of the Renaissance, in 1503. In between, in various collocations, have come the periods in world culture that are valuable to Pound: for example, the Provençal pre-Renaissance (Cantos IV, VI; Canto XX) and the Quattrocento of Malatesta, the Este and Venice (VIII–XI; XXI, XXIV, XXV, XXVI). Their antitheses are taken from the limbos and hells of the nineteenth and early twentieth centuries (VII, XII, XIV–XVI; XVIII, XXII, XXVI, XXVIII). The periods are 'simultaneous' because they are thus interspersed. This has to be so, for without such collocation we could not be made aware, for example, of the Medici element in Thomas Jefferson, or the Sforza element in Napoleon. It is an important principle with Pound that, in time, what matters is (*a*) the waves of cultural causation, which do not respect the clock ('It is dawn at Jerusalem while midnight hovers above the Pillars of Hercules,' he writes, following Dante's erroneous cosmography even in this 'modern' point: *SR*, 6); and (*b*) the recurrence of elements in different eras, without ascertainable cause except perhaps 'human nature'. But there is the other effect of simultaneity, best described by Kenner. In I–XVI:

> The times are mostly transparent, film laid upon film, so that it is equally correct to identify Canto I as Greek fore-time, as Renaissance rediscovery, as Ur-English ('Seafarer') verse, as a reflection of the poet at the start of his career going down to the ship that carried him to the Europe of his great predecessors, and as a piece of writing performed in the 'now' of the poem. Similarly the principal episode in Canto II comes from (1) the Homeric Hymns as rehandled by (2) Ovid in Latin couplets and (3) Ezra Pound in Imagist English [...] There is always a 'now' in which the language on the page before us is being found, analogous to but no longer coincident with the 'now' in which we read it, and the language normally encompasses many times simultaneously. This is perhaps Pound's most profound invention, this way of seeing the past, many pasts, without nostalgia: active now, in the words.[13]

Meanwhile there is a principle of non-simultaneity, in the suggestion that historical causation can be traced in sequence. Pound worried about how to get in the Cantos from Ovid's metamorphoses to now: 'I dare say it wd. be easier to cut the 7 preceding cantos [Canto II stood, when he wrote this, as Canto VIII] & let Acoetes continue = only I dont see how I cd. get HIM to Bayswater' (*PF*, 67). The position of the Purgatorial material at the end of the group I–XVI is evidently part of the answer: it is that arrival at 'now', in the form of the First World War and the Russian Revolution. The position of the Renaissance typecutters and the death of Pope Alexander VI in 1503 at the end of the group XVII–XXX has a similar meaning: that was a significant staging-post in the arrival at 'now'. And these materials would not seem to have significance as causal staging-posts if they were not placed as closures for the two groups.

That suggestion of a sequence of events is reflected in the larger sequence of material in the Cantos, which already, by XXX, is tending to move from past to present. The Italian fifteenth century dominates the group XVII–XXX, while earlier periods were equally important in I–XVI. In XVII–XXX, the essentially eighteenth-century figure Thomas Jefferson appears; the next book of Cantos, XXXI–XLI, will be subtitled in his name. In the Fifth Decad of Cantos, the Renaissance and earlier periods will remain in the background; the centre will be Siena in the seventeenth century and Florence in Jefferson's time. The last prewar group of Cantos will make a huge divagation to cover the whole of Chinese history, but then will devote an equal number of pages to Jefferson's contemporary, John Adams. At that point, what might appear to be a movement towards 'now' stops entirely, and an entirely new set of time-movements begins. By these nods at chronological succession are reinforced underlying arguments about the determination of one cultural era by its predecessors: the usurious nineteenth century, for example, by the moral and spiritual collapse of the Church in the time of Alexander VI Borgia, and by the succeeding vacuum that was filled with the mere philosophy of Jefferson and his contemporaries.

Patterning by theme is a quite different principle, and must tend to run counter to time-patterning. Starting from the simplest divisions, one may see in my earlier theme-sketch of Cantos I–XVI an alternation of the valuable and the hellish. Or one may lay out the aesthetic/moral groupings offered for Cantos XVII–XXX in this chapter, and obtain the following pattern:

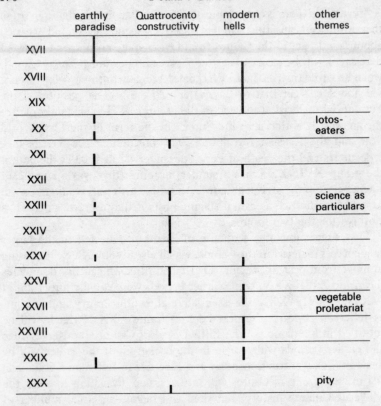

The Earthly Paradise is established in the first Canto of the section, and returned to as a ground-tone roughly every other Canto. The historical past that has shown how to penetrate this sanctum – the Quattrocento – occupies the middle, XX–XXVI, with only one major break. That break allows the anti-theme, modern hells and limbos, not only to straddle the Italian Renaissance (almost beginning and ending the section), but also to place one foot in the middle of it, heightening contrast.

This placing of contrasting materials next to each other is the simplest art practised by any composer who does not want to bore the listener. Looking for more meaningful patterns, one can note with Hugh Kenner that in I–XXX four Cantos, the Malatesta group, which are documentary and concern construction, are followed by fiscal perversion (XII) and Confucius' 'timeless order' (XIII). Then in

XXXI–XLI, the four opening American Cantos, also documentary and concerning construction, are likewise followed by 'Mitteleuropean perversion' (XXXV) and 'Cavalcanti's timeless order' (XXXVI). And, if in this way we consider the Malatesta group as a beginning, we may arrive at sequences of the following kind in the first three books:

		VIII–XVI	*XVII–XXX*	*XXXI–XLI*
1	Revolution/ construction	Malatesta (VIII– XI)	Dionysus (XVII)	Jefferson (XXXI– XXXIII)
2	Materialist mess	Baldy Bacon (XII)	Metevsky (XVIII), Prishnip (XIX)	Mitteleuropa (XXXV)
3	Temple and/or light	Confucius (XIII)	Ideal landscape (XX), Doge's Palace (XXI)	Cavalcanti (XXXVI)
4	Construction		Building Doge's Palace (XXV)	Van Buren (XXXVII)
5	Materialist mess	First World War (XVI)	England in black darkness (XXVII)	Metevsky, Krupp (XXXVIII)
6	Mysteries		Apollo (XXIX)	Flora's night (XXXIX)

NOTES: CHAPTER 8

1 Pound in A. Jung and G. Palandri (eds), *Italian Images of Ezra Pound* (Taipei: Mei Ya Publications, 1979), pp. 144–5: '"Morosini" means palazzo Morosini [. . .] one gondoled on the Grand Canal and the ceilings were LIT from the lights in the Palazzi [. . .]'

2 See V. Contini, *Ezra Pound in Italy* (New York: Rizzoli International, 1978).

3 See my summary of Raffaello Morghen's argument, in 'Pound's Provence and the medieval paideuma', in P. Grover (ed.), *Ezra Pound: The London Years* (New York: AMS Press, 1978), pp. 58–60.

4 It is interesting that in English the usage 'familiar (animal)' arises at about the same time as 'familiar (spirit)', both being later than the general sense 'household, intimate'.

5 Pound consulted Hemingway on the terrain and tactics of some of Malatesta's military activities.

6 From Machiavelli's *Istorie fiorentine*, bk 7, ch. 5.

7 See N. Rubinstein, *Lorenzo de' Medici: The Formation of His Statecraft* (Oxford: Oxford University Press, 1978), passim.

8 'Aver lo stato' in this Canto is sometimes mistranslated. For the usage, see ibid., p. 75; F. Schevill, *The Medici* (New York: Harper & Row, 1960), p. 117; and cf. Machiavelli's usage in the remark next quoted in Canto XXI, from *Istorie fiorentine*, bk 7, ch. 7.

9 ibid., 5.2: 'e così per la guerra non acquistavano gloria ne per la pace quiete'.

10 The history of the text suggests that the current editions' question mark at this point

was not intended by Pound. 'And the rest of it' (p. 87) refers to 'Das thust du nicht' (p. 86).

11 Compare XIX, p. 86, with Lincoln Steffens, *The Autobiography of Lincoln Steffens* (New York: Harcourt Brace Jovanovich, 1958), p. 730; Steffens tells the Mexicans to dig down through the roadsides and stream-beds (as *TC*, p. 79, does not make clear). Also cf. XIX, pp. 86–7, with Steffens, *Autobiography*, p. 590.

12 '*Drafts & Fragments* and the structure of the *Cantos*', in *Agenda*, vol. 8, no. 3–4 (Autumn–Winter 1970), p. 8.

13 ibid.

CHAPTER 9

Commentary: Cantos XXXI–XLI ('Jefferson: Nuevo Mundo')

This new book of Cantos was published in 1934, as *Eleven New Cantos XXXI–XLI* (it received the subtitle 'Jefferson: Nuevo Mundo' in postwar British collections). Since 1930 (*A Draft of XXX Cantos*) Pound had continued, from his small-town Italian base, his long-distance research with the help of correspondents into American history and economic actualities. From these came *ABC of Economics*, in 1933, and *Jefferson and/or Mussolini*, finished in the same year. Pound finally met Mussolini in 1933. His attempts to define the principles of good writing and the canon of world literature were refined down from his early letters to Iris Barry, into *How to Read* (1931) and then *ABC of Reading* (1934). In 1934 the best of his literary essays were collected in *Make It New*, work mainly done (except for the Cavalcanti part) by 1919. (The postwar *Literary Essays* is a slightly refashioned version of *Make It New*.) Perhaps Pound's last involvement with a genuinely new group of writers was with the 'Objectivists', led by his combative old friend William Carlos Williams, and numbering among them the Northumbrian Basil Bunting and the New Yorker Louis Zukofsky. Pound encouraged and criticised and helped to get them published in anthologies. With Bunting's help, Pound gathered a small group of musicians and, beginning in 1933, arranged a series of concerts that included first performances of rediscovered work (William Young, Vivaldi) and early performances of new work, like Bartók's. The concerts were planned on 'ideogramic' principles, so that 'blocks' by different composers should shed as much light as possible on each other. Meanwhile Pound had struggled with the economics of publishing to bring out his edition of the *Rime* of Guido Cavalcanti in 1932; and had summarised some religious thinking in 'Terra Italica' (1931/2). All this bore fruit directly or indirectly in the Cantos.

The concerns of the new group (XXXI–XLI) fall into three areas:

(1)   The intelligence with the special mobility required for political action: Jefferson and Mussolini, with perhaps Hanno as an analogy. (Finance is one of the areas of its action.)

(2)   The developing financial criminality of the eighteenth, nineteenth and twentieth centuries, and the line of heroes against it: Jefferson, Adams, John Quincy Adams, Van Buren, Douglas, Mussolini.

(3)   The matter of love, and resultant deeper knowledges: Cavalcanti (clarity of thought), Eleusis (directed energy).

Among the complexes that will not go into these categories, but clarify them by contrast, are: John Quincy Adams's assumption that there can be probity in public affairs; his deficient capacity for seizing political opportunity, whence his secondary position in the Cantos as prophetic denouncer (compare Tiresias); and, continuing this descent into will-less-ness, the 'tropisms', cultural predispositions as mere vegetable growths, and the crimes that they permit (see again the second category, above). I shall pass over these and dwell on the Cantos and groups of Cantos that illustrate the central themes most clearly.

(i)   POLITICS AND MOBILITY: CANTOS XXXI, XXXII, XXXIII

These three documentary Cantos concern Thomas Jefferson and John Adams, third and second presidents of the United States, and the 'age of usury' that followed theirs. Perhaps the whole disposition that Pound presents in the Jefferson sections is in this single line:

.. difference ascribed to our superiority in taking aim when we fire ..
                                                        (XXXIII, p. 161)

Jefferson wrote this to a friend of the united colonies in 1778 – at which point he was confident that the Revolutionaries would win. The American loss had been about half the British:

In some instances more, but in others less. This difference is ascribed to our superiority in taking aim when we fire; every soldier in our army having been intimate with his gun from his infancy.

The phrases as excerpted in the Canto have a slightly different effect
from the source-passage: they perhaps even carry the suggestion that
our superiority lies in the fact that we take aim when we fire: the others
do not. But at any rate the parable in both cases potentially implies a
contrast between those who act efficiently at the moment of action and
those who put all their effort into inflexible theorising or complex
equipment. The many parallels offered in the three Cantos will realise
these potential meanings in the readers's mind, and also the further
element specified in the source-passage: ability to apply various but
concrete experience. At the same time they will universalise the
applications of these meanings.

The moment of acting is what matters; and so, as George Kearns has
said,[1] these Cantos are full of specifications of time:

> '.. this was the state of things in 1785 ...'
>
>   (Mr Jefferson.)
>   (**XXXI**, p. 156)

(It is not the state of things now). And on the same page:

> .. met by agreement, about the close of the session –
> Patrick Henry, Frank Lee and your father,
> Henry Lee and myself .... to consult ... measures
> circumstances of times seemed to call for ...
> produce some channel of correspondence ... this was in '73
>   Jefferson to D. Carr

Here, as any student with the date 1776 in his head may infer, is a seed
of the Revolution: the establishing of committees of correspondence
between the colony legislatures to counter British measures. It is a seed
planted in due time, like the small beginnings of the 'new economics' in
the *New Age* office during the First World War, when Douglas's
theories began to influence Pound, or Mussolini in the office of *Il
Popolo* (see Canto XLVI).

The Cantos do not suggest a calculus for predicting the due time but,
rather, that circumstances will never repeat in the same combinations,
and so will never call for quite the same actions. It is something like
textures and organisms that count, for which one needs concrete
knowledge. The pre-Revolution French intellectuals had only 'raw
ideology', and hence, in some degree, the horrors of the Revolution
(suggests Adams, looking back):

'When Lafayette harangued you and me and John Quincy Adams
'through a whole evening in your hotel in the Cul de Sac ....
' .... silent as you were. I was, in plain truth as astonished
'at the grossness of his ignorance of government and history,
'as I had been for years before at that of Turgot,
'La Rochefoucauld, of Condorcet and of Franklin.'
　　　　　To Mr Jefferson, Mr John Adams.
　　　　　　　　　　　　　　　　　　　　　(XXXI, p. 155)

Circumstance is a sea, as presented vividly by the first page of Canto
XXXII, covering the Revolutionary period: voyages, gun-running,
fifth columns, using French alliances with Indian princes against the
British enemy. Jefferson is not shown as paralysed; he does not wait for
time-patterns to clear themselves into an easy symmetry before acting,
and is aware that, synchronously, real forces have a very unsymmetrical
relation with patterns seen on the surface. The organising of the
committees of correspondence, and Jefferson's voluminous quoted
snippets of letters on all subjects, indicate this. The committees sought
out live (unofficial) centres of intelligence and activity, and connected
them. Jefferson's quoted letters are communication from unofficial
centre of awareness to unofficial centre of awareness. If Jefferson had
waited for a 'symmetrical education' (as Pound described T. S. Eliot's)
and for proper libraries before putting himself *au courant* with English,
French and colonial economics, history, governmental practice, there
might never have been a Revolution – or the chance (which later came
to him) to found the Library of Congress himself. He went ahead and
educated himself, sought out intelligent men, and put himself in
contact with them, not on the basis of institutional authority but of
what he had to tell them. In these Cantos he lectures Patrick Henry on
provisioning, the French Foreign Minister on taxation systems, and
James Madison on architecture. Superficial minds, Pound noted,
accused him of superficiality,[2] because he was not an expert in all these
things; but it is no use knowing it all if you are too late.

Thus he and his friends set up an unofficial government, which was
the communication between, and propaganda of, a few dozen Samuel
Adamses, Hancocks, Patrick Henrys, and which preceded the institutions set up by the United States, and to a considerable degree persisted
after those had become a reality. Pound's prose of 1933 draws a conclusion for democratic institutions:

Jefferson thought the formal features of the American system would work, and they did work till the time of General Grant but the condition of their working was that inside them there should be a *de facto* government composed of sincere men willing the national good.

(*J/M*, 94–5)

The institutional framework will not preserve freedoms; there must be responsible men willing to act, and they must have the extra instinct for seizing the moment. Jefferson and John Adams both had this quality, but it declined in Adam's descendants; thus in John Quincy Adams, in the Canto immediately following these three. Henry Adams, in the 1860s, lacked

the one quality needful for judging action. Adams never guessed right. Take him in London during his father's embassy. He never foresaw. (*P*, 149)

To take another nugget of 'moral fact':

removal wd. be necessary to more able commissaries rather than to a more plentiful country. (T.J. on provisions.) (XXXIII, p. 161)

Jefferson here says that the problem is the men in charge, not the circumstances. This can become a parable of abundance. Men fail, and then blame circumstance, and erect screens of excuses – such as those Jefferson clears away in the same letter:

If the troops cd. be fed upon long letters, I believe the gent. at the head of that dept. (in this country) wd. be the best commissary on earth. (XXXIII, p. 160)

Men evade problems, deceive, dodge, and then cling to their obscurantisms because they believe that if these little fakes are swept away there will be nothing left for them. They have no faith in themselves or in 'what is' – unlike Jefferson, a radical optimist. Thus fear combines with greed, and the ultimate product is kingship. 'The doctrines of Europe were,' Jefferson says, 'that men in numerous associations cannot be restrained within the limits of order and justice, but by forces physical and moral, wielded over them by authorities independent of their will. Hence their organization of kings, hereditary nobles, and priests. Still further to constrain the brute force of the people' – and here Canto XXXII takes it up – they

... deem it necessary to keep them down by hard labour, poverty, ignorance,
and to take from them, as from bees, so much of their earnings
as that unremitting labour shall be necessary to obtain a sufficient surplus
barely to sustain a scant life. And these earnings
they apply to maintain their privileged orders in splendour and idleness
to fascinate the eyes of the people ... as to an order of superior beings ...
                                            June 12, '23 to Judge Johnson ..

The Canto does not quote those parts of the above letter that relate it
particularly to aristocracy and kingship. This leaves it capable of a more
general application to exploitative cliques, so that it fits with the drift
of the Adams fragments quoted in Canto XXXIII: that in democracies
as elsewhere, human nature tends towards the formation of interested
groups, which perpetuate themselves into overt or hidden aristocracies.

The general movement of these three Cantos is from Jefferson's agile
constructive optimism towards Adams's gloom about the manipulations
to come. The reader will be aware of this movement whether or not he
correlates quotations with their sources; and this movement reflects the
tendency of history in that period (say, 1760–1826), in Pound's view.
Pound's purpose is not to make his reader digest the detail of 'blocks of
three columns of printed matter' (*P*, 313), but to make him aware of a
mechanism, and that it operated in a certain period. But to nail down
the contemporaneity of these concerns Pounds in the last two and a half
pages of Canto XXXIII makes time (hitherto in these three Cantos
involuted upon itself) unroll towards the present. Marx takes over as
the sole source. Each fragment used shows greed, of a persistence and
ingenuity amounting to the monstrous. Not unworthily of the glitter-
ing-coated Geryon in Dante, fraud covers itself with the language of
law. The combined drive accords with that of the source in Marx: that
the working person was driven to death where not inconvenient, and
reforming measures were allowed to go no further than a modicum of
self-interest on the part of the manufacturers dictated. There is a hero –
the Inspector Leonard Horner – but no victory. But the source that
takes over after Marx is Bessedovsky's memoirs of work as a senior
Soviet diplomat under Stalin; and this shows that, whatever Marx's
value as a critic, Marxism is no guarantee of a successful revolution. At
the centre of the American revolution was intelligence, drawing
knowledge to itself; at the centre of the Stalin web was stupidity, and
information was unable to penetrate it:

for ten years our (Russian) ambassadors have enquired what theories are in fashion in Moscow and have reported their facts to fit.[3]

(XXXIII, p. 163)

And so, the last two fragments suggest, the Soviet state was bled by the (Western) bankers and its own functionaries[4] on much the same terms as, according to the Cantos, the English people had been bled for two centuries. And the Americans: the end of the Canto comes from a speech made in the United States Senate on 25 February in the year of publication of this Canto (1931). It shows the Federal Reserve Board, a government-appointed institution, acting as an agent for private interests. A meeting of the Board decides to deflate (which will hurt small businesses); the bankers present pass on this decision confidentially to their big-business customers, who hasten to borrow.

(ii) CAVALCANTI: CANTO XXXVI

The Jefferson Cantos were about a kind of action that is not of the book of rules; can only be justified by the way its totality is seen to fit the totality of its time. Canto XXXVI is likewise about a kind of knowing that is likewise not of the book of rules. It is connected with passion, and a vigorous delight in things – 'openness to experience', in Marianne Moore's phrase, but not as a mere receptacle or videotape, however brilliantly sharp. Concerning this knowing, Canto XXXVI gets a certain number of precisions, wanted by Pound, into his long poem; and demonstrates that such precisions can be got into poems.

The larger part of the Canto is a translation from Guido Cavalcanti's 'philosophical canzone', the *Donna mi prega*. Cavalcanti was Dante's older contemporary and 'first friend'; his verse is difficult and was never popular in the manner of Petrarch's, but has had a certain following, for example among Dante, Boccaccio, Ficino and Lorenzo de' Medici.

Canto XXXVI's kind of verbal precision is to be a correspondence with things, qualities, actions, states genuinely known by the user. (As we shall see, neither 'felt', 'experienced', nor 'understood' is right here.) This proper kind of knowing will necessarily be impassioned knowing; the meaning of which I shall explain later. For this reason, love, as of poet for lady, is a suitable primary subject-matter for the poem.

Getting these precisions into verse, and into the long poem, does not mean merely putting them into a long tract of writing labelled 'poetry'.

The way to communicate is by form; and verse organises forms, major
and minor, into what Pound calls 'as it were one single word. Made
organic' (*OS*, 1265), the whole integrated to enact the meaning. The
Cavalcanti original was a song. It is hard to read it without setting up
dance-rhythms:

> Ond' a'l presENTE
> > chonoscENTE
> > > ChERO
> Perch' i no SpERO
> > ch om di basso chORE

It is heavily patterned with rhymes, inciting this dance; consonant- and
vowel-play add cross-strokes. Pound set himself to render, shape by
shape, an already-shaped artefact; some of which, whether images or
sound-shapes, would have to go. And so he abandons the attempt to
copy the half-rhymes, except once or twice:

> A lady asks me
> > I speak in sEASON
> She seeks rEASON for an affect, wild often [. . .]
> Its being and every mOVing
> Or delIGHT whereby 'tis called 'to lOVE'
> Or if man can show it to sIGHT.

For the Italian foot-tapping partly depends on the unstressed ending,
hard to find in English, as well as on strict syllable-count, hard to follow
in a literal version. Pound can suggest half-rhymes when he cannot hit
them:

> Wherefore I speak to the present KNOWers
> Having no HOPE that LOW-hearted

For the rest he must rely on occasional successes of irregular and
intricate consonant-play:

> ForMed Like a DiaFan FroM Light on shade

– and the vowel-sequence inwoven. Occasionally a line with close
assonance may be liturgical –

> Himself his own effect unendingly

– or with alliteration may be Elizabethan:

> And his strange quality sets sighs to move

These are prize-lines that heighten the whole, since Pound contrives not to detract from their effect with surrounding verse that tries to be splendid and fails; instead he makes the surroundings rather neutral.

He establishes a diction classical ('Who heareth, seeth not form') but not ornate, and avoids banality of iteration in a cadence which, even where prosaic, keeps its suggestion of singability with a leaven of Sappho-like patterns: drawing all to his stillness', 'the white light that is allness'. But a suggestion of the aural form is all that Pound can reach to, since the major interest of the translation is in the image-forms and the way they are articulated into 'grand image' (philosophy).

A great deal of philosophy adheres to the Canzone, though the terms may seem bland and opaque. (In what follows I keep strictly to what seems to be Pound's understanding of this philosophy.[5]) Now in literature, 'seems' is 'is'; if the philosophy is not felt to be there, it is not there. Pound takes two steps concerning this. First, he enriches the image-terms of this Canto with later glosses, throughout the rest of the long poem. Second, in his contemporary prose, he tells us about a cultural material that we would find it worth our while to ponder, so that (among other things) we would bring it to his verse as we bring knowledge of the Bible to a Brontë. Thus reading his essay 'Cavalcanti' (E, 149–200), one may get to know his idea of some of the medieval world-pictures implied by this poem's terms. (Cavalcanti had not this problem; he was versifying a philosophy that at least consisted of variants on philosophies known to all his hearers.)

The thing thus known here is Love. It is known by *contemplatio*:

> In one receipt for 'contemplation' I find that it properly should imply contemplation of divine things, from which *Amore* is omitted. It seems possible that Guido is claiming rank for *Amor*. (E, 186)

The lady has asked, where does love live? She is answered:

> Where memory liveth,
>   it takes its state
> Formed like a diafan from light on shade
>
> Which shadow cometh of Mars and remaineth

Now the diaphanous (transparent) body is not a mere receiving inertness, but is a specifically prepared medium; Pound (*E*, 184) compares the air charged to receive the halo of the moon in *Paradiso*, 10.67–9: 'Thus we sometimes see the daughter of Latona [i.e. the moon] girdled, when the air is so impregnated that it retains the thread that makes her belt.'

The part of the soul where Love establishes itself is 'charged' by Mars, standing for 'impulse', Pound tells us. Here one can consider all Pound's talk of volitionism, 'direction of the will': 'The name of the Fascist era is *Voluntas*.' First, there must be an impulse from within the self, before any registering of this awareness can happen.

Love comes from a Form that is derived from understanding a visual form, and takes its place in the intellect possible:

> Cometh from a seen form which being understood
> Taketh locus and remaining in the intellect possible

This intellect possible is also not, Pound insists, an inert vessel. Renan suggests that the 'passive intellect' might be only the faculty of receiving 'phantasmata'; Pound replies:

> This is exactly what I think it is NOT in Guido Cavalcanti. The terms *intellectus possibilis*, POSSIBLE, and the *Passive* intellect belong to two different schools [...]

(And Pound here lets fly against muddlers of terms.) The intellect possible is the intellect capable of being activated, ready to be activated; and apparently made so – like the memory – by the impulse of the individual himself. Thus love comes from an awareness that can enter and activate a soul *made activable* by some inner impulse. But it also presupposes the light that comes from outside.

This kind of knowing is compatible with – is perhaps enabled by – a sort of vigorous delight in things and sense of attraction towards them. The highest form of it would be Dante's gazing on Beatrice, when he seems to plunge into the god-world like Glaucus. But this understanding is not an Emersonian Idealism, conferred by the activity of the seer's eye and soul on an otherwise shapeless inert world; or an updated version based on Heisenberg. Here it is assumed that shape (which amounts to meaning) pre-exists man's perception of it. It is also assumed that 'informing shape' (inherent in a thing) is continuous with 'understanding of informing shape' (whereby it passes into the apprehender's mind): that the 'meaning' of a thing passes into the human soul and there subsists ('Where memory liveth') without ceasing to inhere in the thing itself. That which in*forms*, gives deep shape/meaning to, the lady – namely her *forma* – is distinct from her mere visual form (her physical shape). When the lover has looked at her visual form, and, by understanding it, realised her underlying inherent Form in his mind, this passes into his possible (activatable) intellect: for Love

> Cometh from a seen form which being understood
> Taketh locus and remaining in the intellect possible

Indeed in such medieval philosophy all true understanding is of Forms, 'Intelligibles' – the deep (not merely visible) structures.

There fixed (in the lover's now-activated soul), love suffers no diminution or change:

> Descendeth not by quality but shineth out
> Himself his own effect unendingly
> Not in delight but in the being aware

As I have noted, 'Himself his own effect unendingly' has a liturgical sound; and this Love seems like an immutable principle, giving light, but not diminishing thereby. The known Form, indeed, is connected to a universal informing Principle, continuously imparting both deep structure to what was mere contingent matter, and understanding of those deep structures.

That is implied in the term 'intellect possible', which fascinated Pound. 'Ready to be activated' implies the existence of something that can activate. Some medieval thinkers considered this to be the agent intellect, within the human soul: the agent intellect took from seen things their Forms, which then 'moved and informed' the intellect possible. But this agent intellect was somehow both light-like, and, in its action, tending in the direction of godhead. For according to a text quoted by Pound in his writings on Cavalcanti (*E*, 186):

The possible intellect, receiving the things that are readied for it to observe, [as intelligibles], takes into itself, with them, the light of the agent intellect, to which it becomes day by day more similar. And when the possible intellect has received all the observed or under-

stood things, it has the light of the agent intellect adhering to it like a
Form.

(Canto LI will take this up: 'That hath the light of the doer; as it were/a
form cleaving to it.')

[...] And the intellect that comes to be composed from the possible
and the agent intellect is the adept intellect, and is called divine; and
at this point the man is perfected [...] And through this intellect
man is made in a certain way similar to God [Canto LI: 'Deo similis
quodam modo'], in that he can thus perform divine acts, and
dispense to himself and to others divine intelligibles, and receive all
intelligibles in a certain measure; and this is that knowing that all
men desire, in which consists contemplative felicity.[6]

Now Canto LI, it will have been noted, translates 'the light of the
agent intellect' as 'the light of the doer'; and has the phrase in a context
of skilled, intuitive, craftsmanlike *making*. In this analogy, the craftsman (or artist) intuitively seizes Forms and imprints them on the
readied understanding;[7] and his 'light', his own mode of perception and
way of being, are always there impregnated into the concepts he has
embodied, and hence into the understanding of the recipient, glowing
from it and from these Forms themselves.

Here a far-reaching analogy suggests itself: for God is the supreme
Craftsman. Accordingly, some philosophers in the 'Arabian background' to Cavalcanti's poem (Pound's phrase: *E*, 158) placed the agent
intellect much nearer to God, outside man. Alfarabi, Gilson tells us,
spoke of

the agent intellect, a subsisting spiritual being, who presides over this
sublunary world and confers both forms on its matter and actual
knowledge on all its intellects [...]

(And here the tone becomes liturgical; compare Pound's Neoplatonising translation of the *Chung Yung – The Unwobbling Pivot –* in *C*, 179–
87.)

The agent intellect is immutable in his action as he is in his being.
Eternally radiating all the intelligible forms, he does not care in what
matters nor in what intellects they may happen to be received.

This agent intellect is a divine principle, part of a chain both coming down from Heaven and connecting man's illumination (his understanding) with Heaven:

> [...] this Intelligence is not the supreme cause. Other Intellects rise in tiers above it according to a hierarchical order, and all are subordinated to the First, who resides in his inaccessible solitude. Man's ultimate end is to be united, through intellect and love, and to the separate agent intellect, who is the immediate immovable mover and the source of all intelligible knowledge for the world in which we live.[8]

Thus as the agent intellect is to the possible intellect; as sunlight is to our eye; so God is to the mind of heaven; the light gives Form to the enlightened:

> Shines
> in the mind of heaven   God
> who made it
> more than the sun
> in our eye.
>
> (LI, p. 250)

In Pound's interpretation of the Cavalcanti poem, Love 'toucheth his aim' – enters the soul – when there occurs a certain concentration of the faculties, later described. This happens, as we have seen, 'Where memory liveth', which, Pound says (*E*, 184), St Albert identifies with the 'possible intellect'. Pound himself takes it that the Form of the lady marks itself on the charged medium within the 'possible intellect' ('The "formato locho" is the tract or locus marked out in the "possible intelletto"': *E*, 188). Two things then occur. First, this internalised Form, gazed upon, arouses the spiritual fire:

> And his strange quality sets sighs to move
> Willing man look into that forméd trace in his mind
> And with such uneasiness [*ira*] as rouseth the flame [*la qual manda fuoco*]

This *ira*, which Pound long wrestled over, is glossed later in the Cantos as a kind of holy rage leading to further knowledge (LXIII, p. 353). Second, this 'forméd trace' (*formato locho*) becomes itself a storehouse of a higher kind of knowledge, purified of the dross of detail as memory erodes the inessential – perhaps entirely reshaping superficies – so that the essential becomes clear. *Dove sta memoria*, 'where memory liveth',[9] becomes a keying-phrase that denotes this effect of sacred memory, which operates only when the original passion was strong; for

> What thou lovest well remains,
>> the rest is dross
>> (LXXXI, p. 520)

Pound gives Cavalcanti further significance for our age. According to him, the history of our culture has left us with an inert world. (Heisenberg's Uncertainty Principle can be taken as an example. In so far as it has 'philosophical' implications, it suggests a world of quasi-particles whose only relation with man in that he is 'made of' the same, and that his very attempts to describe where they are and how soon they will arrive somewhere else are self-annulling.)

Pound was not satisfied with this, and thought medieval philosophy could help. It could see inherent meaning in the world, by seeing inherent, 'essential' shapes, without denying the fact of material detail, knowledge of which is the great contribution of our science. It could thus, as we shall see, be more 'scientific'.

For the modern scientist energy has no borders, it is a shapeless 'mass' of force; even his capacity to differentiate it to a degree never dreamed of by the ancients has not led him to think of its shape or even its loci. The rose that his magnet makes in the iron filings, does not lead him to think of the force in botanic terms, or wish to visualize that force as floral and extant (*ex stare*).

A medieval 'natural philosopher' would find this modern world full of enchantments, not only the light in the electric bulb, but the thought of the current hidden in air and in wire would give him a mind full of forms, *'Fuor di color'* ['beyond/outside colour'] or having their hyper-colours. The medieval philosopher would probably have been unable to think the electric world, and *not* think of it as a world of forms. Perhaps algebra has queered our geometry. Even Bose with his plant experiments seems intent on the plant's capacity to feel – not on the plant idea, for the plant brain is obviously filled with, or is one idea, an *idée fixe*, a persistent notion of pattern from which only cataclysm or a Burbank can shake it. (*E*, 154)

This, I think one can show, amounts to the idea that 'things' (in the widest sense) are Gestalts;[10] plus the idea that there is a sort of 'faculty for being Gestalts' that is common to them (including us among them); plus the idea that our very being part of this community of Gestalt is what enables us to perceive Gestalts – plus, finally, the sense that this all constitutes the 'intimate essence of the universe', which our consciousness is 'incapable of having produced', and is to be respected as divinity (*P*, 49). None of this denies or elides any 'scientific fact'; instead it encourages the scientist to look at fact in a way likely to produce more intelligent results: not as an eye specialist but as an ecologist of the body; not at work/time units but at the economic ecology of the nation. And Pound takes pains to make his reader see Cavalcanti as 'scientific'.

Thus Cavalcanti is to give us the wherefore of Love; but he tells us that he cannot do this without the requisite scientific evidence:

> Be there not natural demonstration
> > I have no will to try proof-bringing
> Or say where it hath birth
>
> What is its virtu and power
> > > (XXXVI, p. 177)

Pound pays much attention to this phrase. He says Guido 'does not definitely proclaim any heresy, but he shows leanings toward not only the proof by reason, but toward the proof by experiment'. Again, 'At times and with some texts before me, "natural dimostramento" would seem to imply almost biological proof' (*E*, 149, 178).

In context here, this 'natural demonstration' will be the personal experience of love. One will never know what Guido means, exactly, until one feels it; the 'thing itself' is more than the catalogue of its attributes, however precisely Guido may deliver that catalogue. In the same way, Love 'is not vertu but cometh of that perfection'; and that perfection is considered to be a perfection, not for reasons, but by feeling. It

> > is so postulate not by the reason
> > But 'tis felt, I say ['*Non razionale/ma che si sente dicho*']

Pound comments: '"*non razionale ma che si sente*" is for experiment, it is against the tyranny of the syllogism, blinding and obscurantist' (*E*, 159; cf. 183). As Fenollosa had said, science and logic are not the same thing; though science may include logic.[11]

The Neoplatonising side of medieval philosophy (of which Alfarabi is a good example) mysticised knowledge: knowledge might be difficult, but when it came it was an 'illumination'. Where, before, one had received mere knowledge of the material details of the thing, at a certain point the *forma* of it entered one's soul; one understood it. It was like a moment of conversion. In modern terms this might be the intuition of a Gestalt: the whole that the 'thing' is.

One can clarify the problem here by pointing out a habit in Pound's literary and cultural criticism. He would merely assert the presence of entities and meanings, without trying to prove it. He habitually talked of presenting and comparing 'slides' (specimens of writing) as if that were a complete experimental act, with results as obvious as a thermometer reading. He said that one should follow poets' judgements in the matter of poetry, just as, in the matter of cars, one would accept the judgement of a car-maker – in particular, that of a man who had made a good car (*ABC*, 30–1). Again, the decline of cultures into greed, he said, was clearly visible in their painting; and in a discussion of aesthetics he would remark as a mere matter of fact that in such a statue 'the "god is inside"' (*E*, 152).

But who proclaims the presence of the god, the quality of the painting, the value of the specimen of writing, or the value of the writing that is supposed to authenticate the poet (this poet) as a judge of specimens of writing?

That is perhaps the standard response of our era. Yet if one takes away such 'direct knowledge' one takes away knowledge. A historical event is a bundle of details that, analysed, instantly diffuse themselves in infinitely branching causal series; no writer can prove that any one of these has priority; we can never 'understand' why things happen in history. In science, as Popper has said, the evidence does not even begin to exist – is not differentiable from the infinity of non-significant detail – until the scientist has a theory; which arises in his mind by a process he does not understand. Darwin was convinced about evolution though the theory depended on mutants, which were a mere postulate in his day. At a certain point the scientist's mind leaps beyond details and he 'knows' the truth of his hunch. But it is not merely that, temporally, one intuits patterns later confirmed. For no shape is ever confirmed in any such solid sense, or known to subsist, according to merely evidential criteria. Where is the 'fact' of a historical event? And where is the human being? He is an ecology whose essential part is nowhere; a system in which no physical molecule (brain, bone or DNA) remains for longer than approximately seven years; neither the beginning of whose existence ('life') nor the end of it has yet been located. It would seem that whole shapes, Forms or Gestalts are (*a*) quite essential to our usable knowledge, and (*b*) arrived at intuitively, not logically.

Thus, according to Pound, Cavalcanti's poem is (at several removes) about God, seen as deep-shaping and the awareness of deep-shaping. It sees God (considered thus) from the angle of psychology, that is, how that awareness-which-is-part-of-God occurs. The phrases in it, Pound said, 'correspond to definite sensations undergone'; he referred to Guido as a psychologist (*E*, 162). When or how is love known?

> Nor is he known from his face
> But taken in the white light that is allness
> Toucheth his aim

This is equivalent to *contemplatio* in Richard of St Victor's sense, which Pound understood not as mere flitting cogitation, nor as meditation (a methodical approach), but as a kind of super-knowing, a seizing of the subject from all sides at once (see above, p. 95). For this 'taken in the white light that is allness/ Toucheth his aim' is Cavalcanti's *Chompriso bianco in tale obietto chade*, which Pound glossed (*L*, 309) with this from the *Purgatorio*:

> [When through impression of pleasure,
>   which some one of our faculties receives,
>   the soul] is wholly centred [on that faculty]
>   (*Purgatori*, 4.1–3)

'Concentrate,' he translated. 'It hooks up with the "bianco" in Guido's "Donna mi prega" and the melody that most draws the soul into itself.' Pound says 'the white light' here because this is a Form, which like all Forms is

> Divided, set out from colour

And around these lines one can group a whole series of clues from Dante and Arnaut Daniel that link, in Pound's mind, the idea of 'whiteness' to the idea of superknowing, superconcentration on a wholeness. 'My final opinion is that *compriso bianco* means understood as a whole' (*E*, 190).[12]

That, then, is some suggestion of what Pound understood and

intended by his translation. It lays no claim to explaining what Cavalcanti's song actually meant. Pound has seized on a very hard text. There are technical terms, capable in themselves of comporting various different (often mutually incompatible) theoretical pictures, depending on the philosophical school chosen; and used tersely by Cavalcanti, that is, without sufficient verbal context to make certain his usage. These are mixed with other terms that may or may not be technical; it is impossible to say, for the use of them is so elliptical. The manuscript texts are fluid and incompatible, making syntax ambiguous. The combined result of this makes possible wholly different readings of the poem. Once more Pound has hit on a scholarly obscurity, on which to build unassailable myth. His method is inspired overinterpretation, helped by autodidactic collateral reading. Without going into any one philosophical tradition of the Middle Ages deeply, he skips about on that vast text-ocean, seeking snippets that seem to tally. These are chosen not because their concepts fit in any extended, thus conclusive, way with Cavalcanti's, but because they share some one term with him (*largiri* from Albertus, *diaphana* from Grosseteste), and because their emotional tone fits with what Pound finds (a critic would say: reads into) the poem. Armed with these he homes in on the insoluble cruces of Cavalcanti, where his freedom of choice between theoretical pictures, and perhaps of image-*making*, is greatest; and indeed he seems to set this forth as a conscious method of avoiding argument (*E*, 180). It remains for the specialist to say whether this use of intuition bears fruit in regard to Cavalcanti's meaning; if, that is, patient detail-work can validly check intuition.[13]

(iii)   VAN BUREN AND THE BANK: CANTO XXXVII

Canto XXXVII's centre is the Bank War: the defeat and termination of the Second Bank of the United States by President Andrew Jackson and his friends, between 1829 and 1836. In this Canto, Jackson's chief 'companion' (in the sense of Roland's peers in the *Chanson de Roland*, or Odysseus' men: cf. I, p. 5; LXXIV, p. 432) was Martin Van Buren. Van Buren in old age 'Remembered this' in his *Autobiography*, from which the central part of the Canto is taken. Jackson's enemy is Nicholas Biddle, President of the Bank from 1823 to its demise. Since the Bank War is one of the base-*exempla* in the corruption of America and the Western world in the Cantos (*Rock-Drill* returns to it lengthily) it is worth some attention.

And inasmuch as its type of historicity has an effect on writing; inasmuch as it makes a difference whether the writing is 'about' Laputa, or Ithaca, or Philadelphia, Pa (not that this need make the writing better or worse, but makes a difference); one of the angles from which this matter should be considered is historicity.

The Second Bank of the United States (1816–36) was a business-government partnership; Van Buren's (and Pound's) thesis is that it became a state within the state. One-fifth of its $35 million capital was subscribed by the government, which appointed one-fifth of its directors. The Bank was authorised to issue paper money to the amount of its capital, but must stand ready to redeem its notes in hard metal. The Bank's advantage was that its notes were made legally acceptable in all payments to the government, which gave them a psychological advantage over the notes of all other private banks; also that it was made the place of deposit of all government moneys. So constituted, it made in its seventeen years of loan finance a profit of somewhat more than $40 million. The United States government's advantage was that it received from the Bank in the same period a total of $4.5 million in bonuses.[14]

When Jackson was elected President of the United States in 1829, and made threatening remarks about the Bank, Biddle, President of the Bank, set about flooding the country with loans. He wanted all to believe that an attempt to wind up the Bank would bring disaster:

> 'To which end, largely increased line of discounts
> 1830, October, 40 million
> May, 1832 seventy millions and then some.[15]
> (XXXVII, p. 183)

He set about using all possible influence to obtain rechartering of the Bank: selective loans, propaganda paid for with Bank money – much of this activity undisclosed to the government directors. Jackson held firm, and in July 1832 vetoed the petition for recharter. He also decided to remove government funds from the Bank, and this began effectively in September 1833; the money was henceforth deposited in local private banks.

Biddle therefore set out to prove that the veto on rechartering had upset the wise courses of the Bank and forced it to drastic measures to prepare for the loss of its official position. He began a sudden and harsh recall of loans:

'employing means at the bank's disposal
in deranging the country's credits, obtaining by panic
control over public mind' said Van Buren

But there was no panic, though widespread distress; and the Bank's
charter was not renewed. Eventually, in 1840, Van Buren inaugurated
an independent treasury, to collect and transfer government funds
without private help. It lasted until 1917, making Van Buren (in this
Canto's closing words) 'Liberator of the National Treasury', 'FISCI
LIBERATOR'. And thus, Pound suggests, ended one phase of the
effort to terrify the public into believing that government could not be
carried on in the United States without the backing of private credit
organised as a tax on the public; by which is meant private banking in
general.

That is the Bank War in its central points according to Van Buren. If
it is a true account of what happened, the point seems proven; whatever
the financial misconceptions of Jackson and his advisers, whatever the
ways in which agrarian fears of finance, or claims of them, were used by
groups that were not agrarian at all, but merely in competition with the
Bank,[16] this was a state within a state. And the central points seem
unassailable, despite the tone of historians towards them. Biddle, in
sole control of the largest corporation in the United States, was
pursuing a national financial policy, one that had greater effects on the
economy than the financial decisions of the government. He inflated or
deflated without regard to national interests but solely for the purposes
of the Bank[17]; directed massive sectional money-movements on the
same principles; had (as he said) the power to break any state bank
when he chose (though he never used it); operated his own propaganda
machine with means larger than the government's; acted to prevent
cancellation of millions in government stock when the government
wanted it cancelled; and invented a form of note-issue that bypassed the
intention of Congress, simply to extend the amount of his credits. All
this was legal. It hardly seems to the point that these powers began to be
exercised most flagrantly after the Bank came under persistent (often
interested and ignorant) attack, from 1829 onwards. From that point
Biddle clearly became Napoleonic;[18] but he simply demonstrated the
power that was vested in his institution under the direction of a power-
seeking man. In the face of all this, the indulgent tone of historians
towards Biddle and his Bank seems to proceed solely from the feeling
that they paved the way for the enlightened central banking of the

twentieth century; which Pound would consider an association of doubtful merit.

Canto XXXVII largely presents Martin Van Buren (Jackson's Secretary of State and then Vice-President) rather than Jackson himself. Thus, as in the case of Washington, Jefferson and Adams, he displaces interest from the rock of firmness towards the agile intelligence. The Van Buren of most histories is a subtle contriver, a consummate demagogue and a verbal evader; Pound rewrites him. Before the main (Bank) sequence, he predisposes the reader by recording a series of humane and unequivocal verbal actions by Van Buren, in behalf of men deprived of the vote (because unpropertied) or of their money (through bank failures), or victims of summary justice on board ship. He also interrupts the main sequence to set Van Buren remembering (like Sordello in *Purgatorio*, 6.66 – see XXXII, p. 159) in a Mediterranean background, with all the connotations of clarity that that now has. But the chief rewriting is done by verbal texture. Quotation marks suggest that Van Buren said

> 'that an immigrant shd. set out with good banknotes
> and find 'em at the end of his voyage
> but waste paper.... [...]'

This blunt man has the pithiness of Pound's Odysseus, who knows where he is going, or will soon find out. But the man who wrote the original was George Bancroft, rhetorising about the humble emigrant in the sticky idiom that Crèvecœur imported from Thomas Gray: 'The modest proceeds of his patrimony', 'the fruits of a life of toil'.[19] The only figures who are allowed in this Canto to mouth the inanities that they originally mouthed are Van Buren's enemies; Van Buren's language is significantly improved. His *Autobiography* is full of tortuous and latinate wadding; and also a difficult irony, that the unalert reader may easily lose track of, which probably gave rise to his reputation of equivocator. On rare occasions it can reach savage intensity: a particular type of intensity that Pound's working of the same material cannot borrow, because he has removed the capacious blandness that this irony requires to play against.[20]

It is a perfectly open and sincere form of attack if the reader has the wit to grasp that it is an attack at all. But the reader soon perceives that the bland-approval level of it is strangely continuous with the *genuine* bland approval that Van Buren felt for the American common people, the inevitable march of their progress, their unalterable virtue, wisdom, and so on. And after all there seems a doubleness in the man, for he who is capable of an irony that point after point lays bare a quite Infernal cynicism of motive in Biddles, Hamiltons and Websters need not have the moral pessimism of a Swift, but can be expected to perceive that the heart of the common man is not pure perfumed soap. This Van Buren never for an instant admits. Pound removes a rhetoric of irony whose moral basis seems doubtful, keeps the amassing of specific charges that makes the value of Van Buren's *Autobiography*, and gives him a voice that he might have done well to possess. Perhaps it is one of those cases where, even if such persons have not existed, we

> 'Should', said H. J., 'for humanity's credit
>
> > > feign their existence
> > >
> > > (CI, p. 726)

NOTES: CHAPTER 9

1 George Kearns, *Guide to Ezra Pound's 'Selected Cantos'* (New Brunswick, NJ: Rutgers University Press, 1980), pp. 83, 90–1, to which this discussion is indebted.
2 Quoted in ibid., p. 88.
3 Grégoire Bessedovsky, *Oui, j'accuse! Au service des Soviets* (Paris: Alexis Redier, 1930), p. 219, which has 'six ans', not 'dix ans'.
4 ibid., p. 223.
5 The Caedmon recording of this Canto (TC 1122, made in the 1950s) clarifies some important points concerning Pound's idea of the sense-division of Cavalcanti's poem. In Ezra Pound, *Pound's Cavalcanti: An Edition of the Translations, Notes, and Essays*, ed. David Anderson (Princeton, NJ: Princeton University Press, 1983), David Anderson has cleared up the very poor text of Pound's Cavalcanti material in *E*, printed previously unpublished material, collated printings and manuscripts and provided a chronology of Pound's work on Cavalcanti.
6 See Ernest Renan, *Oeuvres complètes*, ed. H. Psichari, Vol. 3 (Paris: Calmann-Lévy, 1949), p. 188 n. The attribution of the text to St Albert is doubtful.
7 In a letter of 1922, Pound spoke of D'Annunzio as having the kind of vigour that projects some 'remembered beauty' onto an 'unconquered consciousness' (quoted in Peter D'Epiro, *A Touch of Rhetoric: Ezra Pound's Malatesta Cantos* (Ann Arbor, Mich.: UMI Research Press, 1983), p. 3).
8 Etienne Gilson, *History of Christian Philosophy in the Middle Ages* (London: Sheed & Ward, 1955), p. 187. The original of this passage is on p. 349 of Gilson, *La Philosophie au Moyen Age* (Paris: Payot, 1971), whose 1925 edition was used by Pound.
9 LXXVI, pp. 452, 457; LXIII, p. 353; but see K*PE*, p. 586 (note to p. 453).
10 According to Gestalt psychology, analysing the parts one by one will not yield the attributes of the whole. For Gestalt in Pound, see XCIV, p. 688, and *E*, 188.
11 Ernest Fenollosa, *The Chinese Written Character as a Medium for Poetry* (San Francisco, Calif.: City Lights, n.d.), p. 28.
12 See also *E*, 177, 155, 148; also perhaps the word *alba*, 'dawn', read as 'white'.
13 See Etienne Gilson in E. Homberger (ed.), *Ezra Pound: The Critical Heritage* (London: Routledge & Kegan Paul, 1972), pp. 273–9, and J. E. Shaw, *Guido Caval-*

canti's Theory of Love (Toronto: University of Toronto Press, 1949), pp. 212–13.

The nature of Form and the status of Love are the bases of the Canzone and the points at which Pound diverges most from the mainstream of criticism.

Pound remarked that St Thomas Aquinas had twisted the meaning of the term 'Form' 'almost 180 degrees off its course' (*E*, 188). He referred, I think, to St Thomas's view that the individuation of beings cannot come from Form (since the Form is the same for all beings of the same species); therefore it comes from matter, since the given, delimited amount of matter belongs to the one individual alone. (See Renan, *Oeuvres complètes*, Vol. 3, p. 192.)

Shaw, *Cavalcanti's Theory of Love*, esp. pp. 19, 38–41, applies a similar view of Form (that of St Albert) to the Canzone. To know the Form is primarily to abstract the pure concept (here, Feminine Beauty) from a number of seen instances (such as Betty, Bertha and Sal). There is divine intervention (p. 29), but Form is, first and foremost, the lowest common denominator.

For Pound, it was matter in itself, *hyle*, that was the undifferentiated. Forms were both godly principles, and (first and foremost) the Forms of unique individuals. This view as a whole accords with those neither of Plato nor of Aristotle, but has analogies in a number of medieval thinkers. St Bonaventure could not allow that each individual might have a unique Form (as had Averroes, and as Duns Scotus would later); but each individual had a composite of hierachically graded Forms that made up a unity. The joining of this unique composite to matter was then the individuating principle. (Compare the view expressed in *Paradiso*, 7.139–41.) Robert Grosseteste further held that the Intelligibles were 'not essentially universals, but rather, single things, and it is only by accident that they happen to belong to several individuals' (Emile Bréhier, *La Philosophie du Moyen Age* (Paris: Albin Michel, 1971), p. 244.) Compare also 'form' and *virtù* in Dante's letter to Can Grande, where one is a function of the other; and Pound, *Translations*, introd. Hugh Kenner (New York: New Directions, 1963), p. 18 (citing Pater), on *virtù*.

Most commentators also hold that Love, in Cavalcanti's Canzone, belongs essentially to the 'sensitive', not to the 'rational' soul. That is, in common parlance, it is primarily a physical passion, and cannot therefore have 'power' in the intellect possible (and so on). See e.g. citations in Gianfranco Contini (ed.), *Poeti del Duecento*, Vol. 1 (Milan: Riccardo Ricciardi, 1960), p. 525.

14 See R. C. H. Catterall, *The Second Bank of the United States* (Chicago, Ill.: University Press of Chicago, 1902), pp. 474–6, 504.

15 The current text's '1837' is wrong; cf. *P*, p. 179.

16 cf. B. Hammond, *Bank and Politics in America* (Princeton, NJ: Princeton University Press, 1957), pp. 428–9.

17 Catterall's charitable explanation (*Second Bank*, pp. 142 ff.) for the inflation – that Biddle was not in control – is not borne out by his evidence: cf. pp. 316 ff., 329.

18 ibid., pp. 271, 275 ff., on Biddle's illegal actions.

19 George Bancroft, *Martin Van Buren* (New York: Harper & Brothers, 1889), pp. 160–1.

20 Thus *The Autobiography of Martin Van Buren*, ed. J. C. Fitzpatrick (New York: Augustus M. Kelley, 1969), p. 650 (cf. XXXVII, p. 184):

> But nothing can be further from my intention than to say or insinuate, either in these surmises or by anything I have before advanced or may hereafter say, unless a change of opinion in this respect on my part is distinctly announced, that I believe Mr Biddle to have been capable of abasing his position to advance his own pecuniary interest – as the phrase runs to 'feather his own nest' – by the acquisition in any way of illicit gains. I have always regarded him in that respect as a true disciple of Alexander Hamilton, whom I have considered as free from such reproach as were Washington or Jefferson. Hamilton, who never hesitated to jeopard the general for the support and encouragement of special interests . . .

CHAPTER 10

Commentary:
Cantos XLII–LI
('Siena: The Leopoldine
Reforms')

Cantos XLII–LI were written in serene circumstances, with no disturbance to Pound's base in his beloved Rapallo. The base was provincial, but cosmopolitan connections were possible to a man of alert antennae, as when the New Hungarian Quartet was persuaded to do new music by Bartók in his concert series, or Miss Tseng gave help towards the Chinese-based Canto XLIX. Researches in the Siena archives and Pound's workroom (hung with papers on clothes-lines) went rapidly. The previous section having been published complete by 1934, Pound put out XLV ('*With Usura*') in a monetary-reform journal in 1936, XLVI in the same year in the first issue of his American acoltye James Laughlin's *New Directions*, XLII–XLIV in Eliot's *Criterion* in 1937, and then the whole section (as *The Fifth Decad of Cantos*) late in the same year. What unserenity there was seemed to come from inside Pound, in a flood of angry writings on economics; but his Italy and his Mussolini were becoming polarised from the Western powers, and Pound's sympathies along with them.

Cantos XLII–LI to some extent circle back through the same concerns as the previous sections, but changed by inner changes in Pound, caused partly by the new experiences he had (with the strenuous sense of duty imposed by 'God's gift the universe' on a man out of Thoreau and Browning) gone out to encounter. The book will not fit into the ordering of elements that I have suggested for the earlier books. That is partly because of a new profundity, in the two 'Usura' Cantos and the 'Seven Lakes Canto'. These are not about efforts of construction in a tangible and earthly world, nor are they about paradisal realms where beings are freed from gravitational pull and other mundane necessitations. (Nor are the 'Usura' Cantos on a hellish plane: they are more concerned with presenting the valued things that usury kills.) But the life and objects in them seem so quietly full that one can only speak of an immanence. They thus escape the categories that I have so far dwelled on.

The thematic shape of the book is somewhat as follows. The Siena Cantos, with which the book opens, are on familiar yet different territory: in them, a somewhat anonymous constructivity such as produced the Doge's Palace in Venice is newly allied with nature's fertility. Canto XLIV celebrates Pietro Leopoldo of Habsburg-Lorraine, financially reforming ruler in Tuscany 140 years after the Siena Bank's founding; his son Ferdinando III is fêted in popular procession. It then bridges to Napoleon, in whom, however, Pound is not sufficiently interested to body him forth as more than another Mussolinian swamp-drier and law-giver. There follows the beautiful 'With Usura' Canto, XLV. XLVI is a complex meditation on the socio-cultural history of Western civic irresponsibility, and its relation to the toleration of usury; it grades into a prosecutor's address in the case against usury, listing evidence and effects. For this address all the foregoing historical material was a preparation, and here the poem's genius, like Dante's emerging from Inferno, briefly 'hoists its sails' for clear waters. Then Canto XLVII sings the mystery of the death of Adonis as fertility-figure, associated with Odysseus' descent to Hades, and with the annual ploughing. In this newly grim view, the female principle is mindless and inexorable in its pull; man is wrecked, as by Scylla's teeth, yet his blood appears to give renewal of fertility, and he gains god-like perception.

In the latter part of this book, Canto XLVIII gives fine but perhaps miscellaneous meditations on will-less culture-functions, on a corrupt culture, on craft and on instinct developed to a level that seems characterisable as intelligence. Montségur, the castle-like temple where the heretics of Provence made a last stand, is here presented as ruin, but in the kind of light we find in the Cantos' earthly paradises. There then follows the serene 'Seven Lakes Canto', XLIX. Canto L returns to the level of banal political speech-writing, about Napoleon and the usurers of Vienna; but the final Canto of the book integrates the book's themes convincingly. In a few lines Pound humanises a Neoplatonic God as both sun and source of understanding, in combat (like Napoleon) with an elemental mud of stupidity. There follows a variation on the first 'Usura' Canto. A rich and glistening litany of textures, from a fly-fishing manual, gives the sense both of craft and of immanent beauty, and then St Albert of Cologne is quoted to make God into the Craftsman, leaving the light which is His thumbprint on that which He 'Informs'. Grass returns, for abundance, and the theme of peace (but the speaker is Hitler). There follows a small Hell of greasy usurers; and as the *Draft of XXX Cantos* ended with the demise of the Borgia Pope Alexander in 1503, a convenient marker for the new era of grease and baroque, so this section ends with the League of Cambrai of 1508–10, which extinguished the light of Venice.

The central achievements are perhaps the Siena, Usury and Seven Lakes Cantos, to which I shall devote particular attention.

(i) CANTOS XLII AND XLIII: THE BANK IN SIENA

The first two Cantos deal with the economic discovery of seventeenth-century Siena: an unparasitic source of communal credit. They work in a way now familiar from Pound's 'documentary' passages. Pound perceived a problem: that though Jefferson, Adams and Van Buren saw what was wrong with private banks they found and constructed no alternative.[1] He rooted with his customary carelessness of inessentials among the dark mounds of time's archives for such a glittering construct, secreted perhaps by history and then buried (the diamond is a favourite image: *P*, 22; *GK*, 221; LXXIV, p. 449); and he found it. He then presented it in three simultaneous layers: (1) the formula, the scientist's 'find' – usable elsewhere, and therefore more or less timeless; (2) the peculiar configuration of time's strata round it, giving some idea of causality; (3) the process of his own finding of it.

Time's archives in this case were heaped up in Siena, where few but Pound (unless specialists, who tend to have no interest in how the achievements of 'their' century might apply in the foreign world of now) would have had the foolishness to go. Pound went there and spent peculiarly happy weeks, with results that seemed to come to hand almost too easily to be true. He found that there had been a

> damn good bank, in Siena

> A mount, a bank, a fund a bottom an
> institution of credit
> a place to send cheques in and out of
> and yet not yet a banco di giro [giro bank]

but rather of this nature:

> as third, a Yearly balance
> as 5th that any citizen shall have right to deposit
> and to fruits therefrom resultant at five percent annual interest
> and that borrowers pay a bit over that
> for service (dei ministri) that is for running expenses
> and book keeping which shall be counted a half scudo
> per hundred per year
> (All of this is important)
> and 6thly that the Magistrate
> give his chief care that the specie
> be lent to whomso can best use it USE IT
> (id est, più utilmente)
> to the good of their houses, to benefit of their business
> as of weaving, the wool trade, the silk trade
> And that (7thly) the overabundance every five years shall the Bailey
> distribute to workers of the contrade (the wards) holding in
> reserve a prudent proportion as against unforeseen losses
> though there shd. be NO such losses
> and 9th that the borrowers can pay up before the end of their
> term whenso it be to their interest. No debt to run more than
> five years.
> July 1623
> Loco Signi
> ✚ a cross in the margin   (XLII, pp. 209–10)

The Grand Duke's guardians had already

> gratified
> the city of this demand to
> erect a New Monte [institution of credit]
> for good public and private and to facilitate ...
> .. agreed to accommodate
> ...... and to lend the fund against the Gd. Duke's
> public entries to the sum of
> 200,000 scudi
> capital for fruit at 5% annual
> which is 10,000 a year
> assigned on the office of grazing
> on caution of said security offered
> leaving grounds for other towns that
> wish to participate
> with TTheir HHighnesses
> approbations as follows.
>   (XLII, p. 212)

These two passages (within the first four pages on Siena) contain everything Pound tells us about the bank's workings.

A banker 'is one who borrows money to lend it again at a profit (i.e., at a higher rate of interest)'[2] – thus effectively creating money by doubling it, for in theory the money is still there in the bank for the depositor whom the bank borrowed it from. But this bank differed from usurious banks in that, whether money was transferred by it or created by it, the profit went to the community: distributed every five years to the workers. (Inasmuch as viability of credit and meetability of its demands depend on a communal state of health and creativity – social calm and flourishing trade – the capacity to create and allocate chunks of it, and profit therefrom, should be vested in the people.) The interest was low, for profit–making was not a main aim of the institution. There was a capital, given by the Duke; but the Duke was guaranteed that his capital would ultimately be retrieved, by the assigning, for this purpose, of grazing-land worth 10,000 scudi per year. (Not, that is, unfunctioning real estate, whose value exists in the minds of realtors: *P*, 259; but land producing a product that would stay in demand: wool.)

This illustrates a central point for Pound: nature's nature (unlike the Chase Manhattan's) is to produce, to abound, to be abundant. So this grassland comes back in these Cantos:

> to the sum as of capital 200,000
> for 5% fruitage   that wd. be ten thousand the year
> which attain to the Office of Grasslands
> > (XLIII, pp. 221–2)

Grass is hymned, taking on Taoist tones of serene abundance:

> Grass nowhere out of place.
> > Pine cuts the sky into three
> Thus BANK of the grassland was raised into Seignory
> > (XLIII, p. 219)

This grass-income (for the Duke's extra security) was counter-guaranteed by liens on the property of all citizens; and, further, on the grain dole office, which was poetically called the *Abbondanza*. Pound translates that title as 'The Abundance' (XLII, p. 211), and proceeds, for this liturgy to Exuberant Nature and Man's Direction of the Will,[3] to associate the 'abundance' of this office with the productivity of that grassland and so come to an ultimate formulaic basis, stated as summary at the beginning of the next book of Cantos:

> And I have told you of how things were under Duke
> > Leopold in Siena
> And of the true base of credit, that is
> > the abundance of nature
> with the whole folk behind it. (LII, p. 257)

– that is, 'the responsibility of the whole people'.[4] Pound wanted the rock bottom, like Thoreau, on which he might plant his feet; or, rather, on which the people might 'erect' their Monte ('credit fund', but literally 'Mountain'), to whose diagram ⌂ he has added further height ⌂ not authorised by the original.[5] This 'direction of the will' (Fascist *Voluntas*) is the male principle to mother earth's female:

> there first was the fruit of nature
> there was the whole will of the people
> (XLIII, p. 218)

For this basis he creates a verbalisation not in the original:

> a base, a fondo, a deep, a sure and a certain
> (XLIII, p. 219)

Fondo in such a context in the source-document merely meant 'fund' or 'capital', but here acquires its other meanings: bottom, base, deepest part.[6]

That is the formula, the uncrushable diamond found in these archives. It evokes an emotional response: both 'See, it is not impossible' and 'Yet both success and failure pass':

> wave falls and the hand falls
> Thou shalt not always walk in the sun
> or see weed sprout over cornice
> Thy work in set space of years, not over an hundred.
> (XLII, p. 210)

Layered over the formula, throughout, is the undetachable shape of its period – how and when it was arrived at: haggling administration passes recommendation to higher administration, committee *sits* – 'as we have already been for ten years projecting' – and finally exgurgitates thunderous phrase embodying all the peculiarly Italian elaboration necessary to its self-image:

> sought views from the Senate 'With paternal affection
> justice convenience of city what college had with such
> foresight wherefore S.A. (Your Highness) as in register
> Nov. 1624   (XLII, p. 209)

A 'formula' is only that, and works in one period because someone has the intelligence to graft it into the conditions of that time, and to allow for the fact that events take place in time, and require time, for ideas to sink in, events to occur. To understand the formula at all is to see it in action, observe how it worked, how it grew out of that period; thus what may, and what may not, be transplanted. A cornflower seed can give the secret of germination, but is still a cornflower seed. And that time (Italy, 1624) also shows symptoms, discernible among the 'doggy-mints', that Pound can pick up as continuing into the present in that place. They are symptoms of a *diletto*, a capacity to live, such as Pound observed from the window of his flat in Siena:

> to the end:
>   four fat oxen
> having their arses wiped
> and in general being tidied up to serve god under my window
> with stoles of Imperial purple
> with tassels, and grooms before the carroccio
>   (XLIII, p. 216)

The procession of the Palio at Siena has these splendours, of purple and of gold eagles. God is served with things, in this world (as not in that religion of Pure Mind for which people smashed stained-glass windows in churches). *Laudate, pueri, Dominum*, 'Praise the Lord, O ye children', says the Vulgate (Psalm 112), and the Latin church specifies how: with candles:

> One box marked '200 LIRE'
>   'laudate pueri'
> alias: serve God with candles

Bawling mothers and defecating oxen do not affect this procession; they are part of the general vigour. And to illustrate this vigour Pound brings in a procreative Medici scion's bastards, of whom the Monte's secretary was made 'illegitimate father' (as in Fielding,[7] a super-abundance of generous animal spirits is evidence of a right mind – *homo erectus*?). Of all this the Monte dei Paschi is offered both as the expression, and the furtherance.

The American researcher's interaction with all this is everywhere visible already. Thus

> what college had with such
> foresight wherefore S.A. (Your Highness) as in register

tells us that he finds this gravity funny.

> 1251 of the Protocols marked also
> X, I, I, F, and four arabic
> (XLIII, p. 216)

tells us that he founds these jewels *in* specific folders *on* specific shelves, existing in an Italy that you or I may visit, among material obstacles of railway timetables and midday closings that you or I may struggle against, and sink with fatigue over the effort to decipher old scribblings ('up to (illegible) said to mean, no . . .': XLIII, p. 218), as did Pound. It matters that the discovery of ways out of thickets in which societies may be trapped (at present, in time) be no longer imagined a question of that ideal activity, pure thought, practised by sages somehow translated to a separate plane of sagedom by the gravity of their learning. The discoverer of these presents was not the Jacksonian common man, but the man raised to uncommon perception; not by elite opportunities, but by making use of that which we all have; and so naturally speaking an ordinary tongue –

> get that straight   (XLII, p. 214)

(ii)   CANTO XLV: *'WITH USURA'*

This Canto is famous, and much dwelled upon. It is 'like a single word made organic', opening out with exact movement from beginning to conclusion:

> *With Usura*
>
> With usura hath no man a house of good stone
> each block cut smooth and well fitting

that design might cover their face,
with usura [. . .]
It hath brought palsey to bed, lyeth
between the young bride and her bridegroom
                              CONTRA NATURAM
They have brought whores for Eleusis
Corpses are set to banquet
at behest of usura.

Thus experiment demonstrates: there is no acceptable place at which
to cut it.

Driving out the pictured serenity is not merely inertness, but disease
and corruption. What divinity does not irradiate, here, is not merely
clay (in the Biblical sense), but pullulation of what fetidity breeds.
Pound could never say (with Wilfred Owen)

> – O what made fatuous sunbeams toil
> To break earth's sleep at all?
>   ('Futility')

because it was hard for him to think of the non-divine as merely
inorganic and inert. Evil was active shutting-out of the light; the
opposite of light was a disease, an active going-wrong of the organism.
Thus along with stale rags, dry paper in the mouth, blunting, rust, we
have the thick line (already perhaps suggesting the gross and obscene),
but more especially murrain, gnawing, canker, death of the foetus,
thwarting of desire, palsey, whores (here tainted by association),
corpses. With its insistence, the word *usura* itself perhaps comes to have
some sense of *usure*, wearing, erosion, the unclean decay of disease, as
in Canto XIV:

> The soil a decrepitude, the ooze full of morsels,
> lost contours, erosions.

Thus the Canto builds an emotional centre, against which it posits
another: good building, good design, good art, good food, good social
arrangements, craft using the craftsman's faculties, religious perception
and fertility share the attributes of clarity, sharpness of outline,
distinguishability, and also sense of harmony with the natural world
(sun, stone, wheat, mountain, love-making). They are shown as
incompatible with usury, principle of the diverting and obscuring of the

natural process for short-sighted (greedy, lustful) ends. This is propaganda, in that the poem only sets out two poles, heightening our sense of what life might be in both directions. Other verse must persuade us that the choice of movement along this axis depends on acceptance or rejection of particular practices, economic and other.

The other things named that the Canto depends on include paintings and sculptures, inferred from their makers. They tend, avoiding Vlaminck or Hartung harshness or Rembrandt smoky darkness, towards a body pale and of clear outline. Among these it seems natural that one should emanate visibly; as in an *Annunciation* by Fra Angelico:

> where virgin receiveth message
> and halo projects from incision

And bas-reliefs, like Pietro Lombardo's, seem to become in the Cantos a sign of the *forma* showing itself through stone. The effect of these visual suggestions accumulates and combines with those of the building and the loom, which offer nothing to contradict them, but are quiet and exist in 'freedom from irritants'.[8] They have small, local qualities: local craft, in independent 'economic units', connected with sheep, markets, and a life connected with the local church (suggested by Villon's song for his mother who sees 'harpes et luthes' in her church's painting of Paradise). The hypothesised man here has a stone house, not a mansion.

But the whole would be difficult to locate in history or space. It is all cleaner than any real Middle Ages (where none but the richest merchants had stone houses at all); not as large-scale on the scientific, technical, industrial level as the European Renaissance, when men starved and held strikes. It is not as primitive as the Middle Ages sculpted by the Middle Ages; nor yet as palatial as the Renaissance painted by the Renaissance. The visual model is archaic myth-worlds, and idealised quasi-medieval pasts, painted (as by Fra Angelico) in the Renaissance.

These are the methods of myth, and of course ahistorical and nostalgic. But one should not rule out the possibility that humankind may from time to time live up to myth – as the Ife bronzes, which to European eyes ought to be an imaginative invention of beauty, are found exemplified in living Nigerians.

The metre is in the grand prophetic style: terse, emphatic and denunciatory. The key is the pattern $(\times/)\times\times/\times$, which binds the ends

of lines to itself almost without exception, leaving the beginnings open
and optional; the varied approach to this consistent ending draws
attention to its consistency, and increases emphasis. The pattern is
complete in

> cut smooth and well fitting
>
> thy bread dry as paper

and so on; but its core is in the refrain, 'with usura'. The pattern, being
so often repeated, insists upon itself, and Pound goes all out for
insistence, with syntactical parallelism and repeated phrase. Such
insistence is aesthetically justified just as long as there is violence of
ideation to live up to it, and turns bathetic as soon as that fails. But
Pound has now lived with these concerns long enough to have concentrated them into one interconnected image, which is adequate to
these aural intensities:

> to endure nor to live with
>
> to sell and sell quickly

And he has the mature artist's ability to stop with his material.

(iii)   CANTO XLIX

Now the 'case' concerning present hell has been stated (XLVI), the
Cantos can afford some serenity. It is presented in XLIX, the 'Seven
Lakes Canto', in a peculiar limpidity developed from the English
linguistic lode that Pound opened with his *Cathay* translations.

> For the seven lakes, and by no man these verses:
> Rain; empty river; a voyage

The terseness is as if of a man in the grip of emotion, but ripe with
experience and therefore without gripes, simply uttering as the things
come to him, disjunctly. Yet it is an utterance that is intense and
complete, because of a patterning of sound into which these things
appear to fall of themselves, pre-shaped, like blocks of Inca masonry:

> The reeds are heavy; bent;
> and the bamboos speak as if weeping.

Judicious traces of literary diction ('comes then' – exotic; 'behind hill' –
Pound's own literary tongue) give the sense of an experience that
includes the court as well as the road; this is brought back to unadorned
discourse – for example, in 'where the young boys prod stones for
shrimp'.

The imagery is pre-selected for Pound by a long and very conservative tradition: the eight poems attached to the eight landscape
paintings of Hsiao-Hsiang. Hsiao-Hsiang is a region in Hunan where
two rivers converge and form numerous lakes; a Sung dynasty artist
who flourished in the eleventh century painted eight scenes, and it became a convention to repaint the same eight settings and to write poems
to accompany them. Japanese courtiers took over this convention,
adding a Japanese poem beside each poem newly composed by them in
literary Chinese. A set of these was published in Japan in 1683, and the
poems in it – apparently written not long before that – found their way
(with a quite different set of paintings) into a silk-and-ricepaper
manuscript book that came into the possession of Pound's parents, who
sent it over to him in Rapallo in 1928. There appeared at the same time
in Rapallo a Chinese lady, who helped to decipher. Pound was still
distanced considerably from the manuscript book, which is half in
Japanese; his helper seems not to have attempted the Japanese poems,
and to have made considerable errors with the literary Chinese. Pound
rearranged and cut these materials with great freedom; more indeed as
he continued: he added 'Sail passed here in April; may return in
October', apparently from his imagination, and 'In seventeen hundred
came Tsing to these hill lakes', apparently from some history-book.[9]

Pound's source-manuscript may or may not, for all I know, be a good
reworking of the tradition. Pound, the ignorant, ever fresh up from the
village, sees the whole thing newly. His words show one simple or
compound texture or colour-shade, as if the object were before him
demanding to be shown in words 'as is'; and exactly not either as if it
were some stock overhandled item from some weary iconographic
tradition, or a thing made vague by a language not fully clear to the
translator, who would choose 'horse' where he should say 'nag'. Thus

Sparse chimneys smoke in the cross light

No ready-formed tradition chose the word 'sparse' for Pound, who
seized it from his linguistic experience as being the word for that
visuality he entertained in his mind; which in turn was a product of his

sense of the whole verse's visuality, as is proved by the visual integrity
of the artefact he produces. 'Sparse' is for scatteredness, like hairs or
corn that are un-thick, draughty in this season. Nor are these images
brilliant rarities, from an old collector of Decadent verbal jewels.
'Speak' can be a consummate brilliance of language, in the better sense
of being both exact and powerful:

> and the bamboos speak as if weeping.

The image-work is to evoke an emotion that is consistent and intense.
To reach that intensity the imagery should be as multiple as is possible
without repetition and without mutual weakening; therefore, on different planes.

The following lines evoke something one can only call a sense of
timeless depth; and in the first, third and fourth lines it is aural depth,
visual depth and time-depth:

> Rooks clatter over the fishermen's lanthorns,
> A light moves on the north sky line;
> Where the young boys prod stones for shrimp.
> In seventeen hundred came Tsing to these hill lakes.
> A light moves on the south sky line.

Such verse seems to demonstrate that emotion works by a negative
law: mere absence of aggression, distortion, haste allows us to read into
things (qualified only as to texture, shade and other exact physicality)
powers that favour human well-being. The defining characteristic is
that there is no need of 'more'. It should not surprise that this Canto
comes to have quasi-theological point in Pound's mind, for he has been
sorting things into 'organic categories', thinking through implications,
seeing relationships and clarifying them for a long time now, and has
the experience necessary to passing over that which is not of essential
interest to his inner emotional network – which includes theological
nodes. In 1942 he translated 'the dimension of stillness' in the pen-
ultimate line of the Canto as 'la dimension dell'immoto' – perhaps
'the dimension of the unmoved, or unmoving'. He commented:

Stillness: would be more the concept of the UNMOVING (IMMO-
TO), indeed also the silent unmoving. That which is *still* does not
move and makes no sound. But the concept 'motionless' is more
important in this line. In Dante, above the *primum mobile* is the

immobile, the [heaven] which does not turn. I conceive of a dimension of motionlessness interpenetrating the Euclidean dimensions.[10]

Pound adds certain dimensions to make clear that these evoked emotions can co-exist with social responsibility.

> State by creating riches shd. thereby get into debt?
> This is infamy; this is Geryon.

This violence of language brings the previous perceptions into the field of awareness of a man who also has to live, and conversely brings proper political urges into the field of awareness of a fine sensibility. What follows is a bridge between this language (which we might think of as belonging to a separate world, of Douglas and Social Credit) and the perceptions of the Seven Lakes:

> This canal still goes to TenShi
> though the old king built it for pleasure

Here is an economic asset that was built hundreds of years ago, and (as a measurable cost-cutter) has obviously annulled the cost of building it many times over. It is a good example of effort that may be expended, by the choice of the community, merely creating the credit-slips (money) that will enable it to expend that effort, in the knowledge that wealth equivalent to that issued credit will be created. That depends on the community's 'credit' in the sense of faith in its own future creativity. To pay private individuals for issuing that paper credit is Geryon: fraud.

There follows a chant:

> KEI MEN RAN KEI [. . .]

– which 'means' nothing to the reader, but gives some sense of the aural/visual sobriety of the Japanese–Chinese poem-blocks.[11] Then a folk song: 'Sun up; work [. . .]' The peasant in his field seems by implication to participate in the foregoing beauty; but there is a change of sensibility, from those delicate textures to this rhythm of seasonal work. From this point of view, even that constructivity among high officials is a nothing:

Imperial power is? and to us what is it?

This reminds governors of the limits of the most intelligent power; with what follows, it has something like the effect of 'The blossoms of the apricot/blow from the east to the west,/'And I have tried to keep them from falling' (XIII, p. 60), 'wave falls and the hand falls' (XLII, p. 210). But it also expresses the ideal relation with the governed, in the view of Confucian ethics: the benevolence of the administration should be unnoticeable, or like wind on grass. This is sensibility; which, raised to the *n*th power, transcends:

> The fourth; the dimension of stillness.
> And the power over wild beasts.

Which takes us back to Dionysus, who would be far indeed from the mind of the Confucian calligrapher, but not inappropriate to Pound's ideal China, in which the cults of Shang still exist 2,000 years later in the ideograms of Chu Hsi.

NOTES: CHAPTER 10

1   But Jefferson solved the problem of issue, in theory: *P*, p. 159.
2   Pound, *Impact*, ed. Noel Stock (Chicago, Ill.: Henry Regnery, 1960), p. 186.
3   The last line quoted was created by misunderstanding, and consciously preserved: see B. Kimpel and T. C. D. Eaves, 'Pound's use of Sienese manuscripts', *Paideuma*, vol. 8, no. 3 (Winter 1979), p. 517. Compare perhaps the Chinese character read as 'lord over the heart' (LXXVII, p. 467) and glossed with Dante's 'direction of the will' (*P*, pp. 84, 88, 93).
4   *Impact*, p. 186.
5   G. Galigani, 'Montis Pascuorum', *Yale Literary Magazine*, vol. 126, no. 5 (December 1958), p. 23.
6   B. Kimpel and T. C. D. Eaves, 'The sources of Cantos XLII and XLIII', *Paideuma*, vol. 6, no. 3 (Winter 1977), p. 336. George Kearns has noted the connection with Jefferson's demand that the national bills be 'bottomed' properly: cf. *P*, p. 159.
7   cf. C. J. Rawson, *Henry Fielding* (London/ New York: Routledge & Kegan Paul/ Humanities Press, 1968), pp. 5–6.
8   This is a possible translation of '*enoi gandres*', the key phrase in the Earthly Paradise scene of XX, p. 90 (cf. *MPP*, pp. 177–9, 244).
9   For all this, see *PB*, pp. 304–11; Hugh Kenner, 'More on the Seven Lakes Canto', *Paideuma*, vol. 2, no. 1 (Spring 1973), pp. 43–6; Angela Jung Palandri, 'The "Seven Lakes Canto" revisited', *Paideuma*, vol. 3, no. 1 (Spring 1974), pp. 52–4; and Sanehide Kodama, 'The eight scenes of Sho-Sho', *Paideuma*, vol. 6, no. 2 (Fall 1977), pp. 131–45.
10 Ezra Pound, *Lettere 1907–1958*, ed. Aldo Tagliaferri (Milan: Giangiacomo Feltrinelli, 1980), p. 150 (my translation).

11 After the war Pound tried a paraphrase, quoted in Kenner, 'More on the Seven
    Lakes Canto', p. 46:

> Gate, gate of gleaming,
> knotting, dispersing
>   flower of sun, flower of moon
> day's dawn after day's dawn   new fire

CHAPTER 11

Commentary:
Cantos LII–LXXI:
China and Adams

Cantos LII–LXXI are a very different section from what has gone before. By 1937, when the previous section was published complete, war tensions were already present. It is possible that Pound's plan had envisaged a move direct from the 'discovery' of that economic crime in XLVI – the goal of his journeyings into Hell – to concerns of Paradise. But he felt that it was urgently necessary to avert a conflict; the teaching of history could not be abandoned yet. He was by now so isolated that the Cantos were only publishable thanks to his friends T. S. Eliot at Faber and James Laughlin of New Directions – neither of whom believed in large parts of his current verse. His sense of the relation between what he knew and what the world at large knew was such as to make him journey to the United States in April 1939 to tell Senators and, if possible, the President how to avoid the war. It was in this spirit that he produced Cantos LII–LXXI – digests, successively, of the whole of Chinese history to 1780, and the whole life and times of John Adams. At least one of the China Cantos was ready in time to be recorded in the United States in 1939; and the Adams part was in rough typescript by February 1939, though Pound in January 1937 had not yet clapped eyes on the source of that part (*SL*, 447; *Ibb*, 57). The whole section was published in January 1940: 180 pages written in less time than the previous section's forty-six.

This section fails to have emotive shape, for two reasons. Long stretches are obscure, in a sense properly applicable to poetry: they do not impart enough 'information' through the channels available to poetry (denotative, metrical, of image) to create emotional direction. Second, elsewhere the emotion generated is too uniform in nature. Apparently James Laughlin said that this section was incomprehensible, and where comprehensible was propaganda. But Pound would not budge: these Cantos were 'Plain narrative with chronological sequence'; Laughlin had simply not bothered to read them.[1] Pound could not provide a summary to help the reader, he said: these Cantos were themselves a summary; no further condensing of the material was possible. And they could not be called propaganda just because the philosophy in them was not the reader's: no one philosophy could have privilege as poetic matter. 'Is the Divine Commedia propaganda or not?' – a question expecting the answer: It is. Obviously Pound saw himself as doing battle for a literature intended to affect the world (like Dante's), against the *littérateur*'s predisposition towards mere lyrics and wedding-cakes.

(i) THE CHINA CANTOS

The thesis of the China Cantos somewhat runs in a circle, and thus seems to defeat itself. China offers a harmony between nature and man; awareness of this possibility is religion, which, it is now suggested, should govern the State. Chinese common sense even of the most ancient periods arrived at an understanding of the relations between man and nature that suggested economic programmes identical with those of modern men of sense. China understood that good government occurs when rulers or administrators keep open their communications and sense of identity with the people. Likewise, that when collective inhumanity and greed has brought decay in the state, energy must step in in whatever form is felt to be apt for the moment, 'legitimate' or not: there is the chosen man. From these comes another doctrine, of a Transcendentalist optimism: that certain rules govern the fall of dynasties. The regime that does not care for the people cannot get their best energies from its own personnel, whatever their lip-service; it is felt to have lost authority to rule; it rots; authority is felt to have transferred itself to whatever new man can show himself fit to govern. A new dynasty starts. The chief way in which a regime may lose that authority, the 'mandate of heaven', is by turning to letters without outward relation, and doctrines of unrelated religious inspiration (here read: Buddhism, Taoism), and by losing thereby that 'shell and direction' (*C*, 268) that man needs to accomplish things; dissipating itself in instant pleasure (girls, intrigues). Since these are vices of the intelligentsia, who in any kind of regime are more or less the administrators, they are always a betrayal of the people, with the usual consequences. Therefore, at this link in the chains of emotion, these

Cantos insist strenuously on the need for strenuous practicality, and seem to lash out at all forms of sensuality, relaxation, or merging in the drift of things; and seem to become closed to all that subtle awareness of emanations that they started with.

To go back, then, to that start. The first of these 'China Cantos' is taken from a source different from that of all the rest: the 'Li Ki or memoranda on the decencies and the rites', as translated into French and Latin by Couvreur. 'Les bienséances et les cérémonies', 'the decencies and the rites', is Couvreur's way of translating *Li*, which includes sense of reverence and of propriety, but also the expression of these, both social and religious, in morals, manners and rites. The term does not permit the Western distinction between sense of religion (the reverence for an Omnipotent) and morality (the following of rules laid down by that Omnipotent, which may or may not happen to coincide with the rules of common humanity). A rite is a rite because it is right (felt to be so), and likewise a rule of behaviour. But this does permit Pound's suggestion that sensibility and rite should govern the state.

The *Li Ki* has a superstructure dating at least partly from the second century AD, in which it has degenerated into concern with elaborate marks of humility and the placing of cushions. Pound goes straight for a core that appears to be extremely ancient (it probably stems from the slave-states of Chou). Here the Emperor (HE) seems to belong to a family with goshawk and cricket:

> Offer to gods of the hearth
> > the lungs of the victims
> Warm wind is rising, cricket bideth in wall
> Young goshawk is learning his labour
> > dead grass breedeth glow-worms.
> In Ming T'ang HE bideth
> > in the west wing of that house
> Red car and the sorrel horses
> > his banner incarnadine.
> > > (LII, p. 259)

There is a sense of the tang of odour and the clarity of colour perceived by men who live in clear air –

> cold wind is beginning. Dew whitens.

– and the tactile qualities seem implied:

Steel gray are stallion.

The Emperor (Son of Heaven) binds himself in with this living world by sacrifice –

> with bitter smell, with odour of burning

– and ritual colour and totemic eating:

> Emperor goes out in war car, he is drawn by white horses,
> white banner, white stones in his girdle
> eats dog and the dish is deep.

Like some Neoplatonists, or any folk herbalist, he thus draws on the signs,[2] which are outward expressions of inner harmonisable essences, to manipulate them in 'magic' and to compound, emblematically, the harmony he wishes to produce. But to the *Li Ki* the Emperor was simply drawing on the forces of the dog, or the grain; in the same way as the sparrow hawk, and on the same footing:

> the sparrow hawk offers birds to the spirits.

The form of this part of the *Li Ki* is lists of what you must do in each month. Pound follows it, condensing, to make successive runnings-through in which each of a dozen planes that the West considers to be separate is made part of the same gamut: animals, flowers, Emperor's trappings, public works, agriculture, the procreation of fauna, movements of the stars, change of vegetation. The 'spirits' of all these inhabit the same music. And, as George Kearns has said, Pound has deleted connections to add ambiguity, suggesting a magic world 'where subtle structures of thought move beneath the apparent rigidity of the almanac instructions'.[3]

'Emperor's trappings, public works': this seems to be a change in the religion of the Cantos. So far, by and large, they have expressed that profound distrust of public religion that Pound nurtured as a post-Transcendentalist and perfected by reading Gourmont. Until this point in the Cantos, religion connected with 'empire' has been as bloated as empire itself: either an insulation from consciousness or a means of exploitation. 'Eleusis' has existed between two persons, or has been the property of hidden cults, leaving traces in verse that of its nature has

been incomprehensible to the 'booblik' (Pound's term) and to officialdom.

Now we have the state drawn into rite, and this theme will develop.
It is comparatively easy here: Pound has gone to a period in which all
the state's activities are related to agriculture, or to craft based on
agriculture, or agriculture-based commerce. There appear to be no
relations with other nations; the state is unchanging; no new decisions
have to be taken. For all that appears here, the Emperor is not the
priest-king as in the earliest stages of that role, when he would be a fully
active ruler, but only a *rex sacrificiolus* (a distinction that Pound was well
aware of[4]). It is not hard to have all his functions, and those of the state,
fit in with the rhythms of the seasons. From LIII, the second of the
China Cantos, begins an overview of the Chinese Empire from its
beginnings to the late eighteenth century. Here the concept of the
religious state may become more difficult.

These nine Cantos, LIII–LXI, are a digest by Pound of Father
Joseph de Mailla's *Histoire générale de la Chine*, published in Paris in
1777–85. The first four Cantos of the group summarise volumes I–IX,
which are a translation by Mailla of the standard official condensation of
the Chinese dynastic chronicles, ending at the fall of the Yuen dynasty
in 1368. The remaining Cantos are taken from a supplement covering
the years 1368 to 1780, compiled by Mailla and his editor themselves.[5]

Chinese beginnings are ancient and mythologised, and Pound begins
with the culture-heroes who invented pre-civilised life.

> Yeou taught men to break branches

– that is, in order to make houses, the source says. At this stage he can
continue the harmonies of the immanent without trouble. The characters for writing are 'signs' invented after an example in nature: bird
tracks. The Emperor Yao is complete, inevitable, 'like the sun and rain'
(LIII, p. 262); his deeds are in astronomy and handling floods. Music
goes with honest versemaking, which goes with humane agricultural
distributism, and with a sense of the 'signatures' (in the Neoplatonist
sense) of the textured, grained, differentiated things in nature:

> Yu-chan to pay sycamores
> of this wood are lutes made
> Ringing stones from Se-choui river
> (LIII, p. 263)

– that is, he is to pay sycamores as taxes, and *moly*-grass also.

But by the third page of this Canto these qualities fade, and we have entered (as these Cantos present it) the body of Chinese history, which looks remarkably homogeneous. From many allusive examples we gather that the good rulers understood that values are not materialised labour; that economic activity, the source of wealth, may be castrated by overtaxing; that if you divert your concern to amassing money, you are not amassing real wealth, but making it less likely that real wealth will be produced; and that the exchange-tokens of wealth, and wealth itself, must be circulated to be fertile:

> Earth is the nurse of all men
> I now cut off one half the taxes
> I wish to follow the sages, to honour Chang Ti by my furrow
> Let farm folk have tools for their labour it is
> for this I reduce the said taxes [. . .]
> 'Gold will sustain no man's life nor will diamonds
> keep the land under culture. . . .
> by wise circulation.[6] Bread is the base of subsistence.'
> (LIV, pp. 277–8)

Dozens of examples teach circulation of abundance and distribution – where necessary, promoted by a money handout. Those who carry these out tend (like John Adams at the plough, by implication, and like the Emperor in the annual ceremony of ploughing the imperial furrow) to be seen as enacting their reverence for the Ruler of Heaven (Chang Ti) in such fostering of fertility.

At length one example is treated in detail, and practical proposals are seen in operation.

> and at this time began Ngan
> (or more fully Ouang-Ngan-ché) to demand that they reset
> the market tribunals,
> posting every day what was on sale and what the right price of it
> (LV, p. 296)

Ngan was in favour of a 'just price' fixed by the state. He proposed taxing these markets, lightly,

> thereby relieving the poor of all douanes [customs]
> giving them easy market for merchandise
> and enlivening commerce
> by making to circulate the whole realm's abundance.

This was creative state intervention. The 'bureaucrats' objected, for institutional reasons, and had to be replaced. Ngan persisted, with proposals that Pound considers so important that he has a line placed in the margin (it is not in the current text):

> And Ngan saw land lying barren
> > because peasants had nowt to sow there
> whence said: Lend 'em grain in the spring time
> > that they can pay back in autumn
> with a bit of an increase, this wd/ augment the reserve

The tribunals in charge of this were also to value land for fair tithing; if it were done equitably, the Emperor's receipts need not fall. And as for the currency:

> Ngan made yet a third point
> that was to fix the value of money
> > and to coin *enough* denars
> that shd/ stay always on the same footing.
> > (LV, p. 297)

Then came the controversy. Amid the pessimisms voiced was this from the old minister Ssé-ma Kouang: peasants have no foresight, and will borrow more than they can pay back; in any case, this has been tried, and when the price goes up the whole province is ruined. In the midst of this sniping, and the inflexibility and greed of the mandarins

> oppressing peasants to get back their grain loans,

Ngan's rules were put into effect and

> > worked 20 years
> till Ssé-kouang reversed 'em
> > (LV, p. 298)

As well as methods of economics, Cantos LIII–LXI also show a composite picture of the ideal ruler and administrator. He is sensitive to the needs of the people, thus humane. This is a mysticism of 'the man who knows how'. He is the wind, the people are the grass. But he does not think of men in the mass; that is for the 'bloody rhooshun' (LIV, p. 276), the sort of man who like Stalin consumes 'truckloads of human materials' (*P*, 342):

great works by oppression
by splendid oppression
the Wall was from Yu-lin to Tsé-ho
and a million men worked on that wall.
(LIV, p. 285)

The humane ruler fights the ever-recurring tendency towards graft; he cuts past his institutional advisers, to communicate with the ordinary man; he considers war, hunting across farmland by courtiers, palace extravagance, first and foremost as oppressions. He reverences God and the fertility-spirits in ploughing the annual furrow. His constructive energy cannot be defeated by endless obstacles. Like Malatesta he has a sense of the creative group working together, and also like Malatesta he is aware of the suffering of the men under his command (LV, p. 295). Detail for detail this fits Pound's propaganda for Mussolini, the man with the common touch, the cutter of red tape, the drainer of marshes, the intuitive genius, fighter of oppression, promoter of reverence for grain. Mussolini had a sense of the people's pulse because he came from among them: Pound has selected that aspect of him to put in Canto XLI. His only legitimacy, Pound thought, was his know-how, and this was a point of fascist propaganda; but, put the other way round, it was the chief charge against him among Pound's literary contemporaries: that he had seized power, destroying democracy.

Therefore, perhaps, Pound brings out of China a doctrine of justifiable rebellion. Twenty-two dynasties succeeded each other in China before the revolution of 1912. By definition, each of these was illegitimate, since it was quite separate from its predecessor, and drew no 'royal blood' from it, but was an innovation resting on its ruins. Shakespeare worried about a similar problem, and the answer in *Henry IV* is very pragmatic: better a strong, well-ruling rebel than a rotten king of the right line – but don't do it too often. Henry IV has sins of usurpation to expiate, but on the whole he is a good thing, legitimised by his rule. Pound in 1934 was recommending 'The plays, especially the series of history plays, which form the true English EPOS,/as distinct from the bastard Epic' (*ABC*, 59). And one finds 'hot lords' and other verbal traces of Shakespeare in this versified China (LIV, p. 276; LIII, p. 272). The rebel justifies himself in detail in the person of Tai Tsong, the great founder of the last Chinese dynasty, that of the Manchu. The Ming regime having rotted (from the inside, as always), the tartar Manchu ruler rises. The signs of his legitimacy are that he adopts Chinese law (has a sense of civilisation) and promotes education.

He writes to the Ming Emperor, saying (again with Shakespearian echoes)

> We took arms against oppression
>   and from fear of oppression
>   not that we wish to rule over you
>   (LVIII, p. 319)

and alleging that he has tried every means of peace between their nations. He writes to the governor of Suen-hoa-fou that his aim is justice, and enters his chief argument for legitimacy: that the Ming are no longer civilised:

> you are, indeed, subjects of a great realm
>   but the larger that empire, the more shd/ it strive toward peace
> If children are cut off from parents
>   if wives can not see their husbands
> if yr houses are devast and your riches carried away
> this is not of me but of mandarins.   (LVIII, pp. 320–1)

He trounces an adviser who has misinformed the Emperor,

> Hoping this will teach you not to lie to your Emperor.

Thus he teaches loyalty, acts with restraint, and aims only to end oppression. (These of course are the millennial arguments of usurpers.) Further, Tai Tsong chose to take on the mantle of the true Chinese ancestors:

> Chose learning from Yao, Shun and Kungfutseu [Confucius],
>   from Yu leader of waters

– like Mussolini who appealed back to Roman models. He asserted his own heritage and his 'autarchy' (Pound's word in those years for a proper independence):

> I take letters from China
>   which is not to say that I take orders from any man
> I take laws, but not orders

– like Mussolini, who took over Italy on his own impulse (*J/M*, 108–10). His general, Ousan, receives the Great Seal which is popular acclamation (cf. *J/M*, 100), expressed by Pound as song, like the chants of procession for Ferdinando III of Tuscany and even (factitiously) for John Quincy Adams. The chant is 'A NOI', as they used to chant it for Mussolini, and the ideogram (not in the current text) stands for 'peace':

> in Pekin they cried OUAN SOUI
> > a thousand, ten thousand years, A NOI
> eijen, ouan soui [hail! 10,000 years]; Ousan, Ousan
> > peace maker Ousan, in the river, reeds,
> > flutes murmured Ousan
> Brought peace into China; brought in the Manchu
> Litse thought to gain Ousan,
> > roused Ousan and Ousan
> remembered his father
> > dead by the hand of Litse.
> > > τάδ' ὧδ' ἔχει

p'ing²

(LVIII, p. 323)

Pound insisted that what makes a good regime is not a system; what is needed is active intelligence, accepting no limits on its penetration. A later Canto will have the spokesman of the new house of Chou saying 'Our dynasty came in because of a great sensibility' (LXXXV, p. 543). The most exact knowing is through verse; a ruler with the kind of mind that is impervious to verse will always remain on the surface of events. 'Mussolini has told his people that poetry is a necessity *to the state*', and his associate Delcroix 'is convinced that poets ought to "occupy themselves with these matters"', namely credit, the nature of money, monetary issue etc.' (*GK*, 249); for such reasons, Pound wrote in 1938, the Emperor Chun-Tchi promoted the reading of the Confucian Book of Odes by writing a preface. Canto LVIII has ended with the above-quoted popular chant for the general who supported Chun-Tchi's new house, the Manchu. Now Chun-Tchi opens the following Canto with his prefaced praise of the Odes:

> less a work of the mind than of affects
> brought forth from the inner nature
> here sung in these odes.

Thus the mandate of heaven is transferred, by an inevitable and open process. It is the basis of this whole early-American attitude that 'there is no secret': Confucius said, in Pound's translation, 'The way out is via the door, how is it that no one will use this method' (*C*, 216). (Thoreau translated Confucius: '*Taou* [the way] is not far removed from man. If men suppose that it lies in something remote, then what they think of is not *Taou*.'[7])

But, perhaps as a necessary corollary, these Cantos now deal with all disaster and difficulty by attributing it to wilful obscurantism, and all that is obscure or unknown by assigning it to the realm of evil. A masculine principle is associated with mental clarity and with the elements of good rule; as Pound said later in his Confucian translations, 'The proper man has a shell and a direction' (*C*, 268) (a sort of case-hardened phallus[8]). On the other side are eunuchs (a common curse in Chinese court life), honorary eunuchs, and women. Buddhists and Taoists seem to belong to the second category: they get a spluttering contempt, a charge of blurring, obfuscation, expressed in phonetic metaphors of fizz, swish, blurr; they are always 'Bhud-Foes' creating 'Bhud mess' with their faith in a porcine-sounding 'Boudha', or 'Taozers' and 'Taotsse'. In general women in this section only function as enchanters, leading men astray, incapacitating them for action; or in intrigue, allied with the eunuchs, entangling empire. In frivolity and irresponsibility they are thus associated with the intellectual crimes among ruling classes that cause regimes to rot – solipsistic scholarship in particular:

> The highbrows are full of themselves
> learnèd, gay and irrelevant
> on such base nothing stands
> (LIV, p. 278)

Woman is now Circe only, and Circe no longer makes that beautiful world of 'sharp song' that was shown in Canto XXXIX; her bed no longer leads to Persephone's dark realm and thence to light (as in XLVII). There is now no teaching that confusion or the unknown can be a source of the new. At the same time there is no Ovid or metamorphosis. Everything appears to be known; is it not written on the tablets, which are locked in the caskets, in the hall of the ancestors, 'as check on successors' (LIV, p. 277)? Here we have that old aim of perpetual mental-moral consciousness, as it descended from Augustine to Puritans and their strenuous descendants the Adamses. It creates that taut vigour which is both the verbal form and the only moral commandment of these Cantos:

> Tching ouang kept lynx eye on bureaucrats   (LIII, p. 267)

This ethic seems to make Pound unreceptive to all but the simpler qualities of life. His source itself – Mailla – is without a sense of the qualitative difference of epochs; 800 BC feels no different from 800 AD. Time after time Pound digests off what little authenticity the anecdotes have, and regurgitates mere vicissitudes. Often, since he is in a hurry, he has to 'make it new' by translating into modern equivalents, by means of Mussolinian or history-book tags: 'Quindecennio', '*confino*', 'they tried a star chamber'. Thus instead of making us see deep identity (in an alien culture), Pound merely gives us identity, as if it were both deep and surface; and the result is a cupboard full of Western junk.

Interesting vowel-sequence now becomes a mere trick to apply emphasis to thought that will not bear its weight – as in this hollow 'aroused':

> A hot lord and unlettered, that knew to correct his own faults
> > as indeed when he had first seen palace women, their splendour
> > > yet listened to Fan kouai
> and had gone out of Hien-yang the palace, aroused.
> > > > > > (LIV, p. 276)

Elizabethan diction and word-order have the same effect here. Pound's personal metric converts itself to the portentous tones thus established: 'After 23 years of reign, thăt pénsiŏnĕd thĕ éldĕrs' (LIV, p. 278). Certain stylistic fiddles aim to raise this material above prose: omission/ inclusion of article, inversion of subject and verb, semantic extension of the verb 'to be' – 'and HAN was after 43 years of TSIN dynasty' (LIV, p. 275). They become as wearisome as was once the iambic pentameter, whose grand tensions had fulfilled the same function from Marlowe's to Pound's day. This account of the versification does injustice to a number of passages, but gives the general effect of the whole: Pound is losing 'Eleusis'.

(ii)   THE ADAMS CANTOS

The last date given in the margin of the old Faber edition, in the China section, is 1735; and 1735 is the first date marked in the margin in

Adams's part. It is Adams's birthday. The same number of pages are taken to cover his life as are taken for the whole of Chinese history; thus the two parts form a diptych, as George Kearns has said, and the reader is clearly being asked to look for a continuation in the second part of the same values as have already been found in the first.

Perhaps the central motto of this section is CHENG MING 正名, the Confucian ideograms for the proper naming of things. John Adams was by profession a lawyer. Nervous and emulative, he neglected the province law and plunged into the arcana of the Roman and English fundamentals. He even betook himself to the history of the feudal law, which could bring no income to a struggling family in a small New England town. The times at last brought the 'Cause to Speak to, and exert all the Soul and all the Body I own, to cut a flash, strike amazement, to catch the Vulgar'[9] that he had longed for: in 1761, George III's government instituted the Writs of Assistance, giving (as it seemed to the Americans) illegal powers for the carrying-out of Customs searches. Now there was an issue. From 1765, when the Stamp Act tried to tax all legal and public papers in the colonies, each coercive move by the British government was met with an acute and influential paper by Adams, based on his arcane studies.

Pound undertakes to show that all the British tyrannies were breaches of ancient constitutional rights, operating under cover of verbal sleight of hand. In September 1772 it was announced that the Massachusetts judges would no longer be paid by the elected General Court of the province, but by the Crown; this was Lord North's way of getting the judiciary into his power. One Brattle, an American, thought that it would make no difference to the judges: under English law, all judges were appointed for life. Adams wrote his 'Independence of the Judiciary' articles to show that it was not so:

> It is the wish of almost all good men, replied Adams
> that what Brattle states were good law.
> But from Edward First's time to the present letters patent
> are otherwise worded
> > sic: *beneplacitu nostro.*
>
> (LXVI, p. 385)

That is: the king's official letters appointing judges had always said 'during our good pleasure'.[10] The government in London would therefore wait until the ignorant confusion of the Americans had allowed judges' dependence on the new Crown salaries to be established and accepted, and then, when some judge showed himself rebellious, remove him.

Adams's *Novanglus* papers tried to clear away a similar obfuscation. The struggle against British power was not 'rebellion', for the English had no proper claim to rule within the colonies. The British pretensions to rule over American internal affairs were new (cf. LXVII, p. 389), and based on verbal trickery. The king's rule could only be absolute in conquered countries; America was never conquered by the king. The king granted colonial charters; but these ceased to be valid, in English law, the moment they were exported. Apologists – like Adams's opponent – claimed that the king ruled within the colonies by consent of Parliament; Parliament was the effective and proper ruler. No, says Adams, Parliament granted no charters to colonists. The original colonists owed their fealty to the king; the king is not Parliament; in feudal law, which is the only law governing direct relations with the king,

> homage, fealty are to the person
> can not be to body politic
> (LXVII, p. 390)

English law is a law of the realm. The rule of Parliament, within the fundamental assumptions of that law, is over people within the English realm, represented in Parliament. Parliament has never yet presumed to rule over another people in a foreign land; the common law has no provision for the enforcement of such rule (LXVII, p. 388) But why, if Adams and his fellow-strugglers intended to exert superior force to free themselves from English power, did they bother with arguments based on English law for doing so? Because the whole sense of what they were aiming for (freedom and justice) was drawn from that law, which therefore they had no wish to deny. British governments were simply using confusions of that law for their own purposes. Adams wrote, in Pound's source: 'But "our charter is in the royal style." What then? Is that the parliamentary style?' The king 'governed England by one parliament, Scotland by another. Which parliament were we to be governed by?'[11] To arrive at this deception of the public, Adams's opponent (like the British government he argues for)

> now leaps over law
> now over fact now over charters and contracts
> (LXVII, pp. 388–9)

His writing 'Irritat mulcet et falsis terroribus implet' (LXVII, p. 388)
– 'annoys, appeases, and fills with false fears'. The goal is the
subjugation of one people by another, and the way is the confusion of
terms.

Adams's job was the clarification of the right use of terms: cheng[4]
ming[2] 正名 [12] The phrase appears on the title-page of the previous

section of Cantos, the *Fifth Decad*, London, 3 June 1937, and it closes
the same book. It is fully glossed the following year in the *Guide to
Kulchur*, with great prominence, the gloss being given the second page
of the body of the book and one-seventh of Pound's whole 'Digest' of
Confucius' Analects. This is part:

> *Tseu-Lou asked: If the Prince of Mei appointed you head of the
> government, to what wd. you first set your mind?*
>
> KUNG [Confucius]: *To call people and things by their names, that is
> by the correct denominations, to see that the terminology was exact.*
>
> 正名
>
> [. . .] *If the terminology be not exact, if it fit not the thing, the govern-
> mental instructions will not be explicit, if the instructions aren't clear and
> the names don't fit, you can not conduct business properly.*
>
> *If business is not properly run the rites and music will not be honoured,
> if the rites and music be not honoured, penalties and punishments will not
> achieve their intended effects, if penalties and punishments do not produce
> equity and justice, the people won't know where to put their feet or what to
> lay hold of or to whom they shd. stretch out their hands.*
>
> *That is why an intelligent man cares for his terminology and gives
> instructions that fit. When his orders are clear and explicit they can be put
> into effect. An intelligent man is neither inconsiderate of others nor futile in
> his commanding. (GK, 16–17)*

A second role for Adams in these Cantos is as Odysseus, the plain
man with guts ('THUMON', LXII, p. 345; cf. *Odyssey*, 5.298) and
confidence in his own wits and knowledge. The whole action of
Adams's life as propagandist for revolution is 'very American'. He set
himself to know the constitutional law well enough to be his own
authority on it; to go behind the utterances of those who held the keys
of St Peter, whose only authority was their mystique.

'Authority' was on the side of the British, in law. The British ministers and judges sat in the same halls where the historic developments of English law had taken place; they sat among thickets of the oracular records of law. The American colonies did not possess one complete set of British Statutes, until Adams imported one. Adams had by sweat and persistence to find out what the law was in the given case. From the Statute Books he found what Lord North's government had hoped no American would realise was in them, to wit, a statute expressly forbidding what the British claimed a right to do:

> I had imported from London the
> only complete set of British Statutes
>   then in Boston or, I think, in the whole
> of the Colonies, and in that work a statute
> whose publication they feared, an
> express prohibition of empressment
> expressly IN America   (LXIV, p. 359)

The Adams papers, and Pound's excerpts from them, are full of denunciations of shimmering and deceiving veils:

> pompous rituals theatrical ceremonies
>   so successfully used to
> delude to terrify men out of virtue and liberty
>   (LXVI, p. 383)

Now, it is very interesting that this particular denunciation was published (1767) in the persona of Governor Winthrop, doughty voyager and first founder (1630) of a viable Puritan settlement in New England. Adams will have it that the Puritans left the homeland, in effect, for freedom; thus, in his fictional dialogue, Winthrop addresses Bradford:

> True religion, my friend Bradford, was the grand motive, with you and me, to undertake our arduous and hazardous enterprise, and to plant a religion in the world, on the large and generous principles of the Bible, without teaching for doctrines the commandments of men, or any mixture of those pompous rituals, and theatrical ceremonies, which had been so successfully employed to delude and terrify men out of all their knowledge, virtue, liberty, piety, and happiness.[13]

With 'the large and generous principles of the Bible', it becomes clear that Adams is going to make the Puritans into Enlightenment figures; and this he does. Adams felt very passionately (and very Puritanly)

about the baseless authority of majestic shows. He sweated, with agony
and disgust, over the ecclesiastical Latin of Lancelottus' edition of the
Corpus Juris Canonici, in order that he might justify his sense of the

> fraud and system of bigotry
> on which papal usurpation are founded, monument of priestly
> ambition
> guile wrought into system   (LXIII, p. 353)

And his labours issued in that 'very American' document – Adams's
first important public paper (1765) – *A Dissertation on the Canon and the
Feudal Law*, which is not so much a dissertation on either of those as a
denunciation of

> all that dark ribaldry of hereditary, indefeasible right, – the Lord's
> anointed, – and the divine, miraculous original government, with
> which the priesthood had enveloped the feudal monarch in clouds
> and mysteries [...]14

In this paper, as his editor has noted, Adams is another radical, a Tom
Paine. The reason why the Pilgrim Fathers left Europe was, again, that

> They knew that government was a plain, simple, intelligible thing,
> founded in nature and reason, and quite comprehensible by common
> sense.

In the same paragraph (Adams would never do it later in his life),
Rousseau is invoked, prophet of 'nature', which is one of the chief
items in Adams's mental apparatus in this early stage of his public
career.

The Puritans, as Adams repeatedly insists in this tract, were to
educate themselves with those texts that were open, available to all.
Neither would they be ignorant, nor would they be corrupted by
learning; and Adams exhorts his contemporaries:

> nor suffer yourselves to be wheedled out of your liberty by any
> pretences of politeness, delicacy, or decency. These, as they are often
> used, are but three different names for hypocrisy, chicanery, and
> cowardice.

They were to be nature's men: plain, blunt, unbamboozlable natural aristocrats. And this is how Pound (in 1937) describes Odysseus, never without his poise, as when, naked and caked with salt, he confronts Nausicaa: 'Ulysses the *toff*, liftin his imaginary highhat as he comes out of the underbrush' (*L*, 299).

Thus, as one of Adams's archetypes is 'Romish superstition', and another is the plain blunt Protestant who cuts through it, so the latter comes to take in both Puritans and noble savages and (in these Cantos) both Adams and Odysseus. As with Van Buren in an earlier section, Pound makes Adams Odyssean by diction:

> Be bubbled out of their liberties by a few large names,
> Hume, probably not having read them.
>   (LXVIII, p. 395)

The eighteenth-century circumspection in the source of this has almost been deleted. Pound abbreviates Adams ('wd/'), and gives him the Cockney that he used himself to address Eliot's colleagues at Faber with, or the gangsterese mixed with Brooklyn that he used to address Hemingway. He interpolates anachronisms ('endocrine') and purely Poundian paraphrases ('In fact the oily writer now leaps over law'). Yet he leaves dozens of lines that, though abbreviated, have the decorum of their century: 'its emolument gave but a bare scanty subsistence', 'not less of order than of liberty'. Pound has created a voice, like his own created voice, in which the toff subsists easily with the tough guy, and is a crust sheddable at will. With this, his Adams strides in, Huck Finn among the conmen, and cuts through the cackle:

> '[...] against paying for things we haven't ordered'
>   J. Adams
>   (LXVIII, p. 396)

And having cut through to his point (which is the proper naming of things) in law, he stops ('e poi basta': LXXIX, p. 486; cf. *C*, 269):

> the materials are at the service of the public
> I leave them to jewelers and lapidaries to refine
> to fabricate and to polish.   (LXVII, p. 387)

After CHENG MING, the proper naming of things, and Odysseus's THUMON or straight heart, 'the common law of England' seems to make a third motto for the Adams Cantos. The conception of the

English common law bequeathed by Coke, the great Elizabethan, and his predecessors, was a supra-pragmatic one; this law could never, except by error of interpretation, be in disaccord with 'natural law'; and so its tradition becomes a mystic fount of right, and its ancient phrases, in these Cantos, a litany (LXVI, p. 384; LXVII, p. 387). And finally Pound makes Adams into another Cavalcanti, whose motto here would be 'IRA' or 'rage to know', a sort of enthusiasm or divine anger. The Adams Cantos are dotted with Cavalcanti phrases connoting passion of the intelligence (LXVII, p. 391; LXIII, p. 353; LXX, p. 410).

It seems to me that the Adams section of the Cantos presents the 'paideuma' of its hero (his inherited attitudes and awarenesses) in the best possible light, and that the failings of the section are his failings. Pound's source is *The Works of John Adams*, edited and with a biography by Charles Francis Adams. As a 'found object', this has an ordering that Pound is able to exploit. Unlike Mailla's *Histoire générale de la Chine*, it does not proceed in a straight chronological line. The editor was working with a mountain of heterogeneous artefacts (some of them letters, some three-volume tracts) left by Adams, the first prodigious scribbler in a family of scribblers. And the editor prefaces the bulky *Works* with his own 'Life' of John Adams. Following this shaping, Pound for example must complete the whole chronological cycle of Adams's life, before going back to the start to pick up the earliest diaries. But since almost all the words in these Adams Cantos are John Adams's, the method of writing is drastic cutting; and if a ten-page Canto is to come from a 300-page volume there are considerable possibilities for changing emphasis. In any case Pound does not give equal attention to all volumes, and Volume V does not appear at all. With the thousand mouldings, compressions, excisions and new connections that these means allow, Pound arrives at a sort of onion in the ordering of themes:

XLII: *Overview*, and Adams's *humanity* (defence of Captain Preston).

LXIII: *Ira*, *passion* that gives understanding; Adams the Odyssean explorer in learning ('must dig with my fingers/as nobody will lend me or sell me a pick axe').

LXIV, LXV, part of LXVI: The *struggle* against obscurantism and chicanery: effecting the Revolution, keeping America afloat.

The remainder of LXVI, LXVII, 1½ pages of LXVIII: The *centre*.

The remainder of LXVIII, LXIX, LXX: The *struggle*.

LXXI: Adams's youthful *passion*, seen in retrospect; his *humanity* (pity for coalheavers). *Coda.*

What I have called 'the centre' is taken from what Adams published during his lifetime, therefore naturally the most concentrated expression of him: it weaves together 'cheng⁴ ming²', the right naming; pugnacious Odysseus; English law; and Cavalcanti's passion/knowing. It is thus like Pound's Cantos, a 'great ball of crystal' that lies in the midst of his deeds and recorded analects, formed by the pressure of a life whose lesser evidence lies around it.

What flatness, undifferentiation, the section none the less has seems to come from Adams. Both Adams's morality and his aesthetic seem negative, stoic, Horatian, and naturally to express themselves in a language of ordered and delimited abstractions:

Let every declamation turn upon the beauty of liberty and virtue, and the deformity, turpitude, and malignity, of slavery and vice.[15]

Behind the precisions of Adams's public language, and its gusto and range of observation, we come to a blank wall of awareness, whose nature may be suggested by this remark about the thirteen new constitutions:

[. . .] it will forever be acknowledged that these governments were contrived merely by the use of reason and the senses, as Copley painted Chatham; West, Wolf; and Trumbull, Warren and Montgomery; as Dwight, Barlow, Trumbull, and Humphries composed their verse, and Belknap and Ramsay history [. . .][16]

Painting by Locke is not so different from painting by numbers. Pound (LXVII, p. 393) suppresses this end of Adams's sentence.

NOTES: CHAPTER 11

1 'Verse is a sword: unpublished letters of Ezra Pound', ed. Noel Stock, in *X*, vol. 1, no. 4 (October 1960), p. 265.
2 Compare the doctrines of John Heydon (who appears in *Rock-Drill*) summarised in George Dekker, *Sailing after Knowledge: The Cantos of Ezra Pound* (London: Routledge & Kegan Paul, 1963), p. 83.
3 George Kearns, *Guide to Ezra Pound's 'Selected Cantos'* (New Brunswick, NJ: Rutgers University Press, 1980), p. 130.

4 Lewis and Short, *A Latin Dictionary*: 'the priest who makes offerings formerly made by the king'. See LVIII, p. 316.

5 For Pound's methods, see J. Driscoll, *The China Cantos* (Uppsala: Uppsala University, 1983).

6 But the original 'circulation' here refers to the judicious posting of bureaucrats. See J. J. Nolde, 'The sources for Canto LIV: Part One', *Paideuma*, vol. 5, no. 3 (Winter 1976), pp. 434–5.

7 Henry David Thoreau, *Early Essays and Miscellanies*, ed. J. D. Moldenhauer and E. Moser (Princeton, NJ: Princeton University Press, 1975), pp. 149–50.

8 The relevant character is 'chen' (LXXXIX, p. 635); the bottom part is a shell, and Pound perhaps read the top as 'direction'.

9 *Diary and Autobiography of John Adams*, ed. L. H. Butterfield (New York: Atheneum, 1964), diary entry for 14 March 1759.

10 Frederick K. Sanders, *John Adams Speaking: Pound's Sources for the Adams Cantos* (Orono, Me: University of Maine Press, 1975), p. 296, mistakes the meaning of this phrase, following the *Annotated Index to the Cantos of Ezra Pound: Cantos I–LXXXIV*, ed. J. H. Edwards and W. W. Vasse (Berkeley, Calif.: University of California Press, 1971).

11 *John Adams Speaking*, p. 328.

12 Like so many texts that Pound brings into his system, this one is controversial: its meaning in the Confucius passage may be very broad or very restricted, and the passage itself may be spurious. See Confucius, *Confucian Analects*, trans. J. Legge (New York: Dover, 1971), p. 264 n.; *Les Mémoires historiques de Se-Ma Tsien*, trans. E. Chavannes (Paris: Adrien-Maisonneuve, 1967), Vol. 5, p. 379 n.; Wing-Tsit Chan, *A Source Book in Chinese Philosophy* (Princeton University Press, 1963), p. 40; *KPE*, p. 585 (note to p. 446); *GK*, p. 21.

13 *John Adams Speaking*, p. 280.

14 L. Kriegel (ed.), *Essential Works of the Founding Fathers* (New York: Bantam, 1964), p. 12.

15 ibid., p. 21.

16 *John Adams Speaking*, pp. 345–6.

CHAPTER 12

Commentary
The Pisan Cantos
(LXXIV–LXXXIV)

Pound had put all his credit as a writer behind Mussolini, and for years had put a great deal of his working energy into both gathering support for, and moulding, his regime. The propaganda against usury was both for Mussolini (the enemy was that 'league of lice'[1] the League of Nations, responsible for the Sanctions against Italy), and intended to influence Mussolini's regime (thus Pound's effort to persuade ministers about the Douglas doctrines: Int, 175–6; CI, p. 726). The effort for the Rapallo music programme was both cultural propaganda for Italy, and an effort to lift Italy from cultural torpor. Pound could be said to have worshipped Mussolini in his own way – even D'Annunzio's praise has a ring of falsity compared to Pound's. He had aligned all history and all morality into the struggle between Roosevelt and Churchill – on behalf of the 'loan lice' – and the Axis powers; and Mussolini was the moral energy of the latter. It is known that Fascist officialdom brushed Pound off, but that made no difference to his prewar efforts on both sides of the Atlantic, and these efforts made him allies of some quality among those who had small influence (Uberti, Pisani; in America, Bronson Cutting, George Tinkham and others). Accident or bureaucrats' malice had marooned Pound in Italy when the United States entered the war, and his response was yet more fervently to identify himself with the Mussolini regime. In the eyes of the United States Department of Justice he became a traitor by broadcasting to his countrymen on Rome Radio. The exhausting tension of his whole position is visible in the text of the broadcasts, but also in his testimony to the psychiatrists appointed by the United States District Court when he was later charged with treason. When Rome fell, with the Germans using the length of Italy as a corpse to delay the wolves, Pound made his way north on foot and by what transport was available, amid maximum danger of being shot out of hand by partisans or Germans ('Who *says* he is an American': LXXVIII, p. 478). Instead of escaping to Switzerland, as did many prominent fascists, he stayed to offer his services during the brief hopeless life of the Salò Republic, still trying simultaneously both to mould and to defend the regime with his ever more idealist and Confucian propaganda. It was at this point that he wrote Cantos LXXII and LXXIII, which have not yet been admitted to the canon.

They were both written in Italian, and offered to the regime in November 1944, then to Mussolini himself in early 1945. They are not successful pieces of writing. The value of LXXII would be in its political invective, in which the old Ghibelline Ezzelino da Romano, the brother of Cunizza (*Paradiso*, 9), renews the Dantescan charge that the Church, claiming temporal power, destroyed the Empire. For the present Pope is an arch-usurer, moral ally of the king who has sold Italy to Mussolini's enemies. But the opening of this Canto is mock-cosmic-epic, like a jocular version of the beginning of Ovid's *Metamorphoses*. The work thus seems to apologise for its own pretensions (which was the fault of *Redondillas*, an attempt at epic that Pound printed but withdrew in 1911). And thus the dramatic framework that follows seems to be presented only half-seriously. Nor is it in the least dramatically interesting: the speakers merely appear before the poet, and fade.

In LXXIII the poet listens to Guido Cavalcanti, who has encountered a peasant-girl singing of love. Her love was that which led her, having been raped by Canadian soldiers, to take a group of them to their deaths by guiding them into a minefield. It is clear that the 'love' described is the kind that Pound intended when he wrote, in 1942, that without strong tastes one cannot love or, therefore, exist (*OS*, 1390; *P*, 328). The strong tastes ('forti gusti') evidently include strong disgusts and hate. The Canto picks up some musical interest from Cavalcanti's rhyming half-lines, but has not the smell of life about it, and expects to convert the reader to an understanding of the girl's emotions by a mere repetition of love, splendour and light. It seems like a usual enough example of war hysteria.

When the Salò Republic collapsed, Pound was finally fortunate enough to get into the hands of the United States Army alive. He was taken to the Disciplinary Training Center at Pisa, a prison camp for the army's 'brawlers, killers, rapists, malingerers'. 'Some of the "trainees" were destined for federal prisons in the United States, some were hanged at Aversa, and others were shot down in attempts to escape.

Pound was the only civilian prisoner.' According to notes made later by Pound's attorney,

'At Pisa, Pound was confined in a cage made of air-strip, and in solitary confinement. Cage was in yard with little shelter from sun or rain. Bright lights on stockade shone at night. Two guards outside at all times. Slept on cement floor with 6 blankets. Can for toilet. Allowed no reading matter except Confucius he was working on. Incommunicado. Was told nobody knew where he was.

'After 3 weeks, Pound collapsed. Taken out of cage and put in tent. Partial amnesia. Claustrophobia. Not allowed to talk to other prisoners (told this was ordered by Washington) [. . .] (*NEP*, 397)

He was stricken with 'violent terror and hysteria'; '[. . .] he can now recall only the sensation that the top of his head was empty; also that his eyebrows were constantly taut in a raised position, due to the heat and glare'.[2] He was given a tent and a cot and medical treatment, and it was during this period of convalescence that the Pisan Cantos were written.

Pound's theology, or faith, which was not for him a decoration but a shaper of his life, now came in danger of collapse, as is visible in these Cantos. Pound had spent a good proportion of the wartime years translating the Chinese classic books; he was more and more mystically convinced that Confucius' was the law of all durable government, and that Mussolini had succeeded and failed in precisely the proportion that he was Confucian – as, again, these Cantos tell us.[3] When Pound wished to express the central principle of the Confucian metaphysic he used to terms of the Duecento, the age of Cavalcanti: 'virtù irraggiante', 'irradiating *virtù*'. And he referred his reader to Plato and Guinizelli (*OS*, 504, 591). Thus the Confucian translations that Pound published in Italian were an assimilation of Confucius' thought to the Duecento wisdom. Italy was the chosen land for Confucianism in the West.

The metaphysic of the Confucian *Chung Yung* or *Unwobbling Pivot* (published in Italian in February 1945) is that things are not heaps of contingent dust-drift, but have essential principles, which are durable; which are part of an overarching tendency or Principle in the universe; and which, being a shaping and therefore good principle operative in man as in other things, a man may come to understand. This metaphysic is all about the relation between wholes and fragments. The mosaic is not its little glass and gold-leafed fragments; the Virgin shines

down from the apse at Torcello when, or if, half of the fragments that
make her have fallen, or the whole has been replaced; and so on. This is
merely a matter of faith, inasmuch as no analysis can establish the point
at which the work begins to 'exist'; no psychology can establish the
point at which the individual man 'exists' apart from causalities;
novelists can only suggest points at which an autonomous free will was
exercised, or alternatively (Dreiser) refrain from suggesting that there
were any such points. Sometimes this faith in the existence of whole
entities seems itself contingent. When disintegration in surrounding
things reaches a certain level the stoutest heart may cease to believe that
there is any essential integrity anywhere. Conrad and Ford repeatedly
perform the experiment of removing, one by one, the 'accidental'
(circumstantial or cultural) props to a man's idea of order, and watching
the idea of order collapse in that man's mind. Circumstances in Italy
now performed the same experiment on Pound.

One of the centres of Hemingway's writing can be seen in the rain-
sodden shambles of the retreats in *in our time* and *A Farewell to Arms*.
Pound had particularly approved of the latter novel when it appeared,[4]
but now, describing his own escape northwards among refugees in a
rejected draft for these Cantos,

> Lo sfacelo [the collapse],   understood why Hem had written,
> that is, his values.[5]

Thereafter he was among continual hatred and death.

Pound's Confucian texts in Italian asserted, confidently, coherence.
The principle is not capable of splitting. There is that whose wholeness
is beyond any power to split (*spezzare; OS*, 527; cf. *C*, 117) and thus
render merely contingent. It is possible for a man to find his durable
centre in such a way that nothing can displace him from it: 'The man of
breed can not be split (*spezzato*) in such a way as to be shut off and
unable to rejoin himself' (*OS*, 535). Now, in these Cantos, lengthy and
complex passages are full of reverberations that suggest the opposite. In
the following heap of fragments, few things are new; but they are now
seen from the opposite end of their process:

> E al Triedro [and at the trihedron], Cunizza
> e l'altra: 'Io son' la Luna.' [and the other: 'I am the Moon.']
> dry friable earth going from dust to more dust

        grass worn from its root-hold
      is it blacker? was it blacker? Νύξ animae [the night of the soul]?
      is there a blacker or was it merely San Juan [St John] with a belly ache
                                    writing ad posteros [to posterity]
      in short shall we look for a deeper or is this the bottom?
      Ugolino, the tower there on the tree line
Berlin   dysentery   phosphorus
                        la vieille de Candide [the old woman of *Candide*]
      (Hullo Corporal Casey) double X or bureaucracy?
                                Le Paradis n'est pas artificiel
                                [Paradise is not artificial]
      but spezzato [fragmented] apparently
    it exists only in fragments unexpected excellent sausage,
                        the smell of mint, for example,
                        Ladro [Thief] the night cat;
      at Nemi waited on the slope above the lake sunken in the
                                        pocket of hills
      awaiting decision from the old lunch cabin built out over the
                                                shingle,
      Zarathustra, now desuete
      to Jupiter and to Hermes where now is the castellaro
            no vestige save in the air
      in stone is no imprint and the grey walls of no era
                under the olives   (LXXIV, p. 438)

The reference to the dark night of the soul is more or less abstract, and
distanced by a posture of objective discussion (like most, if not all, of
the speaker's direct allusions to his own state in this book of the
Cantos). But the mythemes assembled here all connote defeat.[6] At some
trihedral structure, it seems, there was once a vision of Cunizza/Venus
with Diana; but this trihedron is to be associated before long with the
Castellaro near Rapallo and the abandoned altars to Zarathustra, Jupiter
and Hermes, a mere pile of stones. It is also to be associated with
Montségur, the 'Eleusinian' cult heroes' stronghold, and the 'stair there
still broken'. Earlier in the Cantos, these held an aura of somewhat
attractive and energising melancholy, of the kind that still inspires
movements of Celtic or Occitanian cultural revival: a mixture of anger
at oppression, and Romantic loss. Now, loss is only loss. Earlier Cantos
are full of broken temples, but the earlier response was determination
to rebuild: to put back the statue of Venus on the cliffs at Terracina, to
'build a dream over the world' (*SL*, 307) (in the form of a stone temple,
projected with Brancusi, or of Mussolini's political 'celestial city'). Now
this Luna (Diana) merely tells us 'I am the moon

and they have broken my house'

the huntress in broken plaster keeps watch no longer
(LXXVI, p. 453)

Zarathustra's temple here is, passively, 'desuete'.

Hence the extremely tentative image of Earthly Paradises (or, simply, Paradise?) that comes in the middle of this passage. It is stated that Paradise is not a wrenched emotional condition, as induced by drugs, sleeplessness, strange music, carrying night into day, and the other apparatus of Baudelaire and his master Poe. Paradise simply exists. On the other hand, how?

> spezzato apparently
> it exists only in fragments unexpected excellent sausage,
> the smell of mint, for example,
> Ladro the night cat

This sausage may be metaphor, or example: the surprise when the palate encounters aroma may be what Paradise is 'like' – sudden and unforeseen; or it may be that this is a Real Presence, that Paradise actually manifests itself in such sudden delights. But, though this sausage-paradise is not a mere joke, it is very tentative ('apparently') and humble (not a magnificent fauns' landscape like that of Canto XX), and also passive on the speaker's part: 'direction of the will' may perhaps have prepared for it, but the causality is evidently too complex for us to understand. It is spasmodic in time, and 'spezzato' in its relations, which is what the Italian version of Confucius' *Unwobbling Pivot* denied the fundamental heavenly Principle to be. This Canto does not, perhaps, deny that principle, but puts man in very tenuous connection with it.

Here the spiritual hero and priest-king, the bard/prophet and grain-hero, is going to be much less the effective stimulator of the heavens' activities on behalf of his people, and much more the mere forewarner of them by his sensitivity (like the tribal chieftain in Upward's description). So when, now, the thought of mint, the sudden paradisal pleasure, takes the poem on to the thought of the cat, it is not the noble sun-worshipper of earlier Cantos, but a night thief. Certainly cats by now can always suggest Dionysus the fertility-god, or his priest, or Pound (depending on their momentary states, these may not be separable), and this connotes a myth of rebirth. But rebirth comes after death – a fact which, though finally emerging in the last Adonis

Canto (XLVII), was even there subsumed in heroism and godly fructiveness of understanding, as well as the seasons' renewal. But the sacrificial priest at Nemi in Frazer's first reconstruction is to be sacrificed when, and because, his verility has failed: when his powers are exhausted. From the point of view of that moment in the story, there is now only a miserable waiting:

> at Nemi waited on the slope above the lake sunken in the
> > pocket of hills
> awaiting decision from the old lunch cabin built out over the
> > shingle

The Cantos now fill with images of sudden miserable death, after 'the mortal fatigue of action postponed' (LXXX, p. 493), such as the author is now enduring, under charge of treason. The speaker is now among the 'po'eri di'aoli [poor devils] sent to the slaughter' by the power of Circe teamed with the power of usury to compass the butchery of all heroes, like the Dionysian bull (associated with the temple of Zarathustra?) that is the image for Agamemnon, brought home to be slaughtered: 'like a dog [. . .] and a good job', as his wife says.[7] Or like Mussolini on the first page of these Cantos:

> That maggots shd/ eat the dead bullock

Governed by such emotions one would not set out to argue points into a programme. And we find that the form of the Pisan Cantos is, first, a simple cry of pain and, second, a naming-over of what has been known, sorrowing over the lost, and trying to find, in what is left, some hope-worthy meaning and reason to go on. The composition took place over a number of months, to judge by the references to seasons and the movements of constellations. And a clear and conscious aesthetic theory governed in some degree its form; as Pound explained to the Base Censor when sending it off to his daughter:

> The present Cantos do, naturally, contain a number of allusions and 'recalls' to matter in the earlier 71 cantos already published, and many of these cannot be made clear to readers unacquainted with the earlier parts of the poem.
> There is also an extreme condensation in the quotations, for example 'Mine eyes have' (given as mi-hine eyes hev) refers to the Battle Hymn of the Republic as heard from the loud speaker. There

is not time or place in the narrative to give the further remarks on
seeing the glory of the lord.

In like manner citations from Homer or Sophokles or Confucius
are brief, and serve to remind the ready reader that we were not born
yesterday [. . .]

The form of the poem and main progress is conditioned by its own
inner shape, but the life of the D.T.C. passing OUTSIDE the
scheme cannot but impinge, or break into the main flow. The proper
names given are mostly those of men on sick call seen passing my tent
[. . .][8]

But this is perhaps largely an editing theory: criteria by which, in
retrospect, the better parts of this writing were considered acceptable as
part of the Cantos. There are indications that long pieces of the poem
were written as continuous outpourings, much as Ginsberg sat in an
apartment and wrote the bulk of *Howl* in an afternoon. The writing was
not at first divided into Cantos, and Pound seems to have had some
difficulty in knowing when he had reached the end of the whole
utterance.[9]

Pound shows how near to the freedom (or shapelessness) of ordinary
conversation this can seem, and yet be quite audibly verse by internal
patterning. Such patterning can exist in what passes for prose; as in
Pound's translation of the *Unwobbling Pivot* into English, set out here
as verse:

> To sleep on a heap of arms and
> untanned skins,
> to die unflinching
> and as if dying were not enough,
> > that is
> Nordic energy
> and the energetic accumulate that sort of energy.
> > (*C*, 111–13)

The converse experiment is to set out some of the Pisan verse as prose;
but some minimal indications of sound-pattern are added here:

and the liars on the quai at Siracusa still vie with Odysseus, seven
words to a b*o*mb; d*u*m capitoli*um sc*andet, the re*st* is explodable. Very
*po*tent, can they *ag*ain put one together, as *the two halves of a seal*, or a
tally stick? Shun's *will* and King Wan's *will* were as *the two halves of a
seal* (½s) in the Middle Kingdom.   (LXXVII, p. 467)

Even the cry or monologued remembrance is not likely to be pure sound; even 'AOI' (LXXXI, p. 519) has associations (with the *Song of Roland*, at least). Pound had been working in his verse on 'the life vouchsafed' (*WW*, 94) during his Odyssey. Pound's Odyssey had been largely in search of Culture – very unlike that of Odysseus. (There were no bookstalls on the *quai* at Aiaia at which to pick up old *Odysseys*, as Pound did: *E*, 259.) That is what Pound's mind was now full of, and what he uttered: 'registered' interpenetrating High Culture and life.

But at last Pound was cut off from massive source-material, from the British Museum and Italian archives and his note-strewn workroom. He tapped what new sources he could. One that left traces was Speare's popular verse anthology, found in the latrine; but that was mostly a stirring of old memory. Pound read the Old Testament, but its tones were not unknown to him. *Time* magazine was present, perpetuating old political rages in Pound's mind, and recording deaths. Otherwise the inputs were conversation with guards and prisoners, sights (shadows and hands passing the tent, the movement of stars and moon, and mist and mountain), and smell and sound, from 'honey-wagon' (latrine cart) to rain on earth and names on sick-call. These mixed with memory.

The Pisan Cantos name over what has been known, like the blinded soldier from the Tyrol who

> '[...] talked of every boy and girl in the valley
> but when he came back from leave
> he was sad because he had been able to feel
> all the ribs of his cow....'[10]
>
> (LXXVI, p. 458)

As in Pound's interpretation of Cavalcanti, memory becomes the storehouse of real knowledge of things because it retains only the essential shapes imprinted there by love – shapes 'truer' than any literally recorded reality. So distance from these experiences helps in the process of sorting out that 'vouchsafed' life and art more exactly, according to a Poundian scale of specific intensity. But this then becomes cultural diagnosis, and in fact the Pisan Cantos are more effective as large-scale analysis of Pound's times than anything he has written before. Pound, as a student of Leo Frobenius the anthropologist, certainly understood and intended this dimension of the book. According to Frobenius, every artefact and gesture is diagnostic of the state of the culture it comes from; from seeing the artefact, the

experienced observer should immediately be able to describe the state
of putrescence or growth of the culture within which that cultural
gesture occurred. Memory, of course, selects the most intense among
the things that the psyche has encountered. These gestures and
elements are likely to be the most profoundly diagnostic of their
organisms; for at the moment of producing them (as Pater might have
said) the organism was most intensely 'itself', and most totally moulded
the medium. Thus

> Said Mr Tancred
>   of the Jerusalem and Sicily Tancreds, to Yeats,
> 'If you would read us one of your own choice
>   and
>   perfect
>   lyrics'   (LXXXII, p. 524)

We hardly need to be told that this is about the art of 'CONversation
. . . . . .', so much is the elegance of Mr Tancred in the phrase 'of the
Jerusalem and Sicily Tancreds', so much the perfection of his choice of
cadence in the remark. That is a symptom of a sensibility, a marginal
clue to a mind and an era.

If we look at the cultural states that the Pisan Cantos diagnose in the
contemporary world, they seem to group themselves into sensibility
and grossness. Sensibility works for wholeness; grossness works for
fragmentation – perhaps by way of greed. 'Facts' are what they are, in
virtue of something complex; but he whose disposition towards the
world is a 'lusting' and 'contriving' (LXXXV, p. 544) has no time, or
humility, for subtleties, but hastens to appropriate. The high-interest
financier converts all activity into convertible self-existent money-
tokens; the economist converts all wealth into 'materialised labour';
Stalin converts people into 'truckloads of human material' (*P*, 307,
342). The fast-food operator sees all consumption as dining-room
customer-space-time units; the genuinely 'academic' critic or philosopher, all knowledge as his demarcated thought-pawns (as village
Vietnam was seen by sociologist-advisors serving the United States
government). Appropriating, these destroy. Conversely, the last book
of the Cantos will say 'That war is the destruction of restaurants' (CX,
p. 780). A good restaurant is as culturally 'factive' as an orchestra, as
vulnerable and as impossible to reconstitute.

According to the Pisan Cantos, usury has led barbarians, incapable of
distinction, to bomb Malatesta's temple, and

the voiceless with bumm drum and banners   (LXXIV, p. 428)

(the simple Brechtian soldier) to be slaughtered by his fellow, led on by mere propagandist noise. And so, later meditating on the later Beethoven, who is fit only for the electric Bechstein or the Napoleonic arena of the Piazza San Marco, we are led back in thought to that 'bumm drum' (out of Speare[11]), and the tones of Caesar's *Gallic War*:

> can that be the papal major sweatin' it out to the bumm drum?
> what castrum romanum, what
>   'went into winter quarters'
> is under us?
> as the young horse whinnies against the tubas
>   in contending for certain values
> (Janequin per esempio, and Orazio Vecchii or Bronzino)
>   (LXXIX, p. 485)

An opportune protest from the horse Pound is watching asserts the value in the clear sound of Janequin, 'as against thickness and fatness' (LXXIV, p. 432).

Thus a great part of the Pisan Cantos is occupied in locating fine sensibility, and demonstrating it. That essential grossness in our declined culture, usury, which produces Rubens, fat lines in art, and machine-carved churches, has destroyed the cakeshops, the joyous fantasy ('en casque de crystal rose') of the Nineties, and Mozart's house (LXXVIII, p. 480). But that sensibility, while it lives, is allied with the political acuteness of understanding of Pound's friends:

> Unkle George observing Ct/Volpe's neck at the Lido
> and deducing his energy. Unkle G. stood like a statue
> 'Rutherford Hayes on a monument'
>   as the princess approached him
> 'You from New England?' barked the 10th District,
>
> and it came over me as he talked:
>   this is Dafne's Sandro –
> How? after 30 years   (LXXVI, p. 461)

Congressman Tinkham discerns energy in a neck; he discerns 'New Englandness' in the princess-by-marriage who has been an expatriate for thirty years;[12] he discerns beauty, doing it homage as did Sandro Botticelli; later we are to learn of his political discernment. The speaker is the one who has discerned each of these facts, and picked out (from among the insignificant) the tone and the phrase that carry them. Each perceived fact is purified of what does not embody fully the speaker's disposition, and subtly aligned with its text-surroundings in order to preserve its force and direction. These active *formae* are bones whitened by memory's sun, which selects from the rest only that cheekbone, that cadence, that word. And the fine sensibilities, among those dispositions recorded here, knew how to live. The delighting mind plays among memories of ebullience; and this delight in not being straitjacketed, as being open and honest, seems to go against obscurantism and (consequently) tyranny.

> but old William [Yeats] was right in contending
>   that the crumbling of a fine house
> profits no one
>   (Celtic or otherwise)
> nor under Gesell would it happen
>
> As Mabel's head was a fine sight
> worthy his minstrelsy
> a tongue to the sea-cliffs or 'Sligo in Heaven'
> or his, William's, old 'da' at Coney Island perched on an elephant
> beaming like the prophet Isaiah
>   and J.Q. as it were aged 8 (Mr John Quinn)
> at the target.
>
>   'Liquids and fluids!'
>   said the palmist. 'A painter?
> well ain't that liquids and fluids?' [To the venerable J.B. bearded Yeats]
>
>   'a friend', sd/ mr cummings, 'I knew it 'cause he
> never tried to sell *me* any insurance'
>
> (with memorial to Warren Dahler the Chris Columbus of Patchin)
>
> Hier wohnt [here lives] the tradition, as per Whitman in Camden
>   (LXXX, pp. 507–8)

The forces of grossness can be divided into three kinds. The first is an as-it-were active, willed grossness, the immediate creator of wars, in which *poveri diaboli* ('poor devils') are set man against man because the usurer has set up international friction with his Gold Standards, flights of currency, rigged devaluations:

>   po'eri di'aoli
>   po'eri di'aoli sent to the slaughter
>   Knecht gegen Knecht
>   to the sound of the bumm drum, to eat remnants

> for a usurer's holiday to change the
> price of a currency
> ΜΕΤΑΘΕΜΕΝΩΝ ....
> ΝΗΣΟΝ 'ΑΜΥΜΟΝΑ
> (LXXVI, p. 463)

The second type of grossness might be the mere inevitable *tropismes* or unwilled quirks of populations, as considered in a meditation in Canto LXXXI, pp. 518–19. In village life, all is not spontaneous piety – there are hired dancers also; and networks of interest on committees, of brothers-in-law (such as would defeat those decentralised local boards for the apportionment of credit that C. H. Douglas had planned). 'The people' have their own momentum, and John Adams feared it. They also have snobbery: ordinary Frenchman does not speak to neighbour as ordinary Frenchman, but in the resounding ring of that literary tongue fixed since the seventeenth century. And conversely you have Malatesta and Federigo d'Urbino, nobles slanging each other at a peace conference like thugs. These are things men do not rise out of; like their economic ideas, these propensities will not be changed 'in less than a geological epoch'.

The third grossness seems to be part of 'the process' itself, including the pattern of natural forces that the hero senses and influences. Desire, in principle the first movement towards enlightenment, may merely dissipate and befuddle the hero: Venus merges into Circe, who is generalised into a principle of stupefaction. Circe seems allied with those usurers who have brought the United States in general between the slaver's decks; Pound proposed Douglas-and-Gesellite economics to Mussolini, who

> Sd/ one wd/ have to think about that
> but was hang'd dead by the heels before his thought in proposito
> came into action efficiently.
> 'For a pig,' Jepson said, 'for a woman.' For the infamies of usura,
> The Stealing of the Mare,   casûs bellorum,   'mits'
> sang Mr Wilson   (LXXVIII, p. 482)

That glamorous quarrel over Helen, which was one of the original impulses for the Cantos, is now a *casus belli* (pretext for war) on a level with usury.[13]

But there are various movements towards the resolution of these agonies, and they produced some of the most famous and prized lyrics in all the Cantos. One comes almost at the start of the Pisan book. It incorporates the legend of the city of Wagadu, built four times and each time destroyed. Wagadu is in fact the Idea of the City, manifested materially and then, because of its own inhabitants' evil, made invisible. But this is a myth of the millennium: 'Should Wagadu ever be found for the fourth time, then she will live so forcefully in the minds of men that she will never be lost again [...]'[14] Wagadu destroyed is, among other celestial cities, Italy betrayed (LXXIV, p. 430) through her own people's sins (which Pound comments on). She is associated with the 'dream' that Pound once wished to build 'over the world', for the 'terrace the colour of stars' alludes to the city of Dioce, a historical city built on theurgical principles (each concentric wall was of a colour appropriate to a different constellation) which in Pound's verbal formulation is insubstantial, yet to be 'built' (LXXIV, p. 425); and that word 'dream' is also the word used (LXXVI, p. 456) for Mussolini's 'effort' (LXXIV, p. 430; cf. LXXVIII, p. 478) to rebuild Italy. The political Italy that Pound tried to help build has been destroyed; but it will be 'resurrected' – 'because it is impossible', the same Canto later says (LXXIV, p. 442). That is, it will remain a dream – such things can never be more than dreams:

> I surrender neither the empire nor the temples
> plural
> nor the constitution nor yet the city of Dioce
> (LXXIV, p. 434)

The constitution is of America; the city of Dioce is of dream. Towards the end of LXXIV this whole meditation incorporates intaglios in general, as well as the Forms which are gods and goddesses; as if the Form which is Venus, seen in Pound's own lifetime, were on the same plane as the city of Achaia carved in intaglio, and cities physically built. All (like Mussolini's mind) are 'diamonds'; all are organised by that 'liquid' Intelligence that radiates from above, as the iron filings are given shape at a distance by the magnet. This seems to leave an ambiguity as to whether the 'dream' of Mussolini was ever actually manifested, and thus to be treasured in the mind like the seen sight of the goddess; or whether it ever can be manifested; or whether the dream itself is what we should be satisfied with – and this latter is the alternative preferred by critics like Noel Stock who wish poets to conclude that political efforts should never actually be undertaken.

In the thought-direction of the whole work, the Ideal City is a resolution soon superseded. Others are attempted. The goddesses who have manifested themselves in Pound's lifetime return, though they are not 'visible to the sergeants' (LXXVIII, p. 483). Towards the end of LXXXI, the thought of Althea, to whom Richard Lovelace wrote from prison, leads to a lyric, whose subtle progression from Ben Jonson's anapaests to Chaucer's iambs has been analysed by Donald Davie.[15] The theme is the arts of instrument-making, lute-music and song; but the suggestion is that in the supreme craftsmen (Lawes, Waller their modern successor Dolmetsch) the art was moved by the goddess: Althea, or that cruel Beauty to whom Chaucer now says

> Your eyen two wol sleye me sodenly
> I may the beauté of hem nat susteyne

These are the eyes of the *Kuthera deina* (LXXVI, p. 456; LXXX, p. 511) (dread Cythera, Venus) who rules this book; and these eyes now manifest themselves:

> there came new subtlety of eyes into my tent

This is the goddess once known: at many points in the Cantos Pound gives her, in her various forms, attributes of his own women, and shows his own women as the Goddess. Passion has engraved the Form in the mind. Perhaps the most famous lyric in the Cantos follows, an assertion of indefeasible mind:

> What thou lov'st well shall not be reft from thee

The same iambic modulates into a demand for humility before the natural world, the ant's green elegance outdoing man's art; but asserts again the constructive act in conclusion.

The final strong note of the Pisan book comes in LXXXIII, before the muted coda of LXXXIV. LXXXIII is a poem of water throughout most of its length. At first this appears in the aspect of a Neoplatonist Neptune (*GK*, 224), and the proper hilarity of such gods and their philosophers, and traces of their eras, such as fragments of sea-blue enamel. Then comes rain, also pure blue; and a Taoist water-calm, as expressed by Confucius (cf. *C*, 217):

> the sage
> delighteth in water
> the humane man has amity with the hills

It is followed by Yeat's folk-song of the grass by the weir: but this is the love that flows, and you cannot do anything about it. 'Olim de Malatestis', that description of the palaces at Fano 'once of the Malatesta', reflects the *former* glory of their house; and that passing is also something that you can do nothing to undo. The poem now alludes to 'Hardy's material', here the recurrent genetic traits of family,[16] 'or πάντα ρεῖ'. That 'all things flow' (Herakleitos) puts this recurrence in the light of those rhythms that have no regard to individual will or hopes – like pretty much the rest of Hardy's material: the non-coincidence of love, and desire out of gear with rational purpose. Confucius now meditates on fluidity:

> as he was standing below the altars
>   of the spirits of rain
> 'When every hollow is full
>   it moves forward'
> to the phantom mountain above the cloud
> But in the caged panther's eyes:
>
>   'Nothing. Nothing that you can do ...'
>
> green pool, under green of the jungle,
> caged: 'Nothing, nothing that you can do.'
>
> Δρυάς [Dryad], your eyes are like clouds [...]
>
>   Dryad, thy peace is like water
> There is September sun on the pools
>
> Plura diafana
>   Heliads lift the mist from the young willows
> there is no base seen under Taishan
>   but the brightness of '*udor*   ὕδωρ   [water]
> the poplar tips float in brightness
> only the stockade posts stand
>
> ¡And now the ants seem to stagger
>   as the dawn sun has trapped their shadows,
> this breath wholly covers the mountains
>   it shines and divides
> it nourishes by its rectitude
> does no injury
> overstanding the earth it fills the nine fields
>   to heaven
>
> Boon companion to equity
>   it joins with the process
>   lacking it, there is inanition

When the equities are gathered together
as birds alighting
it springeth up vital

If deeds be not ensheaved and garnered in the heart
there is inanition   (LXXXIII, pp. 529–31)

This water is inexorable,[17] and seems to combine with the mists hiding the base of the mountain that is a 'phantom' above it. Water flows: mountains, sacred (like Taishan in China) or otherwise, are as nothing. The active impulse is as nothing, as that tiger (active, Dionysian) seems to know. The water participates even in his eyes, which are reminiscent of that black fellow-prisoner's ('night green of his pupil, as grape flesh and sea wave': LXXIV, p. 432; cf. II, p. 10) who was hanged. But peace seems to return with this 'Dryad', another participant in the divine world who manifested herself in Pound's lifetime.[18] 'September sun on the pools' now *combines* that Dionysian principle of fire, light and liquid with the mist and water; the 'brightness of water' is converted into a manifestation, before Pound's eyes, of that essence-imparting out-radiating Principle that is the base-image of Neoplatonism – and which survives through Christianity into the hymnology of Pound's youth or perhaps of this prison camp, 'It breathes in the air,/It shines in the light,/It streams from the hills,/It descends to the plain,/And sweetly distils/In the dew and the rain.'[19] 'This breath'[20] is fluid, light and spirit. It informs man, is his soul, according to no. 260 of the Confucian *Odes* in Pound's version:

> Water above, fire beneath
> so man had, from heaven, his breath,
> > a vapour,
> matter and form compact
> seed and cord held intact[21]

And so it is 'This liquid' that is the Agent Intelligence (as in St Albert and Guinicelli) that is the universal form-giving and awareness-of-form-giving principle, an essential (not 'accidental') element of the mind, that gives it shape as the magnet shapes the heap of meaningless iron dust:

This liquid is certainly a
        property of the mind

nec accidens est [nor is it an accident]   but an element
                    in the mind's make-up
est agens [it is acting/agent] and functions   dust to the fountain pan otherwise
            Hast 'ou seen the rose in the steel dust
                        (or swansdown ever?)
so light is the urging, so ordered the dark petals of iron
we who have passed over Lethe.   (LXXIV, p. 449)

And it is Love: 'Amo ergo sum [I love therefore I exist], and in just that proportion' (LXXX, p. 493); or perhaps Love 'grazeth the light, one moving by other', as in the Cavalcanti Canto. It nourishes, and overarches, integrating; and here even the sense of economic beneficence is brought in, with the 'nine fields' that echo Mencius on the perfect economic relation between state and individual.[22]

What makes this passage more than mere discussion, or assertion, is the way that the thought grows out of pool, mist hiding mountain, poplars and stockade posts. The girlish 'Heliads' that 'lift the mist from the young willows' give the lightness and grace of mist lifting from among delicate trees, as the morning warms. All is shimmering silence and flooding light in which things lose the steadiness of what you can reach out and touch:

                    the poplar tips float in brightness
                    only the stockade posts stand

And the shadow-creator becomes the shadow-catcher, giving the sense not only of the seen moment, but also of the overwhelming magnificence of the creative sun-principle, in its relation with the fugitive ants (and humans) its creatures.

                And now the ants seem to stagger
                        as the dawn sun has trapped their shadows

NOTES: CHAPTER 12

1   *L*, p. 249, referring to Napoleon's usury-backed enemies.
2   Julian Cornell, *The Trial of Ezra Pound* (London: Faber, 1967), pp. 30–1.
3   See 'Chung Ni' (Confucius), LXXVII, p. 470, and LXXVIII, pp. 481–2, where the 'process' ideogram (*C*, pp. 101 ff.) suggests that Mussolini had distanced himself from that.
4   'Ezra Pound and Louis Zukofsky: letters, 1928–1930', ed. B. Ahearn, *Montemora*, no. 8 (1981), p. 159.
5   'From an unpublished draft of Canto LXXXIV', *Sulfur*, no. 1 (1981), p. 8.

6   For Ugolino, see *Inferno*, canto 32, 11. 125 ff.; Pound conflates his action in Hell
    with the manner of his death: cf. LXXIV, p. 436.

7   LXXXII, p. 523; for the bull, see ibid. and *E*, p. 271.

8   'A prison-letter', *Paris Review*, no. 28 (Summer-Fall 1962), p. 17.

9   See 'From an unpublished draft of Canto LXXXIV', pp. 5–6.

10 He had gone home on leave from the hospital: see Mary de Rachewiltz, *Ezra Pound,
    Father and Teacher: Discretions* (New York: New Directions, 1975), pp. 220–1.

11 'Some for the Glories of This World; and some/Sigh for the Prophet's Paradise to
    come;/Ah, take the Cash, and let the Credit go,/Nor heed the rumble of a distant
    Drum!' – a remarkable example of Pound's propensity for seizing financial suggest-
    ions, consciously or not, for it is from Edward FitzGerald's *Rubáiyát of Omar
    Khayyam*: see M. E. Speare (ed.), *The Pocket Book of Verse* (New York: Pocket
    Books, 1940).

12 See Rachewiltz, *Ezra Pound*, p. 84.

13 'Mits' are breasts: LXXVII, p. 469; Pound often refers to Helen's. This follows the
    'usurers' dunghill' and precedes more fatal women.

14 Leo Frobenius and D. C. Fox, *African Genesis* (New York: Benjamin Blom, 1966),
    p. 109.

15 Donald Davie, *Pound* (London: Fontana/Collins, 1975), pp. 92–5, 84–5.

16 Apparently as in Hardy's poem 'The Family Face'.

17 For the source, cf. *The Works of Mencius*, trans. J. Legge (New York: Dover, 1970),
    pp. 463–4; but for the tone here cf. esp. LXXIV, p. 433.

18 She 'is' H.D. the poet: see William French, '"Saint Hilda", Mr Pound, and Rilke's
    Parisian panther at Pisa', *Paideuma*, vol. 11, no. 1 (Spring–Summer 1982), pp. 79–
    87.

19 'O Worship the King' by Robert Grant (1785–1838).

20 In the Mencius passage that is the source of 'this breath [. . .] there is inanition' (cf.
    Mencius, trans. Legge, p. 190), 'this breath' (Legge: 'the passion-nature') seems
    more limitedly of the individual, and less intimately connected with heaven. See also
    ibid., p. 185 n.

21 cf. esp. *KPE*, pp. 458–9, on 'the tensile light'.

22 The nine fields are not in the source; Pound has brought them in from another
    passage in Mencius (cf. *Mencius*, trans. Legge, pp. 243–5 and nn.). See *P*, p. 91.

CHAPTER 13

Commentary:
Cantos LXXXV–XCV
('Section: Rock–Drill')

The *Rock-Drill* Cantos were published in 1954–5, and the *Thrones*
Cantos between 1956 and 1959. They are a product of the same phase in
Pound's life, and the progression in poetics between them is relatively
small, and so I shall discuss those aspects of them as if the two were one
work. *Thrones*' handling of its particular matters may be left for a
separate chapter.

Pound spent six months in the prison camp at Pisa; in the evening of
16 November 1945 he was given two hours' notice, and told that he
would be flown to Washington. On his arrival he was in a state of
hysterical tension, and remained so during the uncertainty of the trial
proceedings. On the evidence of eminent psychiatrists, and to the
disgust of sections of the press that wanted to see him hanged, he was
found unfit to confer with counsel or to understand the charges against
him, and committed to St Elizabeths Hospital in Washington, there to
be held until he should recover his sanity, at which time he would be
tried for treason. He remained there for twelve years, from 1946 to
1958. His privileges were gradually extended, from (at first) fifteen
minutes' conversation with visitors under the supervision of a guard, to
taking his visitors out on the lawns, to (in 1955) 'evening privileges,
that is, the privilege of sitting out on the grounds until about 8:00 P.M.'
Those periods on the lawns apart, he was never for twelve years in a
position to shut out the television, the smell, the wraiths of madmen
drifting in and out, the occasional screams and the endless chatter, for
he was in a mere cubicle, with a tiny table, a grilled window and no
door.

Pound's hysteria departed; but to remain sane must be to have some
sense of direction: for Pound, to work. He was locked in with lunatics,
making immense demands on his ability rigidly to shut out; he wrote in
August 1955, in a letter to Archibald MacLeish:

I can't work here [. . .] The little and broken-up time that I get (with no privacy and constant interruption and distraction) makes impossible that consecutive quality of feeling so important to me [. . .] This daily laceration and frustration of a creative impulse, carried on even a little while [. . .] can and surely will, with me I'm afraid, end with complete artistic impotence.[1]

By then this laceration had continued for nine and a half years.

His whole life's effort was being nullified, in implication, by a thrust that seems to have come as a complete surprise to him. He was forced to submit to it, apparently, because at the time of his trial (in fact simply a hearing of the psychiatrists' opinions) he was exhausted and on the verge of collapse, and in no state to go through with a defence against the charge of treason. It was the psychiatrists' assertion, accepted by the court, that he need not be tried for undermining the war effort because, not only now but for many years past, he had been off his head. His response was bitter scorn against all things institutionally American: America was the madhouse, not St Elizabeths.

So Pound lived in a twelve-year frenzy of correspondence, political agitation among junior extremists, and labour of reading and composing and translating. His new English Confucius had apparently been translated from the Italian version before he left Italy, and was published (as *The Unwobbling Pivot and the Great Digest*) in 1947; the Confucian *Analects* were now translated, and published in 1950. In about 1949 Pound set to work on the Confucian *Odes*, with the help of a Chinese assistant, and these, with the *Women of Trachis* of Sophocles (published in 1953–4), were his most important non-Cantos creative work of these years. One coincidence of image suggests Pound's state – the shirt envenomed with Nessus' blood that kills Herakles in *Women of Trachis*:

> And now I'm in torture, no one to finish it off
> with fire, or with a knife,
>   or do ANYthing useful,
> or even let me alone.

– and Ode 26:

> sorrow about the heart like an unwashed shirt, I
> clutch here at words,
> having no force to fly.

He was deprived of new sensory experience, waves, fields tilled, men working, 'men's minds and their cities' (*Odyssey*, 1.3); and instead flooded with all the printed matter he could wish for, from that Tower of Babel of universal information, the nearby Library of Congress. (At one point his disciples were said to have five desks in permanent use there.) Under these circumstances Pound required of himself that he 'write Paradise' (as the final Canto-fragment has it). Since about 1939 the programme had been for a Paradise, and the aesthetic shape – the upbuilding – of the poem required it, though war and Pisa had put it off. We might expect Paradise to dominate *Rock-Drill*. Or perhaps only to be present in scattered nuggets: for the title was borrowed, with pride, from Wyndham Lewis's description of the relentless hammering action of Pound's mind. The title *Thrones* is intended to suggest the moral–aesthetic splendour of the Just Rulers.

The pattern of *Rock-Drill* and *Thrones* is roughly this: blocks of continuous material from Pound's new reading, occupying perhaps a set of two Cantos, separated by clusters of pre-charged fragments. These fragments are mostly derived from earlier sections of the long poem. In turn, the blocks of new material give rise to further fragments that are used later.

In sections before the China Cantos, the matured method was to develop blocks of new matter with relatively sparse reference back, via fragments, to earlier contexts. Then the China and Adams Cantos (LII–LXXI) used single-book sources, over immense stretches, with even less reference back than before. But suddenly in the Pisan group there were very few sources bringing new matter, and the great bulk was charged fragmentary referrings-back to what had been fully presented before; and there were long passages of immensely agile and complex articulation of these details.

Since the tensing cross-plies in this fabric are tensions implied, not stated – invisible forces between nodes – Pound uses the metaphor of the mosaic, the Form made of chips. As I have said, the 'Thrones' of Pound's title stand for the splendours of the Just; but in another sense they are the splendours of the heavens that are God's fit seats, for which one wants *balascio* (ruby) or topaz,

> Belascio or Topaze, and not have it sqush,
> a 'throne', something God can sit on
> without having it sqush
> (LXXXVIII, p. 581)

In a further sense the whole Paradise part of the Cantos is 'thrones' for God to sit on, being itself an image of the universe's essential structure. And these thrones are to be made of fragments, the *tessere* of the mosaics at Monreale in Sicily;

> tessera, Monreale,
> Topaz, God can sit on.
> (CIV, p. 745)

Pound's readers were evidently already complaining that these Cantos were too bitty – with economic passages skipping from Antoninus to Henry III in ten lines: too frag*ment*ary. That would be a perfectly conclusive criticism according to the ordinary methodology of writing on economics. But Pound replied in the poem to his correspondent (and source) Lewis Maverick:

> Fragmentary:
> (Maverick repeating this queery dogmaticly.
> mosaic? any mosaic.
> You cannot leave these things out.   (CV, p. 750)

Whatever unrelated section the patient librarian might put them in, these things are relevant. However unrelated their sources, put together these fragments set up tensions that make a new thing: the mosaic.

Pound's field of vision was expanding and contracting at the same time, and these fragments are the end-result of the latter movement. From youth he looked for an optimist, energy-rousing faith, and the Coleridge–Browning tradition had given it him ready-made. It lay in a 'coherence', the awe-inspiring holding-together of all that is, and it had said: The evidence is all around you, but inexplicably. Pound had found reaffirmations of this world-view in new science: in Frobenius, and now in the palaeontologist Louis Agassiz. There was a great understructure, present in all things and imparting to them their nature. The whole was in some way intuitable in each part. And he stuck to Dante because, if this Neoplatonic religious sense is relation between macrocosm and microcosm, only Dante had an adequate sense of both: not only the grand image of cosmic integrity but the verbal capacity to enact the sharpness of local texture.

If that mystic macrocosm–microcosm relation exists, there must be few who can grasp both ends of it with equal steadiness. At the point of maximum dilatation you have perhaps Emerson, able (apparently) to participate in Everything but quite unable to make you see anything in particular; also those 'Neo-Platonicks Etc.' described with good humour by Pound in 1938: 'man inebriated with infinity', rhapsodising in prose (*GK*, 222–3). And at the other extreme you have men like John Heydon, as seen in these late Cantos, and Joseph Rock – again, as seen in these Cantos; or, in other words, Pound himself. The sensibility is most aware of the electric godhead in the fine and small.

But many of the fragments that appear in *Rock-Drill* and *Thrones* suggest not a 'coherence' of all that is, but another world. One may illustrate by citing the source of a *Thrones* passage. Joseph Rock was a botanist working in western China, and the following passages, from three pages describing a mountain trail, show the relation of vegetation to landscape:

> [. . .] farther on the slopes were covered with large trees of the same species of oak festooned with the long, beard-like lichen *Usnea longissima* [. . .] Another stream flows from the pass, and this we follow, the rocky stream-bed (ice-covered, December) being the trail, up a narrow valley, which higher up broadens somewhat. To the east a small valley debouches into a meadow, another lovely camping place [. . .]

> Following the east bank of the valley, which becomes broader as we advance, we finally reach a lateral ravine from the east with a stream descending it. The vegetation here is composed mainly of junipers, Larix, *Caragana jubata*, rhododendron and *Spiraea laevigata*, Rosa, and Berberis [. . .]

> A few li beyond we reach the hamlet of I-chia-p'o [. . .] situated at an elevation of 11,500 feet; it stands beside the contact of hornblende-granite with the Devonian sediments. This point is two stages from A-tun-tzu, a distance of about 105 li.

> From I-chia-p'o the trail descends over a rocky slope (green grits and slates) with a stream roaring below. Here the oak forest gives way to pines, *Pinus yünnanensis* and *Pinus Armandi*, with a few scattered oaks and *Rhododendron decorum* [. . .][2]

The sentences come each from a passage describing a different successive stage of the trail. The Latin designations are used for exactitude. But the corresponding passage in *Thrones*:

Forest thru ice into emerald

in 旦 Tan (dawn, that is)

larix, corayana and berberis,
after 2 stages A-tun-tzu
a distance of one hundred *li*
Pinus armandi   (CI, p. 723)

There is still perhaps the sense of a journey, though this may be very
weak unless one has read the Rock. But the 'emerald' appears not to be
in Rock, though corresponding to his meadows, and attracts itself
inevitably in the Cantos to the sapphire and rubies everywhere in them.
The other details are so shorn of connection that they float in magic
suggestion. In such a context the Latin names become not technicalities
but exotica; and Pound is in fact slipping and gliding through Rock's
prose in search of exotica and fantastica to compound together, as the
Symbolist Remy de Gourmont in *Le Latin mystique* dug for sensual
jewels in columns of dense medieval Latin.

This de-location is the principle of dozens of beautiful lines in these
Cantos:

Octonary sun-worshiping Baltic.   (XCVII, p. 673)

Till the blue grass turn yellow
and the yellow leaves float in air   (XCIX, p. 694)

Yao and Shun ruled by jade   (CVI, p. 753)

One may live with such lines for years without wishing to sort out or
justify one's floating, contradictory, instinctive-seeming interpretations
of them. Then one encounters the sources. The first line comes from
the monetary historian Del Mar, who is discussing systems of coinage:
'8 ounces = 1 mark [...] these are hybrid systems, originating
remotely in the octonary numbers and relations of the sun-worship
practised in the countries of the Baltic.' The next two lines seem to
come from a passage where Iong Cheng says he will amplify and clearly
illuminate the intention of his father the Emperor in raising the morale
of the people through education, promulgating good manners.[3] If that is
the source, the Canto lines are arrived at by breaking down the Chinese
characters for 'amplify' and 'promulgate' to find in them 'yellow' and
'blue grass'. As for the last line, 'Yao and Shun ruled by jade' – well,
unfortunately for the magic of the line, they did so in a very down-to-

earth sense: they used it for currency, along with a complicated
revaluation and devaluation system. (See B*FT*, 433–4 n.)

Pound has become a Symbolist, and more effectively so than Eliot in
his late, Mallarméan period, because these lines are so much more
subtle than the lumpy alternation of stress and laboured irrationality of

> Garlic and sapphires in the mud
> Clot the bedded axle-tree.
> > ('Burnt Norton')

Many will be satisfied to see Pound become a brilliant Symbolist, for
to them that is what a Paradise is about: the transition to the purely
spiritual, that which is of the mind only. But something of Pound's
enterprise seems lost. He had attacked both poles of the ancient
Western dualism or 'split' (see *GK*, 342–3) between materialism and
idealism. 'Hindoos' on the one hand treat the body as a sort of sanitary
convenience (according to the 1917 skit in *PD*, 79 ff.), and on the other
seek truth in pure spirit:

> Do not Hindoos
> > lust after vacuity?
> With the Gardasee [Lake Garda] at our disposition.
> 'O World!'
> > said Mr Beddoes.
> 'Something *there*,'
> > sd/ Santayana.
> Responsus [Answer]:
> > Not stasis/
> > at least not in our immediate vicinage.
> a hand without face cards,
> > the enormous organized cowardice.
> And there is something decent in the universe
> > if I can feel all this, *dicto millesimo* [in the aforesaid year]
> At the age of whatever.
> I suppose St Hilary looked at an oak-leaf.
> > (XCV, pp. 646–7)

That leaf was St Hilary's weapon against vacuity. Believers in pure
Spirit, like Yeats, try to lunge at instant understanding, which they
think is available on another plane, ready-made; but the truly religious
man tries to understand what is immanent in the here-and-now (and
Pound suggests that the taking of the apple from the tree of knowledge
was a sin exactly because it was a grab):

Tree of knowledge/error in that: RAPIT [seized] the knowledge, like
Yeats always poking around seances etc./instead of OBserving, let us
say, blue jays. (B*FT*, 264)

The fragments in these Cantos ought to be microcosms suggesting
the macrocosm, as the 'bit of true blue enamel' in the Pisan Cantos
(LXXXIII, p. 528) was a sign that Gemisto's Neptune had been active
there, or as the leaf shows St Hilary the overarching structure. But the
macrocosm–microcosm relation is very difficult to retain and express;
Pound's field of vision, as I have said, had been expanding, to ever
vaster fields of world-relation, as it was contracting towards minute
fragments. When one claims to deduce the shape of the whole from
every single encountered datum, the mind will no longer handle it.
Pound laid claim to an understanding on whose basis he could have
advised Eden, Churchill, Blum, Truman, Hitler and Mussolini in such
a way as to save each of them from his particular disaster, as the poem
shows. Yet at every turn there was a mass of new material to digest, new
scholars to keep in their places, new detail to penetrate.

> mind come to a plenum when nothing more will go into it
> (LXXVII, p. 475)

At this point, it seems to me, the mind begins to retreat into magic.
Thus the Paradisal fragments in these sections, compounding elisions,
cross the thin line between Rock's, Whitman's and Thoreau's gristly
and immanence-conveying 'thisness', and Symbolist unlocated glint-
ings, off there in the mind, untouchable. But these jewels offer small
safety; their gleams and glamours become ever more wisp-like in *Drafts
& Fragments*, as we shall see, losing themselves unattainably in the
atmospheric dimness that surrounds them, amid an overpowering sense
of pathos.

At the macrocosmic pole, there are many symptoms of the over-
stretching of Pound's mind. History loses its differentiations of quality:
the verbal forms that render eighteenth-century China are as those used
for a law-code of ninth-century Byzantium. And conclusions are now
too glib. At earlier stages in his writing, Pound's aesthetic method had
made him capable of important historical diagnoses, however unreliable
in detail. But in those days (with Malatesta or Henry II) he took longer,
multiplied his points of access to a period, relaxed and absorbed, and
claimed far less in scope. Now his claims are almost universal:

> Right, all of it, was under Shang
>   save what came in Athens.
>   (LXXXVII, p. 571)

> so that after one set of damned scoundrels (tonsured)
> another set of damned scoundrels
>   (untonsured)
> the foulest of all these Jimmy Stuart.
>   Coke: the clearest mind ever in England
>   (CVII, p. 758)

And yet behind these assertions about a whole period there are often no more than two or three books.

The sense of vast time and space, archaeological and non-Indo-European, is very salutary for a culture in which the Graeco-Roman tradition can still simply be termed 'Civilisation'. But some of this tends to megalomania, and the claim to explain all significant historical connections: *now* I will fill in the gap between Greece and the Middle Ages, by dealing with Byzantium (and the poem digests another chronicle). Hence the self-assertion against learned authority: hurling the library on to the page, challenging editorial professors. Hence also the manner of the technical note, as if jotted down by the expert in a hurry ('Del Mar examined Gansl': XCVII, p. 674), and of the man who observes (with a present participle) something he pretty much knows about:

> Uncle William frantically denying his
> *most* intelligent statements (re/every individual soul, per esempio)
>   (XCVII, p. 676)

Meanwhile, the invisible financial conspiracy controls the visible world: 'Sodom on Thames sold out Napoleon' (CV, p. 747). Because what Pound has discovered about the Emperor Antoninus Pius shows that he was against usury, and because not much information survives, there must have been a conspiracy to suppress the truth about him: 'Alex, Antoninus in blot-out' (CVII, p. 760). Correspondence of these years suggests a very literal meaning for that line: Antoninus Pius was actually deleted from the manuscripts.

The thought moves endlessly between the two poles of Erebus (condemnation of Tocqueville, of the murder of indigo) and the highest Empyrean, touching them alternately dozens of times in one Canto. Thus the two observations

> But their technique is two lies at once   (C, p. 717)
>
> Shingled flakes on a moth's wing.   (C, p. 717)

are succeeded by multinational finance's networks, the crystal, the futility of Buddhists, the white light, and so on. It does not seem surprising that these Cantos return so often to the goddess Ino (Leucothea) who rescued the drowning hero with her scarf in book 5 of the *Odyssey*, for the mental pressure is painful:

> and he dropped the scarf in the tide-rips
> KREDEMNON [scarf]
>   that it should float back to the sea,
>   and that quickly
>   DEXATO XERSI [(Ino) received it in her hands]
>   with a fond hand
>   AGERTHE
>
>   (C, pp. 716–17)

– that is, 'his spirit returned [*agerthe*] again into his breast'. Leucothea (fused by Pound with Leucothoe) is the 'white goddess'. And since white light has been connected with divinity and god-vision (*alba*, the Provençal dawn-song, read as 'white'?) this takes us back to the scene in XV, where the hero, emerging from Hell, prayed for divine grace to help him past the evil and into the blinding sunlight.

The versification is brilliant and in no way blunts these extremes. The cadence is segmented: small units with full stops. No lyric builds. A terse perception of light is followed by an equally terse and controlled condemnation. Patterns of cadence are not repeated; each seems to have grown with the separate thought that it clothes; and yet the whole seems to develop inevitably line by line because each is densely patterned within itself, and lightly and minimally linked to the foregoing.

> George Second encouraged,
>   the tariff of 1816 murdered indigo.
>   Freemen do not look upward for bounty
>   Barley, rice, cotton, tax-free
>   with hilaritas.
>   Letizia, D*a*nte, *C*anto 18   a religion
>   V*ı*rtù enters.
>
>   (C, pp. 715–16)

(i) ROCK-DRILL: '& THAT GRIFFINS DIG ROCKS'

I shall divide *Rock-Drill* into four major tonalities. The first is associated with John Heydon, the English mystic, and his *Holy Guide*
(1662), of which Pound had first heard from Yeats; with Apollonius of
Tyana, a 'neo-Pythagorean' sage who practised sensory self-discipline
and wandered the world in the first Christian century; and with the *Brut*
of Layamon (who flourished *circa* 1200).

> In the world that Pound creates from Heydon and Apollonius
> the swallows nip celandine (XCII, p. 618)

and

> Pharaotes' tigers worship the sun.   (XCIV, p. 636)

Apollonius' biographer, Philostratus, says that leopards 'delight in
fragrant odours, and scenting their smell from afar off they quit
Armenia and traverse the mountains in search of the tear or gum of the
Styrax, whenever the winds blow from its quarter and the trees are
distilling'. *Rock-Drill* says

> For styrax to Pamphilia,
> leopards
> (XCIV, p. 636)

The tiger that worships the sun is in our world of times and seasons and
ritual; as are those Indians in Philostratus' Life of Apollonius who
follow the Greek rite and worship a fire derived from the sun's rays,
singing a hymn (*hymnon*) to the sun every day (*hemeran*) at midday:
'ὕμνον ἡμέραν' (XCIV, p. 637). Pound creates a certain effect, in
relation to these creatures, with colour; sometimes naming a simple
colour in their context –

> & the 'red' sea named after Erythras
> not from its colour, the cyanine
> (XCIV, p. 637)

– and carefully not putting in compounded hues, thus allowing mere
nouns to suggest a kind of visual simplicity: Heydon's 'swallows nip
celandine', the yellow flower. The verse then moves from simple

picture to simple picture, line by line. That seems to be quite enough to take these creatures away from the limitations of our ordinary world, as it is enough in children's books, or in English folk-songs like 'The Three Ravens'; the visual technique seems similar in the French gothic tapestries.

Apollonius' rite-science finds correspondences between things, but uses them for respect, not for manipulation. Pound's fragments catch his wonder before the multifarious universe. From it come Apollonius' civic ethics, cryptically quoted by Pound; they restate the Confucius of Canto XIII, who said 'each in his nature'. Apollonius celebrates the city of fine and multifariously energetic *men* (who are the real 'plant' of the place), as opposed to the city that merely has beautiful buildings. The analogy, he says, is Homer's many-shaped Zeus, as opposed to the statue of Zeus:

> 'We are the plant.' said Hugo Rennert
> or
> as Homer says:
>   πολλαῖς ἰδέαις [under many shapes]
> not merely set stone
> πράττειν ἕκαστον ... οἵ τι δύναται [that each man should do ...
>   what he best can do]
>
>   (XCIV, p. 638)

Attraction is the basis of societies; that same 'attracting current' (XCIII, p. 624) brings god to goddess and griffin to rocks spotted with gold:

>   Apollonius & Richardus
>   or, as Swedenborg says: 'of societies'
>   & that griffins dig rocks spotted with gold
>   (XCIV, p. 637)

We have seen this interpenetration of human and fauna worlds before, especially in the 'familiar beasts' of Cantos XVII–XXX, but the new element is an almost childlike smallness, intimacy and visual simplicity. Layamon's *Brut* is plundered for it (twenty-six Canto lines taken from a poem of 30,000), to bring the origins of Pound's beloved England into this fairy-animate world:

>   Nor Constance hath his hood again,
>   Merlin's fader may no man know

Merlin's moder is made a nun.
Lord, thaet scop the dayes lihte [who made the day's light],
        all that she knew was a spirit bright,
A movement that moved in cloth of gold
        into her chamber.
'By the white dragon, under a stone
        Merlin's fader is known to none.'   (XCI, p. 613)

Swans attended the birth of Apollonius; a movement in cloth of gold
attends the conception of Merlin, and his first magical deed is a
revealing of dragons. Dragon, mystic conception, strange-seeming
hood of Constance (it is only a monk's), all come into light short lines
tending towards couplets, naïve and simple like the folk-song.

(ii) SHU KING AND IDEOGRAMS

Another major tone brought into the Cantos by *Rock-Drill* is closely
associated with the main Chinese source in this section, the *Shu King*;
and its verbal technique is closely associated with the Chinese characters. The *Shu King* is the 'Book of Documents' or 'History Classic'
that contains the annals of the first three Chinese dynasties. Pound is
most interested in the accounts given (in the form of ethical lectures to
young emperors and to the populace) of the fall of bad dynasties and the
rise of good; and he finds that the elements of civic and personal
morality are (as it says on the first page of *Rock-Drill*) 'All there by the
time of Y Yin': all there by the period of Y Yin, who instructed the
young Shang Emperor who acceded to the throne in 1753 BC.

All depends on interaction between planes that Western public
morality has generally held to be irrelevant to each other. Administration cannot be conducted without self-understanding on the part of
administrators: 'Perspicax qui excolit se ipsum' (LXXXV, p. 545), 'He
is intelligent who perfects himself', or (perhaps) the man who tries to
put off sorting out his own turbulences until he has achieved his
ambitions will in fact just take them out on the public, as we have so
often seen. This self-knowledge is not reached by hermitry (though a
solitary period may steady one down: LXXXV, p. 546), but by
watching oneself in action, and by watching the mirror that is other
men, not the mirror of water (LXXXV, p. 554). There is a proper
steadiness in action coming from full knowledge, as opposed to the
twitchiness of crowds who

jump to the winning side
(turbae)
(LXXXV, p. 544)

This proper kind of movement is of the same kind as the benevolent movements of the universe itself: is

Not led of lusting, not of contriving
but is as the grass and tree
(LXXXV, p. 544)

He who falls away from these high qualities, which naturally involve benevolence, will lose the 'Mandate of Heaven' (LXXXV, p. 558), and men will fall away from him; he will destroy his own dynasty. Conversely, as self-watching requires a fine ear for the unspoken words of one's heart (*C*, 47), so understanding the outer universe requires an ear finer than can be satisfied by public discourse – for things like the solar movements (and this is óne kind of pivot, or *chih*, both a moral hitching-post and emblem of the point at which understanding descends from the heavens at earth's centre):

止 chih³
a gnomon,
Our science is from the watching of shadows;
That Queen Bess translated Ovid
(LXXXV, p. 543)

(That ruler's translating of Ovid, it is suggested, a private activity that would seem quite futile to later generations, was not unconnected with her general effectiveness.)

Thus full moral virtue involves interaction; and Pound asserts that that Chinese character which is flabbily translated 'virtue' (德) *demonstrates* an 'interaction. A shadow?' (LXXXVII, p. 574). It is composed of 'action' 彳, 'eye' 皿, and 'heart' 心; thus 'the action resultant from [the] straight gaze into the heart' (*C*, 21). It involves humanity 仁, expression of the whole man 亻 (*C*, 22); justice; wisdom 智 (the mouth 口 and the arrow 矢, which only fools write without the God-sent sun 日 underneath it: LXXXVII, p. 575); and rite. These 'divagate neither in one direction nor in the other; it is for this that they are called the *exact middle* 衷' (as a note in Couvreur's French translation says[4]). Thus *Rock-Drill* renders this passage:

仁   智

jen² [humanity]   chih⁴ [wisdom]   i-li [justice, rite]
are called chung¹⁻⁴   [the exact middle]

裏

(LXXXV, p. 544)

In that character for 'the exact middle' we find 中 the pivot, for
moderation, which the Cantos make the sign of John Adams (LXX,
p. 413; LXXXIV, p. 540). And so, politically, all depends upon
sensibility: on the understanding of 'shadows' and tones beyond what
can be spoken; on what Confucius heard 'under the rain altars'
(LXXX, p. 512). This is stated in the first lines of the whole section:

LING²

Our dynasty came in because of a great sensibility.
(LXXXV, p. 543)

(Pound read that character, from top to bottom: cloud, three voices,
and the priestess: CIV, p. 766; cf. *KPE*, 14; interpreting the heavens'
changes?)

But Pound's verbal expression contradicts this whole wisdom. 'Way
repeatedly not clean, noisy, & your hearts loveless' suggests no
knowledge of love – for metrical reasons as much as for others. And
likewise

Awáreněss réstfúl & fáke iš fatíguing   (LXXXV, p. 558)

is one of the least serene lines in the Cantos. This contradiction is not so
surprising: in his prose, Pound had been developing a new vocabulary
usable for the *ad hoc* purposes of prose, namely moral and political
outlines: 'awareness', 'intelligence', 'precision', and so on. It had the
merit of shaking up categories, but it was still an abstract language, a
language of categories. Pound had generally kept it out of his verse,
whose method was 'ideogramic'. Now, perhaps a sign of fatigue, it
enters his verse extensively, and shows its incapacity to retain meaning
(a characteristic Pound himself had noted) clearly, while metre and
phoneme-pattern carry the real meaning of this verse quite clearly.

(iii) JADE

Paradise (unless it is considered as hereafter, or elsewhere) is no more than states that are desired or, rather, desirable: not merely those that people do desire, but those that the writer imagines as the most full and delightful states that one might desire. These (if the universe is well organised) would be at the same time the most fruitful for the participant and his personal/social surroundings: making him best disposed to creative actions and profound understandings. Thus it is generally agreed that 'paradise' involves some interaction between serenity, love and understanding. But, because those words are leaky containers, to present such states it is necessary to project them in scenarios: someone doing something or saying something. Dante was able to reorganise scenarios that were already to a considerable extent provided, and which coincided with the general assumption in his time that there was actually a place to which one might, after death, go. For our purposes it does not really matter that they did so coincide: that is, what matters chiefly to the modern reader is the exact quality of the Paradise-myth presented by Dante, not the fact that it happens to be a variant of the mythology of Christianity.

Pound therefore can project Paradisal states by whatever scenarios connote their emotions, drawing them eclectically from anything. In one page he can draw them from a dozen heteroclite traditions, texts, stories, personal experiences, and the actions in them may be of quite heteroclite nature. There may be a suggestion of coming to a suggested *place*, as Borso and Carmagnola came to an unrealised Earthly Paradise in XVII, pp. 78–9, and Savaric de Mauléon to the troubadour-heretics' temple at Montségur in XLVIII, p. 243. (The clue is the word 'hither'.) There may be a suggestion of the great Neoplatonic philosophic fantasia, as in the 'sun's silk', a clear distinguisher of entities and yet an integrator of them, the 'cords' or Pythagorean harmonic 'chords' (XCVIII, p. 693) that bind all together. The commonest Paradise-image may be in the action of rite, performed by human beings described by Pound (XLVII, pp. 236–7) as existing (partly) in the solid world of Naples, setting lights in the sea; or as performed in some action re-fantasised by him from historical rite (the three nights of Venus in XXXIX). But in important passages drawing on all such scenarios, and many more, it is not possible to say on what level the action is:

The GREAT CRYSTAL
                          doubling the pine, and to cloud.
                    pensar di lieis m'es ripaus
Miss Tudor moved them with galleons
from deep eye, versus armada
from the green deep
                  he saw it,
in the green deep of an eye:
          Crystal waves weaving together toward the gt/ healing
Light *compenetrans* of the spirits
The Princess Ra-Set has climbed
                  to the great knees of stone,
She enters protection,
                  the great cloud is about her,
She has entered the protection of crystal
                              convien che si mova
                              la mente, amando
                                                  XXVI, 34

Light & the flowing crystal
          never gin in cut glass had such clarity
That Drake saw the splendour and wreckage
              in that clarity
Gods moving in crystal
                          ichor, amor
Secretary of Nature, J. Heydon.
              Here Apollonius, Heydon
              hither Ocellus
                      'to this khan'
The golden sun boat
                  by oar, not by sail
Love moving the stars παρὰ βώμιον
by the altar slope
                  'Tamuz!   Tamuz!'
They set lights now in the sea
   and the sea's claw gathers them outward.
The peasant wives hide cocoons now
                              under their aprons
                              for Tamuz

That the sun's silk
              hsien   tensile
                              be clear
'Ελέναυς That Drake saw the armada
              & sea caves
Ra-Set over crystal
                         moving
in the Queen's eye the reflection
& sea-wrack –

                    green deep of the sea-cave
ne quaesaris.
            He asked not
nor wavered, seeing, nor had fear of the wood-queen, Artemis
                    that is Diana
nor had killed save by the hunting rite,
                            sanctus.
                        (XCI, pp. 611–12)

Ἑλέναυς was Helen, the 'ship-destroyer', in Aeschylus' pun; Drake, by his historical reaction to Queen Elizabeth, made her live again. Gazing in her eyes he foresaw that there was another Troy for her to burn, but did not hesitate. Thereby he worshipped, in her, the hunting goddess Diana. But the destroying of the Armada was purified in advance by rite, we are to understand – unlike Agamemnon's voyage to Troy, disastrous for his Greeks because their action was sullied by the impious killing of Diana's deer (LXXXIX, p. 602).

All this is brought by Pound into one continuum of light-flooded action. Confucius moves *para bomion*, 'by the altar slope' (compare XIII, p. 58; LXXVIII, p. 481; LXXX, p. 513; LXXXIII, p. 529), but in the same medium as that in which (Dante tells us: *Paradiso*, 33.145) Love moves the stars. In that medium, Ra-Set's boat moves deliberately, as in a triumphal procession ('by oar, not by sail') over a fluid light reminiscent of that in Matelda's stream in Dante's Earthly Paradise. Ra-Set, the goddess, here performs her own rite of self-dedication and is accepted. All these divinities (along with Circe, Helen, Venus, Diana, named or implied in different parts of the passage) Drake sees in Elizabeth's eye, as he sees the doom of men:

        That Drake saw the splendour and wreckage
                    in that clarity
        Gods moving in crystal

The gods move in that crystal because it is the medium, halfway between fluid and stone, that embodies what happens when divine Form shows through: as when Anchises encounters Venus, in earlier Cantos (XXV, p. 119). As this light is a crystal-light, and leads back to the Source of all meaning, so it is natural that when Dante images a river of light from God that abounds with sparks that are his Intelligences/ angels coming forth (*Paradiso*, 30.61; cf. CVII, p. 762) Pound should make it a crystal river (XCI, p. 613), and these Forms 'ghosts' that 'dip in the crystal, adorned' (XCI, p. 617) – or, here, gods moving in crystal. And so, in 'convien che si mova' (*Paradiso*, 26.34), we are told that, loving, we should turn the mind to that Divinity of whose light all other good things are a ray.

(iv) VIGOUR

There is a tone concerned with courage, and generosity, and good humour, and in general vigour delighting in its own manifestation, associated in *Rock-Drill* chiefly with what centres around Thomas Hart Benton and John Randolph. With Benton and Randolph we go back to the era of the Bank War, presented through Martin Van Buren in Canto XXXVII. Benton was colonel of a regiment in Jackson's famous volunteers, then Senator for Missouri for thirty years starting from the date that State was admitted to the Union (1821). He was an independent voice, 'never in any Congress caucus, or convention to nominate a President or Vice-President', as he said; a spokesman for the interests of his section, but as he himself conceived them. His *Thirty Years' View*, Pound's source, is an apex of the self-expression of the Jacksonian persuasion: clearly organising a mass of well-pondered and unprovincial information. It has neither Van Buren's repellent indirection, nor the cheap appeal to folksiness (and evasion of the difficult economic problems) in current apologias for that age.

Pound devotes the bulk of two Cantos to Benton, and elsewhere lists his headings as the duel, the Bank, the Tariff, and Frémont's journeys to California. John Randolph, Benton's ally, is the hero of the duel. Henry Clay has challenged him to fight on the grounds that Randolph accused Clay of a forgery. Randolph has several solid reasons for declining the challenge: Clay has misconstrued his remarks; he is against duelling in politics; and he denies anyone's right to challenge him for a speech uttered on the Senate floor, since free speech is an essential privilege of that institution. However, he is a Southerner, and *noblesse oblige*. He refuses to explain his remarks to Clay because Clay has no right to extort an explanation by such means; accepts the challenge; and determines not to fire back, because of his anti-duelling principles. Fortunately, Clay misses. Pound's selections in Canto LXXXVIII give Randolph's vigour and decision forcefully (omitting, as so often, both the background of the story and its punchline); as in this detail:

[I, Benton] could not ask him [whether he had decided not to fire on Clay]
    but mentioned [Clay's] child asleep on the sofa.
He said:
      'I shall do nothing to disturb its sleep
      or the repose of its mother',
and went on making codicils for things of slight value
                         (LXXXVIII, p. 578)

'Nothing impossible to him who holds honor in sufficient esteem',
according to Guicciardini quoted in *C*, 188; and in Dante's *Inferno*,
10.36, Farinata degli Uberti's countenance seems to express great scorn
(*gran dispitto*) for Hell:

                              'Gran dispitto.'
    'A chi stima . . .'
        (Guicciardini)
        . . .l'onore assai'   (XCII, p. 618)

But in these Cantos physical courage is only a point towards the main
point. The public identification with a cause is much harder, and for a
poet like Pound is what matters. Thus Farinata's descendant Ubaldo
degli Uberti, Pound's friend:

    'Ten men', said Ubaldo, 'who will charge a nest of machine guns
      for one who will put his name on chit.'
                         (LXXXIX, p. 597)

Randolph's gesture combines both physical and moral courage, and,
like the gestures that open Martin Van Buren's Canto, has the effect of
introducing the problem of courage in an easily recognisable language,
to help the reader perceive the more hidden courage that follows.

    Benton's solitary struggle in the Senate against the Bank is given
obliquely by Pound; but Pound gives in magnificent form the speech
that Benton was finally allowed to make. The subversion of government
authority by a private institution could hardly be more clearly stated.
The charter gives the Bank privileges

      'To carry on trade of banking
          upon the revenues,
              and in the name of the
    United States;
              to pay revenues to the

Government
                    in its own (the bank's own) notes of promise. To
Hold United States moneys
                    in deposit, without making compensation;
To discredit other banks and disparage 'em; to
                    hold real estate, and retain a
                              body of tenantry; To
set branches in States without their consent or approval;
to be exempt from liability if they fail;
          To have the U.S. for a partner, and to have partners
                              outside this country;
To be exempt from the regular administration of Justice,
          and to have all this in
                                        Monopoly.
                                        Yeas:
                                        Barnard, Benton, to 20
                                        Nays: 23 Webster,
                                          Willey
                                        (LXXXVIII, p. 587)

This speech aroused the concern that eventually killed the Bank.

Secret shifting was the essence of the whole business, whereby, for example (Benton says), the American government was made to pay interest ($4½ million) on a loan of $7 million from the Bank, when the Bank during the whole of the period of the load held government money averaging the amount of the principal.

Orage remarked on the 'recession of power' (LXXXIX, p. 603)

– that is (*VP*, 23), 'to the dark inner room'. Benton's job, like John Adams's, is simply to shed light in there, to insist that the nominal government be the real government:

          Name for name, king for king

                              王 wang   [king]
                              王 wang   [king]
                              (LXXXIX, p. 591)

Cunizza da Romano, mistress to Sordello the troubadour, who 'greatly enjoyed herself' with numerous lovers 'and liberated her slaves' (*masnatosque liberavit*) (cf. XXIX, pp. 141–2), is brought in here:

          'My fellow slave-holder'
                              sd/ Mr Randolph
                              (masnatosque liberavit)

'Ef my bull-dog' said Mr Bishop
　　to a co-detenuto 'had a face like yours, hang'd if
I wouldn't shave his arse and make him walk backwards.'
And in the time of Mr Randolph, Mr Benton, Mr Van Buren
　　　he, Andy Jackson
　　　　　　POPULUM AEDIFICAVIT [built the people]
　　which might end this canto, and rhyme with
　　　　　　　　Sigismundo.　　　　　(LXXXIX, p. 596)

John Randolph liberated his slaves; the bulldog and the pithy humour
are associated with these people here by authorial insertion. Cunizza
is in Dante's Heaven of Venus obviously because (like the woman
of doubtful fame in Luke, 7) 'she loved much', ἠγάπησεν πολύ. Canto
XC notes this point:

　　　　　'Mother Earth in thy lap'
　　　　　　　　　　said Randolph
　　　　　　　ἠγάπησεν|πολύ
　　　liberavit masnatos.　　　　　(XC, p. 606)

Cunizza in Paradise announces: 'I was called (*fui chiamata*) Cunizza,
and I shine here (*e qui refulgo*)/because the light of this star [Venus]
overcame me' (*Paradiso*, 9.32–3). Canto XCII puts together Farinata's
scorn, Dante's river of light with 'the ghosts dipping in crystal', and
then (as follows) Venus *ex aquis nata* ('born from the waters'), and
Folquet de Marseille, Cunizza's neighbour in the Heaven of Venus:

　　Sanctus
　　　　　that no blood sully this altar
　　ex aquis nata
　　　　　τά ἐκ των ὑδάτων γενόμενα
　　'in questa lumera appresso'⁵
　　　　　　　　　　　Folquet, nel terzo cielo.
　　'And if I see her not,
　　　　　no sight is worth the beauty of my thought.'
　　Then knelt with the sphere of crystal
　　That she should touch with her hands,
　　　　　　　　Coeli Regina [Queen of Heaven],
　　The four altars at the four coigns of that place,
　　But in the great love, bewildered
　　　　　farfalla in tempesta [butterfly in the storm]
　　under rain in the dark:
　　　　　　　　　many wings fragile
　　Nymphalidae, basilarch, and lycaena,

> Ausonides, euchloe, and erynnis
> And from far
>   il tremolar della marina
> chh   chh
>   the pebbles turn with the wave
> chh   ch'u
>   'fui chiamat' [I was called]
>   e qui refulgo' [and I shine here]
> Le Paradis n'est pas artificiel
>   but is jagged,
> For a flash,
>   for an hour.
> Then agony,
>   then an hour,
>   then agony,
> Hilary stumbles, but the Divine Mind is abundant
>   unceasing
>   *improvisatore* [improviser]
> Omniformis [having all forms]
>   unstill   (XCII, pp. 619–20)

Seawater and love; perhaps with some recall of the shore 'by Circeo' where Olga Rudge appears to have come from the waves in Venus' form (LXXIV, p. 435). At the shore where Virgil and Dante first find themselves on Mount Purgatory, Dante is to purify himself. As in Dante's line (*il tremolar [. . .]*, 'from afar/I knew the trembling of the sea': *Purgatorio*, 1.116–17) the sea is distant here, and Pound dwells on its distant whisper, seeming to communicate a nostalgia for a hope no longer felt:

>   the pebbles turn with the wave
> chh   ch'u
>   'fui chiamat'
>   e qui refulgo'

This turns Cunizza's words into floating fragmentary auditory memories of what they once meant. Pound had dwelled on verbal forms into which he might put Homer's famous onomatopoiea, 'παρά θῖνα πολυφλοίσβοιο θαλάσσης' (*Odyssey*, 13.220), 'by the shore of the loud-sounding sea'. Earlier versions by Pound had energy: the definite spondee of 'The sea runs in the beach-groove, shaking the floated pebbles' (VII, p. 25), the attacking consonant-cluster and quick syllable of 'scutter' in 'the turn of the wave and the scutter of receding pebbles' (*L*, 274). These sounds now float:

chh   ch'u
'fui chiamat'
e qui refulgo'

The thought returns to that resigned conclusion of Pisa:

Le Paradis n'est pas artificiel
but is jagged,

– and sets up a swing:

For a flash,
for an hour.
Then agony

'Agony' replies to 'jagged', and is more painful as the '-a-' is more dragged out. Finally

Hilary stumbles, but the Divine Mind is abundant

St Hilary is not seen as some trivial whippersnapper because he fails (even St Anselm is somewhat diminished by his treatment in *Thrones* – 'digestion weak': CV, p. 750). He 'stumbles', but since the speaker in his foregoing lines has been stumbling no distance is set up. The quick 'Hilary' leads to the stooping stress 'stumbles', but with hardly a pause the pace steadies out into these broad syllables: 'but the Divine Mind is abundant'. There is an unfolding from 'stum' to 'but' to 'abundant', giving it a tensile spring and that exuberant grace abounding that both Hilary and the speaker have despaired of.

NOTES: CHAPTER 13

1   C. David Heymann, *Ezra Pound: The Last Rower* (London: Faber, 1976), p. 238.
2   J. F. Rock, *The Ancient Na-Khi Kingdom* (Cambridge, Mass.: Harvard University Press, 1947), Vol. 2, pp. 344–5.
3   See David Gordon 'Thought Built on Sagatrieb', *Paideuma*, vol. 3, no. 2 (Fall 1974), pp. 179–80.
4   *Chou King*, ed. and trans. S. Couvreur (Paris: Cathasia, 1950), p. 109.
5   Rahab, the harlot working for the armies of the Lord, is 'in questa lumera appresso', 'in this light nearby', near Folquet, 'in the third heaven' ('*nel terzo cielo*'); she is another Venus here.

CHAPTER 14

Commentary: Cantos XCVI–CIX ('Thrones')

Some remarks on the biographical background and the poetics of *Thrones* will be found in my introduction to the previous section, *Rock-Drill*. The bearing of the title of this new book is given by Pound in his 1960 interview with Donald Hall. Pound observes that the different sections of his long poem are not intended to deal with different problems:

> I was not following the three divisions of the *Divine Comedy* exactly. One can't follow the Dantesquan cosmos in an age of experiment. But I have made the division between people dominated by emotion, people struggling upwards, and those who have some part of the divine vision. The thrones in Dante's *Paradiso* are for the spirits of the people who have been responsible for good government. The thrones in the Cantos are an attempt to move out from egoism and to establish some definition of an order possible or at any rate conceivable on earth. One is held up by the low percentage of reason which seems to operate in human affairs. *Thrones* concerns the states of mind of people responsible for something more than their personal conduct. (*WW*, 112)

This is an interesting conflation of Dante's suggestions. All the Blessed in Dante's Paradise have seats in the Rose; and Cunizza in the Heaven of Venus seems to refer (*Paradiso*, 5.115) to these seats as 'Thrones'. On the other hand, the 'Thrones' are one of the orders of angels, which according to *Paradiso*, 28.104–5, would preside over the Heaven of Saturn, which is for the spirits of the contemplative. But in *Paradiso*, 9.61–2, Cunizza seems to say not only that these 'Thrones' preside over her Heaven, the Heaven of Venus, but also that they do so in such a way as to reflect down to it God in his judging aspect. And one of the most important inhabitants of the Heaven of Venus is Carlo Martello, who is 'amorous' but appears chiefly in the narrative as a just ruler; which makes an important bridge to the later Heaven which is specifically for the Just – rulers and lawgivers. And these 'Thrones' which are the angels/Intelligences, reflecting down 'God judging' (as Cunizza has said), reflect Him down 'as if mirrored, in nine existences' (*Paradiso*, 13.59), which existences, though they are the nine orders of angels, Pound may well have taken to be, all of them, those 'mirrors' which are 'thrones' reflecting downwards the judging God. That light which is God

> doth, of its goodness, focus its own raying,
>   as though reflected, in nine existences, eternally abiding one.
>   (*Paradiso*, 13.58–60)

– a passage quoted by Pound (XCVIII, p. 693)

All this suggests an intimate connection in the Cantos between justice, goodness (Pound twice brings in from other contexts the God–*bontate* connection made by the above quotation: XCIII, pp. 626, 627) and love – the kind of love shown by Cunizza who 'greatly enjoyed herself' and that woman 'who loved much' in St Luke's Gospel.

> and the greatest is charity
> to be found among those who have not observed
>   regulations
>   (LXXIV, p. 434)

Hence it seems natural that Pound should conflate Dante's image of Folquet de Marseille, Cunizza's fellow-sinner in the Heaven of Venus, as a *ruby*, with the idea that both Folquet and Cunizza are connected with the *Thrones* of the Just; and demand for God, as we have seen, Thrones made of jewels:

> Belascio [ruby] or Topaze, and not have it sqush,
>   a 'throne', something God can sit on
>   without having it sqush
>   (LXXXVIII, p. 581)

Weaving this web tighter, we find that Cacciaguida, Dante's ancestor – another just ruler – is a 'living topaz' in *Paradiso*, 15.85; and 'topazii'

are what all the Intelligences/angels (including of course Thrones) look
like as they pour forth from Above in a river of light (*Paradiso*, 30.76).
So it becomes clear that in the Cantos these jewel-thrones are: (*a*) the
presiding angels; (*b*) the spirits of the Just; (*c*) the places set *for* these
spirits; (*d*) fit seats for God Himself to sit on. And, further, that they
both reward and celebrate chiefly the qualities of responsibility and
joyous exuberant charity. Pound wrote in 1956 of 'The irre-ponsibility
ethic and civic of most of my godamned "licherary" contemporaries'.[1]
And in a quotation aptly adduced by Massimo Bacigalupo (from a
review of a concert in 1934):

> In this music by Telemann one feels the required intensity. One
> understands that the announcement to the Virgin was really 'good
> news' – *incipit saeculum novum*, the new era begins. A 'Hallelujah!'
> which truly expresses the joy of the celestial energies. 'The more a
> thing is perfect, the more it acts, the less will it suffer.' Those
> thrones, spirits, archangels of Dante's *Paradiso* have dominion, they
> are powers that move the great spheres of heaven. Religion is not
> only dejection, grief, sufferance – it is the eternal energy; it is even
> exuberance of energy. This quality is registered in music, in great
> music more than in any other art. In this field one can produce good
> criticism of music by beginning with good theology. (BFT, 332–3)

The fact that all this can be compressed into the term 'Thrones', taken
from Dante, suggests the kinds of care that Pound had and did not have
in reading: care for the emotional currents with which terms were
associated, not care for the theoretical structure in which they played a
part – and, after all, Dante himself is inconsistent about the function of
these 'Thrones'.[2]

Pound in *Thrones* is more intent than ever in bringing this con-
junction between godly love, on the one hand, and justice (including
the political and economic), on the other, up to date. He brings in a
mass of new reading, covering the eras of Napoleon and Roosevelt. The
problem is that the 'literary mind' puts spirituality in one compart-
ment, along with Dante, and econo-politics in another; so Pound
repeatedly couples them:

    Erigena,
    Anselm,
    Cherbury,

Rémusat,
Thiers was against income-tax
'the portal to inquisition'
(C, p. 720)

(The list starts from a ninth-century mystic theologian, passes via a saint and a seventeenth-century Natural Religionist, then his biographer Rémusat and Rémusat's political associate Thiers (1797–1877), whose constructive economics are then cited. There is alleged here a shared benevolence; but also perhaps a continuous influence, since Rémusat also wrote on Anselm.)

This is the last book of the Cantos to present new matters *in extenso* and as argument, and in what follows I shall describe some of the most important of these matters.

(i) BYZANTIUM AND THE REGULATION OF BUSINESS

Seeking as always to bypass the cultures considered 'classic' for our tradition, at the start of *Thrones* Pound goes to Lombardy and Byzantium in the 'Dark Ages'. After a rapid chronological survey we are suddenly in the Eparch's Book, which is to be seen as a pillar of the Byzantine civilisation. Leo the Wise, Emperor of the East from 886 to 911, promulgated a number of regulations (Pound's source contains seventy-four) for the governance of Constantinople's corporations, whose grand master was the Eparch; the manuscript calls them the Eparch's Book. They organise tradesmen into corporations, fitting the principle that Pound thought went into practice under Mussolini: organisation and representation of a profession by those who have some knowledge of it. To this end, qualifications for entry into the corporations are strictly examined, and all mixing of trades is prohibited; for such a corporation has to be a monopoly. The corporations are then rigorously controlled by Leo's regulations. Weights and measures used must be authorised, and prices must be fixed; therefore the place of sale must be an authorised one, so that all may be visible. The merchant's cut is strictly proportioned to the value of the product. The hoarding of commodities against famine and the hoarding of coin are provided against. And export and import are strictly controlled. In all this, item by item, we can see Pound's arguments about the state's relation to twentieth-century capitalism. In his day men thought that liberty was

Liberty, and any restriction on the freedom of big business to trample on individuals was a sin against Jefferson; hence Pound's borrowing of the definition of freedom: permission to do that which does not harm others. Pound felt that the great crime of his age was manipulation of the value of the currency by playing hoarded commodities (copper, silver) against it, or by hoarding it (gold, sterling) as if it were a commodity; Leo provides against that. And the export–import regulation is towards the restriction of dumping, the killing of native industries (like indigo), and the diminishing of a country's independence.

It is possible that Constantinople, 'either as to its "social justice" *or* to its permanent products, art, science, literature', like other 'past forms of the state' (*VA*, 198), compares favourably with what we have in the West in this century. But if the means to Byzantum's cultural health was the Eparch's Book the cost seems enormous. An unimaginable and arbitrary bureaucracy keeps tradesmen in line with continual reiteration of

> shall be smacked, cropped and
> put out
> (XCVI, p. 661)

There seems to be no room for unauthorised young men like Pound's friend Gaudier-Brzeska, who set up shop under the railway arches and invade the territory of the professionals. Between Yeats's Byzantium of tin cockerels in glinting haze, and Pound's of harried shopkeepers, the choice is not attractive.

(ii) BYZANTIUM AND CURRENCY

The Eparch's Book ends with Canto XCVI, and in Canto XCVII we take up with Alexander Del Mar, numismatist and United States government chief statistician; or, to be precise, his *History of Monetary Systems* (1895; Pound used the 1896 edition). Pound develops two chief subthemes. One is profiteering on rates of exchange –

> on which Mr Benton would have reflected, as per:
> the CONtinuous effort to have it different somewhere or other.
> (XCVII, p. 672)

This in itself threatens to diminish sovereign power, but can be tolerated within limits (Int, 179). The other subtheme is the proper form of money: a nummulary system, one where the value of the unit has no connection with the value of what it is made of, but is regulated by adjusting total number of units to changes in available purchasable real wealth. Money is not 'natural' (that is the myth that gold-brokers depend on), 'but is NUMISMA; from custom' (*EPS*, 154):

'limitation is the essence of good nomisma'   (XCVII, p. 672)

and one needs

a proper total proportion
between total issue and buyables,
Ike, '55, had got that far.   (XCVII, p. 672)

Above this there is one fairly simple central theme in the Canto: how national or kingly sovereignty depends on the prerogative of issuing money and controlling its value. (Pound held that Congress had surrendered this Constitution-given power by allowing private institutions to determine the volume of money issued, and its relation to gold (a commodity), both of which affected the currency's value.) Bankers who control wealth, credit *and* means of exchange can quietly dictate policy; a state or king that has lost the prerogative of real control over the currency is delivered, trussed, into their hands.

For historical reasons, gold was the pivot of Roman and Byzantine currency. Surrender the coining of gold, and you surrendered statehood, as Pound explained in the 1950s. Gold in Rome was under the control of the Pontifex Maximus, the Chief Priest;

Caesar usurped it. Gold remained as the basis of Byzantine power. Wherever you get local gold, you have rebellion – from Rothar to Abd-el-Melik [Habdimelich]. The Roman Empire maintained stability. Gold was under the Pontifex or the Empire [. . .] (Int, 179)

The Arab Caliph Abd-el-Melik raised the standard of rebellion against Imperial authority when he 'struck gold coins with his own effigy, holding a drawn sword, as afterwards did Edward III, when he renounced the same dread authority. Abd-el-Melik's dinars bore this challenging legend: "The Servant of God, Abd-el-Melik, Emir-èl-Moumenin"' (Del Mar). Thus the opening of Canto XCVII:

Melik & Edward struck coins-with-a-sword,
'Emir el Moumenin' (Systems p. 134)
        six and ½ to one, or the sword of the Prophet,
SILVER being in the hands of the people

(iii) THE SACRED EDICT, SENSITIVITY
AND ORDER

The next large 'matter' is that of the Sacred Edict: ethical instructions
issued by the Emperor K'ang-hsi (reigned 1662–1723), as mediated for
Pound in three cultural/textual ways. The Edict itself consisted of
sixteen Maxims in terse and highly literary Chinese. K'ang-hsi's son
and successor Yong-cheng thought to make them more accessible to the
people by adding expositions in a simple literary style. But the Salt
Commissioner Wang-iu-p'uh perceived that the whole was still
inaccessible (the divergence between literary Chinese and Chinese as
used was, at that time, extreme). He rendered the expositions into
Colloquial. The third mediation of the Edict is provided by F. W.
Baller, a missionary who published all this with English translations in
Shanghai in 1921. Pound, as is now his wont, uses gleams from all these
cultural refractions of K'ang-hsi's original work, to infer from them the
essential original pattern that cannot (for a modern foreigner) be
embodied in any single one of them; or, often, to gather fortuitous
triggers for his own thought-patterns.

The Edict teaches respect for elders; self-control; strict punishment
of family insubordination; unity in clans; harmony in villages; the
primacy of agriculture; economy and forethought; respect for education
and honesty among scholars; avoidance of religious follies; and so on.
And in this text, stemming from 2,000 years after Confucius, Pound is
able to see glimpses of the Confucian wholeness. A man should have a
'root occupation', the Cantos tell us, a job that he sticks to, for only that
'PEN YEH' will give him 'a developed skill from persistence' (XCIX,
p. 698), thus letting him under the skin of a process. On that basis, the
basis of craft (*techne*: XCVIII, pp. 686–7; *GK*, 327, 351; *OS*, 430), a
man can speak with real knowledge – not merely 'ideas'. Also the
general cultural level is the basis of national stability, and is expressed
in customs; which in turn are beneficently coloured by ancient
relationships with locality:

        and that the equilibrium

t'ai⁴

p'ing²

of the Empire grips the earth in good manners
Earth and water dye the wind in your valley

tso feng   tso feng suh
(XCVIII, p. 689)

But all this is Pound reading the old organic Confucian spirit into a late text that does not have it – unless, with Pound, one takes apart its individual characters and sees this spirit in the interstices. The Edict (to judge by Baller's translation) seems interested in good customs for the sake of stability solely; and takes note of the way climates produce variety of customs only in order to reduce these to order with rules.

Stability is the Edict's sole purpose. This is to be achieved by self-regulation in communities, and individual self-policing. One may find here the bridge to John Adams, 'our norm of spirit/our [pivot]' (LXXXIV, p. 540): in the extraordinary resemblance to the Puritan 'paideuma'. There is the mutual moral surveillance of the early New England communities. There is the ubiquitous internalised father: the Edict inculcates guilt towards parents and Emperor for any kind of wrong-doing, even and perhaps especially wrong towards one's own body (in letting it fall sick). There is the worship of fixity (the Edict does not have Pound's sense of *techne*: it sees nothing between steady one-job workers and vagabonds). There is the dread of religious and social elaboration in all forms, of sumptuousness, of sensuality (incense, incantation). Pound is conscious of a connection with the prewar Adams phase of his teaching, when he reminds us twice that Yong-Cheng figured in the China Cantos, published as one group with Adams's. One is far distant from the Pound of 'Commission' (1913):

> Go to the adolescent who are smothered in family –
> Oh how hideous it is
> To see three generations of one house gathered together!

(iv) EDWARD COKE AND THE ANCIENT ROOT OF JUSTICE

The story implied by Cantos CVII–CIX is of how Sir Edward Coke (lawyer, Chief Justice, and now Member of Parliament) humbled tyranny with law. The rule of James I and of his son and successor

Charles I ignored that sense of usage, and interdependence, that Elizabeth had had; it became ever more absolutist. Charles arrived at imposing illegal loans and imprisoning those who refused them. Over the months in 1627–8 was fought the classic English constitutional battle on the king's right to tax without law and imprison without cause shown. On his side the King had considerable precedent, and the awe of his estate; Parliament had the money Charles needed, and could extort law from him (if it found the courage). Coke eventually proposed a Petition of Right, asking not for gifts freely to be conceded by Charles, but for the restitution and restatement of rights anciently possessed by Englishmen. It appealed past recent precedent to Magna Carta and the great statute of Edward I, *De tallagio non concedendo*. Charles bullied and equivocated and blustered. The Petition of Right was read, and he gave an assent in a form that had no legal force; finally in that late afternoon of 7 June 1628 were spoken the traditional words, *Soit droit fait come il est desire*, and the Petition had legal standing. Thus Pound:

> From the Charter to the Petition
> in June and toward twilight
> DROIT FAIT
> (CVIII, p. 764)

'The Charter' is Magna Carta, the great charter of liberties forced from King John in 1215; this was Coke's moral and legal weapon, according to him and to Pound the basis of English legality:

> the root is that charter.
> (CVII, p. 757)

– and to Pound the weapon that decapitated Charles:

> OBIT, in Stratford 1616, Jacques Père [Shakespeare] obit,
> In 33 years Noll cut down Charlie
> OBIT [died] Coke 1634 & in '49
> Noll cut down Charlie
> Puer Apulius . . . ver l'estate
> Voltaire could not do it;
> the french could not do it.
> they had not Magna Charta   (CVII, pp. 757–8)

But the ancientness of this wisdom allows Pound to 'produce' the lines back to two important complexes. Henry II's reign is, for Coke, a legal Golden Age – Glanville's age – and the Charter codified the good usages of it (cf. CVII, p. 757). It is also the age of the troubadours, and of Henry's queen, Eleanor of Aquitaine: their relations have been presented in Canto VI. Now Pound brings in light from that period to intensify Coke's, whose source was Magna Carta. Pound had seen the gods' mark, the wave in the stone, at Excideuil, birthplace of the troubadour Giraut de Borneil (cf. KPE, 337); so

> Coke: the clearest mind ever in England
> vitex, white eglantine
> as tenthril thru grill-work
> wave pattern at Excideuil
> A spire level the well-curb   (CVII, p. 758)

And he had seen at Allègre the larks whose ecstatic fall in the sunlight was celebrated by Bernart de Ventadorn; they illuminate a page on Coke (CVII, p. 760). 'Naturally' Venus reigns in Coke's London ('Each wench to a pillar'), heretics are left unburned, and 'letizia' or *hilaritas* lives in the words of Coke's goddess, Elizabeth, *Angliae amor*:

> 'JESUS!!'
> quoth the Queen, 1584 anno Domini, 'sterling,
> pund sterling how much? 13,000. It is not to be looked for.'
> (C, p. 715)

But the valuation of this last segment of *Thrones* will ultimately be affected, if the critic succeeds in convincing the reader that the story Pound took to be fit epic matter is schoolbook pap. That conclusion might be drawn from some recent accounts of Coke.[3] According to these, Coke and the Commons represented a rising landed gentry, solidly linked to a merchant class, using their economic power to bring to heel a king who in fact claimed no more absolute power than Elizabeth had. Their great propaganda weapon was the myth of the common law fused with the myth of Magna Carta. For Coke, Magna Carta and the common law circumscribed the powers of the king, and always had, 'time out of mind'. Coke's era arrived at this myth because it had no historical sense; could not well distinguish the habits of Elizabethans from the ways of Normans. Its assumptions put it at the mercy of a mass of legal apocrypha, and a habitual misreading of ancient documents. Thus Coke's contemporaries persuaded themselves that the common law had never changed; and in particular that it had

always, even in the time of Magna Carta, circumscribed the king's
prerogative through the institutions of Parliament and trial by jury, the
antiquity of both being falsely deduced by Coke and his fellows from
their documents.

And all this, some historians hold, is a parent of the Whig Interpretation of History: that image of the glorious and special march of the
English towards cultural (and economic) superiority, in which those
Feet still walk on this sceptred Isle, under the aegis of middle-class
individualism. For the Common Law, foundation of freedom, is un-
iquely British, as Mr Podsnap might have explained to the Foreigner:
Europe has always suffered under Civil Law. (Canto CVII, pp. 757–8,
says 'the french could not do it' – achieve liberty without disaster? –
'they had not Magna Charta'.) But as Donald Davie says:

> to think that the barons who faced King John at Runnymede were
> anything like the Cokes or Hampdens who challenged the royal
> prerogative of the Stuarts in the 17th century, or that these in turn
> had much or anything in common with Sam and John Adams or Tom
> Paine, is to adopt the notorious 'whig interpretation' of English
> history in a sort of parody version for grade-school.[4]

This seems to offer a lump of ammunition suitable for historicist-
minded criticism to heave at the naïf Pound. But the argument I have
summarised from Pocock runs as if the Stuart understanding of Magna
Carta were a myth created by the Stuarts and Elizabethans. In fact it
was the fourteenth century which created, in almost finished form, that
myth, and made it a functioning reality 250 years before Coke. By 1363
the famous chapter 29, 'No free man shall be taken or imprisoned or
disseised or outlawed [. . .] except by the lawful judgement of his peers
or the law of the land', had been statutorily interpreted as requiring
'due process of law', by original writ and trial by jury; 'no free man' had
been interpreted by statute to include even villeins, excepting against
their lords – that is, almost everybody. Coke's extensions of this already
ancient and functioning interpretation of Magna Carta were minor.[5]
And in fact the phrase *nullus liber homo*, 'no free man', already in 1215
included important numbers of non-baronial elements – not specified or
hereditarily exclusive; which is why social groups of various kinds
pressurised successive kings to reconfirm Henry III's version of the
Charter every time they were able to do so. Key pronouncements of
legalists, going back to Bracton (d. 1268), accorded with Magna Carta

to make what amounted to a fundamental law, which, by being a law, circumscribed the powers of the king. Coke: 'the common law hath so admeasured the prerogatives of the king, that they should not take away, nor prejudice the inheritance of any: and the best inheritance that the subject hath is the law of the realme'; *Le common ley ad tielment admeasure* . . . And so Canto CVII, cryptically:

> in commun ley . . .
> ad mesure
> (CVII, p. 759)

Coke's idea of Magna Carta, an ancient declaration of the subject's right to freedom from arbitrary authority, was not favourable to the Whig interpretation of history. It posited an unchanging glory of freedom, while Whig history required a steady progression up from barbarism to the apogee of individualism and rationalism in the eighteenth century and later. In that sense Coke was profoundly conservative; indeed, 'the last great medieval commentator on the common law of England' (Holt). And his conception of what Magna Carta said was no more essentially favourable to the interests of property-holders and merchants than to others: that same conception of it was seized on by Levellers, Wilkeses and Radicals in their turn as the basic declaration of man's rights. Whether or not the Cantos do justice to it, Coke's struggle is full and worthy epic material. In Pound's words:

There *are* epic subjects. The struggle for individual rights is an epic subject, consecutive from jury trial in Athens to Anselm versus William Rufus, to the murder of Becket and to Coke and through John Adams. (*WW*, 111)

NOTES: CHAPTER 14

1 Lee Bartlett and Hugh Witemeyer (eds), 'Ezra Pound and James Dickey: a correspondence and a kinship', *Paideuma*, vol. 11, no. 2 (Fall 1982), p. 301.
2 *Convivio*, 2.5.6, makes them first in the lowest hierarchy, therefore (2.5.13) presiding over the Heaven of Venus; but *Paradiso*, canto 28, 11. 104–5, has them last in the top hierarchy, therefore presiding over the Heaven of Saturn.
3 esp. J. G. A. Pocock, *The Ancient Constitution and the Feudal Law* (New York: Norton, 1967).
4 'Sicily in the Cantos', *Paideuma*, vol. 6, no. 1 (Spring 1977), p. 105.

5   They were that he openly asserted that Cap. 29 applied to villeins (the Six statutes had
    only implied this); that he expanded the term 'liberties' to mean individual liberty.
    Lawyers in his time also argued that Magna Carta gave a basis for *habeas corpus*. See J.
    C. Holt, *Magna Carta* (Cambridge: Cambridge University Press, 1965), pp. 9 ff.,
    from which I have taken much of the foregoing.

CHAPTER 15

Commentary: Cantos CX–CXVII
(*Drafts & Fragments of Cantos CX–CXVII*)

Various important literary figures (among them Eliot, Hemingway, and belatedly Frost) brought pressure to bear to have Pound released, and when the war was no longer so fresh in people's minds the United States government finally gave way. Freed, Pound was full of energy and opinions. He did a small triumphal tour among his friends, and then sailed for Italy on 30 June 1958. He had fourteen more years to live, but only two or three more years in which he would be able to write. His daughter by Olga Rudge, Mary, had married an Italian prince, and what should have been perfect serenity awaited Pound in an ancient castle in a magnificent position under the mountains of the Tyrol. His Gaudier-Brzeska bust, the Wyndham Lewises, his books and papers were there. But his happiness and former ways of working lasted only briefly. One problem was relationships with his wife and Olga Rudge, not to mention Marcella Spann, a young woman he had brought with him from America; another was the irritation of being in the legal custody of his wife. Pound began to complain of not being able to keep up with the world, or to sort out his own affairs. At the end of 1961 he ceased to speak to visitors; he entered an almost unbroken silence, and what appeared to be profound depression. His health became shaky; Olga Rudge moved back in to take care of him, and he was finally estranged from his wife. He died in Venice on 1 November 1972.

The *Rock-Drill* Cantos had been published in 1954–5, when Pound had only three or four more years to stay in the mental hospital, and the *Thrones* began to appear immediately after them. But the collected *Thrones* volume was not finally proof-read until midsummer 1959, back in Rapallo. And that Rapallo summer was Pound's final period of work on the Cantos: the last of *Drafts & Fragments*, probably begun only a few months before, were written then. Published in little magazines here and there over the next few years, some of them included quite weak writing in the first versions, and had to undergo a degree of post-publication revising unknown since the labours over the first half-dozen Cantos between 1917 and 1923. But the final versions are clear of all dross.

The 1968 collected *Drafts & Fragments* does, however, include, as 'Fragments of Cantos', an 'Addendum for Canto C' and a brief paradisal piece, both written in 1941. They are good enough, but do not add anything to the poem; and their tone is out of place here, being that of a man twenty years younger. And the post-1972 American printings have added, as Canto CXX, a fragment originally printed as part of a 'Fragment from Canto 115'. In 1981 the British publishers fell in with the American example. But Pound would not have wanted his long poem to conclude with this fragment: the appeal to the reader's sympathy is not in his spirit.

Drafts & Fragments has received one of the highest compliments that can be paid to verse: critics have simply quoted –

> A blown husk that is finished
> > but the light sings eternal
> a pale flare over marshes
> > where the salt hay whispers to tide's change
> > > (From CXV, p. 794)

– and have forgotten to write criticism, as if the meaning were evident, and nothing needed to be said about the manner of writing. Everything is slimmed down, made lean in words and full in implication:

> To make a church
> > or an altar to Zagreus Ζαγρεύς
> Son of Semele Σεμέλη
> Without jealousy
> > like the double arch of a window
> Or some great colonnade.
> > > (Notes for CXVII et seq.)

The process and the result of abbreviation are like those in Beckett, who cut down and down, from Euphuistic prose to (apparently) mere nomination: one road, with infertile tree; or one mound; or one mouth,

working. Thus the sculptor Brancusi cut down from intricate representation in the manner of Michelangelo to one torso, male, consisting
of a forked steel column as an inverted Y. So we arrive at

> Without jealousy
> > like the double arch of a window
> Or some great colonnade.

This is the result of a progression, and is perhaps not a point that one
could start at.

Both in earlier Beckett and earlier Pound there seem to be phrases
and moments that concentrate whole areas of human behaviour. To
eliminate, later, all the weaker structure that supports them in that
earlier writing, the writer must find a new way of presenting them.
Thus in Beckett's *Happy Days* the phrase '[. . .] this will have been
another happy day.' looks forward so brightly, so determinedly, to
being able to look back. It seems to carry most of the play's vacuous
and plaintive domestic hell. The later Beckett would have replaced the
whole play with a new but equivalent dramatic image. But Pound
instead cuts down to the essential phrase:

> M' amour, m'amour
> > what do I love and
> > > where are you?
> (Notes for CXVII et seq.)

(Who is 'you'? Why should there be any you? The contradiction is
open, complete and hopeless.) Or again: in *Waiting for Godot*
Lucky and Pozzo are an epitome of sado-masochistic dependence-
relationships. In these last Cantos, the horrors of love relations are cut
down to one centre, jealousy, without elaboration, but with an image
that carries all self-pitying and demanding possessiveness:

> Under the Rupe Tarpeia [the Tarpeian Rock]
> weep out your jealousies

In *Krapp's Last Tape*, all unselfconscious emotion, seen from the stasis
of a consciousness that watches its own emotions, is suggested in a brief
memory of a day in sunlight on a river. Here an emotion from some
specific day and time, now equally out of reach, is in the grey fullness of

Twilit sky leaded with elm boughs.

Pound's way of presenting these concentrations without supporting substructures is not, like the later Beckett's, to develop each into a brief independent drama, but to string them together. Each line, or, more often, pair of lines, seems to point in a new direction; the linking is according to the development of a mood, and is more or less open-ended. These nodules reinforce each other not by semantic focus on one central point, but because they are all equally powerful, and there is none that does not seem to reach out to half-remembered, known, intuited experience:

> For the blue flash and the moments
> > benedetta [blessed]
> the young for the old
> > that is tragedy
> And for one beautiful day there was peace.
> > Brancusi's bird
> > > in the hollow of pine trunks
> or when the snow was like sea foam
> > Twilit sky leaded with elm boughs.
> Under the Rupe Tarpeia
> > weep out your jealousies –
> To make a church
> > or an altar to Zagreus Ζαγρεύς
> Son of Semele Σεμέλη
> Without jealousy
> > like the double arch of a window
> Or some great colonnade.
> > > (Notes for CXVII et seq.)

When the unit of art comes down to two lines, one may feel very insecure about asserting what any one unit suggests, or whether it acts as metaphor or metonym. A window: space, light, and with an arch, for strength and firmness; a colonnade, marching across space. There is no such thing as 'mere naming', and word-order, choice between 'synonyms' and diction all condition the effect. 'A window's double arch' would have suited earlier Cantos, but would be too clipped for this ease and spaciousness. 'Big' would never have done here, and *-ade-* needs the repeat of *great* for its magnificence. A further mystery of this technique of glimpses is that 'like the double arch of a window/Or some great colonnade' does not really qualify the church or the altar. In some way it seems a direct description-by-negative of what 'being without jealousy' is: an ease, an order.

The reader might not at first guess it, but this section is extremely allusive; sources (if the term is justifiable in relation to such a technique) have been teased out for almost every line.[1] But of the many new matters brought into the Cantos by these few pages there is room to mention only one or two. Various references obscure to most English readers when the book was published show Pound still fighting his own version of the war, with a harrowing passion. There is the victorious cavalry charge of the Savoia Regiment at 'Ibukerki' on the Russian steppes in 1942. It is paralleled with the spirit of the Italians fighting Austrians in the First World War, when

> At Oleari, the Divisione Sforzesca
> disobeyed into victory,
> Had horses with them.
> (CX, p. 779)

There is the earlier case (in the same Canto) of the rising of the people of Brescia in 1849 against the Austrians. All these instances seem to be subsumed into the Brescian stone lions with their damaged heads:

> not with jet planes,
> The holiness of their courage forgotten
> and the Brescian lions effaced

The following lines make this part of the battle between stability and rootlessness/fragmentation, with lonely 'resisters' against the encroaching evil 'blacked out', while yet the sun renews light. The next Canto gives us Napoleon (whose enemies in the Cantos work for the usurers of Europe) and the Banque de France; and also current skulduggery and truth-hiding in the fight for control of China:

> And 600 more dead at Quemoy –
> they call it political.
> (Notes for CXI, p. 783)

That instance is linked with Napoleon's era, through his former minister Talleyrand, who speaks of the shifting of the meaning of words in diplomacy. Geryon appears, and the Canto ends with the subversion by Abd-el-Melik, who rebelled, coined gold, and brought disorder to the

Byzantine Empire. Thus in this conspiracy theory of history the Italian
cavalry regiment on the Russian steppes in 1942 was on the side of
light, order and stability, against erosion, obfuscation and greed.

With the passages concerning 'Rock's world' we come to the last
statement of the dream of Thoreau-modified-by-Frobenius: a dawn
world where there is nothing between man and a unitary flowering
universe, except reverence for it; plus a sense of tribe and culture as
another unitary (but changing) flowering, built especially around the
rites that worship that nature-universe's complexities. Joseph F. Rock
was born in Vienna in 1884. As Pound, a linguist-Odysseus, moved
from Provençal under the tutorship of W. P. Shepard to the landscape
of southern France, so Rock fell in love with Chinese characters at the
age of 15, and 'It created a desire in me to explore the vast hinterland of
China and to learn to know its history and geography at first hand'.[2] In
1922, Rock came to one of the least-known areas of China, the rocky
and vertiginous region on the borders of Yunnan, Szechwan and Tibet.
There he encountered the [1]Na-[2]khi.

The [1]Na-[2]khi herd sheep on the alpine meadows at altitudes of 10,000
feet and above. Their brown, weathered faces smile in Rock's magnificent photographs in front of houses that look like heaps of rocks, with
Yangtze torrents or white peaks in the background. They had, when
Rock knew them, a rich literature of romance and rite, recorded by the
priests in pictographic script, and largely unknown to the world. Rock
stayed with them for twelve years, recording and translating. His four-
volume assemblage of [1]Na-[2]khi writings was ready for the printer in
1941; the half-tone blocks were already made, and destroyed when the
Japanese entered Shanghai. Rock still had the manuscript and his
eighteen volumes of notes; but they were sunk by a submarine when he
was forced to ship them out in 1943. Rock returned in 1946 to find his
chief interpreter dead – a severe setback because the [1]Na-[2]khi script is
merely a few pictographs per sentence, the rest being in the priest's
memory. Rock began again, found and 'trained' another interpreter,
and produced editions and translations of ceremonies and stories, until
the communists forced him out in 1949. At that time he observed that
those priests who still remembered the old literature were denying any
connection with it, in face of the communists' hostility to religion. He
foresaw that the [1]Na- [2]khi culture would soon die. That is the bearing
of Pound's lines

> his fragments sunk (20 years)   (CX, p. 781)

and

> Rock's world that he saved us for memory
> a thin trace in high air
> (CXIII, p. 786)

The ^{1}Na-^{2}khi setting in Rock's descriptions is snow-range and meadow, quartz, granite and Yunnan oak. After labours with Baller's Sacred Edict and the like, or among the cabbage smells of that institution in Washington, to emerge into such a text-field must have seemed a deep breath of clear air. But it is not just a tourist's freshness: the literature shows that the entities of the landscape have penetrated every element of the ^{1}Na-^{2}khi imaginative life, as (in the ^{1}Na-^{2}khi eyes) beauty.

The ^{1}Na-^{2}khi seem to have carried with them from their ancient nomad home (where 'they beheld only the great expanse of heaven and the vast grasslands, with here and there a grove of junipers in remote and shallow valleys'[3]) a reverence for the juniper. It is worshipped as the central god-principle in a ceremony called 'The Sacrifice to Heaven', in which it is flanked by one oak representing Heaven and another representing Earth. The juniper is in effect another Tree of Heaven, like the great ash Ygdrasail that offers strength in *Rock-Drill*:

> That you lean 'gainst the tree of heaven,
> and know Ygdrasail
> (LXXXV, p. 545)

For 'the head of the Juniper supports Heaven, therefore the vast Heaven is immobile, the foot of the Juniper is attached to the Earth; the vast Earth therefore does not move; the green Juniper has thousand spreading branches; the ^{2}Non-^{1}ö has thousand branches';[4] and Rock's footnote tells us that this ^{2}Non-^{1}ö implies both in gods' medicine or nectar (Amṛta) and the protection and support offered by the ceremonial objects. One part of the ceremony is the 'Impurities Smoke Out', which is to drive out ^{3}Ch'ou, all kinds of impurity, imperfection, incapacity.[5] Its chanted preamble lists ways of purification: a certain high mountain was purified by the snow, a lower mountain by the rain; ^{2}Ndu attained old age by purifying himself with *Artemisia vulgaris*. Also a certain pheasant purified itself by going to the juniper, and its female by going to the oak; another (the stone pheasant) purified itself with the dew. And so Pound:

                    Quercus [oak] on Mt Sumeru
                            can'st'ou see with the eyes of turquoise?
                        heaven   earth
                            in the center
                                is
                                juniper
                    The purifications
                            are snow, rain, artemisia,
                            also dew, oak and the juniper

                    And in thy mind beauty, O Artemis,
                            as of mountain lakes in the dawn
                                            (CX, p. 778)

This is Pound's last blast against the dualism that divides all into
Amassed Matter and Ideal Abstraction (and which of course produced,
by reaction, this particular Thoreauvian Protestant and his attempt to
de-Protestantise the West). Once more he tries to re-divinise the
universe, to see (as he said in 1912) 'about us the universe of fluid force,
and below us the germinal universe of wood alive, of stone alive' (*SR*,
92). It is, as Jamila Ismail suggests,[6] the proper culmination of a long
poem full of gods, trees and familiar beasts. It is a very logical
development, but the thought-movement and image-choice of *Drafts &
Fragments* undercuts what it affirms.

The sensibility implied by the whole is in the grip of revulsion and
despair. There seems to be an encroaching disorder, which is a
blackness because it is something that this sensibility cannot forget.
Every positive act that might seem a reason for limited contentment
serves only to remind of its own fragility: the beautiful road cut through
the lakeside rock –

            Cozzaglio, Dino Martinazzi made the road here (Gardesana)
                                            (CX, p. 778)

– gets entangled with those futile and beautiful cavalry charges in an
endless war that seems passioned with desperation. All that is desired
is

                        a nice quiet paradise
                            over the shambles
                                (CXVI, p. 796)

– a small enough claim, a little walled garden or *hortus conclusus*, for a voice that has sought to show Paradise in the All. But a shambles is a slaughter-house, which may take the mind back to CXIII, p. 789:

> And the bull by the force that is in him –
> not lord of it,
> mastered.

(Thus 'The bull runs on the sword,/*naturans*': XLVII, p. 237. The source of the present passage is Remy de Gourmont, where he describes the awesome spectacle of the bull driven to his coupling not by the lure of a pleasure but by 'a force exterior to the individual though included in his organism': *NPL*, 57.) It may even take the mind back to the butchering of Agamemnon-as-bull and Dionysus-Mussolini-as-bull in the Pisan Cantos. In the interview with Donald Hall in 1960, Pound said that the lowest division of his moral cosmos was for 'people dominated by emotion' (*WW*, 112); as in the Pisan Cantos, this category here seems very inclusive.

The long poem had progressed towards a theological enlightenment and certainty by building certain images which (despite all their external sources) are particularly Pound's: the temple, the crystal, the white light. Dioce's city was theurgically designed to draw down the heavens' forces; on the tower at Ecbatan, the 'god's bride' (IV, p. 16) lay awaiting a cosmic copulation. Troy was the citadel of a culture, and when it fell (XXIII, p. 109) the priest-king Aeneas (guided by the chthonic deities) took the heritage to Italy, where his descendants planted Rome: ROMA/AMOR, in the palindrome given by *A Visiting Card*, the city of the 'sacred' language Latin (*P*, 327, 317). The city and the temple fuse. The Albigensian heretics 'behind' the troubadour culture had their citadel, Montségur, whose cult (Pound suggests: cf. *MPP*, 238 ff.) derived ultimately from Eleusis. Savaric de Mauléon and Gausbert de Poicibot retreat to Montségur amid the disaster of the Albigensian Crusade and the fall of their culture in XLVIII, p. 243. 'Mont Ségur', as Pound writes it, means 'secure mountain' (compare the Luther hymn 'Ein feste Burg ist unser Gott' ('A Tower of Refuge is our God!') included by Pound in *Confucius to Cummings*). But as the god's bride and the city of Dioce are in some way the 'cunt of the world', focusing the gods' forces, so Pound hints at a mystical meaning in Arnaut Daniel's obscure reference to entering the lady's castle (*SR*, 89). This passage in Pound's comment on Gourmont's *Natural Philosophy of Love* appears to be connected:

The mind is an up-spurt of sperm, no, let me alter that; trying to watch the process: the sperm, the form-creator, the substance which compels the ovule to evolve in a given pattern, one microscopic, minuscule particle, entering the 'castle' of the ovule. (*NPL*, x)

There is the emotion of penetration and form-imparting; but there is also the emotion of 'entering protection', as does the god/goddess Ra-Set in XCI, p. 611, a passage which clearly denotes the attainment of Paradise.[7]

The 'cult' of the aware in the Cantos has always been presented as local and vulnerable; in the ruins of Pound's Mussolini-effort at Pisa, Montségur is grey, broken, like Diana/the moon's 'house'. After that phase of the poem there is even more emphasis on how few are the true believers, how frangible the line of their tradition: 'a little light from the borders' (XCII, p. 622). *Thrones* takes an image for this from Joseph Rock:

> The hills are blue-green with juniper,
> the stream, as Achilöos there below us,
> here one man can hold the whole pass
> over this mountain, at Mont Ségur the chief's cell
>
> you can enter it sideways only, TSO 筰 is here named
>
> from the rope bridge, hemp rope? a reed rope?
>
> (CI, p. 725)

A pass that Rock says 'can safely be guarded by one man'[8] is here conflated with the Chinese character for the slender rope bridges that cross ravines in the ^{1}Na-^{2}khi area. These seem narrow paths, that the elect may pass and easily hold against barbarians, to the sacred donjon: the room at Montségur which, as archaeology has discovered, is aligned with the annual movement of the sun's rays.

All this building of the impregnable Paradise-sanctum culminates in the first line of these *Drafts & Fragments*:

> Thy quiet house   (CX, p. 777)

– that is, 'thy quiet house at Torcello' (CX, p. 780), the church at Torcello where the Virgin in mosaic dominates the apse. But from here there is no development, except in rare and oblique reference, or in contexts of great uncertainty:

> Falling spiders and scorpions,
> Give light against falling poison,
> A wind of darkness hurls against forest
> > the candle flickers
> > > is faint
> Lux enim –
> > versus this tempest.
> The marble form in the pine wood,
> > The shrine seen and not seen
> From the roots of sequoias
>
> > > > > ching[4]
> > 敬
> > pray   pray
> > > There is power
> Awoi or Komachi,
> > the oval moon.
> > > > > (CX, p. 781)

Awoi in the Japanese Noh-play connotes jealousy, and 'All neath the moon' in *Thrones* is 'under Fortuna' (XCVII, p. 676).

A number of image-chains, built up through the whole long poem to affirm that (as Browning's Fra Lippo Lippi says) this world 'means intensely, and means good', now come to an end that denies them. The book opens exuberantly:

> Thy quiet house
> The crozier's curve runs in the wall,
> The harl, feather-white, as a dolphin on sea-brink
>
> I am all for Verkehr [intercourse, circulation] without tyranny
> > – wake exultant
> > > in caracole
> Hast'ou seen boat's wake on sea-wall,
> > how crests it?
> What panache?
> > > paw-flap, wave-tap,
> > > > that is gaiety,
> Toba Sojo,
> > toward limpidity,
> > > that is exultance
> > > > > (CX, p. 777)

It is of dolphins to leap, *exsultare*, a word Ovid likes; also of the phallus, and of the mind. Delight makes for understanding, and is of many planes, and Ovidian metamorphosis bodies forth these understandings. The crozier's curve in the wall here, like the wave in the stone earlier,

puts liquid in solid; and the main image for that has been crystal, whose
inner waves 'weave' together. Crystal appears at the moment of god-
showing. But the line of crystal images ends here:

> I have brought the great ball of crystal;
>   who can lift it?
> Can you enter the great acorn of light?
>   But the beauty is not the madness
> Tho' my errors and wrecks lie about me.
> And I am not a demigod,
> I cannot make it cohere.
>   (CXVI, pp. 795–6)

The waves 'weave' in the crystal as light, and light brings together all
that is associated in the Cantos with dawn, illumination, coition; the
'white light that is allness' (XXXVI, p. 179) and Form; and the
synaesthetic fusion of sound and light in 'the sharp song with sun under
its radiance' (LXXIV, p. 439). That song is now reaffirmed, but as
something that this sensibility cannot reach:

> A blown husk that is finished
>   but the light sings eternal
> a pale flare over marshes
>   where the salt hay whispers to tide's change
>   (From CXV, p. 794)

And the very crispness-in-clarity of Rock's world, that is the sign of
intuited structure, seems unstable, going towards the ultimate horror
(as noted in the China Cantos: LIV, p. 280), seepage:

> In mountain air the grass frozen emerald
>   and with the mind set on that light
>   saffron, emerald,
>   seeping.
> 'but that kind of ignorance' said the old priest to Yeats
>   (in a railway train) 'is spreading every day from the schools'
>   (CXIII, p. 789)

If one asks what makes this light, or unmakes its power, the answer
seems to be: sense of order. Does knowledge bring worthwhile fruit?
Does any phenomenon have stable relations with any other? Is a
lifetime's constructive effort likely to leave any durable result at all?
Here the 'resisters' against evil and fragmentation are 'blacked out';

everywhere in this book the chaos is imaged as darkness. The beginning
of Canto CXIII seems to offer hope:

> Thru the 12 Houses of Heaven
> > seeing the just and the unjust,
> > tasting the sweet and the sorry,
> Pater Helios [Father Sun] turning.
> 'Mortal praise has no sound in her ears'
> > > (Fortuna's)
> θρηνος
> And who no longer make gods out of beauty
> θρῆνος   this is a dying.
> Yet to walk with Mozart, Agassiz and Linnaeus
> > 'neath overhanging air under sun-beat
> Here take thy mind's space

Here is a place reserved for beauty (which is the 'gold thread in the
pattern/(Torcello)' that one must 'affirm': CXVI, p. 797). But Helios
seems more or less indifferent to it all, gold threads or black threads. It
is a delightful image, full of humour; but his function seems not to
differ from Fortuna's: to smile, and just keep rolling along. What is the
relation of his light to the light that battles against hate? The problem of
evil remains.

The beautiful first page of the book launches gaily:

> – wake exultant
> > in caracole
> Hast'ou seen boat's wake on sea-wall,
> > how crests it?

And that vigorous all-participating imagination seems to take us back to
the first line in Pound's definitive collection of his short poems –

> I stood still and was a tree amid the wood   ('The Tree')

– with:

> can you see with eyes of coral or turquoise
> > or walk with the oak's root?

But the reader who has followed up Rock knows that this is from the
lover's plea to his dead girl in the [1]Na-[2]khi romance described by him.

The ceremony that placates the suicide's wandering spirit connects strangely with the Dante line before it:

> toward limpidity,
> > that is exultance,
> here the crest runs on wall
> che paion' si al vent'
> > ²Här-²la-¹llü ³k'ö
> of the wind sway   (CX, p. 777)

It is called the 'Wind Sway' ceremony, and the meaning of that title here bends to coincide with the wind-driven wraiths in Dante's Hell who 'seem to be on the wind thus [light]': Paolo and Francesca, condemned lovers, lost, with nothing but the memory of their own passion. The vigorous Odysseus seems finally to have been replaced at centre stage by Elpenor, the companion whom he met in Hades in Canto I, 'unwept, unburied'; this autobiographical poem has registered a deep change.

NOTES: CHAPTER 15

1   esp. in E. Hesse's notes to Pound's *Letzte Texte (Cantos CX–CXX): Entwürfe und Fragmente* (Zurich: 'Die Arche', 1975).
2   J. F. Rock, *The Ancient Na-Khi Kingdom* (Cambridge, Mass.: Harvard University Press, 1947), Vol. 1, p. vii.
3   J. F. Rock, 'The ²Mùan ¹bpö ceremony', *Monumenta Serica*, vol. 13 (1948), p. 7.
4   ibid., p. 21.
5   ibid., pp. 22–3.
6   '"News of the Universe"', *Agenda*, vol. 9, no. 2–3 (Spring-Summer 1971), p. 78.
7   cf. also XCII, p. 618, 'And from this Mount were blown/seed'.
8   Rock, *Ancient Na-Khi*, Vol. 2, p. 444.

CHAPTER 16

The State of the Text

The present text of the Cantos, as published by New Directions in New York and Faber in London, puts together all the sections of the long poem that Pound authorised for inclusion. Most, if not all, of these sections were proof-read by Pound in earlier, separate publication. Pound exercised great care in adjusting spelling, spacing and punctuation to articulate his meaning in every fine joint. (In only eleven Cantos there are about 200 changes of detail between *A Draft of the Cantos 17–27* (1928) and the Faber *A Draft of XXX Cantos* (1933); each is an improvement in clarity or pacing.) Large parts of the separate sections were composed in the printer's shop from corrected sheets taken from the previous magazine printings of the separate Cantos. Further, when Faber collected all the sections up to and including the Pisan, in 1950, Pound made more changes, and there were later errata lists. The following two sections of the poem, *Section: Rock-Drill* and *Thrones*, were typeset in an expert and scholarly printing shop in Verona, under Pound's close supervision. *Drafts & Fragments* was heavily revised and corrected between magazine publication and the separate version. Since the present collected text simply gathers all the previously published sections, it ought to be satisfactory; but no textual scholar would consider it so.

The principal reasons are three: (*a*) the nature of Pound's care with words; (*b*) the fact that the current text does not incorporate many of the corrections Pound authorised from 1950 onwards; (*c*) the fact that a large number of changes *not* authorised by Pound were made. (The details are in Barbara Eastman's *Ezra Pound's 'Cantos': The Story of the Text, 1948–1975*.)

Pound was very conscious of spelling, punctuation and spacing where they affected the sound of words. He knew that magic compromise between idiolect-reproducing phonetic spelling and the orthographical norm, which is necessary to catch the culturally diagnostic ways in which people speak: '"mi-hine eyes hev"' (LXXX, p. 498),

'"Part o deh roof ma'am"' (LXXX, p. 508). He used spelling to bring out the elements of an utterance that add up to musical cadence:

> not a slivver, not a spare disc of sunlight
> Flaking the black, soft water   (IV, p. 14)

He was less conscious of spelling as reflecting (non-orally) 'period' or 'place', but he used it here also, in a rather hazier way:

> No more do my shaftes fly
> To slay. Nothing is now clean slayne
> But rotteth away.   (XXX, p. 147)

These functions apart, he was not very conscious at all of spellings as elements of self-consistent conventional systems: his own spelling and his awareness of spelling in the texts he used were poor.

He was also half-unconscious of grammatical systems in the languages from which he drew. The Cantos and Pound's other writings are full of impossibilities like '*Lei fassa furar a del*'[1] and 'vacuos exercet aera morsus' (*E*, 152[2]). And his attitude to facts was doggedly Yeatsian. Yeats would not have cared in the slightest if someone had pointed out that his 'arch-King Ardrigh' meant 'arch-King High King';[3] nor Pound, if one had told him that his 'River Kiang' ('Separation on the River Kiang') meant 'River River'.

But finally, like everyone else, Pound was subject to mere error in proof-reading. He was quite conscious that it mattered for his poetic purposes that Canto XX, p. 89, should read 'The viel [stringed instrument] held close to his side', and not 'The veil [. . .]'. But when the compositor got that wrong Pound (like all proof-readers at some time or other) saw what he had intended, not what was on the page in front of him; and that error passed into the printed American text, where it stayed until 1971. More important, his sense of what worked well in the poem was not always consistent (naturally), and he did not necessarily correlate one occasion with another. Hugh Kenner gives examples: a strange compositor's line-repeat that cropped up in XIII was explicitly welcomed by Pound on one occasion, but apparently rejected on another; typescripts from which the Pisan Cantos were set by New Directions and Faber apparently did not agree with each other; and Pound did not catch at their first appearance the discrepancies between British and American texts that were eventually to amount to two printed traditions.[4]

New Directions' printing methods made it too expensive for them to adopt the Faber changes requested by Pound; and these changes were still not adopted in bulk when New Directions began to use offset, in which changes are much cheaper. And then, in 1975, the British text, incorporating those changes, was scrapped. Faber's text since that date has been a photographic reproduction of New Directions', identical except for the temporary omission of Canto CXX.

Meanwhile a revision committee had been proposed in America; it boiled down eventually to Eva Hesse in Germany and Hugh Kenner in the United States. 'Master copies' of the Faber text were marked with the changes proposed by Hesse (more than 800 in number) and by Kenner. But by the time that Pound was approached for his approval in detail (in 1964) he was too depressed and fatigued to devote more than sporadic attention to this labour. New Directions none the less went ahead with piecemeal changes to their text: in the two printings of 1970 and 1971 some two hundred were made, and the 1972 and 1975 texts add four more. Some of these follow an errata list made by Pound; the authorisation for others is uncertain; by far the greatest number were certainly not authorised by him. The changes are of every kind, from correction of indubitable spelling errors (unpronounceable Greek, for example) to putting Chinese characters the right way up, to correcting errors of fact.

The text of the future, one might think, should revert to the last readings proof-read or otherwise definitely authorised by Pound; with, as footnoted variants, those whose authorisation is uncertain, and (clearly distinguished) those that the editor thinks might have had Pound's approval had he been asked. However, a very large number of the changes made between 1970 and 1975 were made on principles that would deny such a proposal. It appears that Eva Hesse wished to have the text corrected not merely according to Pound's intention in the given case, stated or surmised, but according to correctness itself. This effort was always either meaningless or damaging to the poem.

> The pines at Takasago
> grow with the pines of Isé!

was changed to

> The pine at Takasago
> grows with the pine of Isé!
> (IV, p. 15)

The former reading had been passed by Pound without correction in all the earlier printings of any importance (this point applies in all the following examples). It fits with XXI, p. 99, which the editors appear not to have noticed, for they did not change it: 'Grow with the Pines of Ise'. Evidently it was quite firmly fixed in Pound's mind that the pines at Ise and Takasago were more than one in number, whatever the source said.[5] The editors have 'corrected' Pound's version of the Japanese myth (as, no doubt, they would have corrected Ovid's versions of the Greek); somewhere, it will eventually be discovered, some part of the Pound myth-web will have been torn by this.

In 1970 Pound's consistent Provençal spelling '*e lo soleils plovil*' was changed to '*e lo soleills plovil*'. Now the editions of Arnaut Daniel that Pound used (Canello, Lavaud) have 'soleills'; but it is of little relevance to check against the printed source that Pound is likely to have taken the phrase from, since for him (as for the Provençal poet) any given written text was merely a 'window' to the aural artefact. 'Soleils', as it happens, is a perfectly respectable Provençal spelling; but, whether or not, Pound was simply using it to get down his sense of the word, as aurally remembered. Pound was born after Dr Johnson (1709–84), lexicographer, and Karl Konrad Friedrich Wilhelm Lachmann (1793–1851), professor extraordinarius of classical philology in the University of Königsberg; but he might as well have been born in the age of the maker of Provençal manuscripts, for whom spelling was, not a matter of indifference, but a series of local compromises between broad conventions and the dictates of his ear. If editors succeed in conventionalising Pound's spellings as far as they scientifically can, there will be as much difference in feel between what he wrote and what the reader buys and puts on his desk as there is between an Arnaut manuscript written in Italy in the thirteenth century and any modern monumental scholarly variorum printed edition of Arnaut.

In 1971 Pound's 'San Bertrand' at XCV, p. 645, was changed to 'Saint Bertrand', which is more correct because Saint-Bertrand-de-Comminges is a place-name in modern France. But this is effectively a change of locus from Old Provençal to modern French. It is true that 'Saint' is also a Provençal spelling; but Pound wanted something that was obviously Provençal as opposed to French. The point of this opposition connects with the whole heretic-troubadour drama of XLVIII, p. 243.[6]

The specific oral direction of Pound's word is altered when the publishers change his venomous 'Pullizer' to the correct 'Pulitzer' on the same page; and his thin-lipped 'petrified terd that was Verres' to the much heartier 'turd' (XIV, p. 62). As well change his 'Bhud'/'Bhudda'/'Bhudd-ha'/'Bhuddists' to the proper 'Buddha' and the rest.

A whole tangle of cultural indirections is cut away, as Hugh Kenner has pointed out, when Pound's Japanese spelling of Chinese names is sinicised ('Ran-ti' to 'Hsiang': IV, p. 15;[7] the adviser also wanted 'So-Gioku' on the same page to become 'Sung Yü'). On those principles we should also change most of the Chinese names in the Chinese Cantos from French spellings to those of the Wade-Giles system (or the new mainland Chinese system) – except that Pound has given a reason for the French, on page 254 of the Cantos. When we get round to it, we should certainly produce a direct and authoritative translation based on a proper text of book 11 of the *Odyssey*, to replace that wholly unreliable artefact (mediated via the language of Rome and the attitudes of the Italian Renaissance) that now forms the bulk of Canto I. (Whether we should satisfy ourselves with an Oxford or Leipzig text, or reconstruct our own, to be changed if new papyri surface, is not clear.) And then there is the problem of Pound's erroneous 'Maison Quarée' (cf. XXXI, p. 154). The adviser requested that this be changed to 'Carée' (unfortunately omitting to double the 'r'), but then discovered that Pound's error was authorised by his source (Thomas Jefferson). Yet consistency with former principles of correctness would certainly require that the building be named in the language of its builders (Latin).

One could establish the principle (already apparent above) that the spelling should be as in Pound's source; but who is to say finally what Pound's sources were? Thirty years of research have left a great many uncertainties. Various recondite sources are listed by the *Companion to the Cantos* for the beautiful composite lyric on Malatesta's lady Isotta at the end of Canto IX; but it is not very likely that Pound consulted them, for all the bits used are there in Yriarte's *Un Condottiere au XV siècle* (a source we know he used) on pages 142 and 155. Pound was not one to reject a good 'found poem' when he saw it. The *Companion* is not able to adduce a source for Eleanor's gallivanting with Saladin in Canto VI, though it notes that the story probably originated with the *Chronique de Rains*; as I have demonstrated at length,[8] Pound's source was a seventeenth-century collection of *Intrigues galantes*, which to-

gether with a nineteenth-century student anthology of history documents provided the material of a good part of the Canto (the *Companion*
lists neither). All this illustrates the difficulty of being right about
Pound's sources.

Pound's quite conscious method of haste will probably have made
some sources unascertainable, as well as so distant from his final poem
as to be irrelevant. Facing his document, Pound tried to penetrate it
intuitively, 'to pick out the element of immediate and major importance' in the 'tangle' (thus at least he described the working of
Mussolini's mind: *J/M*, 66), without being clogged by detail. He then
jotted, rapidly, disconnectedly, elliptically. (See, for example, the notes
for Canto XX at Yale; or the form of a typical Pound quotation, '*mezzo
oscuro rade*', missing the '*luce*': *E*, 154.) In composing his verse he
would apparently pick up these notes, without referring back to their
source, without necessarily remembering their immediate verbal context, and perhaps sometimes without remembering which book they
came from. Having forced the core-meaning of the passage in note-
taking, he then forced the core-meaning of his notes, it would seem:
rearranging phrases, travestying syntax and sense of the detail of
original situation. Each step took him farther from the words of his
source, but not, he would say, from the meaning. When Marianne
Moore asked his advice about translating from French, he replied:
'WRITE the sense in plain english, PROSE, and then versify the
SENSE of your prose' (N*EP*, 440). In editing the letters of John Butler
Yeats in 1916, Pound wrote of what appeared to be an error:

> The omission of 'mentem' in the quotation on page fifty five is, so far
> as I am concerned, deliberate. Anyone might have quoted the line
> correctly and any editor might have emended it. As it stands now the
> latin is, to my mind at least, more a part of the writer's own thought.
> The unessential word has been worn away, and with such attrition I
> leave it.[11]

'What thou lovest well remains,/the rest is dross' (LXXXI, pp. 520–1).
And, besides this conscious use of the unconscious shaping effect of
memory, there is also conscious word-metamorphosis. Pound consciously conflated Leucothoe, she of the incense-bush, and Leucothea
(who rescued Odysseus); a learned critic took this for error, and New
Directions tried to correct XCV, p. 645, to make the goddess into
Odysseus' rescuer only. Fortunately, there survives a letter from

Pound setting an earlier publisher right on the point (see B*FT*, 376).

In 1975 New Directions, advised by Hugh Kenner, decided to make no more unauthorised changes, which would seem to suggest that the text will eventually revert to the readings authorised by Pound, perhaps after the long-term project of a variorum edition has been realised. Meanwhile the reader might consider that the semantic distortion brought to the poem by the weaknesses of the text is, so far, about at the same level as the scratches on a record, and that it is generally audio fanatics who care about such things; the musician is at a loss to understand why they do not listen to the music.

NOTES: CHAPTER 16

1 V, p. 18; cf. *MPP*, p. 291, n. 48.
2 Pound rejected correction of this phrase in the *Hugh Selwyn Mauberley* text: see K. K. Ruthven, *A Guide to Ezra Pound's 'Personae' (1926)* (Berkeley, Calif.: University of California Press, 1969), p. 141.
3 W. B. Yeats, *Uncollected Prose*, ed. John B. Frayne and Colton Johnson, Vol. 2 (London: Macmillan, 1975), p. 84 and n.
4 See Barbara C. Eastman, *Ezra Pound's 'Cantos': The Story of the Text, 1948–1975* (Orono, Me: National Poetry Foundation, 1979), pp. xiii–xiv; also collation of Faber and New Directions texts in *Annotated Index to the Cantos of Ezra Pound: Cantos I–LXXXIV*, ed. J. H. Edwards and W. W. Vasse (Berkeley, Calif.: University of California Press, 1971), pp. 313–22.
5 Cf. T*C*, 13. The source in this case would be the Fenollosa notes on the Noh.
6 The same applies to the garbled correction of 'Montrejau', ibid.
7 This change also corrected a fact (Ran-ti was a palace, not a person).
8 *MPP*, pp. 86–92, 308–12, 261–70.

CHAPTER 17

Trends in Criticism

Material not otherwise identified here or in the Select Bibliography is represented by excerpts in one or more of the following collections: J. P. Sullivan (ed.), *Ezra Pound: A Critical Anthology* (Harmondsworth: Penguin, 1970); Eric Homberger (ed.), *Ezra Pound: The Critical Heritage* (London/Boston, Mass.: Routledge & Kegan Paul, 1972); Walter Sutton (ed.), *Ezra Pound: A Collection of Critical Essays* (Englewood Cliffs, NJ: Prentice-Hall, 1963).

(i) 1917–45

The critical response to Pound's Cantos before the Second World War was inadequate. T. S. Eliot in these years maintained silence on them, except (for example) to say in 1928 that they were of the greatest importance and a storehouse of verse technique for the young poet – but not discussable except with 'those who accept his poetry as I accept it'. But he did pay detailed attention to the 'Hell Cantos' in 1934, attacking the theology manifest in their technique (see above, Chapter 7). Joyce offered praise, avoiding anything specific enough to suggest that he had read the Cantos; in private he parodied them. Yeats in 1928 offered his version of Pound's explanation of the structure, in such a way as to make it seem the structure of a kaleidoscope, with the mere 'found-object' interest of endless permutations. He hoped vaguely that, if he thought about this 'mathematical' structure more, he might find that 'here is no botch of tone and colour – Hodos Chameliontos – except for some odd corner where one discovers beautiful detail'. Then and in 1936 he gave it as Pound's aim to withdraw mind from what was experienced, presenting it as intermingling flux. His opinion of the qualities of the verse divided it into Paterian nobility, and crude, stammering revolutionism. Wyndham Lewis, in *Time and Western Man* (1927) suggested that Pound was a man without an independent sensibility, but with a remarkable faculty for vicarious emotion. Thus in his verse he could relive pasts in a perfectly convincing manner, and was indeed intent on rescuing the whole of the past for the modern age. Pound's Cantos were 'admirable' (*Men without Art*, 1934) but, despite his claims to be a modernist, the poet was in fact a believer in Golden Ages: a brawl in modern Wigan or Detroit was never as interesting to him as a brawl in fourteenth-century Siena. To compensate for this, Lewis wrote, Pound strove for modernity through the unconvincing voice of the tough guy, the 'strong silent man'.

Poets and university critics in general may not have been less intelligent then than now, but to launch into something as massive and as different as the Cantos without any guides (none of us now has to do this) required some determination. The reader's unconscious inclination was to find reasons for not bothering. This is why the critical action of men like Eliot, Joyce, Yeats and Lewis was all-important: only their influence could have overcome such shrinking back. But the mixture offered by Eliot, Joyce, Yeats and Lewis was general vague praise plus specific and brilliant attack. (Why this should have been is a difficult question; perhaps they felt that Pound the impresario needed no help; or perhaps it is merely that Pound's freedom from professional jealousy is more or less unique.) Pound, of course, unlike Eliot, entirely failed to 'manage' his audience. He gave them no philosophy in prose that they might subtly and unjustifiably identify with the verse, making the latter easier to handle. He offered no reassuring aura of scholarly authority; and in replies to critics he wrote as if economics were the whole point of modern literature, and as if they were witless not to have seen this.

Critics of minor talent tended to echo Yeats and the others, on the theme of empty brilliance on the one hand and lack of major form on the other. To say that the Cantos were a poem was to say that callisthenics were ballet (John Gould Fletcher, 1928). There was much burying of Pound, with sighs, as the necessary but now superseded educator of a past generation (Harriet Monroe, 1925; A. S. Amdur, *The Poetry of Ezra Pound*, 1936). Meanwhile, more independent and acute critics of the tendency now known as New Criticism developed anti-Cantos arguments. In 1932 F. R. Leavis found that the Cantos' techniques gave no values to the allusive materials they worked with. By contrast, the methods of *The Waste Land* subserved 'an urgency pressing from below: only an austere and deep seriousness could have controlled them into significance'. The Cantos appeared to be 'little more than a game'. Yvor Winters (1937, 1943) found the Cantos' method anti-rational: there was no framework of theme, but only a principle of 'unity of mood, carefully established and varied'. His general argument was that removal of rational meaning from the whole removed at the same time a principle of differentiation, hence also the possibility of strong structure; and a similar argument was developed against unsymmetrical verse-forms. R. P. Blackmur added to such ideas his own arguments about obscurity – sometimes acute, sometimes quite mistaken. (Thus the purpose of presenting the anecdotes in the Cantos was, he said, always secondary, as in Canto I, which was there for a point about the relation between ourselves and the Renaissance: 'the actual subject-matter translated has no substantial bearing upon the rest of the Cantos'.) He concluded that not only the structure and the key to the meaning were hidden, but also 'the substance of the poem itself'. These varyingly meritorious and discussion-worthy arguments were written in a tone that carried its own message. From it the student could perceive quite clearly that the critic had, after all, better things to do than to spend much more time on this rather minor writer. His colleagues thus having performed the necessary stable-cleaning for him, Cleanth Brooks in 1939 was able to publish his *Modern Poetry and the Tradition* without any discussion at all of Ezra Pound.

In general it was left to poets – with no more than a coterie audience – to demonstrate in detail how, in the Cantos, new matter marched with new measure; and at the same time to give some indication of the Cantos' real status. Glenway Wescott already in 1925 had made useful contributions in this line; thus also Basil Bunting (1931), Marianne Moore (1934), George Barker (1935), Edwin Muir (1937, 1940). So also did Louis Zukofsky, especially in the 1931 article I have frequently quoted, which further considered the Dantescan relation between moral values and structure in the Cantos. In 1931 William Carlos Williams said useful things about measure and content – though he also pointed out that Pound's 'training' was evident in a predilection for over-poetic hyphenated noun-modifiers ('god-sleight', 'sea-swirl'). In 1935 he attacked readers' indifference to Pound's American-history themes, and pointed to the cultural results of such indifference (*Selected Essays*, pp. 162–9).

(ii)   1946–60

The critical act of 1949 was the award to Pound of the Bollingen Prize for Poetry, by the Fellows in American Letters of the Library of Congress (Eliot, Robert Lowell, W. H. Auden and others), for the

Pisan Cantos. Controversy followed, since this was interpreted as an official reward for treason. Little critical sense emerged from the controversy. But in reviewing the book the poet John Berryman (1949) gave a good analysis of the way in which the form-and-material seeds of the Cantos as a whole were implicit in the first three. He added: 'The Cantos have always been personal; only the persona increasingly adopted, as the Poet's fate clarifies, is Pound himself.'

Irritable dilutions of Yeats, Leavis and Winters continued. But one interesting symptom of a change was the number of recantations. In 1946, Eliot was once more vague in his praise and brilliant in his negatives. After taking in the Pisan Cantos, he added (1950) a belated and unnoticeable note, recanting. D. S. Carne-Ross found in the Pisan Cantos failure and 'no real religious comprehension' (1950); in 1973 he seemed to find in them a new Gospel for Catholicism. Thom Gunn (1960) savaged *Thrones*, but in 1969 refused absolutely to allow his review to be reprinted: it had been a mere sneer at 'probably the greatest poet we have had in this century'. (And in 1969 Charles Tomlinson regretted his damning review of the *Literary Essays* in 1954, and its 'ignorance, safeguarded by the certainties of Cambridge English'.)

Peter Russell in 1950 tried to stir the embers by assembling valuable earlier pieces by Edith Sitwell (1934) and Allen Tate (1936), along with good new explications of the background to the earlier Cantos about Italy, and of economics. In university circles, interest grew slowly. The *Pound Newsletter* (1954–5), edited by John H. Edwards, was an important beginning. Lewis Leary in 1954 assembled useful essays. Earl Miner's 1958 book on Japanese–English poetic influences was expert and perceptive on image-juxtaposition in Cantos passages. Clark Emery in 1958 quoted Pound at great length in setting out his theoretical frames. David W. Evans in 1957 brought out finely the movement of the personal situations hinted at in the Pisan poem.

But Hugh Kenner's *The Poetry of Ezra Pound* (1950) can be said to have rescued Pound. At the time of its writing, *Instigations*, *Gaudier-Brzeska*, *Guide to Kulchur* and *ABC of Reading* were all out of print, and the *Letters* and *Literary Essays* not yet published. Kenner justified the Cantos' structure by justifying Pound's ideogram theory, and justified that in turn partly by tracing, over the centuries, the rise and fall of the sense that the poet's job was to present 'substantial form' in the world outside him, not merely to arrange 'essence', as mind addressing mental entity. He showed that important elements in Pound were not new, but

were buried in over-familiar *loci* like Aristotle and Wordsworth; and
that these 'traditional' elements were genuinely renewed by Pound,
being modified by colourings and liberations common to the age of
Eisenstein, Einstein and Joyce. Kenner paid a good deal of attention to
placing Pound within particular culture-streams, but without falling
into the cultural determinism that swamps the author in question under
a mass of trivia, each alleged to be a factor determining his action, and
each (apparently) equally significant. Kenner's style reflected much
knowledge of cultural differentiations. All this had the effect of
transforming Pound from a naïf and an exotic to a man of responsible
intelligence. And with the Cantos Kenner bullied readers into bringing
to bear the knowledge that they themselves could deduce from Pound's
page. The book should be reread, along with other contemporary
pieces, such as the comparison with Milton in Russell's collection, and
the *Rock-Drill* article of 1956 (reprinted in *Gnomon*, New York, 1958),
still the most convincing effort to read that section without heavy use of
sources.

The *Annotated Index to the Cantos of Ezra Pound*, edited by J. H.
Edwards and W. W. Vasse (1957), was hamstrung by its principle of
organisation (alphabetical listing of names and foreign words, which
chopped up each passage of poetry into unrelatable miscellanea). But its
great quantity of information has been fruitful for later Pound scholarship. In London, the journal *Agenda* (1958 onwards), edited by William
Cookson, carried Pound's writings and some Pound criticism. But
some of the most important Pound criticism of this period is in the stray
remarks of Robert Creeley, Charles Olson, Allen Ginsberg and their
contemporaries, poets whose verse in the 1950s was renewing Pound's
lines of development.

(iii)   1961–70

Perhaps because Kenner had now assured them that the Cantos had
some independent value, critics were now ready to look at some of the
Cantos' sources, to see what effect this would have on their opinion of
the poetics. One of the earliest book-length surveys in this style was
George Dekker's judicious *Sailing after Knowledge* (1963). Noel Stock
edited a useful collection in 1965, and in 1964 and 1967 adduced much
inside information (he had been a disciple of Pound's) while adjudging
the Cantos a failure for their amateur 'expertises' and their avoidance of
the culture's traditional basis. But his *Life* (1970), full of useful data,

reduces Pound's whole effort to a series of miscellaneous gestures. The book of the decade was Donald Davie's *Ezra Pound: Poet as Sculptor* (1965). It followed the line of earlier poets' criticism in its sensuous apprehension and skilled verbal re-evocation of the 'total content' of the verse, sometimes with the help of the writings of Pound's friend Adrian Stokes. The book showed the weakness of Enlightenment elements, tending towards abstraction, in the Cantos; but finely demonstrated the radical difference between ego/nature relations in Yeats and in the Pisan Cantos, with Coleridge's and Ruskin's notebooks and Keats's letters as the true predecessors of the latter.

Eva Hesse, Pound's German translator, furthered such studies with her 1969 collection; Earle Davis had clarified one area with *Vision Fugitive: Ezra Pound and Economics* (1968). Daniel Pearlman's (1969) *Barb of Time* has remained influential, arguing that the Cantos set up a duality of mechanical time and of escape from that into a mystical time-lessness. In 1970, Walter Baumann, with a scholarly care not yet common in works on Pound, showed how two Cantos (IV and LXXXII) branched out into the meanings of the whole poem. All these studies were furthered greatly by the publication in 1963 of the exemplary *Bibliography of Ezra Pound* by Donald Gallup. And by the end of the decade university research into the Cantos was respectable.

(iv) 1971–83

The book of this period was Kenner's *The Pound Era* (1971). It extended understanding of elements in the traditions that had led to Pound (such as James's), and scientific parallels to Pound's concepts (such as Buckminster Fuller). It watched 'ideograms' of typically Poundian perceived detail grow through his prose and verse, and showed how Pound's fundamental structural insight repeatedly triumphed over his local ignorance. It described the development and dispersal of the energy-centre constituted by Pound, Eliot, Joyce, Lewis and Williams. And it held its encyclopaedic information together with a recurrent theme, which was about the precedence of immaterial shapes over material constituents, in art, physics, biology, phonology and myth. Like the engineer, the despised artist created such shapes, alleged to be useless in their immediate context, but organising the human ecology's future.

Donald Davie's brief *Pound* (1975) overturned some assumptions by showing Pound's great literary conservatism and his Edwardian idea of what Europe consisted of (the Latin-derived cultures). It read Cantos metres to show unperceived ways in which Pound developed verse tradition. Massimo Bacigalupo in *The Forméd Trace: The Later Poetry of Ezra Pound* (1980) illuminated the fine layerings of Pound's image skills, and also some contradictions in his attitudes, adducing much new information. And the explosion in the quantity of information now available is largely the result of Carroll F. Terrell's efforts since 1972 as editor of the Pound journal, *Paideuma*. He has printed important critical articles, memoirs, Pound documents, and numberless local source-discoveries, and has encouraged the line-by-line correlation of the Cantos with major source-texts reprinted *in extenso*. The results are being edited down into Carroll F. Terrell's *Companion to the Cantos of Ezra Pound*, of which the first volume (up to Canto LXXI) appeared in 1980. It clarifies the poem passage by passage, adducing comment, fact and cross-reference pragmatically, according to the requirements of each case rather than of a lexical rigidity. It is indispensable for the consideration of sources. The Canto-by-Canto clarification of Pound's materials proceeds in articles scattered in other journals, as well as in major undertakings like those of Wilhelm (1977), Hesse (1975) and Fender (1977). Other works like Makin's *Provence and Pound* (1978), McDougal's *Ezra Pound and the Troubadour Tradition* (1972) and Sieburth's *Instigations* (on Gourmont; 1978) investigate Pound's revaluation of particular cultural areas. Essays such as Mottram's on Pound and Merleau-Ponty (see Select Bibliography: Bell) consider fundamental questions of outlook. It will be obvious from this brief survey that Pound criticism is at a peak of activity.

SELECT BIBLIOGRAPHY

BIOGRAPHY

Rachewiltz, Mary de, *Ezra Pound, Father and Teacher: Discretions* (New York: New Directions, 1975).

Stock, Noel, *The Life of Ezra Pound* (Harmondsworth: Penguin, 1974).

BIBLIOGRAPHY

Gallup, Donald, *Ezra Pound: A Bibliography* (Charlottesville, Va: University Press of Virginia, 1983) (an expanded and corrected version of the author's *A Bibliography of Ezra Pound*, 1963, rev. 1969).

TEXT OF THE CANTOS

Pound, Ezra, *The Cantos of Ezra Pound* (New York: New Directions, 1972; and London: Faber, 1975 [i.e. 1976]). This is the text to which reference is made in all current study-aids and criticism, including the present work; but, for reasons which will be clear from Chapter 16 ('The State of the Text') above, I have generally preferred the variant readings of the 1954–68 Faber collected editions.

Pound, Ezra, *I Cantos*, Vol. 1, *I Primi Trenta Cantos*, ed. and trans. Mary de Rachewiltz (Milan: C. M. Lerici/V. Scheiwiller, 1961). One of the more important among the innumerable places in which authorised variants may be sought.

Pound, Ezra, *Selected Cantos of Ezra Pound* (London: Faber, 1967). Pound's selection, made in 1965.

Eastman, Barbara C., *Ezra Pound's 'Cantos': The Story of the Text, 1948–1975*, with introd. by Hugh Kenner (Orono, Me: National Poetry Foundation, 1979).

CONCORDANCE

Dilligan, Robert J., Parins, James W. and Bender, Todd K., *A Concordance to Ezra Pound's 'Cantos'* (New York: Garland, 1981).

MANUSCRIPT MATERIALS

Many American universities have Pound letters and papers; Yale and Columbia have particularly important Cantos manuscripts.

COLLATERAL READING: POUND'S WORKS

There is little in Pound's huge written output that does not shed some light on the Cantos, the central focus of all his efforts. Perceptions are often set out in anecdotal form in his prose, and later given tighter expression in the Cantos; and since, in these 'perceptions', thing seen is usually inseparable from demonstration of new way of seeing, 'source-material' is here entwined with 'theoretical frameworks for Cantos-writing'. The following are particularly useful; most of the books have both a British and an American edition. The student who is short of time will find many of the best pieces in J. P. Sullivan (ed.), *Ezra Pound: A Critical Anthology* (Harmondsworth: Penguin, 1970).

Personae: The Collected Shorter Poems of Ezra Pound (New York: New Directions, 1971). The best collection of the short poems.

Literary Essays of Ezra Pound, ed. and introd. T. S. Eliot (London: Faber, 1960).

The Spirit of Romance (New York: New Directions, 1968).

Guide to Kulchur (London: Peter Owen, 1966).

Confucius: The Great Digest; The Unwobbling Pivot; The Analects (New York: New Directions, 1969).

Selected Prose, 1909–1965, ed. and introd. William Cookson (New York: New Directions, 1975).

Fenollosa, Ernest, *The Chinese Written Character as a Medium for Poetry*, ed. Ezra Pound (San Francisco, Calif.: City Lights, n.d.).

The Confucian Odes: The Classic Anthology Defined by Confucius (New York: New Directions, 1959).

ABC of Reading (London: Faber, 1961).

Translations, introd. Hugh Kenner (New York: New Directions, 1963).

'Ezra Pound: an interview', with Donald Hall, in the *Paris Review*, no. 28 (Summer-Fall 1962), pp. 22–51; reprinted in Kay Dick (ed.), *Writers at Work: The 'Paris Review' Interviews* (Harmondsworth: Penguin, 1972), pp. 92–113.

Gaudier-Brzeska: A Memoir (Hessle, East Yorkshire: The Marvell Press, 1960).

The Selected Letters of Ezra Pound, 1907–1941, ed. D. D. Paige (New York: New Directions, 1971).

Opere scelte, ed. Mary de Rachewiltz, introd. Aldo Tagliaferri (Milan: Arnaldo Mondadori, 1970). A few important items in Italian not collected elsewhere, and the Italian versions of Confucius.

SOURCES AND PASSAGE-BY-PASSAGE COMMENTARY

The most complete listing of source-texts for individual Cantos is in Carroll F. Terrell, *A Companion to the Cantos of Ezra Pound* (Berkeley, Calif.: University of California Press). The first volume (Cantos I–LXXI) appeared in 1980; the second volume is forthcoming. This work also lists exegeses of individual Cantos, and gives a passage-by-passage key to the meaning.

Annotated Index to the Cantos of Ezra Pound: Cantos I–LXXXIV, ed. J. H. Edwards and W. W. Vasse (Berkeley, Calif.: University of California Press, 1971), has largely been absorbed into the foregoing, but contains genealogical, chronological and other tables that are still useful.

Kearns, George, *Guide to Ezra Pound's 'Selected Cantos'* (New Brunswick, NJ: Rutgers University Press, 1980). Balanced, accurate.

Brooker, Peter, *A Student's Guide to the Selected Poems of Ezra Pound* (London: Faber, 1979).

D'Epiro, Peter, *A Touch of Rhetoric: Ezra Pound's Malatesta Cantos* (Ann Arbor, Mich: UMI Research Press, 1983). Excellent on Cantos drafts.

Fender, Stephen (ed.), *The American Long Poem: An Annotated Selection* (London: Edward Arnold, 1977). Cantos XXI, XXXVII, XXXVIII and XXXIX.

Pound, Ezra, *Letzte Texte (Cantos CX–CXX): Entwürfe und Fragmente*, ed. and trans. Eva Hesse (Zurich: 'Die Arche', 1975). Contains a very full annotation of *Drafts & Fragments*.

Sanders, Frederick K., *John Adams Speaking: Pound's Sources for the Adams Cantos* (Orono, Me: University of Maine Press, 1975).

CRITICISM (see also Chapter 17)

Criticism of individual Cantos is listed in the *Companion to the Cantos* (see foregoing section). Full bibliographies of the criticism published in various periods since the Cantos' inception have been published in *Paideuma* from time to time. The following brief list includes only books.

Alexander, Michael, *The Poetic Achievement of Ezra Pound* (London: Faber, 1979).

Bacigalupo, Massimo, *The Forméd Trace: The Later Poetry of Ezra Pound* (New York: Columbia University Press, 1980). Full of insights.

Baumann, Walter, *The Rose in the Steel Dust: An Examination of the Cantos of Ezra Pound* (Coral Gables, Fla: University of Miami Press, 1970).

Bell, Ian F. A. (ed.), *Critic as Scientist: The Modernist Poetics of Ezra Pound* (London: Methuen, 1981).

Bell, Ian F. A. (ed.), *Ezra Pound: Tactics for Reading* (London/Totowa, NJ: Vision Press/Barnes & Noble, 1982). Includes Eric Mottram, 'Pound, Merleau-Ponty and the phenomenology of poetry'.

Bernstein, Michael André, *The Tale of the Tribe: Ezra Pound and the Modern Verse Epic* (Princeton, NJ: Princeton University Press, 1980).

Brooke-Rose, Christine, *A ZBC of Ezra Pound* (London: Faber, 1971).

Bush, Ronald, *The Genesis of Ezra Pound's Cantos* (Princeton, NJ: Princeton University Press, 1976). An informative account of influences on and problems with the first Cantos.

Chace, William M., *The Political Identities of Ezra Pound and T. S. Eliot* (Stanford, Calif: Stanford University Press, 1973).

Davie, Donald, *Ezra Pound: Poet as Sculptor* (London: Routledge & Kegan Paul, 1965). Very influential.

Davie, Donald, *Pound* (London: Fontana/Collins, 1975).

Davis, Earle, *Vision Fugitive: Ezra Pound and Economics* (Lawrence, Kan.: University Press of Kansas, 1968).

Dekker, George, *Sailing after Knowledge: The Cantos of Ezra Pound* (London: Routledge & Kegan Paul, 1963).

Emery, Clark, *Ideas into Action: A Study of Pound's Cantos* (Coral Gables, Fla: University of Miami Press, 1969).

Géfin, Laszlo, *Ideogram: History of a Poetic Method* (Austin, Tex.: University of

Texas Press, 1982). Relates Pound's poetics to those of Williams and post-1945 successors.

Hesse, Eva (ed.), *New Approaches to Ezra Pound* (London: Faber, 1969). Numerous valuable essays.

Juhasz, Suzanne, *Metaphor and the Poetry of Williams, Pound, and Stevens* (Lewisburg, Pa: Bucknell University Press, 1974).

Kenner, Hugh, *Gnomon: Essays on Contemporary Literature* (New York: McDowell, Obolensky, 1958). Essential essay on *Rock-Drill* included.

Kenner, Hugh, *The Poetry of Ezra Pound* (Millwood, NY: Kraus Reprint, 1974). Essential.

Kenner, Hugh, *The Pound Era* (Berkeley, Calif.: University of California Press, 1971). It may be best to tackle the first few chapters *after* such chapters as 'The Invention of Language', 'Knot and Vortex' and 'Imagism'.

McDougal, Stuart Y., *Ezra Pound and the Troubadour Tradition* (Princeton, NJ: Princeton University Press, 1972).

Makin, Peter, *Provence and Pound* (Berkeley, Calif.: University of California Press, 1978). Chapter 4 and footnotes analyse Canto VI.

Mancuso, Girolamo, *Pound e la Cina* (Milan: Giangiacomo Feltrinelli, 1974).

Nänny, Max, *Ezra Pound: Poetics for an Electric Age* (Bern: Franke, 1973).

Pearlman, Daniel, *The Barb of Time: On the Unity of Ezra Pound's 'Cantos'* (New York: Oxford University Press, 1969).

Perloff, Marjorie, *The Poetics of Indeterminacy: Rimbaud to Cage* (Princeton, NJ: Princeton University Press, 1981). Includes a section on the poetics of the Cantos.

Read, Forrest, *'76: One World and 'The Cantos' of Ezra Pound* (Chapel Hill, NC: University of North Carolina Press, 1981). Numerological, but containing some good sense on Pound's view of history.

Russell, Peter (ed.), *An Examination of Ezra Pound: A Collection of Essays* (New York: Gordian Press, 1973). Good pieces on Pound and Milton, on the Chinese character, and on money.

Sieburth, Richard, *Instigations: Ezra Pound and Remy de Gourmont* (Cambridge, Mass.: Harvard University Press, 1978). The importance to the Cantos of many elements in the French tradition.

Stock, Noel (ed.), *Ezra Pound Perspectives* (Chicago, Ill.: Henry Regnery, 1965). Includes Hugh Kenner, 'Leucothea's bikini: mimetic homage'.

Stock, Noel, *Poet in Exile: Ezra Pound* (Manchester: Manchester University Press, 1964).

Surette, Leon, *A Light from Eleusis: A Study of Ezra Pound's 'Cantos'* (Oxford: Oxford University Press, 1979).

Wilhelm, James J., *Dante and Pound: The Epic of Judgement* (Orono, Me: University of Maine Press, 1974).

Wilhelm, James J., *The Later Cantos of Ezra Pound* (New York: Walker, 1977).

Williams, William Carlos, *Selected Essays of William Carlos Williams* (New York: New Directions, 1969). Three Cantos pieces.

Zukofsky, Louis, *Prepositions: The Collected Critical Essays of Louis Zukofsky*, expanded edn (Berkeley, Calif.: University of California Press, 1981). See 'Ezra Pound' and 'American poetry, 1920–1930'.

INDEX